Jesuit Studies

Contributions to the arts and sciences

by members of the Society of Jesus

Jesuit Studies

JESUIT STUDIES

King and Church

THE RISE AND FALL OF THE

PATRONATO REAL

W. Eugene Shiels, s.j.

LOYOLA UNIVERSITY PRESS

Chicago, 1961

© 1961

LOYOLA UNIVERSITY PRESS

Printed in the United States of America

Library of Congress Catalog Card Number: 61-11113

P-TAP-P-P-E

T his book grew out of a smaller study made by the author twenty-five years ago. The subject was Gonzalo de Tapia, founder of a mission system in Spanish North America. Every step in the narrative revealed the decisive role played by the king in the area of church affairs. From the choice of missionaries to their dispatch into specific fields overseas, their material support, the control of local movements, the establishment of policies, and the expansion or retrenchment of operations, there was seen a clearly delineated over-all direction as carefully mapped in the large as in its smallest details. Further study disclosed the same procedure in every other part of the Spanish empire, whether in booming capitals or on barbaric frontiers, and that for nearly three hundred years. The thoroughness and uniformity of this royal intervention argued the existence of a vast systematic institution, perhaps the most pervasive organization in the commonwealth that Spain was building across the world.

It appeared that this phenomenon called for further inquiry. In itself it was a fact in imperial history as novel as it was important. In its prime objective, the Christianization of a new world, its results were most impressive, and this is well known. Not so clear are other aspects of the question. Scholars have indeed produced an immense literature on various problems inherent in the subject. But the very wealth of writings, not to speak of their diversity of interpretation, confuses rather than clarifies the essential character of the Patronato Real.

The maze of difficulties thus raised would seem to justify an attempt to draw the basic outline of the system through a straightforward and simple exposition of origins, growth, and decline. There is need to confront the documents fundamental to the institution. Using this controlling idea, and with the concurrent advice of several experienced historians, the book is projected as a presentation of the exact words of those who created, modified, enlarged, and finally terminated this adventure in government which affected so large a part of mankind.

To his advisers the author owes deep gratitude, particularly to his late academic director, Professor Herbert E. Bolton, the late Professor Arthur S. Aiton, Professor John F. Bannon, S.J., Professor Paul S. Lietz, Ernest F. Burrus, S.J. of Rome, and Mathias C. Kiemen, O.F.M. of Washington, D.C. The Newberry Library through Mrs. Pierce Butler gave priceless help in obtaining materials. The Loyola University Press and its Canisius House for Jesuit writers provided the unique opportunity of an entire year of endowed freedom for the labor of composition and professional editorial guidance.

It was at first intended to place the documents and the author's translations on opposite pages. Reconsideration, however, made it evident that the English version served better to illustrate the running narrative and that the originals should rather form a separate section. These are accordingly grouped together to form Part 2. Some originals, though given in full translation in Part 1, were nevertheless not reproduced in Part 2 because their place in the story was judged to be rather secondary than substantive. Such is the case with the *Omnimoda*, the establishment of procurators for the missionaries in the Indies, and the instruction of Pius V to Philip II.

The reader is asked but one favor: not to expect the book to do more than it promises. Its object is to lay out in ready form the foundation stones of the Patronato Real, to let the fathers of the institution speak their own sentiments with all the flavor of a genuine and authentic address to posterity. There is no effort to prove anything unusual, unless it be the grandeur of concept and achievement, and of tragic unfulfillment, that lay in that epochal story. Done at Canisius House, Evanston, Illinois, August 24, 1959.

W. E. S.

CONTENTS

PART ONE

The Narrative

CHAPTER I

The Spanish Patronato Real

In the year 1755 Don Antonio Joaquín de Ribadeneyra y Barrientos dedicated an important book to his Catholic majesty, Ferdinand VI. It was a handsome, compact manual for the use of officials in the Patronato Real de las Indias.[1] The Mexican advocate, a skillful writer though a frank regalist, designated this patronage as "the most precious pearl in the royal diadem." His metaphor has often been repeated, and with obvious satisfaction, although it permits of double interpretation. Assuredly the kings were most jealous of their patronal power, but there is something further in the phrase. Possibly Don Antonio gave to posterity a valuable synthesis of history. The idea deserves some examination.

Undoubtedly the Patronato went far to establish the church and to construct the growing empire of Spain, yet many a question haunts the students of this institution. Primarily needed is a clear picture of the thing itself. How did it come to life and arrive at its full stature? How broad was its impact? Was it in continuity with medieval practice, both in papal provisions and

---

[1] The work was entitled *Manual compendio de el regio patronato Indiano.* It was published in Madrid by Antonio Marin. The author had large experience in this area of the law as a councilor of the *audiencia* of Mexico. The book is beautifully printed in two colors and bound in black leather. The copy used is in the Newberry Library of Chicago.

1

in royal administration, or did it constitute a new venture in religion and in politics? Was its development accidental, or did the kings foresee the broad future in its simple beginnings?

Further questions concern its religious value. The missionary success under its auspices has never been surpassed. Yet out of its very way and manner of life arose a peculiar subordination of the clergy to the civil administration, to the royal will, and to national policy, all of this tending to dissipate the ties that should unite the head and the members of the clerical body and ensure them the freedom of decision expected in matters of conscience. Somewhere in the Patronato there lay a radical distortion and antagonism. And in the end it fell apart under the stress of the American independence movements, though even then it left a seriously divisive residue in the successor republics.

An attack on all the problems involved in this centuries-old and worldwide institution would demand much labor and many minds. Others have of course addressed the matter from their special points of view.[2] Here the approach aims directly at the central question: What was the Patronato Real? To clarify this fundamental issue and to facilitate probing into various aspects of the subject nothing serves so well as the genuine message of the prime documents. They brighten an area where there has been much shadow. With their aid the search for understanding may find its reward.

Spain inaugurated her overseas empire in 1492. Had the discovery come a century earlier, she would have been totally unprepared to take advantage of this good fortune. But in the reign of Ferdinand and Isabella great national forces reached maturity. The climax of that era, the victory of Granada, demonstrated internal cohesion of a high order, expansive confidence,

---

[2] See the various manuals listed in the bibliography, such as Encinas, Frasso, Puga, Solórzano Pereira, as also the commentators mentioned.

and a stoutly militant spirit. This dynamic power broke through the barrier to the Great Frontier.[3]

Isabella, queen of Castile since 1474 and in time sole sovereign of the Indies,[4] changed her country from a chaotic kingdom into the vital core of Spanish life. At her accession few believed she could succeed. During the preceding reign her brother, Enrique IV, had piled onto frivolity and indecision a rank disdain for the rights of his sister. Warrior nobles, notably the dukes of Medina Sidonia and Cádiz and the archbishop of Toledo, engaged in constant civil warfare. This, coupled with lawless brigandage of highwaymen in the open country, kept the realm in fear and distress. Economy was stifled under this regime. Justice generally lagged amid a senseless confusion of laws and widespread violence. Sporadic invasion from Portugal and Granada met a faltering defense, and a generally prevalent corruption of morals weakened regard for culture, peace, and order.

Into this situation the young queen of twenty-three now brought her personal integrity and charm and her surprising gifts of administrative ability. Ferdinand—they were married in heroic circumstances at Valladolid in 1469—inherited Aragon from his father ten years later, and the couple formed a rare team in government. While she lived he was a model of kingship, and to his death he retained his love and regard for his

---

[3] William Hickling Prescott, *The History of the Reign of Ferdinand and Isabella the Catholic* (McKay edition. Philadelphia, 1893), II, 100-03, gives a full summary of the results of the campaign on the morale of the Spaniards.

[4] The same author, in I, 201 and 237-39, summarizes the details of the marriage agreement of January 7, 1469 and of the convention arrived at in Segovia when on December 13, 1474 Isabella proclaimed her accession. Both sharply limited Ferdinand's power in Castile. Though the monarchs jointly signed all edicts, each retained sovereignty in his own kingdom. Isabella alone had title to the Indies, having commissioned Columbus, guaranteed the contract, paid the royal contribution, issued orders for the voyage, and directed overseas developments until her death in 1504.

esposa carísima, as he often wrote of her. Now the writ of the crown began to carry full conviction. Nobles found themselves no longer able to dominate the *cortes,* and townsmen voted on equal terms with them in passing national legislation. Judicial decision, based on a recodification of law and lively respect for the royal arm, supplanted the rule of party spirit and intimidation. Within the eight years from 1474 to 1482 internal trade increased sixfold. A sound currency was created, together with an army of quality and a naval force so powerful that in the last-named year seventy ships could be detached for the defense of Naples. The Inquisition beclouded a period that might otherwise have been wholly fair. Its methods were needless and inhuman,[5] though it helped to nullify any tendency toward a fifth column during the Moorish wars. On her chestnut mule Isabella rode widely, to calm local jealousies, to do swift and merciful justice in Seville or Cádiz, to direct the providing of munitions and supplies for the armed services. She and her consort gave an unusual example of clean living and dedication to the national cause. They kept the promise made at marriage to unite the country and destroy the power of Granada, and on January 2, 1492 they saw the *reconquista* completed.

In the midst of that campaign the monarchs got into their hands a political power of the first magnitude. This was the famous Bull of Granada, given by Innocent VIII on December 13, 1486. In order to understand why these powers should have been requested by the monarchs and granted by the papacy, it will help to review very briefly certain salient facts concerning the war against the Moors. To Spaniards this deadly conflict had from its start the character of a holy war. After 1064, when Alexander II sanctified the cause and blessed its banners, it was

---

[5] Sixtus IV took vigorous steps to check its cruel and arbitrary processes. See Ludwig von Pastor, *History of the Popes from the Close of the Middle Ages* (English translation. London, 1891-1934), IV, 402.

a crusade.[6] Such is the constant position taken by the monarchs, a position accepted and approved in the papal documents of the fifteenth century studied later in this book. Sixtus IV ennobled this idea with special marks of confirmation, a nuncio sent specifically to promulgate the crusading bull of 1482, and as a gift to the sovereigns a gorgeous banner with a massive silver cross. This latter emblem Ferdinand brought to every battle, and in brilliant ceremony set it high on the altar of the church in each captured town.[7] Donation and patronage were a regular part of the campaign. During the course of the long war, Prescott writes:

> Scarcely a town was reconquered from the Moors, without a considerable portion of its territory being appropriated to the support of some ancient, or the foundation of some new, religious establishment. These were the common reservoir, into which flowed the copious streams of private as well as royal bounty.[8]

As leaders in the war the royal couple took full part in these acts of devotion. They had, too, a serious interest in making sure of the loyalty and dependability of clerics appointed to the bishoprics, abbacies, or local prebends of these benefices. To ensure the vital allegiance and to encourage zeal and service in the crusade the monarchs asked Rome to give them control of all patronage in Granada, including the right to nominate to all major prelacies as well as to hold in trust all tithes and endow-

---

[6] For a good brief statement on this matter see D. Mansilla in *Hispania sacra*, XX (1957), 494-96, where he reviews José Goni Giztambide, *Historia de la bula de la cruzada en España* (Vitoria, 1958). He holds that, from the first bull of Alexander II to the Bull of Granada of Innocent VIII, there is a continual series of papal proclamations of crusading war coupled with indulgences, the specific notes that characterize a crusade. Moreover, he asserts that this first bull of Alexander II inspired the Clermont Council and the proclamation of Urban II in 1095.

[7] Prescott describes the ceremony as it was performed in the capture of Moclin. See *Ferdinand and Isabella*, I, 457; for the ceremony at the Alhambra, see II, 95.

[8] *Ibid.*, I, 66.

ments assigned to the support of religion. In Chapter 4 the complete text of this bull is reproduced. The bull is pivotal in the Granadine conquest, as it is in the entire subsequent story of the Indies.

It will be recalled that Columbus signed the capitulations of Santa Fe guaranteeing his voyage of discovery just three months after Granada fell. Then, in one of the strange conjunctions of history, at the moment of highest common action and most exciting interest—the phrase is Prescott's—the nation was presented with its epic opportunity in the transatlantic world. And the apparatus of royal patronage was taken over completely into the new discoveries by force of the bulls of Alexander VI and Julius II, with the result that the entire construction of the American church lay in the hands of the crown. The monarchs now selected every cleric who would cross the seas for religious purposes.[9] They singled out the location of each cathedral and minor chapel. As they alone knew the geography of the distant territories, Rome had to depend on them for what information it needed to guide the expanding church. The documents to be found in later chapters throw much light on that dependence. In the circumstances the monarchs were quite free in the making of ecclesiastical arrangements; and when future letters from the papal curia might seem about to restrict their liberty, they could always rely on a broad interpretation of the already broad concessions.

In Granada, then, and afterwards in the Indies they made and guaranteed all economic arrangements for the support of

---

[9] Many examples of this selection from the first days are found in Joaquín F. Pacheco, Francisco de Cárdenas, y Luis Torres de Mendoza, *Colección de documentos inéditos, relativos al descubrimiento, conquista y organización de las antiguas posesiones españoles de América y Oceania, sacados de los Archivos del Reino, y muy especialmente del de Indias* (Madrid, 1864-1884, 1885-1932). See, for example, on the sending of Padre "Broil" and his companions on the 1493 voyage, I 30, 178.

religion, including the unrivaled 1512 Concordat of Burgos, wherein they redonated the tithes to the American bishops after Alexander VI had given them full possession of the same tithes. They regulated the procedure of ecclesiastical courts, the manner and time of worship, and rules for lay and clerical behavior, even to causes of excommunication and the lifting of the same. They were masters of all local patronage and of the presentation of every incumbent, as they also guided his choice of policies and his local movements from that time onward. Frequently they placed clerics in civil offices and sometimes had them investigate the whole gamut of civil administration, as in the noted Jeronymite episode of Hispañola in 1513-1516, when the commission of religious was ordered to find an answer to the pregnant question: Can the natives maintain themselves in the condition of free men of Castile?[10] The office of protector of the Indians was unfailingly entrusted to a religious person, as though to signify that this post, so symbolic of the solicitude of both church and state for the welfare of the natives,[11] should fall properly under the control of the Patronato Real. Not infrequently an *oidor* of an *audiencia* who had shown extraordinary talent gave up lay life to accept the charge of bishop, as happened to Vasco de Quiroga of Michoacán and San Toribio of Lima.

A multiplicity of landed investments connected with tithes, benefices, and church properties and the supervision of missions, *encomiendas*, and parishes were likewise under the control of the Patronato. Entire staffs of a host of institutions worked under its orders. Viceroys and governors as vice-patrons were assigned special assistants to take care of these matters, and they soon came to have need of the manuals prepared for official use.

---

[10] For materials on this affair see Lewis Hanke, *First Social Experiments in America* (Cambridge, 1935).

[11] See the letters of Ferdinand to Governor Ovando printed later in this work.

The over-all concept of the patronal grant appears to have had feudal and contractual overtones. Possession of the privilege depended on fulfilling the missionary charge. In this matter the pope remained the judge and the final court of appeal. As to the contractual notion of subordinate jurisdictions, the medieval organization of society was clear. And thus the king-patron tended to see in himself the head of an enclave in the church, the management of which was delegated to him through papal concession. He had but to rule his patronal commitment properly, and the lord-in-chief would be satisfied of his fealty and reliability. This seems to have been the case in early America, where the entire charge of conversion was "entrusted" to the patron, and that in an area which was certain to enlarge both in territorial scope and in the number of subjects who would fall to his care. As the operation went on in the expanding feudality, it encountered problems in political theory that had not previously been met in a Europe, whose peoples lived in severely limited territories and under age-old restrictions on the mutual conduct of lord and subject. There were few who, like Ferdinand, foresaw the possible enlargement of the role of patron into that of ruler of an empire. In this respect the Patronato de las Indias took on an aspect different from that seen in the Granada of 1486, although the basic grant of patronage was expressed in similar terms for both districts. The end result gave the monarchs an opportunity to push their patronal rule beyond the original powers into a quasi-pontifical rule of the clergy.

Historians generally give favorable mention to the work of the church in the building of America. What has been overlooked is the functional use made *of* the church by the crown, a fact possibly obscured by the striking deeds of individual characters who made effective the work of the Patronato. An investigation devoting serious attention to that problem may help very much toward an understanding both of the history of the Western Hemisphere and of the development of the science of politics. The church was employed there in a unique fashion not paralleled by any other people except the Portuguese, and by them somewhat less profitably in comparison with their Hispanic neighbors. Civil and sacred interests were intertwined in a system so thorough and complex as scarcely to be separated, so permanent and pervasive that the organic union escapes any but a careful observer. Speaking from the standpoint of politics, it was as though one took the admittedly skillful and persistent use of the attributes of sovereignty under Isabella, Ferdinand, Charles V, and Philip II and advanced it geometrically by endowing these monarchs with an almost total papal vicariate. So broad a power of government has seldom been devised.

And yet there was little of the spectacular in this history, aside from a few brief crises that momentarily challenged the settlement during its three centuries of life. The operation of this supercharged regal machine proceeded smoothly in a day-to-day routine that matched the mills of the gods, regular, constant, and effective—so much so that a hurrying critic may err badly in castigating either of the parties involved. If anything, it was a most conservative arrangement, though, as will be seen, it could in bad hands be turned into something revolutionary.

Geoffrey Barraclough in a much-lauded essay cautioned scholars not to hunt for deliberate shifts of policy in the evolution of provisions, and in this he put in his debt all students of medieval times.[12] Provisions, as the eminent legal historian remarks, followed a consistent pattern of legislative and administrative progress, toward which even the most extreme of popes would have had to yield unless he altogether abandoned his own code and the chancery that used it for him. So it was with the Patronato Real. For long its motion was as quiet and orderly as that of the stars, and as unnoticed. Rare was the pen that was used against it.

----

12 Geoffrey Barraclough, *Papal Provisions* (Oxford, 1935).

Some find in the Patronato a revival of Justinian caesaro-papalism. Such parentage is occasionally claimed in the manuals used by its officials.[13] Ribadeneyra, whom Bancroft considered a reliable author on the subject,[14] asserted that the Patronato was an inheritance from Justinian, a view quite in keeping with his subservience to the king and his misreading of ancient history. Since both empires followed a definitely Erastian course, the judgment might seem well taken. A short inspection, however, would appear rather to indicate marked differences between the two systems, the one a protectorate of the church, the other a patronage within the universal body.

Justinian (527-565) came to office in a regime that had already begun the tradition of exaggerated imperial interest in the rule of the church. His predecessors, Constantine and Theodosius, were two whose intervention would make the papacy pay dearly in subsequent times.[15] The new emperor now took up this customary role of "protector" of Christianity, assuming prerogatives that ignored the difference between *sacerdotium* and *imperium*. He should have had that division on record from the time of Gelasius I; but if he did recall it, he had no mind to follow it. Plainly he exercised a plenitude of power, and that with no grant from the spiritual authority. He issued a decree condemning fourteen propositions of Origen. A similar decree condemned the alleged errors in writings of Theodore, Theodoret, and Ibas. To the see of Constantinople he promoted a heretical bishop. He convoked a general council of the church through the agency of Pope Virgilius. And after himself adopting the Monophysitic doctrine, he required all bishops to accept

---

[13] Antonio Joaquín de Ribadeneyra, *Manual compendio de el regio patronato Indiano* (Madrid, 1755), p. 104.

[14] Hubert Howe Bancroft, *History of Mexico* (San Francisco, 1883), III, 685. At that point he has a useful three-page sketch of the patronage.

[15] Philip Hughes, *A Popular History of the Catholic Church* (New York, 1951), pp. 25-44, analyzes this general problem.

it and removed from their sees those who refused to do so. He likewise introduced a new marriage impediment, that of abduction, after he had made it a capital crime in civil law.[16] Nevertheless it must be added that, in his *Novels,* his own special contribution to the *Corpus juris civilis,* he expressed utmost reverence for the head of the church and its bishops.

Spanish monarchs, in contrast with Justinian, claimed no power over doctrinal matters and exercised administrative powers only insofar as they found them in their patronal grant. Alexander VI had commissioned the crown, in a series of bulls, to do a missionary task. Although the privileges there contained and the universal patronage in the Indies conferred on them by Julius II in 1508 reflected a break from a tradition of papal provision dating at least from Innocent III, these concessions were not without justification, in the imperative need to choose a trustworthy agent and then to give him full delegation, so that he might go on with his weighty task of constructing Christianity in a wholly new sector of the globe. Soon the kings obtained permission to alter boundaries of dioceses, a surrender to civil power unknown to canon law. Yet the Council of the Indies knew its geography; Rome did not. And the transit of a letter might be a matter of six months. In those circumstances the church overseas grew up as an appendage of the crown that gave the directions and met all costs. Such a crown—and it was energetic—obviously intended to continue in control, for while making the church it was likewise making the Spanish empire. When changes were in order, as in the shift from management by religious orders to diocesan organization, hardships came to early tillers of the hard soil. The newness of the terrain opened up a wide field for overdisplay of powers, and suits followed.

---

[16] *Corpus juris civilis: Codex Justinianus* (Krueger edition. Berlin, 1904), IX, xiii, p. 378, wherein Justinian made abduction a capital crime absolutely diriment as an impediment to marriage.

The novel feature was settlement by royal decision rather than by recourse to Rome. Policy on that point was fixed, not without a clash of wills, in the Junta de Madrid in 1568. No true cleric liked to take religious commands from a civilian king, but this was apparently the constitutional position, particularly after the decision of the Junta and the express approval of St. Pius V.[17]

Few would underestimate the efforts made by Spanish royalty for the advantage of religion, and every succeeding crisis left the rival bodies in understanding and peace. Only after the Bourbons took the helm in 1701 did dangerous trouble come.[18] The crown then undertook to extinguish in all Spanish territory a large religious order, the Society of Jesus, under charter by the head of the church. At the same period, in 1768, the king absorbed under his personal aegis the Holy Office of the Inquisition, despite its direct institution by the Holy See under Sixtus IV.[19] Regalist claims fogged the vision of Charles III and made a "pious villain"[20] into a plague of the papacy. The sequel showed the crown at this final stage as a more formidable adversary of the church than was its "protector," Justinian, and no reader is surprised to hear in Madrid the threat to abandon unity if the royal will were crossed. In 1831 the crown actually announced its decision to follow the example of Henry VIII if a particularly disliked cardinal (Guistiniani) was elected pope.[21]

---

[17] Pastor, *History of the Popes,* XVIII, 330-44, on Pius V and the Patronato.

[18] This matter is treated in Chapter 15.

[19] Richard Herr, *The Eighteenth Century Revolution in Spain* (Princeton, 1958), p. 19, note 14, also citing the *Novísima recopilación de las leyes de España* (Madrid, 1805), II, iii, ley ix. More broadly, he instances the advice given to Charles III by the Consejo de Castilla on November 30, 1768 regarding his powers: "The king, as patron, founder, and endower of the Inquisition, possesses over it rights inherent in all royal patronage." See Herr, p. 28. See also Pastor, *History of the Popes,* IV, 396-405 on its institution.

[20] Manuel Giménez Fernández, *El Concilio IV Provincial Mejicano* (Seville, 1939), p. 11. The phrase is *beato pernicioso.*

[21] W. Eugene Shiels, "Church and State in the First Decade of Mexican Independence." *Catholic Historical Review,* XXVIII (July 1942), 206-28.

So much for comparison. As a system the Patronato almost defies definition. It would not do to speak of it as a state church, for it was not so conceived or spoken of. Much less was it a church state. Yet the two were almost one, even though this oneness will be seen to involve an insoluble tension.

On the debit side the crown so encompassed religion that its rule has been referred to, and correctly, as a "servitude of the church." And yet this can be overstressed, for the monarchs almost uniformly carried out their patronal mandate with a strong sense of duty. Mecham in his thorough factual study[22] ventures the opinion that they put the good of religion ahead of their state interests. Second, it is well understood that the church does not think of itself as a being of this world only. Its ends are beyond present life; and while it uses its mundane elements, this is nevertheless but sounding brass unless it be viewed, as it is by its members, as the preparatory movement toward eternal life. In its organized operation it must employ the most diverse types of human personality, human resources, human potential for good. And it would oppose any royal attempt to convert its society into political slavery.

The difficulty more immediately threatening was a tendency induced by this arrangement pointing toward undue conformity with regal desires, a fact more noted in Bourbon times.[23] This was only one of the dangers of the Patronato. A greater came in the too-ready, too-casual, assumption of high virtue in this extreme compounding of human associations.[24] And when the monarchs were able to make and unmake the personnel directing the work of the church, to order about a vast body of the be-

---

[22] J. Lloyd Mecham, *Church and State in Latin America* (Chapel Hill, 1934), pp. 1-44. This chapter on "Church and State during the Spanish Regime in America" is a judicious legislative history.

[23] See Chapter 15, for example, pp. 254-57.

[24] For some fine observations on interlocking associations see Carl Gustavson, *Preface to History* (New York, 1956).

lieving membership with no juridical check beyond the royal conscience, to enjoy a dominion that included the entire corporation of Hispanic Christianity, and especially to estop its contacts with the independent, trusted, and competent head at Rome, then, no matter how sincere the intentions of the early Habsburgs or how fully they used the *hombres de Dios* in the betterment of society, it needed no prophet to foretell a day of reckoning. It was, in a sense, a magnificent illusion. The wonder is that so many centuries passed before that day of reckoning arrived.

As time went on a complacent national approval hung over the work of the Patronato.[25] It came to be looked on as a purely Spanish royal invention. This had its pitfalls. Many felt that the crown could not miscalculate when their king so thoroughly supported every facet of religious belief and, often, of conduct. Not a few found it to their interest to sing the praises of royal virtue while battening on royal favors. Others developed a haughty bearing toward their foreign, and sometimes competing, coreligionists. Most had no notion of what happened in the halls of the Escorial or the Prado when legates of Rome quietly asked for justification of some royal decision. And a generally self-congratulatory spirit finally terminated in that hideous travesty of politics, the regalist principle that deep in sovereignty lie the roots of right over every public and private action. Very close to that principle there lay a threatening chasm.

This negative criticism will serve to maintain balance of judgment while the benign influence of the powers granted to the Patronato is under consideration. And there is no doubting the fact of benignity. In no other time or place has paternal government done so much for the expansion and improvement of religion. The Spaniard took his belief seriously. He had a

---

[25] Frasso, Solórzano, and especially Ribadeneyra unblushingly adopt this attitude.

mission in America: the commitment to uplift the native and to help him save his soul.[26] The epitome of that mind shines through the biography of Mexico's first bishop, Juan de Zumárraga.[27] And the agency for most of this accomplishment was the Patronato Real. The immense largess of hospitals, refuges, loan funds, schools, universities, seminaries, magnificent and artistic churches, gives concrete proof of its efficacy. Particularly is this seen in the status of the Indian; for the survival of the native, his civilizing, his elevation to final equality with his fellow man, were a persistent aim at law and in administration, where a large part of the work devolved on officialdom in its religious operation. The number of tribes brought from barbarity to mission to pueblo has never been counted but their gratitude was real, even if it appeared in silent acquiescence to this enormous social benefit. Elizabeth Weismann in her *Mexico in Sculpture* draws a close-up of Indians at Tepotzotlán in the seventeenth century donating one full year of labor to build a marvelous church, which to them meant more than all the wealth another might win in that time.[28] If today the Indian, as some hold, constitutes the backbone of defense of religion in those lands,[29] the cause undoubtedly goes back to the missions that

---

[26] See the thought-provoking introductory essay in Silvio Zavala, *Philosophy of the Conquest of America* (México, 1953).

[27] Joaquín García Icazbalceta, *Biografía de D. Fr. Juan de Zumárraga, primer obispo y arzobispo de México* (México, 1881), an unsurpassed biography of this heroic man.

[28] Elizabeth Wilder Weismann, *Mexico in Sculpture* (Cambridge, 1950), pp. 125, 134. The work throws needed light on the rise of the Indian and their views regarding their religion. She writes of these workers: "Nothing emphasizes this [absorption of the worshiper in mystery] like the effect of entering a humble Mexican church, roughly plastered, perhaps thatched, to find the interior rich in luminous gold. Socially and economically the implications are enormous. Here, somehow, is relief from political oppression and curtailment of life. Here in a first-rate work of art, in its fabulous convincing opulence, is surcease from poverty."

[29] Philip M. Hannon, "Going In through Their Door." *America*, C (January 10, 1959), 419.

brought his forefathers from beyond the frontier into the full society of the Spanish realm.[30]

In 1492 this institution of a Patronato Real was a comparatively recent phenomenon.[31] For centuries the papacy, through its unquestioned doctrine of spiritual supremacy and the silent force of a majestic legal and chancery machinery, had slowly but definitely made it clear that the church was not a federal but a monarchical body.[32] When once the Dark Ages came to an end and men found freedom to pause from warfare while they thought on life, and when the university-trained clerics had changed the entire character of episcopal patronage,[33] the tendency toward order and justice took hold of the whole church, and appeal to its supreme head became normal expectation in any suit for relief or benefit. During the same period appointments to many benefices fell under the reservation of the sovereign pontiffs. The decree *Execrabilis* of John XXII canonized long custom rather than caprice and novelty.[34] Protests were few

---

[30] History records remarkable cases of this rise in status, such as that of Padre Rincón, five times rector of colleges, best professor of canon law in colonial New Spain. See Gerardo Decorme, *La obra de los Jesuitas en México durante la época colonial* (México, 1941), *passim*. John Tate Lanning, *Academic Culture in the Spanish Colonies* (Chapel Hill, 1940), treats their scholastic opportunities, particularly of the *mestizos*.

[31] Chapter 2 will offer materials on the question of an earlier Patronato Real. Writers with regalist views on the subject show a strong inclination toward reading history backwards, or anachronism.

[32] Barraclough, *Papal Provisions*, p. 130: ". . . the papal office as comprising an active, direct participation in local church affairs, the Roman pontiff himself as more than *primus inter pares*, the church more as a monarchy than as a federation of dioceses."

[33] *Ibid.*, p. 161: "Among all the different classes seeking preferment none could with greater reason complain of the localization and preponderance of personal influence in the disposal of benefices than the graduates of the universities; and it was because they . . . called in the central authority to redress the balance in their favour, that the papacy was led to intervene in the disposal of benefices."

[34] *Ibid.*, pp, 9, 60: "Such constitutions as John XXII's *Execrabilis* mark a definite attempt to hold the evil for which the German *Eigenkirchschenwesen* was responsible, in check."

and quiet, in view of what Edward II and Philip IV had done to episcopal freedom. Barraclough suggests that the noisy clamors of German aristocracy against provisions may have resulted from their fear of losing benefices for their sons and not from any numerical superiority of Italian beneficiaries over the German in Teutonic lands—a complaint embraced, he says, by historians who prefer literary materials to the statistics of Roman and episcopal chanceries.[35]

The appearance of the Spanish Patronato Real and the Portuguese Padroado Real in the fifteenth century marks a sudden and decided break in this long-established beneficiary pathway to Rome. Instead of holding firm to full papal appeal and reservation, the popes now in two outright grants handed over to the crowns of these nations the fullness of presentation, tithe, and reservation, in the second grant extending this control from Gibraltar to India. To date, this about-face has not been convincingly explained. Some facts are known, and they may help to clarify what seems so contradictory in the Roman policy, which is normally consistent and conservative.

In the afterswell of the Great Schism its memory lingered on. The parallel and continuing conciliar movement posed a repeated danger for Rome down to the middle 1500's. Around the Eternal City Italian *condottieri* (and Neapolitan forces) were generally on the warpath, while the curia could not muster funds enough to ensure the safety of the city. In this situation the popes were caught in a dilemma. They had had enough of overbearing royalty in the late and recent past, yet without the close support of the better kings there could be recurrent threat of a break in the loyalty of cardinals and also danger that hostile powers might rally round the characters who—chiefly in France—persisted in waving the challenge of a council before the pope. This made the Roman circumstances bad enough. Then

---

[35] *Ibid.*, pp. 45 ff.

a thunderclap sounded in the East. The Seljuk Turks took Constantinople and advanced almost unopposed into the Balkans, meanwhile sallying forth with their ships of war right into Italian harbors. Nicholas V, taken out of the gentle atmosphere of humanism and raised to the papal throne, was struck with stark fear at the victories of the Crescent. His immediate predecessors had watched the advance with trembling. Undoubtedly the popes were ready, from this double cause of anxiety, to confer unusual favors on various kings, especially on those who had shown strong support for the counterattack of the Crusades.

On her part Spain was in mortal combat with a much-feared —and hated—adversary. Her queen commanded the fullest confidence at the Roman curia, and the same was true of Henry the Navigator, sponsor of crusade and white knight of the African campaigns. The *Romanus pontifex* of Nicholas V gave him a long and deserved eulogy.

Whatever may have been the other supposed reasons behind these grants, there is no question that, in sponsoring these two great exploring and colonizing nations, the papacy helped to bring on a profound change in history. For Spain the Bull of Granada was one key to American success. It contained all the elements of the Patronato Real de las Indias: the right to choose the officers of the church, to hold and distribute the funds necessary for their material support, to convert the people of the conquered land, and to maintain these converts in their Christianity. Ferdinand and Isabella saw in these powers a means of creating in the newly discovered lands a pattern of life similar to that of the homeland. Accordingly they asked the popes to concede like privileges for the overseas areas, acquired or to be acquired. This petition had the result that, after the *Universalis ecclesiae regimini,* they had the counterpart of the Granadine grant for the New World.

For Spain itself they and their successors could get no similar concession until after two hundred and fifty years had passed. Then Benedict XIV, on January 11, 1753, granted the patronage throughout Spain.[36] This completed the Patronato Real Universal: Granada, the Indies, Spain.

Only once in its long life was the institution under full attack: in 1568, when Rome made a determined move to reverse the entire arrangement and regain immediate control over the Hispanic church, only to draw back when Philip II showed how complete a disorganization this would cause in the infant Christianity of the Occident. Otherwise the Patronato Real enjoyed permanent respect, obedience, and credit for its American accomplishment.

As this study now proceeds to unravel the various strands of patronage and its historical development, it may not be impertinent to suggest that certain social results connected with the process deserve further attention if one is to find the true measure of the part played by the Patronato Real in the making of the Spanish empire. Four such phenomena were obviously important. First is the stimulus given to Spanish thought and public debate. It is recognized that the "national question" which so exercised the universities in the sixteenth century—"By what right is Spain in America?"—and its subsidiary problems, such as the place that the Indian could hold in society, came naturally from the direct contact of Patronato agencies with the native. Another extremely interesting social result was the very evident rule of law that prevailed during these three centuries in the Indies and that is today an almost vanished reality. Trust in contracts, assurance of title, security of enterprise, expectation of court justice, reliance on the word of his majesty, are of course a galaxy of intangibles, in a sense; but their prevalence and their origin are matters of import. A third and striking quality of those times was the character of officials appointed by the crown for this service and the reasons that attracted men

---

[36] This matter is the subject of Chapter 14.

of high professional talents, such as, to name one, Vasco de Quiroga. The list of bishops, teachers, viceroys, *adelantados*, and missionaries of caliber beyond the ordinary indicates an unusual condition of order and opportunity to achieve. A last and intriguing point is the affection of the Indies for the crown and the loyalty that made it possible to police their entire American field with never more than three thousand soldiers up to the year 1763, when Spain began to face Britain as the one great competing imperial power in the Western Hemisphere. Spaniards are proverbially hard to govern. How much of this grateful regard could be traced to the Patronato Real?

CHAPTER II

Patrons and Patronage

Some prosaic lines must introduce the history of Spanish patronage if one is to interpret the documents that lie back of it. When these documents speak of law there is a technical sense in the language.

A *patron* is a person who endows a place of divine worship and who is in turn endowed with particular rights. And the *right of patronage* at law amounts to the sum of privileges and duties belonging to the founders of churches and other ecclesiastical enterprises. As the whole purpose of these actions and the persons consecrated for them are spiritual, primary jurisdiction over them belongs to the spiritual power, at law and in fact.

There is a *private* patronage, restricted to the single or corporate donor, and a *public* or crown patronage wherein the sovereign endows the spiritualities of the land and is vested with quasi-religious rights over the royal territory. The former may be held either by king or by commoner. The latter becomes part of the machinery of government. Both have elements in common as social institutions with wide bearing. But in the realm of politics crown patronage may attain great power. Such a patronage was the Patronato Real, first (1486) of Granada and the Canaries and Puerto Real, next (1508) of the Indies, and finally (1753) of all continental Spain. The totality then became the Patronato Real Universal.

For the sake of later discussion it is well to recall the famous
definition of patronage given by Alfonso X of Castile (1252-
1284), justly remembered as El Sabio. He wrote:

The Latin *patronus* means "father of his trust." And just as one's
father is charged with the care of his son, with his raising and protection and doing all the good for him that he can, so he who will build
a church must meet its costs, be interested in all its needs, and protect
it after he has built it.

And patronage is the right or power that they gain over a church,
the benefit that those who are its patrons obtain. And a man wins that
right in a threefold manner. First is the land he gives on which the
church is built. Second is the building of the church. Third is the
landed property that one gives when he leaves an endowment from
which the clergy who serve it find their living, and with which they can
fulfill their other duties, according to the title "How they should build
their churches."

Similarly three things belong to the patron by reason of the patronage. The first is honor. The next is the support that he deserves when in
trouble. The third is the care he should have to watch over the [spir-
itual] work. And when the church is vacant, he is entitled to present
the priest for it.[1]

The heart of patronage lies in the last short sentence of the
definition. *Presentation*, to a layman, is the act of bringing the
candidate to the bishop for installation. At law it is the right of
the patron to name to the ecclesiastical authorities a suitable
cleric, thereby conferring on him a *jus ad rem*.[2] It is the first
and chief privilege of the right of patronage, for it enables the
patron to advance into the holding the person whom he considers
most fit to bring about desirable spiritual, economic, social, and
political effects of the position. He who controls the presentation

---

[1] *Las siete partidas del rey don Alfonso el Sabio, cotejadas con varios códices
antiguos* (Madrid, 1807), Part. I, Lib. I, tit. xv. This translation, and all
others hereafter, are by the author except that on pp. 28-29.

[2] "Praesentatio est jus designandi clericum idoneum ab ordinario loci in beneficio
vacante necessario instituendum" (Stephanus Sipos, *Enchiridion juris canonici*
[Roma, 1954], p. 662).

of personnel has more than the power of the purse. He can expect that personnel to follow his policies in the organized life of the flock. He produces, as it were, the vital human center of the organism. It is his, for himself and his heirs. As a consequence patronage receives a prominent place in the law of every Christian country, and not least in the canon law of the church.[3]

What the patron endows is a *benefice*. Popularly the term is often understood to signify the properties donated or the duties of the beneficiary, but in its strict sense it is the right of the cleric presented to receive ecclesiastical revenues on account of the performance of spiritual work. This service could run from attendance on an oratory to the care of an archdiocese.

The possessor of this right is, after due installation, the *incumbent*. The chain of events, from his naming to his entry into service, is designated as *provision*. Provision denotes canonical induction into a benefice: the naming of the person, confirmation by the proper ecclesiastical superior of the one selected, collation (or concession or institution) of the vacant benefice by one who has authority to take this action, and entering into the actual possession of the benefice. The *jus in re* accompanies the last step of provision. It has already been noticed in Chapter 1 that the four acts in provision came under the competence of the sovereign pontiff by the historical process so thoroughly examined in the previously cited work of Barraclough.[4] The point of his findings must not, of course, be missed. Though Rome became the high court of appeal, it did not in fact grant a majority of the provisions in the period mentioned, for provisions in the form of a *motu proprio* were rarely bestowed.[5]

---

[3] *Codex iuris canonici . . . fontium annotatione . . . auctus* (Roma, 1917), Lib. III, tit. xxv, cap. 4, "De jure patronatus" embraces Canons 1448-71. The code is printed in Latin for clarity and universality. Translations are never official.

[4] See Chapter 1, p. 16.

[5] Barraclough, *Papal Provisions*, p. 92.

With these preliminaries dismissed, a short sketch of the history of patronage is in order. At the outset it is clearly seen that Christianity began operations as a human society compounded of spirit and matter. Each primitive unit needed edifices, ministers, and support, and it got them through offerings made by members of the unit or as gratuities from similar groups. These spontaneous acts had important implications. The custom fused the many into a commonalty of thought and, in time, of law. It created initiative, public spirit, traditions of magnanimity, and a strong desire in the donors that, as El Sabio wrote, they be given the right to look after the use made of their gifts. It furnished a distinctly inspiring outlet for lively faith. Lastly, not to overlook its broad economic aspects, it provided new bases of group interest in the exercise of political life, the type of corporation whose strength influences the direction taken by government. This fact helps to explain how Europe survived the crumbling of the old Rome. An entirely fresh drive replaced the decadent world outlook of the passing Empire and went on to assist in the revival of civilization. Patronage became an element of structural stiffening in the new society as it cemented civic and religious foundations.

Pre-Christian Rome employed the term *beneficium,* or reward, for parcels of land conveyed by the emperor to veteran soldiers in consideration of past services performed and as a retainer for future support. Some time after Constantine had legalized the right of Christian assemblies to hold title to property, the word took on a purely religious sense at law. Benefice now meant the juridical claim to have a living in view of spiritual functions. To the donor belonged the naming of the incumbent, and in the passage of time additional benefits accrued to him.

Ordinary support for pastors in the primitive church did not come from contributions or funds of individual churches but from the income of the head of the diocese, and he apportioned it according to need. As the faith spread beyond urban districts, early evidence indicates a modification in diocesan economics. Possibly to encourage the building of country churches, givers of funds and artisans who donated their labor began to receive episcopal favors in return for putting up the edifice and supporting its pastor. At the Council of Orange (441) in southern France, Canon 10 decreed that a bishop who built a church as a donation in the diocese of another bishop might nominate the priest for the church, but he could not consecrate it nor institute the cleric.[6]

The *Corpus juris civilis,* monumental inheritance from Emperor Justinian, provides good proof that during the century after the Council of Orange patronage became sufficiently common to call for imperial legislation. The *Novels,* the fourth part of that compilation and itself the personal contribution of the emperor, treats extensively of the clergy. *Novels,* 57, Chapter 2, reads:

> This too we decree for the honor and service of your [patriarchal] see, that if someone builds a church or expends funds otherwise in the support of its ministers and should wish to appoint clerics, no right allows them to oblige Your Reverence to ordain them. They are to be examined by Your Holiness, and, on your judgment and that of him who holds their episcopal see, you will always grant them ordination as it may seem opportune in the divine ministry and their merit deserves.[7]

Novels, 123, Chapter 18, decrees:

> If any man should erect an oratory and desire [you] to ordain clerics therefor, through himself or his heirs, and if they furnish a sufficiency for the clerics and nominate worthy men, those nominated are to be ordained. But if those whom they nominate be unworthy, the

---

6 P. Guerin, *Les conciles* (Parisiis, 1868), I, 296.

7 *Corpus juris civilis* (Schoell-Kroll edition. Berlin, 1912), III, 313. The original is of course in Greek.

sacred canons prohibit their ordination, and the most holy bishop should arrange to ordain those whom he judges most worthy.[8]

It may be interesting, before considering Spanish patronage, to take a brief look at its English correlative. In England this spiritual trust is an *advowson*, from "avowing" the merit of the candidate. It has had a long life. The king, now known as the "patron paramount" (though his is a private patronage), holds nearly one half of the English benefices. To him belong all disabled *advowsons*, as do their first fruits, or first-year revenues. The remainder are found among people of all classes except Catholics. These last must by law surrender any such inherited rights to the universities: to Oxford if they live south of the Trent, to Cambridge if to the north.

Early English practice conformed with that of other lands; and during the two centuries after St. Augustine of Canterbury landed at Dover, custom had it that pastors should receive their income from the cathedral church, with all nominations in the hands of the bishop. This would follow naturally from the monastic character of the clergy, descendants of the forty Benedictines who re-established the church in the southern kingdoms. Similarly, older Christianity deriving from Ireland and extending across the north and east had been altogether monastic, as one learns from Venerable Bede.[9] But in the time of Alfred *advowsons* increased in number, indicating the privileges granted for religious donations as he reconquered his kingdom and rebuilt what the Northmen had devastated. Not long afterward, in the disturbed times following upon the death of William the Conqueror, the institution got out of hand. For some decades patrons installed pastors without the consent of the bishops and sometimes against their will. Further abuse

---

[8] *Ibid.*, III, 608.

[9] Venerable Bede, *Ecclesiastical History of the English Nation* (New York, 1910), *passim*.

found clerics with two or more benefices. This usage also abounded on the Continent. At this point the Fourth Lateran Council (1215) stepped in to block the new habit of pluralities.[10] The effort was not wholly successful, for dispensation might be found; and difficulties mounted until Trent put a full stop to this prolific source of anticlericalism. In England, meantime, after its separation from the papacy, the archbishop of Canterbury exercised the power to dispense, on the basis of a concession granted to specified prelates by Clement VII in 1529. Later on the Establishment experienced times of vexation in the matter. The Pluralities Act of 1839 narrowed the use of multiple benefices. More recent check was written into the Clergy Pension Measure of 1926.[11]

In Spain and Portugal, whose clergy rested on apostolic foundations, patrons built the first churches, but the institution of patronage was saved from many troubles by the wide influence of the spirit of Roman law and its strenuous defense of the rights of individuals. Thus the records of the councils held at Toledo testify to the continuous election of bishops in the Roman manner until in the time of the last Visigothic kings there came an abrupt change. These unstable barbarians insisted that they themselves must name the bishops. It appears that they copied the example of the Merovingians in France. In the days of King Ervigio the Twelfth Council of Toledo (681) in Canon 6 decreed the following:

> When one [bishop] dies, and the king is so far away that he cannot at once be advised of the vacancy, the archbishop of Toledo names and invests his successor, who with the approbation of the king remains as prelate of that church. If there be no king, then in the bishoprics to

---

[10] Giovanni Dominico Mansi, *Sacrorum conciliorum nova et amplissima collectio* (Martin-Petit edition. Parisiis, 1901-1924), XXII, 979.

[11] For the specific details on English patronage the author is in debt to the works of Walter George Frank Phillimore, particularly his *Ecclesiastical Law* (London, 1921).

which the king ordinarily provides they allow to the metropolitan of Toledo a certain manner of confirmation.[12]

When Mohammedan conquest replaced the rule of the Visigoths, the new sovereigns continued this custom until the Spanish countermove got under way. The great monarchs of the Reconquest now outdid each other in founding new churches and converting old mosques into Christian edifices. Canonical election was reestablished—with royal consent, and undoubtedly demanded by the very independent *cortes*—and this method of choosing bishops carried on down to the fourteenth century.

Alfonso el Sabio left in *Las siete partidas* a clear statement of medieval Spanish practice in episcopal elections:

What Right the Kings of Spain Possess with Regard to the Election of Prelates, and for what Reasons

There was an ancient custom of Spain which still prevails, that when the bishop of any place died, the dean and the canons communicated the fact to the king by means of their church messengers, who carried a letter from the dean and chapter stating that their prelate was dead, and that they asked him to permit them to hold an election without hindrance, and that they did surrender to him the property of the church; and when this is done, the king should grant their request, and send and collect his dues; and after the election has been held, he directs them to present to him the person chosen, and orders that what he received be delivered to him.

This preeminence and honor the kings of Spain enjoy for three reasons: first, because they conquered the country of the Moors, turned their mosques into churches, banished from them the name of Mohammed, and placed there the name of Our Lord Jesus Christ; second, because they founded churches in localities where none ever previously existed; third, because they endowed them, and, in addition to this, conferred many favors upon them; and so for this reason kings have

---

[12] This citation is taken from D. Ignacio Jordan de Asso y del Rio y D. Miguel de Manuel y Rodríguez, *El ordenamiento de leyes que D. Alfonso XI hizo en las Cortes de Alcalá de Henares, El año de mil trescientos y cuarenta y ocho* (Madrid, 1847), p. 121, note 2. The book appeared first at Madrid in 1774.

the right to be petitioned by chapters in the matter of their election, and to have their request complied with.[13]

Meanwhile there is abundant record of widespread private patronage. The building and rebuilding of churches, monasteries, oratories, hospitals, and the houses of the military orders made what practically amounted to a patronal society. And thus when Alfonso el Sabio wrote his classic definition, he was recounting the well-recognized story of over a thousand years.[14]

Students may be confused by the complete lack in that definition of any hint of lay investiture. It should be noted that Spanish patronage before 1486 was altogether private, if one except the short Visigothic interlude. Unlike the German system, it operated as an act of largess. It recognized the juridical necessity of papal preconization and assignment of subjects. And the bishops rarely served in royal government. Only at the end of the medieval period are a few unique personalities such as Ximenes and Fonseca summoned for official duty near the crown. Undoubtedly Spanish patronage had political overtones, but only because of its religious bases.

In investiture the king or emperor acted in his royal capacity, and he performed as of right every act of provision short of consecration. He examined, nominated, confirmed, installed, gave subjects. Upon the demise of the incumbent diocesan he

---

[13] Taken from *Las siete partidas* (English translation by Samuel Parsons Scott. Chicago, 1931), p. 57. It is in Part. I, tit. v, ley xviii. The translator there added a brilliant footnote on the manner in which Visigothic kings appointed, transferred, and invested prelates, as they likewise presided over ecclesiastical councils. When Moorish *khalifs* replaced them and took over the royal functions, they continued to "provide fully" in making prelates, often with shocking scenes arising from simony. The strange point is that a Mohammedan ruler might appoint a Christian bishop.

[14] Spaniards for centuries learned the facts concerning patronage from Juan Mariana, *De rebus Hispaniae libri XXX*, translated into Spanish and published as *Historia general de España* at Toledo in 1601. It is still widely cited because of its style, its broad concept of history, and its use of sources.

chose the successor, gave him charge of the land as a prince, and this by formal presentation of the insignia of episcopal rule, the ring and crozier. In solemn court he pronounced over the kneeling candidate the forthright words: *Accipe ecclesiam*— Receive your church. Investiture saw these acts as properties of the royal estate. At least it so appeared to his subjects, and German bishops thus instituted were notably ready to side with the sovereign, as well against the royal subjects as against the papacy, and this notwithstanding that the spirituality could alone give power over a spiritual flock. Investiture, finally, was held to be good jurisprudence and good government, and thus the hierarchy became almost totally feudalized by the end of the tenth century. Spain never had a *Hohenstaufen*.

Perhaps the chief contrast between German and Spanish churchmanship resulted from the collision of the latter people with the Moslem. The eighth century dealt them a blow never felt by their fellows to the north, and one destined to shape their national character on rugged individualistic lines. Out of Arabia the armies of the Crescent swept with hurricane force. In 711 under Tarik and in the next years they swarmed across the straits and drove through the peninsula toward its farthest borders. This searing blast broke up the geographical unity and nascent political society of the Visigoths, and it brought on subjection to a hated and alien race. Under various Moslem dynasties the natives felt alternate waves of tyranny and civilization. Mozarabic Spaniards accepted the new rulers and retained their religion. Stouter heroes, among them the fabulous Don Pelayo, disputed the change, and from the Asturias initiated an epochal struggle, the *reconquista*, fundamental memory of every Spaniard. Out of that conflict came a new nation, and a hardy type of man, the type that would stand in the *cortes* of Aragon and reportedly take oath to each new king in these words: "We, who are as good as you, swear to you, who àre no better than we, that we will accept you as our king and sovereign lord, provided you observe all our liberties and laws; but, if not, our oath is void."[15] It is hard to picture that *cortes* accepting a royal right of lay investiture.

Thus it fell out that, while other Europeans took the cross to campaign for the holy places in the Near East, warriors in the peninsula were long at crusade in their own homeland.[16] Toledo fell to them nine years before 1095, the year of Urban II and Clermont, of Geoffrey de Bouillon and Peter the Hermit and the movement for the recovery of Jerusalem. For years kidnaped children had been recruited as future janissaries, trained to serve as civilian and military officials, put to withstand the on-slaught of their own kindred. Hostile Moors, wise and rich, challenged Hispanic Christians with possession of their sacred shrines, curtailment of trade and travel, selective obligation to pay tax, inferior standing in society, scorn for their faith. The effect of this on Spanish life is understandable. They fought for religion and home. Contest with successive emirs of Córdova meant deadly enmity. Chivalry used its weapons with finality. A loyalty higher than feudal ties summoned up immense sacri-fice, and this, incidentally, left Spain far less feudal in land tenure and personal allegiance than was true of England or France. Priests and bishops joined the fight, buoyed up by the common promise of glory in death or in survival. That they might win back or rebuild a church in heathen land and thus obtain the rank of patron stirred them to the quest for honor and to efforts to gain repute for prowess. In the battle for free-dom in both fields—civil and religious—kings and nobles real-ized the strength of a holy citadel set up in recaptured territory. This concept was an anchor more firm than bounty land or lordly title; and it prevailed for centuries.

---

[15] The historicity of the language of the oath is questioned by Prescott, *Ferdinand and Isabella*, I, 81, note 6.

[16] See Chapter 1, note 6, for the meaning of a crusade.

To the modern mind there is a question ever recurrent in this narrative of war fought by medieval Christians against their nonbelieving neighbors. One might get the notion that to them it was a case of "the only good Indian is a dead one." Spaniards of course could make a case of resistance against enemy attack, of regaining unjustly taken territories. Yet the theory of a crusade went farther. For were not the Moslem of Spain in, say, the thirteenth century *in possession* when there was question of the right to rule and to repel aggression? How could popes and bishops approve of a war of conquest in the name of a just divinity? Was it right to despoil the enemy of goods and dominion? What would an educated mind of that day think on the matter?

Fortunately there is in the works of St. Thomas Aquinas (1225-1274) a thorough contemporary analysis, to show that men of the time faced the issue and thought it through. His *Summa theologica,* in the *Secunda secundae,* allots the entire Question 10 to an inquiry into the problem.[17] In his treatment he uses a definite terminology and a consistent frame of reference. This he explains in Article 12. The first norm of conduct taken is the practice of the church, the second the law of nature, the third some practical judgments formed upon examination of the results of particular actions. To ensure clarity and candor in this difficult matter, the entire discussion must drive straight at the focal point. Accordingly the meaning of infidelity is immediately proposed:

I reply by saying that infidelity can be taken in two ways: in the first way, according to simple negation, where he is so named for this only that he does not have the faith. It is understood in the second way as the contrary of faith, whereby he refuses to hear it, or even contemns it . . . and this is the proper definition of infidelity, and so taken

---

[17] The quotations have been translated by the author from the *Summa theologica* (Taurini, 1928).

infidelity is a sin. If, however, it be accepted as pure negation, it has no mark of sin but rather of pain, for such ignorance of divine things is a consequence of the sin of the first parent.[18]

The material here considered will deal only with the first type. In Article 12 he asks whether children of Jews and others outside the faith must be baptized against the will of their parents. In reply he gives a categorical negative. He explains:

. . . under the natural law the child, before he comes to reason, is under the care of the parent. So it would be contrary to natural justice if the child, before arriving at reason, were to be withdrawn from the care of his parents, or if any order were given to it against their will. But after he begins to have the use of his free will, then he begins to belong to himself [*esse suus*], and he can provide for himself what things are proper under divine and natural law.[19]

He inquires in Article 11 whether the rites of those outside the faith are to be tolerated. His thinking is broad:

I reply by saying that the regimen of men is derived from the divine government and ought to imitate it. God, however omnipotent and altogether good, sometimes allows evils to happen on earth which He can prevent, lest by their removal much greater good be hindered or greater evil follow. Hence those in charge of human government rightly tolerate some faults to avoid impeding certain good actions or to prevent greater evil.

And he enforces the point by quoting Gregory the Great in regard to the Jews:

All their festivals, just as they and their fathers have kept their custom for so long a time, they may observe and celebrate with freedom.[20]

---

[18] Art. 1, under *Respondeo*. It is interesting to note that the Council of Trent (Sess. xiv, cap. 2), at the end of the era, declared: "The church passes judgment against no one who has not previously entered through baptism." See Henrici Denzinger, *Enchiridion symbolorum* (Twenty-ninth edition. Freiburg in Breisgau, 1953), p. 313.

[19] See under *Respondeo*.

[20] See his *Conclusio* and *Sed contra*.

Article 10 discusses a question that has no small bearing on modern controversies over the relation between religion and government. It inquires whether those outside the faith can have legitimate authority over Christians. In what has been and is a Christian commonwealth, they are not to be given authority *de novo* over Christian society. But if they have long held authority, they are entitled to continue to exercise it:

We can see this in another light, in a dominion or rule already existing. There we must consider that dominion and rule were introduced by human right. The distinction between the faithful and those outside the faith is of divine right. But divine right, which comes along with grace, does not remove human right, which rests on human reason. And so in itself the difference between the faithful and those outside the faith does not take away the dominion and rule of the infidel over the faithful.[21]

Lastly, to the heart of the question, he asks in Article 8: "Are those outside the faith to be compelled into the faith?" His summary conclusion reads:

I respond by saying that there are those outside the faith who never accepted it, such as gentiles and Jews. And such are in no way to be forced into the faith in order that they may become believers. For to believe is an act of the will. They are, though, to be put under control, if means are at hand, so that they do not impede the faith, either by blasphemies, or by evil persuasions, or also by open persecution. And for this reason the faithful of Christ often war against the infidel, though not indeed to make them believe; for even if they overcame them and held them captive, they would leave them in their liberty as to belief; but for this, that they may compel them not to impede the faith of Christ.[22]

---

[21] See the *Conclusio*.

[22] *Conclusio*. The bull of Nicholas V, *Romanus pontifex* (1454), lists among the ends of the crusade: ". . . so that through these measures he may bring back to the one fold of our Lord the sheep entrusted to him by divine mandate." Following the original charge of Urban II, this supposes peaceful conversion. See the bull below in Part 2, pp. 266-72.

Stark words, yet that was the theory of the crusade.[23] In its essence the enemy had many rights, and these must be respected, for natural right is inalienable wherever it is found. An underlying supposition was that Christians, like everyone else, had the right to live wherever they would, so long as they committed no crime. Another was the right, or duty, of Christians to propagate the orthodox faith. When others blasphemed, openly impeded, or persecuted, protection against such harassment, even by force, was considered perfectly just, as Suárez would later say at Salamanca.[24] The crusading bulls show how this principle would be interpreted, not by an independent judge—for none was available—but by the head of Christianity when his subjects asked for relief. Until the 1600's a haunting fear of the Moslem hung over Europe, and this, coupled with the drive to expel the interloper from the homeland, made the affirmative side of the argument seem invincible. Between Christian and Moslem there was no contemporary possibility of a workable *jus gentium.* Accordingly the crusader rode out to battle with good conscience. As he rode, and smote, his stroke helped bring freedom and unity to his people. Sometimes he gained signal political and economic advantages, and these were confirmed to him by documents rewarding his success with new material possessions. The doctrine of spoils in a just war was held to justify their retention. The chance to spread the faith brightened the entire picture, for he believed in it and used it as the groundwork for his civilizing plans. His sincerity was proved by the effort he made to build a permanent religious organization in the lands "con-

---

[23] The same pope says: ". . . who . . . not only repress the ferocity of the Saracens and the other infidel enemies, . . . but beyond that conquer lands . . . and . . . bring them under their dominion." The bull considers these as legitimate purposes and favors which the popes granted to crusaders. This subjection was in the case considered necessary to guarantee that infidels would not "impede the faith."

[24] Francisco Suárez, *De fide* (Vives edition. Parisiis, 1858), p. 439.

quered or to be conquered." Forthrightness may have been tinged with acquisitiveness; it was not tainted with hypocrisy.

Spain's *reconquista* finally united Goth and Hispano-Roman in one society. Geography took a hand in the process, and Castile at the center bore the brunt of the fighting. Portugal first won full independence. The conquest of the Algarves in 1253 completely ended Saracen rule. Aragon fulfilled her share in the campaign with the capture of the Balearic Islands (1229) and Valencia (1238) under Jaime El Conquistador. The middle theater belonged to the sons of Covadonga and Compostella. Those precarious victories begot the typical Spanish proverb "A dead hero is worth twelve live captains." After many advances and retreats, at last in 1212 they broke through the Guadarramas and, driving southward, won the heart of enemy country along the Tagus and Guadalquivir, never again to be turned back. The fall of Seville (1248) saw them sweep down to the Atlantic. Only Granada—and for a while Córdova—remained as a small, tight bastion, rich and cultured, but, as Prescott remarked, destined after two centuries to pay the cost of her "effeminate luxury" before the insistent pressure of superior power.

During the fourteenth century the *reconquista*, and with it patronage, made little progress. External factors were somewhat to blame for the setback. For in 1305 Clement V was elected pope and moved the papacy to France. Ominous events followed. First came the condemnation of the Knights Templars and the call for all princes of Europe to imprison them.[25] This deed, for which Philip Hughes asks clemency while not condoning the action,[26] hurt the military orders and brought embarrassment to

---

[25] Pastor, *History of the Popes*, I, 60.

[26] Hughes, *Popular History*, p. 131: "from the beginning of his reign an invalid racked with all the horrors of a painful cancer." This matter receives fuller treatment in Philip Hughes, *A History of the Church* (New York, 1934-1947), II, 90-93.

crusading kings, notably Díñiz of Portugal (1279-1325) and
Alfonso XI (1312-1350) of Spain. His successor, John XXII,
in 1319 reserved to himself all minor benefices falling vacant
during the next three years, and because of his great needs in
the absence of support from the states of the church collected
annates from each of them as often as they were conferred by
the pope. His extensive reservations exercised a prejudicial
effect on ecclesiastical life.[27] He then found himself in conflict
with the emperor over the latter's coronation, and the upshot
was a furious debate stirred up by Marsiglio of Padua and
William of Ockham and seriously questioning the rights of the
pope. To complicate the situation, new Avignon methods of
financing the church introduced what was perhaps a necessary
change, but one that certainly disturbed international relations;
for England took the position that the pope, whose funds were
in French investments, fought on the French side of their long
war. The same English, though for less disinterested motives,
passed their Statute of Provisors against foreigners appointed
to sees in the kingdom. And the very residence of the pope in
France roused nationalistic passions everywhere. As a result of
these troubles European kings began to take a livelier interest
in the presentation of their own bishops, and that without canonical election—a trend that would reach serious proportions
in the next century.

Some scholars find reflections of this spirit in a great Spanish
legal document, the *Ordenamiento* given at Alcalá de Henares
in 1348 by Alfonso XI. The last law in that pronouncement of
cortes and king reads as follows:

It was ancient custom, and it is kept in Spain, that when any prelate or archbishop or bishop dies, the canons and others to whom the
right and custom of election pertains, ought at once to notify the king

---

27 J. P. Kirsch, "John XXII," in *Catholic Encyclopedia.* (New York, 1907-1914),
   VIII, 431-34.

of the death of the prelate, and they ought not elect another until they so inform him; and likewise that every aforesaid prelate, after he is confirmed and consecrated in due manner, before he goes to his church is to come and do reverence to the king. Because some chapters and prelates do not regard the right which we have according to this said custom, we order every chapter of cathedral churches, and all arch-bishops and bishops who will be named from now henceforth, that they uphold us and the kings who come after us in our right by reason of the same custom. And let those who oppose it in any way know that we and the kings who shall come and reign after us will be against the elections that may be done to our prejudice, and we shall go counter to the prelates and chapters that do not regard the said our right, with all our power, and we will uphold our right in such manner that our dominion will always be recognized as it should be, and respected.[28]

The editors find in the above law a proof of a true Patronato Real at this early date. In the preface to the ordinance they write: "To this precious document we owe the important evidence of the right of Patronato Real over the churches of the kingdom; for the last law of the ordinance teaches us that, although in those times the use of the elections was prevalent, these had no effect unless they were at once confirmed by the authority of the sovereign."[29] A contemporary Mexican scholar, Jesús García Gutiérrez, sees in the same law a foreshadowing of the full Patronato Real.[30]

It would appear that the document makes no claim to the right of presentation, though its threats might have the effect of a veto. As the same right was exercised by earlier kings,[31] such as St. Ferdinand I of Castile and Alfonso VI, and by all later kings down to Isabella and Ferdinand, this should cause no surprise. The king, as he spoke, saw himself surrounded by a

---

[28] Jordan de Asso y Miguel de Manuel, *Ordenamiento*, tit. xxxiii, ley lviii.

[29] *Ibid.*, p. xxviii.

[30] See his *Apuntes para la historia del origen y desenvolvimiento del regio patronato Indiano* (México, 1941), p. 11.

[31] Jordan de Asso y Miguel de Manuel, *Ordenamiento*, p. 121, note 2, citing laws and customs of these and other Castilian kings.

stout *cortes,* including warrior bishops, who in those days felt no terror at a royal presence. The language reveals no more than the obvious fact that bishops play a part in the great commonwealth—feudality would be the term if this happened beyond the Pyrenees. They have a patent obligation to notify the king of their coming into office—undoubtedly with papal confirmation in that day. The king must be apprised of the decease of the incumbent. The proper conduct of the electoral process—including a ban on traitors, which was upheld by papal excommunication—was very much his concern in his body politic, where the episcopate held a key position in that highly charged religious society. The "reverence" to the king indicates the dual function of the bishop in those times: regard for his own duties in the ever-imminent task of crusading and the providing of leadership in the church. As a coadjutor of the king, who himself must shoulder all responsibility for crusading warfare, he should assuredly be an acceptable person, not alone in sacramental matters but in his capacity as a public figure.

If Avignon altered the sensitivity of kings toward the higher clergy, a worse calamity now struck, the Schism of the West. Those forty years (1378-1418) caused turmoil. Obscurity in the election of Urban VI gave a flimsy excuse for Francophile cardinals to inject duality of papal rule into what was already coolness toward Avignon. It would end only in the high sacrifice of Gregory XII.

This interlude, and the shaky years that followed, gave open opportunity to European kings ambitious for the plunder of power. Morale tottered in the courts and pretension verged toward absolutism. Royalty acquired the habit of supervising clerical discipline and of gross interference in the hierarchy. Popes made serious compromise with independence in an effort to keep the nations in religious unity. With irritating frequency kings arrogated to themselves the right to provide sees for bishops, and from that they went on to solicit from Rome the privilege of bringing forward petitions that they hoped to convert into true presentations.

Among Spanish kings symptoms of this tendency appear. Enrique III of Castile (1390-1407), El Doliente (the Sorrowful), decreed for his council the reservation of the right to present petitions for new prelates in disregard of the canons.[32] Juan II (1407-1464), son of Enrique, with the connivance of the procurators of three monasteries named in his order to prepare the petitions, authorized his council to prepare such petitions and to intervene in getting the desired candidates for cathedrals and monasteries.[33] This intervention should not, however, be read out of context. Juan II was on good terms with Rome. Eugene IV in 1436 gave him a generous grant of faculties in consideration of his renewed crusade against Granada. He received the right to hold and support the churches that he would there conquer, to have patronage over those which he endowed with his own wealth, and to present suitable clerics to the bishops for installation when these churches fell vacant.[34] These, of course, were not cathedral churches but simple oratories or parishes.

It is reported that Enrique IV (1454-1474), son of Juan II and brother of Isabella, found himself brought up sharp close to home. On September 29, 1464 representatives of the "three arms of the state"—*real, eclesiástico, militar*—meeting in Burgos signed a petition of complaint to the king that unfit and unworthy prelates and dignitaries had been advanced "for a price received by persons close to Your Highness."[35] That persons in the curia of his majesty would be paid for these advancements reflects to the discredit of Enrique IV, indicates the

---

[32] García Gutiérrez, *Apuntes*, p. 12.
[33] *Ibid.*, p. 13.
[34] See the bull *Laudibus et honore*, Chapter 4, pp. 64-65.
[35] García Gutiérrez, *Apuntes*, p. 13.

corruption of his rule, and suggests some royal tampering with church administration. And "the three arms" assuredly registered their protest.

A new device entered at this period into royal treatment of the papacy. It is the use of the king's *placet*, or *exequatur*, much later to receive in Spain the euphonious name of *pase regio*. It will have much to do with relations with Rome and with the patronage. Pastor finds its first occurrence during the Great Schism,[36] when its legalization in Sicily was published in the *Monarchia Sicula*. By this new prerogative the crown refused admittance to any papal communication that opposed the designs of the state. Alfonso V of Aragon employed this tool of Sicily in a particularly striking case of bumptious royalty. In 1425, with Martin V seven years in office after the Council of Constance, the pope dispatched a legate, Cardinal de Foix, skilled diplomat and relative of Alfonso, with an embassy to the Aragonese court. Pastor tells the story succinctly: "But the King of Aragon had assumed an attitude which at once rendered all negotiations impossible. He forbade his subjects to hold any intercourse with Rome, prohibited the publication of papal Bulls, and let the Cardinal-legate know that in the event of his presuming to enter his kingdom, he would have his head cut off."[37]

Ferdinand and Isabella both showed something of this irritation in the early years of their government. The former clashed with Sixtus IV in 1478. Cardinal Ferrici, bishop of Tarragona,

---

[36] Pastor, *History of the Popes*, I, 142, note 1. The *beneplacitum regium* was widely used during the Avignon period. For French instances of that time see R. Hedde, "Pragmatique sanction," in *Dictionnaire de theologie catholique* (Paris, 1930-1950), XII, parte 2, 2780-85.

[37] Pastor, *History of the Popes*, I, 275. In V, 240 an account is given of the breakdown of morals in the same court of Aragon. It should be noted that Aragon felt the moral results of the crusading spirit much less than her neighbor Castile, and also that the Foix of Navarre were bitter enemies not stopping at assassination.

died in that year, and the pope conferred the bishopric on Andreas Martínez. Ferdinand wished it to go to the gifted Cardinal Pedro González de Mendoza, and he accordingly ordered Martínez to resign and threatened him with exile if he refused. The frightened candidate thereupon complied. Four years later, when Cuenca of Castile fell vacant, Isabella had a similar dispute. Her pious and able confessor, Alfonso de Burgos, was her choice for the diocese; but the pope had already appointed his nephew, Raffaello Sansoni, to the post. At once she recalled her ambassador from Rome and declared that she would summon a council unless Sansoni, a great lord "with essentially worldly interests," as Pastor puts it, were withdrawn.[38] Sixtus IV, to calm the storm, granted her the right in future to recommend the names, without formal presentation, of her bishops. Sansoni was allowed to hold the office for a short period and then yielded to Burgos.

In this case Isabella, though justly insisting on the religious welfare of her people, nevertheless lost sight of sound jurisprudence, for her civil authority did not empower her to cut the chain of ecclesiastical right, no matter how excellent the men she chose on this and later occasions. The case illustrates both the advance in royal claims—she held that her responsibility for her people demanded that she have a voice in excluding unworthy prelates—and a restoration of proper relations between churchly and political concerns. It might well be seen as foreshadowing the reform begun in the time of Paul III.

In summary, up to the reign of the Catholic monarchs no royal Patronato power had appeared in Spain. Patronage wielded great influence both in times of peace and in crusading war. Bishops held no civil office. Kings had long demanded

---

[38] On these two cases see *ibid.,* IV, 397. Sansoni was known as a man of no ecclesiastical spirit (*ibid.,* IV, 412). See also Prescott, *Ferdinand and Isabella,* I, 301-02.

from the bishops an act of "reverence" upon election and latterly had entered actively into their appointments. Aragon in particular, under the impact of the schism, promoted antipopes and vetoed papal appointments. But no extant law approved immunity from papal directives or power of presentation. Religion in the peninsula operated on altogether positive lines, ready to throw its full weight into the making of the New World.

CHAPTER III

The Portuguese Precedent

While the Europe of the Great Schism and its aftermath seethed in a ferment of councils and antipopes, counterforces produced results of great importance. They were to inaugurate two royal patronages, bring Hispanic rule to two new continental areas, and in the process change the course of history.

In 1439 the last antipope, Felix V, emerged from the Council of Basel. He had short shrift. Weariness with both radicalism and disunion soon ended further interest in tampering with the papacy, and the personal rapacity of the Savoyard Amadeus merely hastened his failure. Tough-minded, arrogant Alfonso V of Aragon turned him away in 1443, and six years afterward he submitted to Nicholas V.

Now at the southwest end of Europe the Atlantic gave birth to a fresh outlook in western civilization. Portugal and Spain began the search for outward development. Their motive was larger than competition for the Canaries and other islands. An intensive crusading spirit came back to life, first in the Orden de Cristo under João de Aviz, then in the marriage of Aragon and Castile. From these crusades developed the Padroado Real and the Patronato Real. The Portuguese foundation acted as exemplar and proving ground for its Spanish counterpart. The documents establishing this foundation will form the subject of the present chapter.

The great bulls of patronage in the fifteenth century rest
their grants squarely on the idea of crusade. It is clearly written
in the texts. Critical eyes have occasionally discounted both the
crusading clauses and the ingenuous directness of the language.
The popes, however, had no intention of doing dishonor to their
office as they conceded these novel and extensive privileges. Examination of the typical bull of crusade, *Orthodoxe fidei propagationem*,[1] proves that censure to lack justification. One glance
at the document brings instant admiration at the mastery of
form, style, and procedure that marked the work of the papal
chancery. In content the breadth of the grant is exactly bounded
by the caution of experience, the care that there be no misunderstanding of its limits or its obligations. Its blunt "We ratify no
other right than that of patronage and presentation as herein
described" shows the control of a firm hand, the overview of a
mind sovereign in this area. It has been suggested that Ferdinand
and Isabella had minute knowledge of papal difficulties—
worldliness at the curia and military threat from Italian powers—and this might create the impression that the pontiff was
forced or cajoled into the agreement.[2] Closer inspection leads
to the conclusion that the pope acted with full freedom and
understanding, that in fact no papal bull was ever more carefully drawn up.[3] It exhibits a combination of genuinely paternal
regard for his spiritual children and their achievement, of support for their just expectations, of provision that the gifts be
not misused or overinterpreted, of readiness to cancel the entire
grant should they forget the origin of the powers conceded.

---

[1] See Chapter 4, pp. 66-70.

[2] García Gutiérrez, *Apuntes*, p. 28. He thinks that the pope yielded "for political
reasons," that "for him it was a great trial." He cites the Spanish translation
of Pastor. The English edition has no like citations, nor the German original
(Freiburg, 1895), III, 304.

[3] Neither the pope nor any man alive at the time could have foreseen to what
lengths the discovery of the Indies would widen the application of the grant,
nor indeed of the later bull of Julius II.

In regard to the Portuguese bulls, it must be kept in mind that these were pioneer steps in the direction of royal patronage and that they dealt with territory not yet included in European maps. Moreover, they were addressed to a military order, not to the crown. This order, the Orden de Cristo, deserved the confidence put in its integrity. Its master prior, Enrique the Infante (1394-1460),[4] got his promotion from the crusading victory at Céuta (1415) in his twenty-first year and held that post during forty-five years of dedicated service. As long as he ruled, he tried to keep his men at spiritual service, though after 1450 they engaged in slaving and commercial dealings. From his castle at Sagres he directed the campaign against the Moslem, his aim being to find another Christian prince (in Ethiopia) and join him in surrounding the sons of the Prophet. Later he would win the sobriquet of Navigator, though it is well to note that his navigational activities, notable as they might be, were the result of an overpowering consecration to the cause of crusade. He was a knightly person, and a gifted one.

His order had a venerable tradition. It was in effect the revived Knights Templars of Portugal. Portugal was the first country in which the Knights settled (1128).[5] When Clement V suppressed the order Portuguese bishops held a trial at Lisbon and found it guiltless of the charges made. King Díñiz then appealed to the new pope, and meantime sequestered the properties of the suppressed body in expectation of their return. To keep alive the crusading spirit he organized the ex-Knights into a *militia Christi* and found the pope ready to approve them

---

[4] He was the third surviving son of João I, retaining his title of *infante* through two succeeding reigns. On the Navigator see Edgar Prestage, *The Portuguese Pioneers* (London, 1933).

[5] Charles Moeller, "Christ, Order of the Knights of," in *Catholic Encyclopedia*, III, 698-99. Note the opinion of Edgar Prestage in the preface to his *Chivalry: A Series of Studies To Illustrate Its Historical Significance and Civilizing Influence* (London, 1928): "We have no adequate account in our language of chivalry in Germany and Spain, and none at all of chivalry in Portugal."

(1319) under the title of the Orden de Cristo. In the time of
João I they manifested a flourishing growth and a zeal for
bringing Africa under the Christian banner. Martin V and
Eugene IV, as the *Romanus pontifex* recounts, gave them possession of lands conquered, rights of presentation, and the indulgence for those dying on campaigns of crusade.

While emphasizing the crusading nature of both the Granada warfare and the conquest of the Atlantic coast of Africa,
another factor deserves attention. Both the Granada conquest
and the move into Africa carried overtones of imperial character. The use of patronage to further this acquisition of external
lands and to direct their subsequent development is a new departure in politics and one deserving close attention. In the first
place, though Portugal had Céuta several decades before Granada fell, it was Spain that ultimately realized the possibilities
of crown patronage. How she established her uniquely successful
system is a point for history to explain, though it might be
compressed into a single statement: she had the good fortune
to find an untrammeled space for empire building. Reorganizing
Granada provided her immediate preparation. Then she went
west. The immense stretches of America were near to no other
political entity comparable to hers. Moreover, they contained
two civilizations, the Aztec-Maya and the Quechua-Amarú, previously unknown but now offering challenge to the newcomer's
power to assimilate what was best in these cultures and to adapt
himself to his new environment. Similarly, the same factor of
external expansion made the stories of these two patronages far
different from that of France, although the French crown received from Leo X in 1516 a grant identical in essentials to what
the other two obtained, Portugal just two years before.[6] France,

---

[6] In 1514 Portugal received for the crown all religious rights previously held by
the master prior of the Orden de Cristo. In 1516 the papacy induced France
to abandon claims of pragmatic sanction and accept presentation to bishoprics
and application of their revenues.

busy with democratizing the papacy through a series of councils and then with the geopolitics of Calvin, engaged at the time in no serious outward movement that might stir the soldier or statesman, the thinker or the businessman. Nor did she then have in mind establishing any colonial empire.

This push outward by Hispanic peoples released unsuspected powers, as they contacted primitive peoples, old civilizations, and vast stretches of open land. They had a magnificent field for experimentation and for improvement in method. It was not the daring of desperation that urged them on, but a thrill in discovery, victory, invention, broadening of knowledge, free rein to enkindled imagination, the making of a new world. The Portuguese, when once they passed the forbidding promontory of Cape Boxador (1434), struck for something more than a few unknown capes. They were on their way to the other end of the earth. By 1471 they had St. Thomas in the Gulf of Guinea. In 1486 they rounded the Cape of Storms, renaming it the Cape of Good Hope because their path to India was cleared. This had been their objective before 1454, when Nicholas V wrote it into his grant.

In confronting the fact that these bulls put large quasi-religious powers into the hands of laymen, it is recognized that medieval times made no sharp distinction between church and state. What is found there is two parallel laws, civil and canon, and two parallel courts. Both often dealt with the same matter, though on different grounds, and no static unanimity affected thought on the subject. It was understood that *sacerdotium* and *regnum* were not rivals but coworkers, that neither could interfere with the other in his rightful sphere: sacraments and civil administration belonged in different orders. Not so was the case of a church building. It belonged to the entire family of the people. Full social acceptance was accorded to patronage, with its right to oversee both the condition of buildings and lands and the service of the incumbent, so that the social acts of re-

ligion would have proper care. Patron never summoned priest
on matters of substance, on faith or sacerdotal powers. But
on the point of performance of duties, the worldly lord might
well call upon the bishop to insure timely amendment.[7]

Another matter calling for comment was the conferring on
a layman of religious power over a cleric. The *Inter caetera
quae* of Calixtus III has interesting examples of this seeming
inversion. But take the case in the concrete. Those responsible
for fulfillment were the Orden de Cristo, a group of fighters
among whom many were priests. The entire order shared in the
privileges and obligations of the bull. To its master—a layman—went the regulation and application of these injunctions.

In the history of royal patronage the beginnings are found
in grants given in the 1450's to Enrique, infante of Portugal, as
master prior of the crusading order. The first came from
Nicholas V (Tommaso Parentucelli), a name never mentioned
by scholars without reverence for his distinguished character as
a humanist. He entered the cardinalitial college a meek and
gentle man in December of 1446. Four months later he was
pope, ruling from 1447 to 1455. In that position of exalted
responsibility he saw the Turks overthrow Constantinople. This
event was for him a turning point, as it was for all the West.
Now he, and many others, felt that only a crusade would save
Christendom; that what was needed was not defensive measures
but a bold attack to force the enemy everywhere to respect the
freedom of the faith. Affonso V of Portugal, alert to the same
concept and relying fully on his military knights, asked Rome
to approve his African crusade with broad grants of power. The
upshot was the *Romanus pontifex* of Nicholas V and the *Inter
caetera quae* of his immediate successor, Calixtus III.[8]

---

[7] Roman law greatly influenced this unity of outlook. See Walter Ullmann, *The
Medieval Idea of Law* (London, 1946). Chapter 5 is particularly pertinent.

[8] During a crusade it was customary to ask formal proclamation from each pope
regnant in the course of the campaign.

The former bull was saved for posterity by the coincidence that it is included entirely in the second, which is its complement. The two contain, beyond the main story, several data that are rarely noticed. They are printed in the rich and reliable collection of Hernáez,[9] and in abbreviated form in the recent work of García Gutiérrez.[10]

[Romanus pontifex]

Nicholas, bishop, servant of the servants of God. For a perpetual remembrance.

The Roman pontiff, successor to the heavenly key bearer and vicar of Jesus Christ, surveys all the regions of the world and with paternal care considers the condition of all nations that dwell therein. In his thought and desire for the salvation of each of them, he is accustomed after serious deliberation to give helpful directives, and to dispose matters as seems pleasing to the Divine Majesty, so that through these measures he may bring back to the one fold of our Lord the sheep entrusted to him by divine mandate, thus to gain for them the reward of eternal happiness and to win pardon for their souls.

Now we believe that under God we shall more fully attain that goal if, with deserved favors and special aids, we encourage those Christian kings and princes who, as athletes and intrepid warriors for the Christian faith, not only repress the ferocity of the Saracens and the other infidel enemies of the name of Christ, but beyond that conquer lands situated in the most remote parts even unknown to us, and without sparing effort or cost bring them under their dominion. And we have definite assurance that the kings and princes themselves, if relieved of certain outlays and handicaps, will be much heartened to further so salutary and laudable a project.

Latterly word has come to us, not without great satisfaction, that our noble and beloved son Enrique, infante of Portugal to our most

---

[9] Francisco Javier Hernáez, *Colección de bulas, breves, y otros documentos relativos a la iglesia de América y Filipinas* (Brussels, 1879), II, 824-30. For the orignal Latin see pp. 266-72.

[10] See Jesús García Gutiérrez, *Bulario de la iglesia Mexicana* (México, 1951), pp. 11-12 for the abbreviated bull of Nicholas V; pp. 13-15 for that of Calixtus III. This is a documentary on each bishopric of Mexico, fully annotated by a competent scholar.

dear son in Christ Affonso, illustrious king of Portugal and the Algarves, follows closely in the footsteps of his father, João of renowned memory, former king of the same domain. Burning with zeal for the saving of souls and ardent in faith, this true Catholic soldier of Christ the Creator of all is a fearless and brave defender of the faith and an intrepid warrior. Fully devoted to spreading the praise and veneration of the most holy name of the Creator throughout the world and into the most remote and unknown regions, from his early years he has striven to bring into the fold of that living and redeeming faith the pagan enemies of the cross, that is, the Saracens and other infidels. Under the direction of King João he took the city of Céuta in Africa and added it to the national territory. Through many other battles he fought under the royal standard against these said hostile infidels, at great risk to his own person and immense labor and expense, together with the loss of many of his companions in warfare; and in spite of a very dangerous career he continues the arduous campaign. In lonely islands of the Ocean Sea he has planted groups of the faithful, had churches and other holy places founded and built for the celebration of divine worship, brought many natives of the islands in that sea to the knowledge of the true God and to baptism, and in this way enlarged the praise and glory of the Lord while he assured the salvation of souls and the propagation of the faith.

Moreover, when he learned that ships could sail to southern and eastern shores where never, or at least not in the memory of western man, anyone had ever gone, places totally outside our knowledge and human beings hitherto unmentioned in our histories, with the thought that this would give the greatest service to God, he turned his efforts on the sea toward contacting the people of India who honor the name of Christ. With their consent he would enlist them as auxiliaries of Christ against the Saracens and other enemies of the faith, including in his plans many gentiles and pagans not yet defiled with the sect of the impious Mahomet. These he would first subdue in the king's name and then preach to them the unknown Christ. For the past twenty-five years, leaving behind his native auxiliaries, he has kept to a course of exploration. In swift ships called caravels he has searched the sea and the maritime lands to the south, aiming almost every year for the antarctic pole. Thus it fell out that his ships touched many ports, islands, and waters, and came at length to the Province of Guinea. After claiming various islands, ports, and seas adjacent to that region, he sailed on and reached the mouth of a great river[11] [Senegal] that was by many thought to be the Nile. For some years he made war on the people of those parts in the name of the king and himself the infante. Many islands there fell to his arms and accepted peace, and they are now in his control along with the adjacent sea.

Numerous inhabitants of Guinea and other Negroes, taken into captivity through legitimate exchange or in lawful contract of sale, were brought to the same region. Of these a considerable number embraced the Catholic faith. It is hoped in the divine clemency that, if his success continues with them, the whole people will be converted, or that at least the souls of many of them will be gained for Christ.

Now we have word that the king and infante desire our assistance. They have borne heavy risks, labors, and costs. Many of the natives among these kingdoms are lost in the wars. As lawful rulers who with the help of the natives have marched through such extensive provinces and gained possession of the ports, islands, and seas, they fear that others may in cupidity be led to sail into those regions and spoil the good and laudable work or usurp its fruits, or at least impede their success. In the hunt for profit, or out of ill will, they may bring in forbidden articles of iron, weapons, wood, and other materials to the infidel, or even teach the infidel the arts of navigation. Should this happen, the natives might reinvigorate their courage and strength to the point where progress would be slowed or perhaps altogether stopped, and this not without great offense to God and the scorn of all Christianity. To prevent these reverses, and for conserving their own right and possession, they have published decrees sanctioned by heavy penalty against anyone navigating there or doing business in the ports or presuming to fish in the seas, except in ships manned by Portuguese sailors and after the paying of a certain tax, and this only after obtaining express permission of the same king or infante. Still in the passing of time it could occur that persons of other nations or kingdoms, through envy, malice, or the desire of gain, might approach that area without care for the decrees or payments of tax, and pass through their provinces, ports, islands, and waters, trade there, and make bold to fish. From this they could come into conflict with King Affonso and the infante, who are under no delu-

---

[11] D. Cyriaci Morelli [Domingo Muriel], *Fasti Novi Orbis et ordinationum apostolicarum ad Indias pertinentium breviarium cum adnotationibus* (Venetiis, 1776), p. 4, states that they believed the Senegal—which they named for a native chief—to be a branch of the Nile.

sion on the point, and there would arise from this presumption hate, rancor, dissension, war, and scandal, from which the greatest offense to God and danger to souls might rightly be apprehended.

We have given due thought to these premises. In a former letter we conceded full and free right to King Affonso to invade, attack, defeat, and subjugate any Saracens and pagans and other enemies of Christ wherever they are situated, and to take the kingdoms, duchies, principalities, dominions, possessions, mobile and immobile goods wherever obtained and held and to reduce their persons to perpetual servitude;[12] and to apply, appropriate, and convert to their own and their successors' utility the kingdoms, duchies, counties, principalities, dominions, possessions, and goods. Using our patent, the same King Affonso or his representative and the infante do lawfully and justly hold the lands, ports, and seas thus acquired. They all pertain by right to King Affonso and his successors, nor may any other of the faithful of Christ, without license of the same King Affonso and his successors, intervene therein in any way whatsoever. Thus will King Affonso, his successors, and the infante more earnestly prosecute this holy work, so famous and worthy of the reverence of all future ages, the salvation of souls, the growth of the faith and the depression of its enemies, thus bringing glory to God and the faith itself and to the whole republic of the church. They now justly petition that further assistance be offered and that through us and the Apostolic See they be more amply fortified with graces and favors.

Acting on very full information in all and each of these things, of our own motion and not simply because of petition by King Affonso and the infante or at the instance of another addressing us in their name, after mature deliberation, by our apostolic authority and with certain knowledge we desire the aforesaid letter of faculties to be taken as inserted here word for word with each and every clause. Céuta and the other conquests and whatever may have been acquired even before our letter was given, and those lands that in future will in the name of King Affonso and his successors and the infante be taken in conquest from the hands of the infidels or pagans in those regions and environs and in places distant and remote are their own of right, this to include everything whatsoever of these provinces, islands, ports, or seas. They are all comprehended in the faculty of the same letter. By virtue of that letter

---

[12] Perhaps on the theory that prisoners taken in a just war could be made the slaves of the victors.

and the present patent, what they have acquired or will in future acquire pertains after the acquisition to the same king, his successors, and the infante. And the same conquest, extending from the Capes of Boxador and Nam [Nun] throughout all Guinea, that is in that southern area and in the same series of possessions, we declare to belong and appertain to King Affonso and his successors and the infante and to no others, and forever to be their own by right. And the same may there publish statutes, prohibitions, and mandates with sanctions, may impose a tax, and dispose and ordain for the natives and their rulers now and forever licitly and freely.

Further, since on many counts it may be fitting for these purposes to grant what King Affonso asks with Enrique the Infante, and this too for his successors and for whatever person or persons to whom they may commit the undertaking, noting that among the Roman pontiffs our predecessors Martin V of happy memory did grant the same for King João at his request, and on another occasion Eugene IV, by indults to the famous Duarte, king of the same kingdoms and father of King Affonso, therefore we do of free will and right act decree that these parties may undertake the following course of action: namely, to buy and sell to certain Saracens and infidels any goods or foods as seems proper, and also to enter into pacts of any sort for exchange, contract, traffic, or negotiation, and to transport to the regions of those same Saracens and infidels goods of any description, provided that they be not made of iron or wood or rope, nor ships or arms.[13] They may sell to the said Saracens and infidels all and single of those mentioned articles, and make, handle, and use whatever is necessary in these transactions. The same Affonso, his successors, and the infante may found or cause to be founded and built, in the provinces or islands or regions he has acquired or will acquire, churches, monasteries, and other holy places. He may likewise transport to these localities any ecclesiastical person whatever, seculars or members of any mendicant religious order, with the permission of their superiors. And those persons may dwell there; and in any whatever of the places described, whether already settled or to be settled, they may hear confessions and absolve upon salutary penance any reserved cases except those reserved to the Holy See, and may administer the sacraments of the church. We concede and

---

[13] This restriction indicates an existing regulation the origin of which is unknown to the author.

bestow these powers upon Affonso and his successors on the throne of Portugal and on the infante.[14] . . . Given at Rome, at St. Peter's, the year of the Incarnation of our Lord 1454, January 8, the eighth year of our pontificate.

Calixtus III was a man of interests and background quite different from those of Nicholas V. During his pontificate of three years (1455-1458) he was absorbed in organizing Christian Europe against the Turk. With the abnegation of a St. Jerome, firm of will, inflamed with devotion, he wrote with clarity but without perception of what was implied in his policy of crusade. In the Balkans he saw Scanderbeg a tower of strength against the invader. Now, as he looked westward, he found a similar dynamic power driving against Africa. This may well be the reason why he entrusted such unusual faculties to Enrique the Infante and to his successors. In this he far exceeded moderation in what he handed over to the master prior, and his grant forms the first important step in presenting to posterity a crown patronage. It would be completed for Portugal by Leo X in 1514. If later the Patronato Real became an irreplaceable system in the Hispanic world, the cause may be laid to this pope's zeal for present success in a holy cause. The *Inter caetera quae* may be found in García Gutiérrez.[15]

[*Inter caetera quae*]

Calixtus, bishop, servant of the servants of God. For a perpetual remembrance.

Among the many duties laid on us by the Divine Clemency, most ardently is our heart drawn to this, that in every place and particularly in those regions bordering on the land of the Saracen the divine worship flourish to the praise and glory of the omnipotent God and the exaltation of the Christian faith, and that it undergo constant expansion. And those favors which our predecessors, the Roman pontiffs, have conceded to the well-deserving kings and princes for legitimate causes, we shall

---

[14] Hernáez omits here the customary injunction and warning.
[15] García Gutiérrez, *Bulario*, pp. 13-15. For the original Latin see pp. 272-75.

ratify with our apostolic power, so that, all doubts being removed, these
may endure in perpetual vigor.

Not long since, our predecessor of happy remembrance, Pope Nicholas V, granted letters patent to the following effect:[16] . . .

Now the aforesaid King Affonso and Enrique the Infante are extremely solicitous that the Apostolic See concede forever to the said
Order of Christ, from whose revenues the said infante was reportedly
enabled to gain those lands, the spiritualities in those remote islands,
regions, ports, and localities situated on the Ocean Sea near the southern shore of Guinea, which the same infante took by force of arms from
the hands of the Saracens; and that the declaration, constitution, donation, concession, appropriation, decree, petition, exhortation, support,
inhibition, command, and will, moreover the very rescript of Nicholas
our predecessor himself, and all and each part contained therein, be
confirmed.

Wherefore humble supplication comes to us, on the part of the said
king and infante, to add the vigor of apostolic confirmation to the declaration, constitution, injunction, inhibition, mandate, and will, and the
rescript of the same; moreover that we deign to concede forever, and of
our apostolic benignity provide fully and opportunely in these premises,
the spiritualities and complete ordinary jurisdiction,[17] both in the aforesaid acquisitions and in other islands, lands, and localities to be acquired in future by the same king and infante in the regions of the
said Saracens.

We, therefore, aware that the religion of the same order can, in
those same islands, lands, and localities, gain salutary fruit in the Lord,
and yielding to such petitions, do hold as ratified and acceptable, and
with our apostolic authority we do, by these presents and with certain
knowledge, confirm, approve, and declare to subsist in perpetual firmity
the declaration, constitution, donation, appropriation, decree, petition,
exhortation, support, injunction, inhibition, command, will, rescript,
and the contents of the same and whatever intent is there involved; sup-
plying all defects if perchance any lie therein. And beyond this, we of
our authority and knowledge do for the aforesaid parties perpetually
decree, enact, and ordain that the spiritualities and complete ordinary

---

[16] Here the entire previous *Romanus pontifex* is repeated.

[17] Here one meets the famous phrase that marked the broad powers given the
Franciscan order in Spain. See below, pp. 212-14.

jurisdiction, dominion, and power, so far as spiritualities extend, in the islands, towns, ports, regions, and localities from the Capes of Boxador and Nam [Nun] down to all of Guinea, and beyond the southern shore even to the Indies, both acquired and to be acquired, belong and pertain to the military order of the same for all future time. And these sites, number, quality, names, designations, boundaries, and situations we wish to be held as expressed in these presents. This we now, from this time forward, concede and grant to the aforesaid parties by our word, authority, and knowledge.

And this in such sense that the prior major of the said military Order of Christ holding office at the time is to confer and provide to each and all ecclesiastical benefices, whether with care of souls or without, both secular and religious of whatever order, in the islands, lands, and localities aforementioned, whether the benefices are now founded or to be founded, instituted or to be instituted, of whatever rank and value they be or have been, as often as they happen to be vacant.

And he may issue sentence of excommunication, suspension, and interdict and other ecclesiastical judgments, censures, and penalties, as often as there may be need and the character of the actions and negotiations going forward at the time demand it, and all and each other sentence which the ordinaries of places are *de jure* or by custom enabled to issue and dispose; and further, insofar as they are spiritualities, in no wise other than ordinaries can and should issue, dispose, ordain, and conclude. Over all and each of these matters we by these presents do concede, with full and free exercise of right, that in these islands, lands, and localities, whether acquired or to be acquired, no diocese exists. And it is invalid and of no effect if any other person should there attempt to rule by whatever authority, whether knowingly or in ignorance.

And this, notwithstanding apostolic constitutions and ordinations, or statutes, customs, privileges, usages, prerogatives in the oath of the same military order or confirmed by apostolic or any other power, all contrary decrees of whatever kind notwithstanding. Therefore let no man infringe or unwarily dare to go against this document of our confirmation, approbation, constitution, fulfillment, decree, statute, ordination, will, concession, largess. But if any should[18] . . .

Given at Rome, at St. Peter's, the year of the Incarnation of our Lord 1456, March 15, the first year of our pontificate.

---

[18] Omitted in Hernáez and García Gutiérrez, for brevity, is the threat of punishment to opponents of the papal brief.

This striking concession proved to be an experiment for the papacy, and later grants will exhibit at least tacitly far more careful assignment of jurisdiction and provision for the normal organization of the church under episcopal direction. *Inter caetera quae*, which gave most unusual powers to the infante of Portugal in his capacity as master prior of the Orden de Cristo and to his successors in the same role appears to exceed any previous crusading grants in its inroad into the province of ecclesiastical jurisdiction. In fact, it confounds the understanding of one who attempts to read it in the context of the twentieth century. To judge it sharp distinction must be kept between sacramental power and juridical rule over subjects. Excommunication belongs in the latter field, and a layman might conceivably enjoy this delegated power, no matter how repugnant it may sound to good ecclesiastical thinking.

So, too, of the extreme concession to confer all ecclesiastical dignities. This goes beyond the idea of patronage as described in later privilege. Yet in the document there is no suggestion of the master prior's receiving sacramental powers for his own use or of giving them to the clergy, through ordination, consecration, or the conveying of faculties. If indeed the words "complete ordinary jurisdiction" were to be taken in their present meaning, the master prior would be a bishop, as the term "spiritualities" seems to indicate. The clause stating that "no diocese exists" compounds the confusion if again it be read as not only excluding other bishops but giving the episcopal sacramental power to the master prior. The sense here is plainly that there is no diocesan in all that territory—a huge section of the church to be without a bishop—and that the nonsacramental episcopal powers are held by the order in its highest officer. Nevertheless it must be agreed that, if these tremendous ecclesiastical rights had been not merely vested in the head of a military order but had instead been conferred upon the crown, there would come into existence a close church-state union.

Aside from the qualifications just mentioned, it is evident that, in giving to the military director of the vast Portuguese conquests the complete possession and control of that extensive region, the pope set up something of unique significance. Religion is to a certain extent jeopardized, for it is put into a position of competition with secular right.

The question of the right to approve crusading warfare has already been discussed. The papal right to assign islands and uncivilized mainlands, well treated in the work of Luis Weckmann (with a highly laudatory preface by Ernst Kantorowicz),[19] need not be discussed here. What concerns a reader at this point is in a sense preliminary. These grants formed the pattern of thought for Ferdinand and Isabella. They saw in this new design what possibilities lay in royal patronage, how effective it might be in the conquest of Granada, and—once Columbus had reported—what a tool it could be for the organization of the Indies. They had full opportunity to review what the Orden de Cristo had been doing since Céuta: first a fierce crusade, then a period of exciting discovery, next the economic developments with much more to come in gold-bearing territory and remote ports where a handful of cowries could buy a useful slave; and India surely called to the Portuguese before Nicholas V put it into *Romanus pontifex*. These signal economic gains the Portuguese were now pursuing, in the constant advance of a campaign over the ocean culminating in territory placed under military rule where the Portuguese would settle down to profitable business. These forward movements begot a sense of dignity and grandeur in empire and—something more than feeling—a quite

---

19 Luis Weckmann, *Las bulas alejandrinas de 1493 y la teoría política del papado medieval* (México, 1949). He traces the "omni-insular theory" back beyond Urban II to the influence of the Donation of Constantine. Contrary to Francis I, he holds that Alexander VI did not at all give away what he did not have, for during many centuries the papacy was accorded the feudal right over these uncivilized territories.

tangible and perhaps formidable military and naval power that would confront the Catholic monarchs as soon as Columbus brought home the news of Castilian discovery. During the fifteenth century the two nations exhibited considerable rivalry over the recently found island groups. Now, after a brief skirmish of diplomats, they would compete in a rivalry of accomplishment, out over the waters that washed their new empires. It is time to turn to the Spanish Patronato Real.

CHAPTER IV

The Bull of Granada

As one approaches this document, which provided the first full royal patronage, it may help to recall the distinction between private and royal (crown, or state) patronage. Though the bull concedes patronage over only one of the kingdoms of the Spains, then in process of recovery, it establishes something new. In the privilege the king is now taken as more than a single person; he is the representative of the whole community. Accordingly a grant of royal patronage, or a Patronato Real, implies a special compact between the papacy and the head of the state. The crown accepts the burden of furnishing support for all religious actions within the territory: the building and endowment of places of divine worship and the maintenance of its clergy in carrying out the duties annexed to that charge. And it receives the right to constitute the personnel of the clerical body through the establishment of the episcopate (and other higher clergy such as abbots of monasteries) by the process of presentation. Lesser presentation usually remains with the bishops. The papacy guarantees to honor the royal presentations unless fraud is evident and to confirm and provide for them up to installation in their benefices.

In passing, it is clear that in this system the crucial point of royal obligation is likewise the focus of possible conflict: the maintaining of its clergy in carrying out their duties. The crown has certain undoubted rights to see that these duties are carried out, and one of them is the right to loyalty, or patriotism. How far these rights will meet with ecclesiastical objection depends upon a multitude of unforeseen factors that may become operative in the future, among which geography and time will play their parts.

In 1456, despite the broad concessions of *Inter caetera quae*, the grant of Calixtus III lacked the two essential elements of royal patronage. A military order, and not the crown, received the privileges, and thus held a private patronage; and no right of presentation to the episcopacy was accorded. No bishops, but the master prior of the Orden de Cristo, ruled this new segment of the church. It was conceived at law as a purely missionary corporation within the framework of a crusade. The master prior had full prerogative for presentation of priests, with the disciplinary power of an ordinary—that is, of a bishop. This was truly remarkable; but he did not have the great sacramental powers which are the center of episcopal right.

This Orden de Cristo now proceeded to demonstrate a pattern for the assimilation of conquered people into the Christian and Portuguese way of life. Witnessing that demonstration were Ferdinand and Isabella, as they pressed their high purpose of incorporating Granada into the unity of the Spains.

On August 29, 1484 Innocent VIII became pope. Shortly after his election, on November 21, he addressed the European powers on the imminent danger poised for the church and western civilization by Turkish advances.[1] An imperative summons went out for all Christian states to act in a situation so serious as to forbid delay.

Spain at that juncture faced the critical moment of her ten-year war, the campaign against Málaga,[2] which as the key to

---

[1] Pastor, *History of the Popes*, V, 288-90.
[2] For the campaign see Prescott, *Ferdinand and Isabella*, II, 24-25.

Granada blocked the military attack headed south and southeast from Córdova. After a long and severe siege the stronghold capitulated on August 18, 1487. The campaign (from May to August) followed upon the diplomatic effort whose outcome was the *Orthodoxe fidei propagationem* of December 13, 1486. To Ferdinand and Isabella the effect of this bull was decisive for immediate success and momentous because of the effect that it would have upon the future.

To prepare the way for obtaining this bull Isabella had her Roman ambassador, the Conde de Tendilla, request the Holy See for an exact copy of a former grant of patronage made to her predecessors of Castile.[3] The return letter brought a rarely mentioned document. It is fortunately preserved in a manuscript of 1488 now at Simancas.[4] This formal state paper was drawn up by Pedro de Toledo, bishop of Málaga, member of the royal council and chief almoner, at the order of their majesties, for important purposes of state. It contains two papal briefs. The first is the copy desired by Tendilla. Signed by Innocent VIII, it simply transcribes word for word from the regestrum of Eugene IV, with no introductory or concluding remarks other than verification of authenticity and the usual injunction of obedience, the *Laudibus et honore* sent by Eugene IV on August 9, 1436 to King Juan II of Castile (1406-1454), and the enclosure is dated on May 8, 1486. This bull, as will be seen, grants to Juan a personal patronage over churches recovered in the crusade of Castile. The second is the copy of the epochal Bull of Granada of December 13, 1486. Following the latter is a large and precise authentication of the two letters by the

---

3 Though Ferdinand and Isabella both signed the request, as is clear from the two bulls taken together, the grant was to affect Isabella alone in her own kingdom of Castile.

4 The 1488 reproduction is in the archive of Simancas, Sección Patronato Real, legajo 69, 1. The author has the film copy, and of course its enlarged reproduction in the original size.

same bishop of Málaga and three members of the royal council of Castile.

The reproduction of 1488, interesting primarily, of course, because of the *Orthodoxe fidei propagationem,* offered so many difficulties in paleography—its script is the monastic letter of the Pyrenees, and it is badly folded and sometimes faded—that the author sought an original of this prime document of the Patronato Real. Fortunately a note of Father Leturia provided the necessary lead, and the film of the authentic bull soon arrived from the gracious director of the archive.[5] Because of its perfect condition and exquisite execution—it appears almost as a fine engraving—the reading offered no serious problem. This is the document spoken of in Chapter 3. The bull of Eugene IV reads as follows:

[*Laudibus et honore*]

Eugene, bishop, servant of the servants of God. For a perpetual remembrance.

Most worthy of praise and honor are the works and deeds of our very dear son in Christ, King Juan, illustrious ruler of Castile and Leon. Wrestling mightily for Christ like the celebrated champion *[6] he fell upon the wicked Saracens, those enemies of the Christian name, and in scorn of all personal danger attacked them headlong and subjugated their lands and settlements under the rule of the faithful of Christ. His splendid victories for us and the Roman church are justly famous.

Wherefore, considering in the quiet of our mind his wholehearted dedication, we hold it only proper that his legate get favorable hearing

---

[5] This original Bull of Granada, so called because the grant embraces the Moorish kingdom of Granada as of 1486, is in the same Sección Patronato Real, legajo 38, 4. Pedro Leturia, in "La bula del patronato de las Indias españoles que falta en el archivo Vaticano" (*Studi e testi,* No. 125 [1946], p. 402, note 3, and p. 404, note 9), located the original of 1486. His article is the famous reconstruction of *Universalis ecclesiae regimini,* the Roman original of which can no longer be found, but copies of which are in Simancas. The film of the original Bull of Granada was obtained through the courtesy of Mrs. Pierce Butler, director of the Ayer Collection in the Newberry Library, Chicago. For the original Latin see pp. 275-77.

[6] An asterisk always indicates a missing or illegible word or words.

for graces that the king asks, thus to encourage him and his successors
in further prosecuting these fruitful campaigns. We recall that our
predecessor of happy memory, Pope Urban II, duly conscious of the
heroism of the then king of the Spains [Alfonso VI] and his religious
devotion to the same Roman church, conceded by his written patent to
this king, his successors, and his valiant warriors the churches and oratories that they might capture or construct in the realm of the same
Saracens. King Juan reminds us that under this same concession his
predecessors as true Catholic fighters for the faith, struggling against
great odds and constantly pouring out money and labor, did recover
and hold many lands taken from these Saracens, and that they were
enabled to bestow very many dignities and to dispose of other ecclesiastical benefits, and in certain places to have the right of patronage over
those churches, oratories, and chapels. We, therefore, fully in sympathy
with this petition and cognizant of the facts, confirm and approve by
apostolic authority the extension of the aforesaid grant, and by these
presents we communicate the patronage. Moreover we broaden the right
of patronage, to all and each of the lands, mosques, and sacred places
that King Juan and his successors take from the hands of the Saracens
and adapt to the praise of the divine name. And the said King Juan and
his successors will have, for other churches that they will with their
own funds found and endow in the kingdoms of Castile and Leon and
in the aforesaid acquired territories, the right of patronage and of presenting suitable persons to the ordinaries of the places, as often as they
fall vacant. By our aforesaid authority we reserve these rights to King
Juan and his successors, though always with the right of every other
person intact.

Therefore let no man dare to infringe this document of our confirmation, approbation, strengthening, and reservation, nor in rashness
to contradict it. But if anyone should presume to attempt so to act, let
him know that he incurs the indignation of the omnipotent God and His
blessed apostles Peter and Paul. Given at Bologna, the year of the
Incarnation of our Lord 1436, July 24, the sixth year of our pontificate.

On December 13, 1486, Innocent VIII sent to Ferdinand and
Isabella the central document of this entire study, the Bull of
Granada.[7] It follows at once.

---

[7] In the archive of Simancas, Sección Patronato Real, legajos 38, 4 and 69, 1.
For the original Latin see pp. 277-82.

[*Orthodoxe fidei propagationem*]

Innocent, bishop, servant of the servants of God. For a perpetual remembrance.

Our chief concern and commission from heaven is the propagation of the orthodox faith, the increase of the Christian religion, the salvation of barbarian nations, and the repression of infidels and their conversion to the faith. Hence it is that Catholic kings and princes, athletes of Christ and tireless warriors battling in that cause, never fail to find in us their deserved assistance and favor. For the more precarious that freely embraced combat for the sake of the immortal God, the greater their insistence on diligent and expert pressing of the contest and the better they realize that, beyond the salvation of their souls, the Apostolic See grants to them most abundant recompense. This we gladly confer, and as a reward of their crusade make them rulers, guardians, and keepers of the lands they conquer and the people there resident. They have a right to be assisted in a manner helpful to them and generally beneficial, so that they may possess and control the churches, monasteries, and other ecclesiastical benefices and occupied territories regained by them in the enterprise to which they consecrated themselves by vow.

Now surely our dear son and daughter in Christ, King Ferdinand and Queen Isabella of Castile and Leon, are by the grace of the most-high maker of all things and founder and author of all good, the omnipotent God, illustrious among all other Christian kings and queens. With a broad empire of most ample kingdoms and diverse other provinces, they possess the obedience and sense of duty of rulers subject to the Lord, the insight and decision proper to all great sovereigns. Noble in their affluence and resourcefulness, with brilliant youth, spirit ready for every redoubtable undertaking, provident counsel, constancy in administering justice, merit for many valorous deeds, skill in warfare, and stalwart courage and audacity—for all these gifts they return thanks to their author and enter into whatever bold campaign brings honor to the same omnipotent God and the expansion of the Christian empire. They have not limited their enterprise to the task begun in the attack on the infidel in the islands of the Canaries, but the effort carries on to wider fields.

Before their eyes is the kingdom of Granada, part of their own racial family. In former years this realm, the true inheritance of the Spains, was held by those fierce enemies of the Christian name. They now come back in battle to subject it to their dominion. In the lands taken and to be taken from the same Saracens they have created churches, monasteries, and ecclesiastical benefices. To the support of these institutions and to their endowment they have applied fixed portions of the tithes, fruits, revenues, and rentals of the said ecclesiastical properties. And not by their own prowess, but trusting in the power and guidance of the same omnipotent God, they won a victory from every angle most difficult, carving out cities, camps, towns, many holdings; almost a third of Granada, we have been told, fell to their control under the divine assistance and the favoring madness of the enemy. And neither in the domain of Granada nor in the aforesaid islands do they halt in the daily progress of their crusade.

They plan for the people of the cities, fields, and camps captured, and those ready for future capture by themselves and their successor kings of Castile and Leon, preservation under their rule and the upholding of the same faith therein, as our beloved and noble son, Enecus López de Mendoza, conde de Tendilla, captain of the same King Ferdinand and Queen Isabella and their representative to us and the Apostolic See, has in their name described for us. They consider it of great moment at this time that for the cathedral churches, monasteries, and conventual priories in the regions they have recently captured in the same islands and the realm of Granada, in the villa of Puerto Real of the Cádiz diocese, and in such other parts of the country of Granada and the islands as are about to be mastered by Ferdinand, there be appointed ecclesiastical persons of integrity, diligence, and zeal for the orthodox faith, men of clean life and moral uprightness along with genuine spirituality, provident too and experienced in government, and both beholden to and acceptable to the same rulers. Men of this character will obtain the canonries, prebends, portions, and dignities of the same cathedral and collegiate churches won back or to be recovered and organized in time to come. These must be persons whose manner of life is laudable as is their conversation on divine things, whose divine celebration is frequent and devout, and whose persuasive example is an exhortation to a holy life, thus to bring those now living there to abstain from all wickedness and to strive for virtue. By their unwearying zeal they will work for the salvation of their own souls, forward the estate of their kings, and altogether shun rebellion.

In earlier letters of ours, responding to the prayer of the same king and queen, we conceded the faculty to create for certain prelates a number of ecclesiastical foundations, monasteries, and other benefices in the aforesaid localities, and in those places to apply as an endowment the ecclesiastical fruits, revenues, and rentals. It was our hope that, if there were conceded to King Ferdinand and Queen Isabella the right of patronage over the churches, monasteries, dignities, priories, canonries, prebends, and portions of this kind, then surely, to make certain the conservation and maintenance of the inhabitants of the same acquired regions and those that would be acquired in the future, and keeping in mind the integrity of devotion in the same kings and their perseverance in the Catholic faith, opportunity could be found to name persons to preside in the same churches and monasteries and priories, and to obtain the dignities, canonries, prebends, and portions mentioned. Thus fortified by the protection of the same kings as patrons, and by their help and favor [these prelates] could more easily recover and preserve the occupied properties of the churches, monasteries, priories, dignities, canonries, and prebends, be defended against all oppression, receive relief in every necessity, willingly support the preservation of the faith and the estate of the same kings in the same regions, and see to the welfare of the churches, monasteries, dignities, priories, canonries, prebends, and portions of this kind, not to speak of the persons obtaining these posts. We are in full accord with this policy.

On this entire problem we have held mature deliberation with our brethren. Wherefore, relying on their counsel and their express consent, we confer the full right of patronage and of presentation of suitable persons to the Apostolic See for the cathedral churches and, when their fruits, revenues, and rentals exceed two hundred florens of gold *de Camara* per annum according to the common estimate, of the monasteries and conventual priories in the same lands of the kingdom of Granada and the Canary Islands thus far acquired by the same King Ferdinand and Queen Isabella or that will, by them or their successor kings of the Spains at the time, be acquired and organized anew as it may come to pass in the future, and similarly those churches and properties standing in Puerto Real, and also the postpontifical offices in the same cathedrals and the principal posts in the collegiate churches; and to the ordinaries of places the right to the other monasteries and lesser postpontifical dignities, canonries, prebends of the same type, complete or half portions of cathedral and collegiate churches already erected in the same places; and in others that happen to be created, after their erection the fruits, revenues, and rentals when, as said, they have been applied canonically, even in a vacancy after their first erection. For all time forward we by our apostolic authority and the tenor of these presents concede to King Ferdinand and Queen Isabella and to their extant successor kings of the same kingdoms these grants in perpetuity, and we desire that they pertain to them from henceforth completely and without restraint. And in regard to the presentations of this kind, for the sees which may be created through the same King Ferdinand and Queen Isabella and their successors, those persons presented at the time to this see for the cathedral churches and monasteries are to be placed in the same churches and monasteries respectively as diocesans and abbots, and likewise for the sees in conventual priories and major and principal dignities in cathedral and collegiate apostolic churches, just as the ordinaries of places are bound and obligated to institute, by their ordinary authority, persons presented at the time to other dignities, canonries, and prebends, full or half portions of this kind. And the special and general reservations made at times through the Apostolic See and its legates for churches, monasteries, priories, dignities, canonries, prebends, and portions [are theirs,] and whatsoever other graces and licenses that are not by law included in ecclesiastical benefices of lay patronage to the churches, monasteries, conventual priories, dignities, canonries, prebends and portions, and which pertain to the right of patronage of this kind.

Nevertheless, if they [the monarchs] act beyond the provisions and completions established by the Holy See and the ordinaries, or otherwise than in the manner of presentation here described, their acts are null and void. With the advice of our same brethren and on the aforesaid authority we establish, ordain, and decree to be unratified and invalid the action of whoever attempts anything contrary to these presents, from any motive and with whatever authority undertaken, whether knowingly or in ignorance.

Beyond the aforesaid, by apostolic letter we command our venerable brethren, the archbishop of Toledo and the bishops of Palencia and Cuenca, that in as far as they or two of them or one, by himself or through another or others, in whatever circumstance or time come to realize that the aforesaid grant is challenged, and they be lawfully summoned, by solemn publication they must uphold King Ferdinand and Queen Isabella and their successors as enjoying peaceful possession of the right of patronage and of presentation. The persons presented by them are to be received at the time and admitted, and upon the presentations themselves (if canonically carried out) they are to be put in charge and instituted according to the tenor of the above statute, withholding by our authority those who deny the same, for subsequent appeal.

And all this notwithstanding the apostolic constitutions and ordinations and oath or apostolic confirmation, or support by any other grant, or by the statutes and customs of churches and monasteries of this kind and of the orders indicated, and all things else to the contrary, or if there exist an indult from the said Apostolic See for the ordinaries of localities or any others held either in common or separately to the effect that they may not be interdicted, suspended, or excommunicated, through apostolic letters not making full and express and word-for-word mention of such indult therein, regarding the said kings in the same churches, monasteries, priories, dignities, canonries, prebends, portions, and ecclesiastical benefices.

We ratify no other right than that of patronage and of presentation as herein described. Nor do we intend by this grant in any other way to do prejudice to the liberty, supremacy, and jurisdiction of the Apostolic See and the other churches. Let no man whatever make free to infringe this patent of our concession, statute, ordination, decree, mandate, and will, or dare in temerity to attack it. But if anyone should presume so to attempt, let him know that he will incur the indignation of the omnipotent God and His blessed apostles Peter and Paul. Given at Rome, at St. Peter's, the year of the Incarnation of our Lord 1486, December 13, the third year of our pontificate.

The magnificent exordium of this bull proposes its general objective, to approve the conversion of the Saracens and the maintenance of the faith in reconquered territory, with both tasks allotted directly to the Catholic monarchs. The crusading formula, "the repression of infidels and their conversion to the faith," found also in the two previous Portuguese bulls, is no serious modification of what Aquinas allowed, although it seems to connote forceful conversion. Yet this force was neither approved nor anticipated; the subsequent action of Ximenes in Granada bears out the point. "Maintenance of the faith" recalls directly the Aquinas dictum concerning the "impeding" of the faith; it affects first the Christian inhabitants—hundreds now in Moorish prisons—and second the prospective Moorish converts. To this formula is added the usual plenary indulgence for a crusader dying on campaign: "cognoverint se . . . animarum salutem . . . quesivisse."

In the eulogy given the monarchs by Innocent, unlike the common papal practice of suggesting what is hoped for rather than what has been going on, the picture conforms to actuality. Hence when the pope proceeds in his third section to discuss the proposition offered by the ambassador, he relies on calm reason and accomplished fact.

As to the *ius patronatus* conferred, its precision matches the breadth of the concession. Royal endowment and royal presentation for the cathedral churches, including that of postpontifical offices, establish crown support and crown construction of the hierarchy. Reservations, though not essential, become an integral extension in the continuance of the organization. The three great bishops are called upon to support the kings in any demurrer against their new position.

For six years the kings will now carry on a furious drive to end the weakness and disunity of Spain. Meantime Christopher Columbus, with steady support from Isabella, rounds out his waiting time and appears at the war camp of Santa Fe, there to sign the capitulations and set in motion his famous discovery.

CHAPTER V

The Challenge of New Lands

In the year 1492 three separate events conspired to give birth to the Spanish empire. The surrender of Granada on January 2 fulfilled long dreams of unity and vitality for Spain. August 11 found Pope Alexander VI elevated to the papal throne. October 12 brought renown to Columbus and glory to Castile. Within twelve months the great admiral set off on his momentous second voyage that would begin the transfer of European civilization to the *Novus Orbis*.[1]

Soon after Christmas of 1492 Columbus, with his *Santa Maria* wrecked and the *Pinta* off on a diversion, took sail from Navidad in the *Nina* for his dead-reckoning course to the Azores, and on March 6 he entered Lisbon. Nine days later he sailed into Palos harbor. Meantime his overland messenger reached the monarchs at Barcelona, and on the thirtieth they wrote him to come quickly, stopping on the way at Seville to make arrangements for the next trip.[2] In mid-April he had a royal welcome

---

[1] Peter Martyr, who gave currency to the phrase, receives an extended notice in Prescott, *Ferdinand and Isabella*, II, 76-79.

[2] The letter is in Martín Fernández de Navarrete, *Colección de los viajes y descubrimientos que hicieron por mar los españoles desde fines del siglo XV, con varios documentos inéditos concernientes a la historia de la marina castellana y de los establecimientos españoles en Indias* (Second edition. Madrid, 1859), II, 27-28.

at Barcelona, and plans went forward for the full exploitation of his discovery. Pivotal in that enterprise was confirmation of right and possession by the papacy. Urgent dispatches[3] were carried to the ambassador at Rome for immediate presentation in person to Alexander VI. On May 4 the pope took action in that fundamental document of international law, *Inter caetera divinae.*[4]

This prompt settlement required no more than three weeks, and it evidences professional expertness in the court at Barcelona,[5] the Spanish embassy in Rome, and the Roman curia. Alexander, despite his glaring personal deviations, has a large record of support for missionary activity. The embassy but recently had given a splendid account of itself in the formulation of *Orthodoxe fidei propagationem.* As to the court, Antonio de Herrera summarizes the case that it submitted to Rome.[6] In his lines can be seen the kings' respect for the informed and alert administrator at the head of the church who, though of their nation, was nevertheless a man of parts in official business and could act with an independent mind. Herrera writes:

Such was their obedience and regard for the Holy See that, despite their decision to send the admiral back at once to the Indies to expand

---

[3] Apparently the first dispatch went soon after the first message came to the monarchs. This was to insure their conquest against Portuguese complaints. The second dispatch must have included the idea to divide control of the oceans, and this explains the difference between the May 3 and May 4 texts of *Inter caetera divinae.*

[4] This three-word title is used herein to distinguish the above-mentioned bulls from others beginning *Inter caetera.* The May 3 bull given in Navarrete is not printed here, for reasons explained shortly below. It would constitute merely a matter of record, not advancing the story.

[5] Pacheco y Cárdenas print sixty-six *cedulas* issued in regard to the discovery during May of 1493. See Ernesto Schäfer, *Índice de la colección de documentos inéditos de Indias* (Madrid, 1947), I, Nos. 54-120.

[6] Antonio de Herrera y Tordesillas, *Historia general de los hechos de los Castellanos en las islas i tierra firme del mar oceano* (Madrid, 1601), Dec. I, Lib. II, cap. 4, for these instructions regarding the presentation of the request to the curia.

his discovery and at the outset plant the Catholic faith in those parts, their first move was to acquaint the pope with what had occurred. . . . They told their ambassador to let the holy father know that the discovery was made without prejudice to the rights of Portugal. Columbus had had a precise order to stay one hundred leagues away from La Mina and Guinea and any other holding of the Portuguese, and he had complied with that injunction. As to their retaining possession of new lands found by the admiral and other discoveries, wise counselors thought that, for them to enjoy just possession of this new world, there was no need of papal confirmation or donation. However, the Catholic monarchs, as obedient children of the Holy See and devout princes, directed the same ambassador to ask the holy father if he might arrange for this favor to be granted to the crown of Castile and Leon; namely, the discoveries and what would be there discovered, and to give them bulls to this effect.

They felt that the holy father would be most pleased by this request, for he did not want the natives there left in their infidelity; the Castilians would not hinder their conversion, but by the hand of Columbus they would share their gifts with the natives, and the Roman court would reap great joy and pleasure at news of such an event.[7] He remembered too what the monarchs had already sacrificed for God as they financed that journey of discovery and what they must now spend to improve it; that no other Christian prince had wealth or means sufficient for such a task; that none had so boldly battled the infidel, nor set in motion so grand a discovery, nor so completely driven Mahomet out of their land as did Spain by the valor of the Catholic kings after 720 years of continuous combat. Better hope for the faith than exists in Spain could not be found among the nations, for planting and conserving the faith in the Indies.[8] The greater propinquity of Spain to the new provinces urged her appointment to the work of their conversion, and it appeared as if God had used her to cure the ills and misfortunes of the natives. . . . And now that the Holy See must dispose of these temporalities, would his holiness most considerately move to concede this petition of the Catholic kings.[9]

---

[7] The words are *gran novedad.*

[8] For the sincerity of these words consult the fragment of the will of Isabella, p. 99.

[9] The translation is by the author.

A peculiar question arises when one examines the papal bulls relevant to the petition of the sovereigns. It would seem that, immediately after the request for papal approval of the Spanish plans, a second message was sent to Rome to suggest the drawing of the Line of Demarcation. Navarrete prints the bull of May 3, 1493, in which there is no mention of the line.[10] This bull, like its fellow of the next day, begins with *Inter caetera divinae,* and the two continue identically (with very minor changes of phrase) for seventy-eight lines. At that point the bull of May 4 introduces the Line of Demarcation in a passage of twenty-three lines, after which identity resumes. Then the sentence beginning "So that you may with greater liberty" (in the Latin, "Et ut tanti negotii") returns to the demarcation theme; and after a short passage substantially identical with the parallel passage in the bull of May 3 the bull of May 4 reiterates the decrees concerning the line in the sentence beginning "We expressly exclude" (in the Latin, "Ac quibuscumque personis"). The bull of May 3, near its end, introduces data on Portuguese claims similar to those found in the *Eximiae devotionis,* also of May 4, but not found in the May 4 *Inter caetera divinae.* From "This ordinance stands" (in the Latin, "Non obstantibus constitutionibus") both bulls run in identical language to the end. Both bulls are undoubtedly genuine, but it would appear that the bull of May 3, if published at all, was not meant to be final.

A number of writers continued the *Annales Ecclesiasticae* of Baronius after his death.[11] One of his successors offered a pe-

---

10 Navarrete, *Colección,* II, 29-33. H. Vander Linden, "Alexander VI and the Bulls of Demarcation," *American Historical Review,* XXII (October 1916), 1-20, has an illuminating investigation into the relationship between the early Alexandrine bulls in point of provenance and date.

11 Note that Baronius wrote only through Book XII. He had brought the *Annales* down to the year 1198 when he died in 1597. A writer known as Raynaldus was responsible for the years 1198-1565.

culiar explanation for the royal decision to request the papacy
to substitute the May 4 form of the bull instead of the earlier
draft issued on May 3. The documents, as noted above, differed
widely. Before either was published, he wrote, João II ordered
the Portuguese navy to deploy near the Andalusian (Canary)
Islands. The frightened Spanish rulers, as a delaying action,
then dispatched peace envoys to Lisbon while they sent the pope
an appeal to change the contents of the May 3 bull and put into
the May 4 edition the ruling on the Line of Demarcation.[12] This
story seems to offer nothing to clarify the overnight revision
of the document of May 3. Spain did in fact send peace envoys
to Lisbon, but only to explain the truth rather than as a delaying
action. Moreover, to observe the sailing and action of that fleet
and to report back to Barcelona within so short a time would
have been remarkable. This author, moreover, asserts errone-
ously that Ferdinand had long cherished the desire to discover
distant lands as Portugal had done,[13] though it is known that at
the start the king opposed the whole plan of Columbus,[14] and
this was one reason why Isabella assumed direct responsibility.
From their letter to Columbus on September 5, 1493[15] it is plain
that the admiral had during his Barcelona visit given them
specific data on locations and a suggested line of division, and
it is fair to conclude that the shift in instructions was then decided. Its insistent speed may also be explained by the will of
Isabella, wherein the queen wrote with unquestionable integrity:
"Our principal intention was . . . that he would grant to us the
said concession so that we could . . . send to the said islands and
mainland prelates, religious, clerics, . . . to instruct the natives
and dwellers there in the Catholic faith . . . and give them all due

---

[12] Cesare Baronio, *Annales ecclesiasticae* (Mansi edition. Lucca, 1738), XVIII,
387d. On this see Prescott, *Ferdinand and Isabella*, II, 162-64.
[13] Baronio, *Annales*, XVIII, 386d.
[14] Prescott, *Ferdinand and Isabella*, II, 122.
[15] See in Navarrete, *Colección*, II, 123-25, cited in part below on p. 85.

care."[16] Ferdinand accepted this purpose of his spouse, without of course losing sight of its political connotations.[17]

Inter caetera divinae, unlike the Bull of Granada and its predecessors, does not derive from a crusading movement but from a new experience in European activity, the discovery of what would now be called "open land." Accordingly, when addressing the papacy, Ferdinand and Isabella asked for a departure from past papal practice that would demand a fresh approach. The pope is requested to confirm possession of islands and mainlands without reference to past views on a crusade and solely on grounds of justly acquired territory previously unpossessed by civilized peoples. Thus a new problem is created. Alexander VI solved it by a double decision. There is the time-honored right of appeal to the Roman pontiff for adjudication of causes between sovereigns—today one would say governments. That appeal he hears, and he provides the settlement.[18] To this arbitrament he adds a seemingly unimportant clause in political thinking. He entrusts the Catholic kings with the duty of conversion of the natives in the Indies. He, too, gives them the means for accomplishing that purpose: the privilege of building the structure of the church there. He has at hand no missionary organization capable of entering a distant and primitive area and of supporting itself by its own resources. That will be a later ecclesiastical development. Instead he allows the kings to act as patrons, thus opening the way for Julius II in 1508 to confer on them the full Patronato Real de las Indias.

---

[16] See below, p. 99.

[17] His candor in this matter is obvious in his instructions to Columbus, and definitely in the instructions sent to Ovando. For the charge given Ovando on his entry into office see below, pp. 95-97; to Columbus, see below, pp. 93-94.

[18] H. de la Costa's critical review of Luis Weckmann, *Las bulas alejandrinas de 1493 y la teoría política del papado medieval,* in *Traditio,* VII (1949-1951), 516-18, opposing the omni-insular theory and preferring that of arbitral decision between conflicting claims.

At once the monarchs proceed to act on this privilege. Father Buil has a letter from the court on July 25 advising him that the bull has arrived "concerning both what touches your part in the enterprise and what must be our broad undertaking in the Indies."[19] Unlike the *Romanus pontifex* of Nicholas V, *Inter caetera divinae* does not hand over the natives for subjugation or enslavement. The prime right is not conquest but conversion, and the first clerical ministers immediately go west. The May 4 draft of the bull follows.[20]

[*Inter caetera divinae*]

Alexander, bishop, servant of the servants of God. To our very beloved son and daughter in Christ, King Ferdinand and Queen Isabella, renowned monarchs of Castile, Leon, Aragon, Sicily, and Granada, health and apostolic benediction.

Among other duties pleasing to the Divine Majesty and dear to our heart, the most impelling indeed is that the Catholic faith and Christian religion be particularly exalted in our day and everywhere spread and enlarged, so that souls be saved and barbaric peoples be humbled and brought to the faith.

When we were called to this sacred see of Peter by the divine clemency (though we little merited it), we recognized in you truly dedicated rulers and princes as we had always known you to be and as your glorious deeds proclaim to almost all the world. You not only aim high, but work and devote your whole spirit and effort to these purposes, sparing no labor, expense, risk, even to the shedding of your blood, as is testified by your recovery of the kingdom of Granada from the tyranny of the Saracens in these times, with such glory to the divine name. We deem it, then, not unmerited, and we owe it to you and do freely and graciously grant those favors that will help you to further such holy, laudable, and acceptable projects, with a daily advance in attachment to the honor of God and the increase of the Christian realm.

---

[19] Navarrete, *Colección*, II, 89.

[20] In Hernáez, *Colección*, I, 12-14. The bull has been widely printed. For a Latin-English text see F. G. Davenport, *European Treaties Bearing on the History of the United States and Its Dependencies* (Washington, 1917). Other texts examined, including that of Navarrete, *Colección*, II, 34-43 (Latin and Spanish), is guilty of some small omissions. For the original Latin see pp. 283-87.

News now comes that you have set out to search and find new islands and mainlands remote and unknown, and never yet reported by other princes, so that you might bring the natives and inhabitants thereof to the service of our Redeemer and the blessings of the Catholic faith. Up to this time you were so intent upon the attack and recovery of the kingdom of Granada that you lacked the means to prosecute this holy and laudable purpose to its desired conclusion. But now that the Lord was pleased in the aforesaid recovery to complete your plans, you dispatched our devoted son, Christopher Columbus, one indeed worthy and well commended and skilled in such affairs, with ships and able men. At the cost of much labor, daring, and expense, he set out to search diligently for mainlands and remote and unknown islands over the sea where hitherto no discoveries had been made. Sailing on the Ocean Sea they came at last, with the help of God and their own unbending effort, to certain distant islands and mainlands that were never yet reported, where very many people live who, so it is said, go naked and eat no meat. As far as your messengers can relate, the peoples of these said islands and regions believe that the one God and Creator is in heaven and that the Catholic faith should be embraced and good morals practiced, and they are sufficiently civilized to offer hope that, if they be instructed, the name of Christ our Savior and Lord can easily be brought to those lands and islands. Moreover, we learn that the said Christopher has already placed, erected, and constructed a stronghold on one of the principal islands, for the protection of those Christians who went there with him and as a base from which they might search out other islands and distant and unknown mainlands. In those islands and mainlands now discovered, gold, spices, and many other precious things of diverse kind and quality came to light. Being apprised of these events, you at once, as becomes Catholic kings and princes, took thought on how to exalt and spread the Catholic faith. After the example of your renowned royal progenitors, you proposed with the divine blessing to take control over these mainlands and aforesaid islands, their natives and inhabitants, and to bring them to the Catholic faith.

We therefore commend in the Lord your sacred and laudable intentions. And we desire the enterprise to come to its fitting consummation, so that the name of our Savior may be brought to those countries. This we earnestly exhort you to do in the Lord, and to bring them to receive the holy rite of baptism as the apostolic command obliges.

Through the mercy of our Lord Jesus Christ we seriously urge that you undertake such measures at once. With the zeal of the orthodox faith, look on these peoples with great consideration and make every effort to induce them to receive the Catholic religion. Let no dangers or hardships at any time deter you. Have firm faith, and trust that the omnipotent God will second your endeavor.

So that you may with greater liberty and forthrightness assume the duties of these arduous tasks, we of our own motion, not at your instance nor on the expressed petition made to us by anyone else, but of our own largess, clear knowledge, and the fullness of the apostolic power, assign to you all islands and mainlands, discovered or yet to be discovered, sighted or not yet sighted, to the west and south of a line set and drawn from the Arctic or North Pole to the Antarctic or South Pole, the line to stand a hundred leagues to the west and south[21] of the so-called Azores and Cape Verde Islands, whether these mainlands or islands discovered or not yet discovered, be in the direction of India or any other territory. All these islands and mainlands, discovered or not yet discovered, sighted or not yet sighted, to the west and south of the aforesaid line, if they were not actually possessed by another king or Christian prince by the day of the Nativity of our divine Lord just past, or which day began the present year 1493 when some of the aforesaid islands were discovered by your representatives and captains, we, by the authority of the omnipotent God granted to us in blessed Peter and the vicarship of Jesus Christ which we hold on earth, by these presents do donate, grant, and assign, and with them all their towns, camps, territories, villages, and the rights and jurisdictions and all appertaining thereto, to you and your heirs and successors, the kings of Castile and Leon. And we make, constitute, and depute you and your heirs and successors as lords of the same, with full, free, and all-embracing power, authority, and dominion. We decree nevertheless by this our donation, concession, and assignment that no right is understood as withdrawn from, nor can it be extinguished for, any Christian prince who actually possessed the aforesaid islands and mainlands up to the said day of the Nativity of our Lord Jesus Christ.

---

[21] The whimsicality of Prescott (see *Ferdinand and Isabella*, II, 161) scarcely makes allowance for the infancy of ocean geography as it was known in 1493. The king was as much in the dark as was the pope, but he put a man to work on it and got results. See reports of Mosen Jaime Ferrer in Navarrete, *Colección*, II, 111-20.

Moreover, we order you in virtue of holy obedience (for as you promise, so we do not doubt you will do, in your noble dedication and royal magnanimity) that you dispatch to the designated mainlands and islands virtuous and God-fearing men endowed with training, experience, and skill, to instruct the natives and inhabitants before mentioned and to imbue them with the same Christian faith and sound morals, using all speed in the premises.

We expressly exclude all persons of whatever rank, even imperial and royal, or status, grade, order, or condition, under pain of automatic excommunication—which they incur *ipso facto* if they act contrariwise—from presuming to approach those islands or mainlands whether discovered or to be discovered, sighted or not yet sighted, to the south and west of the line set and drawn from the Arctic Pole to the Antarctic Pole, whether the islands and mainland discovered or to be discovered lie toward India or any other region, this line to stand a hundred leagues west and south of the islands commonly called the Azores and Cape Verde, whether they come to trade or for any other reason, unless with the special license of yourselves or your heirs and successors. This ordinance stands despite any apostolic constitutions or orders, anything else to the contrary notwithstanding.

We trust in Him from whom all empire and dominion proceeds that, with the Lord guiding your deeds as you advance in this sacred and praiseworthy campaign, your labors and efforts will in a short time win most happy fulfillment, to the joy and glory of the Christian people. However, since it will be difficult to circulate this document to each place where it might be expedient, we will, and with like act and knowledge decree, that copies transcribed by hand and certified by a notary public summoned for the purpose and with the seal of any person holding ecclesiastical dignity or witnessed by an ecclesiastical curia be given the same trust in court and in every other place where it is used as these presents would demand if they were opened and exhibited. Therefore let no man infringe this document of our commendation, exhortation, requisition, donation, concession, assignment, constitution, deputation, decree, mandate, inhibition, and will, or in temerity oppose it. If, however, anyone presumes so to attempt, let him know that he will incur the indignation of the omnipotent God and His blessed apostles Peter and Paul. Given at Rome, at St. Peter's, the year of the Incarnation of the Lord 1493, May 4, the first year of our pontificate.

CHAPTER VI

Later Alexandrine Bulls

Between 1493 and 1501 Alexander VI held to the two policies affirmed in *Inter caetera divinae*. Both Portugal and Spain received papal assistance in cementing titles to new land, and the latter saw a gradual development that would give firm foundation for the complete patronage in overseas territories. Innocent VIII had put narrow limits on the grant for Granada. His successor, perhaps unknowingly, pushed these limits beyond all hope of future restraint. The letters most concerned with the later settlement follow below. They begin in *Eximiae devotionis*, published the same day as the parent bull. Ferdinand and Isabella undoubtedly intended to have the full patronage for their Indies. Here they ask for a grant qualitatively equal to those made to Enrique the Infante.

[*Eximiae devotionis*]

Alexander, bishop, servant of the servants of God. To our beloved son and daughter in Christ, King Ferdinand and Queen Isabella, illustrious monarchs of Castile, Leon, Aragon, and Granada, health and apostolic benediction.[1]

The genuine integrity of your service and the complete faith with which you revere ourselves and the Roman church assuredly deserve

---

[1] In García Gutiérrez, *Bulario*, pp. 21-22. It is found also in the works of Hernáez, Pacheco y Cárdenas, and Ribadeneyra previously cited. For the original Latin see pp. 287-89.

that we graciously grant to you the aids that will enable you to fulfill with ease and expedition your holy and laudable decision to search out remote and unknown lands, for the honor of the omnipotent God, the propagation of the Christian empire, and the exaltation of the Catholic faith.

We have this day, of our own decided will, acting on certain knowledge and with the plenitude of our apostolic power, forever donated, conceded, and assigned, as is shown more fully in our letter to that effect, to you and your heirs and successors in the rule of Castile and Leon, all and each of the mainlands and remote islands, even unknown, lying to the west in the Ocean Sea, which those whom you sent at the cost of great labor, risk, and expense have discovered or will discover, and which are not actually under the temporal dominion of any Christian princes, with all their realms, cities, camps, territories, villages, and general jurisdictions.

Since, however, certain indults have previously been conceded to the kings of Portugal who in the regions of Africa, Guinea, and Mina Auri received other islands from a grant and apostolic donation similar to yours, and these kings have acquired through the Apostolic See various privileges, favors, liberties, immunities, exemptions, faculties, and letters patent, we, who (as is proper and fitting) do not wish that you and your aforesaid successors should have less in grants and prerogatives, of our own will and not at your instance or that of any other making petition for you in this matter, but of our own liberality and knowledge and the plenitude of our apostolic power, desire for you and your above-mentioned successors that in the islands and lands by you or in your name thus far discovered and in the future to be discovered you have all and each of the favors, privileges, exemptions, liberties, faculties, immunities, letters patent, and indults conceded to the kings of Portugal, just as if the intent were word for word inserted in your present grant. These you may explicitly use, employ, and enjoy, and this you should do in every case and cause, just as if all of them were specifically conceded to you and your heirs and successors by our apostolic authority. By the tenor of these presents we extend these favors in all matters and situations to you, your heirs, and specified successors, in equal measure and fullness and in the same form and mode, forever. And this notwithstanding constitutions and apostolic ordinations, and all grants conceded in letters patent to the kings of Portugal, or anything else to the contrary.

However, since it would be difficult to send this present document to every single place where it might be expedient, we will, and with like knowledge decree, that copies of the same transcribed by hand and certified by a public notary summoned for the purpose and with the seal of any person in ecclesiastical dignity or witnessed by an ecclesiastical curia be given the same firm trust in and outside of court wherever it be used as these presents would have if opened and exhibited. Therefore let no man infringe this document of our indult, extension, amplification, concession, will, and decree, or in temerity oppose it. If, however, anyone presumes so to attempt, let him know that he will incur the indignation of the omnipotent God and the blessed apostles Peter and Paul. Given at Rome, at St. Peter's, the year of the Incarnation of the Lord 1493, May 4, the first year of our pontificate.

From this bull it is arguable that the Catholic monarchs sought possession of powers granted to the master prior of the Orden de Cristo. Though it is known that they obtained for the crown the grand mastership of the Knights of Calatrava in 1487, Alcántara in 1494, and Santiago in 1499,[2] whatever similar transfer of powers was implied in the bull seems not to have been employed in the American Indies, nor did the knights of the military orders take any particular part in their organization. Perhaps it is better to see in the above document a desire to fortify their general position in the competition which was then beginning with the Portuguese expansion.

A much more portentous bull appeared on September 26, 1493, the *Dudum siquidem*, which actually threw the whole question of mutual rights into the arena of early international law. A letter of the Catholic monarchs to Columbus dated September 5, 1493, and highly confidential, asks advice of the discoverer who, they write, "understands better than any other person" the impact of the Line of Demarcation on Portuguese holdings in the South Atlantic.[3] They feel that Portugal will

---

[2] Prescott, *Ferdinand and Isabella*, I, 297-98.
[3] The letter is in Navarrete, *Colección*, II, 123-25 (no. 71).

come to no amicable agreement, since João II does not know what Columbus found or where it is. A caravel has set out from Madeira—without, it is said, royal approval—to search through the Indies of Castile, "and you know this." But in one way or another they want to discover "what is ours."

Look this over carefully, and do not let that caravel, or the three that have been sent to intercept it, get into what pertains to us. . . . Some say that Mina del Oro and Guinea are on our side of the line, and the Portuguese think that too. . . . Write us before you set sail if that is a true statement derived from your measurements of the Demarcation. If it is, we will have the bull changed. . . . But do not waste an hour in starting your [second] voyage. If you meet with enemies, handle them as you think best. As to your armed escort suggested earlier, tell us what you think best. But hurry off. Pray God this event will have an ending as happy as was its inception.

One must at this point keep clearly in mind that what Columbus had intended from start to finish was to get to the east by going west. The monarchs, on the other hand, were intent on prosecuting their new discoveries in the Indies, and the above-cited letter to Columbus unmistakably states their will to have no trouble with Portugal over the issue. Both were interested in a geographical area that was extremely hazy, and for all they knew their Indies might be very close to India. They now got a grant that led inevitably to the Treaty of Tordesillas. In that little town of the Province of Valladolid the next June would see international law founded.

[*Dudum siquidem*]

Alexander, bishop, servant of the servants of God. To our beloved son and daughter in Christ, King Ferdinand and Queen Isabella, illustrious monarchs of Castile, Leon, Aragon, and Granada, health and apostolic benediction.[4]

Recently we donated, conceded, and assigned of our own motion and with certain knowledge and apostolic right all and each of the

---

[4] In García Gutiérrez, *Bulario*, pp. 23-24. For the original Latin see pp. 289-91.

islands and mainlands discovered and to be discovered, to the west and south, and not under actual temporal rule of other Christian lords, to you and your heirs and successors as kings of Castile and Leon in perpetuity. And we invested,[5] constituted, and deputed you and your heirs and successors aforesaid in these prerogatives, with full, free, and all-embracing power, authority, and jurisdiction, as is more fully contained in the letters patent drawn up by us. And we wish the tenor of that grant to be held as if the rights were here enumerated word for word in these presents.

Now, because it might happen that your representatives and captains or vassals, in sailing to the west or south, should come to the regions of the Orient and chance upon islands and mainlands that were formerly or are now there situated, we, who desire to forward your progress with most benign favor, do by our own like decision and knowledge and full apostolic power extend and amplify the donation, concession, assignment, and letters patent and all appertaining thereto.

All and each of the islands and mainlands, discovered or to be discovered, already sighted or to be sighted, those which may exist or have existed or which appeared while sailing or voyaging toward the west and south as was said, whether they be in the regions of the west or south and the Orient and India, are conveyed by these presents just as if there had been in the aforementioned letters full and express mention of them. And we concede to you, your heirs and successors, the full and complete liberty freely to take physical possession of the indicated islands and lands by your own authority, to retain them in perpetuity, to impede any adverse force, and to defend them through your own agency or that of another or others. And we expressly restrain any persons of whatever dignity, status, grade, order, or condition, under penalty of automatic excommunication which those who so act incur *ipso facto*, from sailing in those parts, fishing, spying into the islands and mainlands, or presuming on any other ground or pretense to go or send others there, without your precise permission or that of your heirs and successors. And this notwithstanding the constitutions, faculties, or assignments of ourselves or of our predecessors regarding

---

[5] The word "invest" might give color to the feudal-grant idea on which Luis Weckmann based his study of the Alexandrine bulls. It is plain, however, that the pope uses words that imply origin of title from various sources without particular concern to fix it in any one area.

the aforesaid regions, seas, islands, and lands, or other areas, whether their cause be piety, or the faith, or the redeeming of captives, or other most urgent motives, no matter with what mandates, even if derogating derogations or stronger or more effective or unusual, even any judicial sentences whatever, or censures or penalties thereto attached, made to whatever kings or princes, infantes, or any other persons or orders or military bodies who have not attained actual and effective local possession, even though they formerly voyaged there by right of donations and concessions of similar tenor. Those donations, by the intent of these presents to be taken for sufficient proof, we altogether revoke, and the titles to lands and islands not actually possessed by them are to be held as intrusions and void clauses, together with all others which in this document we declare to have no force, whatsoever to the contrary notwithstanding. Given at Rome, at St. Peter's, the year of the Incarnation of the Lord 1493, September 26, the first year of our pontificate.

This reference to India and the Orient and the revocation of former political grants in the same area threw open the race for new lands and precipitated the diplomatic question that was concluded at Tordesillas.[6] Portugal could not openly challenge the papal jurisdiction, but she at once began the quiet process that, on June 7, 1494, pushed the line to three hundred and seventy leagues west of the Azores and Cape Verde, extended it round the poles, and recognized the right of possession when the land was occupied.

In the establishment of the Patronato Real de las Indias, the main contribution of Alexander VI was—after conferring title of ownership—the right and duty of constructing the church in those lands. Closely connected with this basic charge of evangelization laid on the Catholic monarchs was their right to obtain in the Indies the funds necessary for carrying out their obligation. Two bulls became the foundation for that prerogative. The first gave them power, though in a limited way, to tax

---

[6] These events are carefully investigated in Charles E. Nowell's essay, "The Treaty of Tordesillas and the Diplomatic Background of American History," in *Greater America* (Berkeley, 1945), pp. 1-18.

for a religious purpose. The second allotted to them all tithes due from the inhabitants.

[*Eximie devotionis*]

Alexander, bishop, servant of the servants of God. To our beloved son and daughter in Christ, King Ferdinand and Queen Isabella of the Catholic Spains, health and apostolic benediction.[7]

The genuine integrity of your service and the complete faith with which you revere ourselves and the Roman church assuredly merit that we give favorable reply to your candid petitions, in as far as in God we can relieve the necessities that at this time press heavily on the Christian republic.

We now learn from your message and from the account of your ambassador the extent of your concern at the evils and losses wrought in the past year by the most perfidious Turks, enemies of the name of Christ with a constant thirst for Christian blood. And there is no letup to their work of preparing an immense maritime fleet and a no less formidable land army for the invasion of the Christian lands and realms. We learn too that yourselves, in the manner of Christian kings and princes and because of your singular love of the same Christian republic, propose to confront the perfidious Turks with your best strength and are now putting together a large fleet. And as you will necessarily incur huge and unbearable costs to get this under way, it is incumbent on you to impose in your kingdom, islands, lands, and dominions certain exactions and subsidies—*sisa*, as they are called in those parts—on the produce of farmers and townsmen of your said kingdoms, islands, lands, and dominions, as you have customarily done at other similar times of crisis.

Your humble petition now asks that, if the imposition of the said *sisa* falls upon secular and ecclesiastical persons of the kingdoms, islands, lands, and dominions aforesaid, we would deign to concede our license, so that you may demand its payment after their [*cortes*] agreement to the tax, or that we make other opportune provision in our apostolic benignity.

Noting, therefore, that when there is question of the defense of the Christian faith and of the very Christian republic itself it is befitting

---

[7] In Pacheco y Cárdenas, *Colección de documentos inéditos*, II 5, 4-7. For the original Latin see pp. 292-93.

that ecclesiastical as well as secular persons freely choose to do this
and even gratuitously offer their votes for new imposts of this kind, and
hearkening to your suppliant pleas, we do grant that if, in your aforesaid kingdoms, islands, lands, and dominions, the said *sisa* for the
requirements of this extraordinary defense should be imposed on seculars and ecclesiastics and religious persons of both sexes, of whatever
dignity, status, grade, order, or condition, in the aforesaid kingdoms,
islands, lands, and dominions, and they agreed to pay it freely, for one
year only and not to be used except for the specified work of defense
nor converted to other uses, then, by the tenor of these presents, as a
special gift of our favor, you may with liberty and honesty exact and
levy it. Notwithstanding the apostolic constitutions, ordinations, statutes,
and ecclesiastical customs, or those of whatever monasteries or other
religious houses or orders, or of oaths, apostolic confirmations, or
on whatever other basis established, or all other things whatever to
the contrary.

Therefore let no man dare to infringe this document of our concession or to contradict it. If, however, anyone presumes to attempt to
do so, let him know that he will incur the indignation of the omnipotent
God and the blessed apostles Peter and Paul. Given at Rome, at St.
Peter's, the year of the Incarnation of the Lord 1499, March 21, the
eighth year of our pontificate.

It has been contended by many Spanish and Latin American
authors, notably Frasso, Solórzano Pereira, and Ribadeneyra,
that in the *Inter caetera divinae* the full Patronato Real was conferred on the Catholic monarchs by Alexander VI. The above
document proves how hurriedly that judgment was formed. The
bull does not approve the royal overriding of private corporations, but rather assumes the right of these groups to continue
with their customary medieval freedoms, which are here supported both by the pontiff and the crown. Transition from this
system to the subsequent omnicompetence of the king will be
slow. Finally, one finds in the bull merely a slight beginning
in crown use of ecclesiastical properties for a merely popular cause.

The final Alexandrine bull here offered shows behind the
scenes the hand of a man who understood the art of politics. He

asks simply for the crucial grant, the tithes of America. He got it. Within seven years Julius II will confer full patronage.

[Eximiae devotionis]

Alexander, bishop, servant of the servants of God. To our beloved son and daughter in Christ, King Ferdinand and Queen Isabella, Catholic monarchs of the Spains, health and apostolic benediction.[8]

The genuine integrity of your service and the complete faith with which you revere ourselves and the Roman church assuredly deserve that you be enabled with freedom and alacrity to fulfill your plans, those particularly which respect the exaltation of the Catholic faith and the humbling of the infidel and barbarian peoples. And indeed the petition you have just brought to our attention shows on your part a marked zeal for the exaltation of the Catholic faith such as you proved some time back when you undertook a campaign demanding great expense and arduous struggle. And you do not lessen that zeal as you go on from day to day, but employ it for the gaining and regeneration of the Indies and the regions of the Indies, to the end that in them all obnoxious cults be removed and the Most High be worshiped and honored.

Now, since you will be burdened with a heavy outlay to recover the islands and regions alluded to and exposed to the risk of great dangers, it is proper that you ask and obtain the right to receive and levy tithes from the natives and inhabitants now living there, for the conserving and retaining of the said islands after they are acquired and regenerated and for the costs necessarily incurred in that conserving and holding. Wherefore on your part you have made respectful supplication that, in the premises, we deign of our apostolic benignity to provide timely aid for you and your estate.

We, therefore, who desire with intense fervor the exaltation of the same faith and its further increase, especially in these our times, commend your pious and praiseworthy proposal earnestly in the Lord. Thus moved by your prayer, on our apostolic authority and by these presents we grant this special favor of our grace to you and to your successors ruling at the time, that from the natives and inhabitants in the aforesaid islands, dwelling even for the time being in the said acquired and recovered regions, you receive the tithes as previously assigned in fact

---

[8] In García Gutiérrez, *Bulario*, pp. 25-26. For the original Latin see pp. 294-95.

and effect, according to the ordination of the bishops then in the localities, whose consciences we burden in this matter.[9] These tithes will be used for the building of the churches in the said islands by you or by your aforesaid successors out of your and their resources, and for a fund sufficient for the proper sustenance of their ordinaries and rectors, as also to meet the demands made from time to time on the said churches for the fitting support of the divine worship and praise of the omnipotent God, and for the episcopal rights. And this notwithstanding the decrees of the Lateran Council, and any other constitutions and apostolic ordinations to the contrary.

Therefore let no man infringe this patent of our concession nor in temerity attempt to do so. But if anyone should presume so to dare, let him know that he will incur the indignation of the omnipotent God and His blessed apostles Peter and Paul. Given at Rome, at St. Peter's, the year of the Incarnation of the Lord 1501, November 16, the tenth year of our pontificate.

---

[9] Icazbalceta, *Zumárraga*, pp. 161-62, has a splendid note on this cession of the American tithes to the crown. Some say that tithes cannot be secularized, but the fact is that they were. The bull took effect, so that later—after the redonation of 1512 at Burgos, on which see pp. 121-26—when the crown retained two ninths, it was no usurpation but a right. This concession of Alexander VI recompensed the kings for the expense and care connected with the conquest and conversion of the natives and for the added charge to give proper endowment to the churches. Their redonation was magnanimous, but lower officials were wont to play favorites or punish unfriendly prelates by their inequities in disbursing the funds. The whole system, however, puts the church into vassalage to the royal patron.

CHAPTER VII

Spade Work in America

It is a familiar story that things went hard for both Spaniards and Indians in the West Indies during the decade after their discovery.[1] The entire situation teemed with strange elements, and Columbus could do with them no better than other men. By 1501 the crown decided that no grantee would be capable of mastering the problems presented by the fledgling empire. The monarchs accordingly took over the powers that Columbus had exercised and assumed direct charge. Appointments and assignments now came immediately from the court. In this way arose a solid overseas administration under the firm and supple guidance of a governor on the scene and a council of Indian affairs in Spain. Nicolás de Ovando, first governor (1501-1509) and knight of Alcántara, formed this structure so well that he is called the founder of Spain's empire in the Indies.

Isabella, Castilian sovereign of the new world, always surpassed her consort in directness of perception and integrity of character, and their joint policies reflected her interests throughout this fundamental period. Deeply religious in principle, she

---

[1] For a concise account of these years that represents careful research and contains a report of recent findings see John Francis Bannon and Peter Masten Dunne, *Latin America* (Milwaukee, 1958), pp. 65-74.

envisaged a twofold relationship between religion and the success of the enterprise. If the native were to be won to Spain, he must be converted. If the Spaniard were to become a dependable colonial, he would need the help of strong church organization. And Alexander VI had embedded this charge and right in his basic grant. Wherefore, when Columbus was readying his second and most important voyage, the monarchs gave definite instructions in their letter of May 29, 1493.[2]

Instruction of the king and queen our lords for Don Christopher Columbus, admiral of their highnesses for the discovered islands and mainland and for discovery in the Ocean Sea among the Indies, and their viceroy and governor there, and also captain general for the armed fleet that their highnesses are sending to the said islands and mainland: concerning the manner of prosecuting this voyage that he makes by command of their highnesses and the use to be made of the armada, as also of the route and what he must do when, God willing, they reach their destination, among which are the following:

First, it has pleased God our Lord in His exalted mercy to make known these islands and mainland to the king and queen, our lords, through the skillful guidance of the said Don Christopher Columbus, their admiral, viceroy, and governor of those places. Moreover, he reported to their highnesses that he found the people living there quite ready to be converted to our holy Catholic faith, for they have no laws or customs [that hinder this conversion]. Their highnesses are most pleased and grateful for these benefits. It is, then, altogether just that first thought be given to the service of God our Lord and the exaltation of our holy Catholic faith. This their highnesses desire, that our holy Catholic faith be promoted and increased; and therefore they order and charge the said admiral, viceroy, and governor that in every way and to the fullest extent possible he labor and strive to win over those who dwell in the said islands and mainland, so that they may be converted to our holy Catholic faith. To further this purpose their highnesses are sending thither the learned father Fray Buil, together with other religious whom the said admiral is to take with him. He will see

---

[2] This letter is in Navarrete, *Colección*, II, 77-83. For the Spanish original see pp. 295-97.

that these men, when they reach the Indies, use all their talents and zeal to acquaint the natives with the truths of our holy faith. For this they should come to know and understand our language, and so their teachers, using all their skill, will take care to instruct them in the use of Spanish. Moreover, the chief concern of this expedition, when once the armada happily arrives, is the promotion of our good relations with the natives. The admiral will therefore take great precautions that those who travel with him and those who will later on come from here treat the said Indians with truly considerate attention. These men should give them no offense. Rather, with each and all of them there should be close association and friendship. They should do every good they can for the Indians. Likewise, the admiral will be liberal toward them and give them presents out of the merchandise of their majesties that is taken along for barter, and he will show them much honor. And in case any person or persons mistreat the said Indians in any way whatever, the admiral as viceroy and governor of their highnesses will chastise them in exemplary fashion, using the powers of their highnesses which he brings with him. And now, because spiritual deeds cannot long endure without material arrangements, the admiral will look after the temporalities according to the following schedule.[3] . . . Done in the city of Barcelona, May 29, the year of the Nativity of our Lord 1493. I the King—I the Queen. By order of the king and queen. Fernand Álvares.

These simple instructions announced the appearance of royal patronage in the Americas. The crown accepted its duty as laid down in *Inter caetera divinae,* and in so doing began to exercise its right to choose a staff, direct operations, fix terms of support, and judge the results achieved by the ecclesiastical body. When in 1501 Nicolás de Ovando received appointment as royal governor of the Indies, a similar though much more in-

---

[3] Seventeen other items following the prologue touch on rule, discovery, and protection. Regarding clerics Prescott (*Ferdinand and Isabella,* II, 158) writes that twelve were assigned for this voyage. Four actually went: besides Fray Bernardo Buil, Benedictine, there were Fray Ramón Pane, Hieronymite; Frailes Juan de la Duela (Bermejo) and Juan de Tisín, Franciscans. Others came soon afterward, in all twelve clerics before 1502, when Ovando brought ten Franciscans.

cisive set of instructions accompanied his official induction as crown administrator. The directive[4] clearly reveals the growing sense of command in churchly matters, and the patent skill of an understanding ruler.

Granada, September 16, 1501

The King and Queen

The duties which you, Fray Nicolás de Ovando, commander of Lares, of the Order of Alcántara, must fulfill in the islands and mainland of the Ocean Sea, where you are to be our governor, are the following:

First of all you are to look with much diligence to the matter of the service of God. See that the divine worship is performed with great edification, good order, and reverence, as is proper.

Item: Since it is our desire that the Indians be converted to our Catholic faith and save their souls—for that is the greatest good that we can wish for them—and since in this it is imperative that they be taught the truths of our faith so that they may come to a knowledge of it, you will give your heart to the work. As the religious do who are there, let no pressure of force be used. Teach and urge the natives with all kindness, in such manner that you will soon have them in the fold. And furnish every favor and assistance that will bring success to the effort.

Item: In line with the policies that we commended to you, see that all our subjects dwelling in the said islands and mainland accept your regulations as individuals and groups and that they obey you as our governor in every ruling that you make in our name. Give much thought to keeping all of them in constant peace and concord and the course of justice, and in your administration treat everyone with equity and with no acceptance of persons. For this choose capable and effective assistants and officials, and punish in due manner what needs chastisement.

Item: Take care that the Indians be well treated and are enabled to walk in peace throughout all their land. Allow no one to hurt them or rob them or do them any other harm. Have fixed penalties that you find salutary, and carry them out on those whom you find guilty. For this you will issue the necessary proclamations and orders.

---

[4] In Pacheco y Cárdenas, *Colección de documentos inéditos*, I 31, 13-25. For the original Spanish see pp. 297-99.

Item: You must act as we would toward the caciques [chiefs] and other principal men. We wish the Indians to be dealt with kindly, as they are our good subjects and vassals, and let no one dare to do them evil or hurt. And so you must publish our royal will on this point. And if from this time forward any man do them any damage or injury whatever or forcibly take anything of theirs, and knowledge of this comes to you, castigate the evildoers in such fashion that in the future no one will venture to bring on them any ill, mischief, or wrong.

Item: As we have word that some Christians in those islands and chiefly in Hispañola did take from those Indians and hold their women and chattels and other goods against their will, on your arrival order that they give back whatever was removed against their desires. Protect them with sentences so severe that from now on none will attempt to do such a thing. If they should wish to marry with the Indians, let it be done freely on both parts and with no coercion.

Item: It is our wish and will that the Indians pay our tribute and it is right that they pay just as our subject citizens do in our kingdoms and realms. However, since the amount which they pay and contribute depends on the productivity of the land, speak in our name to the caciques and other principal persons and show the Indians what you consider the proper amount, and agree with them on what they are to pay, each one for each year, in point of tribute, and let them see that in these matters there will be no injustice on your part.[5] . . .

Item: Since it is our desire that the Christians who dwell in the said Island of Hispañola and who will live there from now on should not live in prodigal style, see that none dwell outside of the settlements which they have built in the said island, and each should have his patrimony of a hut or small house to be his shelter and family home.[6] . . .

---

[5] Four *items* are omitted here as lacking reference to patronage.

[6] Five *items* are omitted here as lacking reference to patronage. After "in our dominions" in the next paragraph come two final *items* which are omitted here for the same reason. In sum, the eleven omitted *items* deal with these matters: pay a just salary to Indian workers; provide an office for Bobadilla; list our debts to Admiral Don Christopher Columbus; select sites for settlement on good, well-watered land; set up three fortifications and other strong points for defense; estop the payrolls padded by Bobadilla; correct the wasteful habits employed in cutting brazilwood; collect the lawless element and ship them back home; watch out for fraud in the gold mining; sue Bobadilla for the cattle he attached; keep strangers out of the land and pick up their credentials; and, finally, rule with a firm and strong hand.

Item: Inasmuch as we have the grant from our most holy father of the tithes and first fruits in the said islands and mainlands, give order that all, both Christians and Indians, give tithes and first fruits from their work, trade, and produce in maize and that they render the first fruits according to the schedule that you bring with you, which is the most reasonable that is paid in our dominions.

On March 29, 1503, King Ferdinand wrote to Governor Ovando from Zaragoza in reply to a long set of administrative questions sent him by the governor.[7] Passing by matters not connected with the patronage, the following extracts are of some interest:

Zaragoza, March 29, 1503

To Commander Fray Nicolás de Ovando, governor of the Island of Hispañola. . . .

In regard to the salary that you say has to be given the clerics who are in the islands for the service they do in confessing, baptizing, and administering the holy sacraments, for this service Commander Bobadilla had assigned to each of them a hundred and fifty pesos of gold annually. It was thought to be too little, and so you later paid them each sixty pesos more, and the friars turned back what they had left over. We decide that the most we approve as provision for that service is that each of the said clerics receive annually a hundred pesos of gold. When that has been used, let them be advanced whatever amount is needed above what they have received.

In regard to the paragraph in which you say that it would be well if the pope conceded plenary bulls of composition[8] for those living in the islands, at present it seems to us that this is not necessary.

On your report that Fray Juan de Robles brought a memorial on the ornaments proper for use in the churches there, my order is that you provide as you see fit from the materials that are sent for that purpose.

As to your paragraph wherein you say that the clerics are conceding certain indulgences to those who give alms for the churches and

---

[7] The meticulous concern of the sovereign is very evident.

[8] *Compositio* is a type of reparation, something like voluntary bankruptcy, that is allowed to one holding the *bula cruzada.* For current Spanish practice see *Acta apostolicae sedis,* XXI (1929), 18-19.

hospitals, on that point we have written to our most holy father that he approve these as they are now conceded.[9] . . .

In regard to your other notation concerning our order for them to pay us tithes on the cotton and other products that they have in the Indies and in other regions outside the boundaries of the settlements and that to preserve the liberties conceded by us to the Indians no one [no Spaniard] may have anything of theirs in his possession unless it has been purchased, in which matter you say that the settlers in the said islands have suffered some injury, we command you to find the solution that we should order carried out in this contingency, and in a problem so important to follow the policy that you see is most agreeable to our service and to the good of the people in those said islands.[10]

On October 12, 1504 Isabella executed her will.[11] This document, done in the full vigor of statesmanship despite the near approach of death, was improved by three codicils on November 23, three days before her departure. Of these the first two bear directly on the present study. The initial paragraph appoints a commission to form a code of Spanish law. It reads:

Moreover, inasmuch as I have always wanted to prescribe the reduction of the Fuero, the ordinations, and the pragmatics[12] into one corpus where they might be found more briefly stated and better arranged, clearing up doubtful clauses and certain contradictions and rectifying the costs resulting therefrom for my subjects and citizens, a project that failed of enactment because of my infirmities and other preoccupations, therefore I beg the king my lord and spouse, and I command and charge the said princess[13] my daughter and the said prince[14] her husband, and I direct my other heirs at once to form a commission made up of a prelate who is knowing and honorable, with

---

[9] This was common custom in those days.
[10] In Pacheco y Cárdenas, *Colección de documentos inéditos*, II 5, 45-46. For the original Spanish see pp. 299-300.
[11] Prescott, *Ferdinand and Isabella*, III, 161-66, gives a fine summary of the entire will. He himself had at hand three copies.
[12] The *Fuero* was perhaps *Las siete partidas* of Alfonso el Sabio. Ordinations were enactments of *cortes*. Pragmatics were royal edicts.
[13] Princess Juana, heiress of Castile and Aragon, mother of Charles V.
[14] Prince Philip of Burgundy, husband of Juana.

some persons who are well trained and wise and experienced in the law, and let them survey the said laws of the Fuero, the ordinations, and the pragmatics, and take and reduce them to a corpus arranged in short and compendious form.[15]

The second codicil is famous. Gross abuses had arisen in the New World, and the grand ideals of Isabella seemed in danger. Hence she added to her testament this eloquent plea for justice to the Indian:

Next, inasmuch as at the time when the Holy See conceded to us the islands and mainland, discovered and to be discovered in the Ocean Sea, our principal intention was that we petition Pope Alexander VI of happy memory that he would grant to us the said concession so that we could gain and take over[16] their homeland and convert them to our holy Catholic faith, and to send to the said islands and mainland prelates, religious, clerics, and other learned and God-fearing persons to instruct the natives and dwellers there in the Catholic faith and to teach them the blessings of good morals and give them all due care, as was implied in the bountiful letters patent of the same concession, to that end I pleaded very earnestly with the king my lord, and I charged and commissioned the said princess my daughter and the said prince her husband, that they embrace and comply with that intention and let it be their principal aim, and that in it they be most diligent and not consent to or offer any opportunity for the natives and inhabitants, won in the same Indies or to be won, to receive any hurt in their persons or goods, but to give orders that they be well and justly treated; and if any harm be received, they remedy it and take good care that they exceed in no point what is enjoined and commanded in the apostolic letters of the same concession.[17]

---

[15] In Jordan de Asso y Miguel de Manuel, *Ordenamiento*, p. xv. For the original Spanish see p. 301.

[16] Note that among the causes of war considered just in *Las siete partidas* was "first, to augment the people's faith and to destroy those who would oppose it" (Part. II, tit. xxiii, ley ii).

[17] In Pacheco y Cárdenas, *Colección de documentos inéditos*, II 5, 92-93. This section was apparently the only fragment of the original available in the Spanish archives when the *Colección* was published. For the original Spanish see pp. 301-02.

Just eleven days before Isabella died Pope Julius II signalized the growth of the church in the Indies by establishing the first three bishoprics of America. Julius, whom many writers see, as did Prescott, in a distinctly dark cloud,[18] succeeded by this letter in throwing the first check into the machinery of the Patronato Real, while at the same time he inaugurated the hierarchy of the new world. He was a most gifted man, compared by Pastor to Cortés and Michelangelo, a trio said by that historian to outmatch any three who ever lived at the same time. His ecclesiastical arrangements with Spain will reflect the Italian alliances by which he made good the independence of the Papal States. Ferdinand stood firmly at his side in driving Louis XII out of Italy.[19] For Isabella he had the admiration shared by his countrymen, one of whom, Prospero Colonna, paid her this tribute spoken to Ferdinand on his visit shortly before her death, that he had come to Castile "to behold the woman who from her sick bed ruled the world."[20] The bull of Julius II follows.[21]

[Illius fulciti presidio]

Julius, bishop, servant of the servants of God. For a perpetual remembrance.

Fortified by the strength of Him who holds in His hand the quarters of the globe, who sees the thoughts of men and governs and directs them by His ordering providence, we readily embrace the fullness of the office entrusted to us from on high, to the end that in all this darkness those who wish for enlightenment may approach the true light who is Christ. To carry that light to all lands as their need and reasonable cause demand, we employ the pre-eminent power of the Holy See to

---

[18] He writes, *Ferdinand and Isabella*, III, 114: "The belligerent pontiff made his tiara a helmet and his crosier a sword."

[19] Prescott tells the story of these wars with precision, *ibid.*, II and III, *passim*.

[20] *Ibid.*, III, 160, for the quotation from Sandoval: *"Ver una señora que desde la cama mandava al mundo."*

[21] In Pacheco y Cárdenas, *Colección de documentos inéditos*, II 5, 86-91. See *ibid.*, II 5, 38-86 for a preliminary discussion and the meaning of the bull. For the original Latin see pp. 302-05.

plant new archiepiscopal and episcopal sees. These new plantings add new sectors to the Church Militant, whereby the profession of the Christian religion and of the Catholic faith spring up, grow, and flourish everywhere. Thus the most humble places become resplendent; and their inhabitants, the flocks of the new dioceses and of their honorable prelates, with the assistance of ministers in sufficient numbers can now under our Author and Lord more easily attain to the reward of eternal felicity.

In this day our dear son and daughter in Christ, King Ferdinand and Queen Isabella, illustrious monarchs of Castile, Leon, and Sicily, press on eagerly toward the increase of the new Christianity, for the glory of God and the exaltation of the said Catholic faith. They have not rested up to this time; nor do they now, in as far as lies in them, slacken that daily effort. Not alone in Europe, but in Africa and in the parts of Asia, they struggle to remove the lands and dominions of the infidel from the servitude and tyranny of the same infidel,[22] that the same Catholic faith may be planted there and, once planted, spread out in wide expansion.

Among the other kingdoms and dominions thus recovered from the Moors and Saracens and other infidels, one notable island in the so-called islands of the Indies, or adjacent to the said islands, was by the divine aid recently captured from the said infidels by the valiant and powerful army and the maritime fleet assembled for the campaign, and it was brought under the domination of the same king and queen. To show that they were not content with a purely temporal rule after the recovery and submission of this same island, they gave it the name of Little Spain, as if to make plain the full character of their intention in the spiritual realm, the exaltation of the Catholic faith. Hence they sent over to the said island religious and learned men to bring thither the word of God and by their preaching convert the same infidels to the Catholic faith. These religious and other persons destined to the work were unable to build their house upon the rock and to maintain it. Nor did the same fruit come forth that would appear if in the said island there were appointed persons who would have permanent residence, and with it make progress by word and example.

Now we have held mature deliberation on this problem with our venerable brethren. Following upon their counsel and the prayer and

---

[22] See Zavala, *Conquest of America*, preface by Rafael Altamira.

petition of the aforesaid king and queen, for the praise of God Himself and the glory and honor of the blessed and glorious Virgin Mary and the joy of the whole heavenly court, acting in the plenitude of our apostolic power and authority, by the tenor of these presents we apply to the provinces of Hyaguata, Magua, and Bayuna, regions or communities in the said island, the name of cities. We assign one metropolitan with the rank of archbishop to the Province of Hyaguata. This province, in which lies the port of Santo Domingo, is to be under the invocation of the Annunciation or Incarnation of the Blessed Virgin Mary.[23] To Magua and Bayuna, now to be called cities bearing the name of the regions in which they lie, we assign cathedral churches and bishops, one for each. In the aforesaid island they will preach the word of God, convert the said infidels and barbarous peoples, instruct and teach the converts in the true faith, bring them the grace of baptism and the sacraments of the church, and minister to them and to all other Christians now living there. Let them determine the size and style of the metropolitan and cathedral churches named above, and see to their building. And let them erect and institute the respective ecclesiastical dignities in their cities and dioceses, the canonries, prebends, and other ecclesiastical benefices with or without charge of souls. And let them conserve and plant other spiritualities, as they think expedient for the increase of the divine worship and the salvation of souls. They shall have and enjoy the archiepiscopal and episcopal insignia, jurisdictions, privileges, immunities, and favors which other archbishops and bishops possess and enjoy or can possess and enjoy by law and custom, and the same in like matters for the future.

We designate the entire Island of Hispañola as the archiepiscopal province for the same church of Hyaguata, and for its resident archbishop. His diocese, however, will embrace these regions, places, and towns: the aforesaid port of Santo Domingo ac-Ceni ayucubet, Guayagua, Azua, Iguanama, Higuei, Nicao, Aramana, Aycagua, Magaren, Canobocoa, Camuti, Elbonao, and Elmanie; and he will have the cathedral churches of Magua and Bayuna as suffragans. The bishop of

---

[23] It is not customary today to speak of the incarnation of the Blessed Virgin, for it was the Second Person of the Trinity who became incarnate. Since this occurred, however, at the Annunciation, when the angel Gabriel appeared to Mary, one can understand what the pope had in mind and what was customary nomenclature in that day.

Magua will have Magua as his city, and for its diocese and district the towns and places named Marien, Macorix, Huatiguana, Abaraco, Cauxina Himatanoex, Manguato, Caono Hyavaroex, Coaxec, Cibao Himatanoex, Cubao, Lostiguaos, Elma-corix, Elcotrix. The bishop of Bayuna will have as his see the city of Bayuna and for his diocese and district the regions and towns and places of Maguan, Jabonico, Xinabuer, Jacahuer, Iguanuco, Atryco, Cleahex, Guacaci, Xurugua, Taxguanuo, Camaye, Elcahayseto, Elbaoruco, Jaquimo, Laxaguana, Guahyqua, and Haniguayagua. These we designate in perpetuity, so that both the metropolitan archbishop himself in his metropolitan province and each of the said bishops of Magua and Bayuna in his province, see, and diocese may respectively exercise episcopal jurisdiction, authority, and power, and may receive and demand the tithes, first fruits, and other episcopal dues. And the king and queen receive and may receive, in their archiepiscopal and episcopal cities and dioceses, what is theirs by law or custom, or by privileges conceded to them.

Let, then, no man whatever take leave to infringe, or rashly attempt to contradict, this document of our designation, erection, institution, and assignment. But if anyone should so attempt, let him know that he incurs the indignation of the omnipotent God and of the blessed apostles Peter and Paul. Given at Rome, at St. Peter's, the year of the Incarnation of the Lord 1504, November 15, the first year of our pontificate.

In the *Illius fulciti presidio* of Julius II the sentence beginning "Let them determine the size and style" caught the sharp eye of Ferdinand. Julius wrote as though entirely oblivious of the royal desire for patronage. From the expressions used by the pope there developed a controversy the outcome of which gave Spain all the power that she desired in the direction of the church.

CHAPTER VIII

Julius II Grants the Patronato Real de las Indias

The death of Isabella on November 26, 1504, threw the nation into a most unexpected state of disunion. Ferdinand, firm in Aragon, found the nobles of Castile chafing to regain their former independent powers. Beyond this, Philip of Burgundy, his son-in-law and father of the future king, developed an ambition for power far beyond his temper, his rights, and his abilities. His conduct made him so troublesome an adversary that the bereaved sovereign saw himself unwanted and reviled. In these circumstances the able ruler might justly and successfully have resorted to force. Instead he decided to resign his regency and to go off to Naples until the influence of Ximenes could restore some sanity to the kingdom.[1]

It is in this light that one must attack the imminent question: why did Ferdinand not immediately appoint the bishops for whom Julius II provided in *Illius fulciti presidio?* Ten months elapsed before this able and prudent man could formulate and dispatch instructions to his ambassador at Rome. By that time his former courage and clearheadedness had been somewhat renewed. He now directed a frank plea for the pope to reconsider

---

[1] He sailed from Barcelona on September 4, 1506. Philip I died on September 25.

the principles implicit in the bull that founded a hierarchy in the Indies. His request had important results. The letter follows.[2]

The King. To Commander Francisco de Rojas, member of my Council and my ambassador at Rome.

When at my request I was shown the bulls that were sent to create and provide for the archbishopric and bishoprics of Hispañola, [I found that] they do not concede to me the patronage over the said archbishopric and bishoprics, nor over the dignities, canonries, prebends, and benefices with or without care of souls that have to be chosen in the said Island of Hispañola. It is necessary, then, that his holiness concede the patronage of all these in perpetuity, to me and to the kings who will succeed in these kingdoms of Castile and Leon. In the said bulls there is no mention whatever of these matters, as there was in the bulls for the kingdom of Granada. Moreover, the erection of the said dignities, canonries, prebends, and ecclesiastical offices of the said island is committed to the said archbishop and bishops, but there is no mention made of presentation.

Now it is desired that, in the said bull of patronage, the pope should order that none of the said dignities or canonries may be erected unless it is done with my consent as patron. And the said erection is to be committed to the archbishop of Seville, so that he may do it with my consent. And he should order that no one can be provided or instituted, in the first vacancy after the first erection, unless each of the [provided] archbishop and bishops be persons presented and at the time chosen by me and my successor kings of these kingdoms, and no others at all. And if those said archbishop and bishops or any others are requested by the person presented, through their legitimate procurators, to institute them, they may not agree to do so. The said archbishop of Seville at the time will institute them. Moreover, because of the great distance between these kingdoms and the said Island of Hispañola the future kings will not be able to present them within the term of four months that the law demands. Hence you must obtain that the said four months be extended to ten or eight months.

You are aware that I and her most serene majesty, my wife who is now in saintly glory, held through the apostolic donation all the tithes and first fruits of the Indies and mainland of the Ocean Sea. As we

---

[2] In Pacheco y Cárdenas, *Colección de documentos inéditos*, II 5, 80-83. For the original Spanish see pp. 306-08.

agreed at the time to constitute the said archbishopric and bishoprics in the Island of Hispañola, so we intended to make over to these archbishop and bishops, their churches, and beneficed clergy, the said tithes and first fruits, reserving to ourselves those tithes which in these kingdoms are called *tercias,* and all the tithes on gold, on silver and metals, on brazilwood and precious stones, on pearls and clinkstones. You must arrange that his holiness restrain the said archbishop, bishops, churches, and beneficed clergy that are or may be erected in the said Island of Hispañola or the other islands and mainland of the Ocean Sea from the enjoyment of any part of the tithes named in the above enumeration, and that what we reserve of this last for ourselves and our successors we make perpetually reserved. Despite the content of the apostolic collation for the said archbishop and bishops, let it be clear that they must be content to possess their tithes in the aforesaid manner, and see that it is put into the apostolic letters.

Further, it is evidently committed to the same archbishop and bishops, by the same apostolic letters and the provision of the said archbishop and bishops, that they are empowered to bound and to divide the area of the said archbishopric and bishoprics. Now, since it may well happen that they will not on that subject be forever in agreement with one another, it is necessary that his holiness order that I, or the person or persons to whom I entrust the matter, make the said division and partition, and that the said archbishop and each of the said bishops must accept the ambit of territory that is thus marked off for him. Consequently, I charge and order that you at once speak for me to his holiness, and beg him to concede everything that is here put down. Use all diligence in forwarding this business as rapidly as you can, and send me the result dispatched with a trustworthy courier. For as to the bulls of the archbishopric and bishoprics, I do not see how to give them provision until your answer arrives. In doing this you will give me much pleasure and service. From the city of Segovia, September 13, 1505. I the King.

By command of the king, my lord. Gaspar de Grizyo. Signed by Doctor Ángulo and Licentiate Zapata.

After ten months spent in Naples and its environs Ferdinand at last decided to return to Spain, and on July 20, 1507 he disembarked at Valencia. At once he pressed forward to Castile, and this time he found his presence eagerly expected. Once more in the regency, he again took up the direction of affairs in the Indies. Evidently he had word that the pope would soon publish a bull containing the rectification that Rojas had sought. Meantime, in a *cédula* to Ovando in Hispañola, he sent the following instruction regarding the bishops. It is dated October 21, 1507. After discussing mines, trade, and discovery he wrote:

> The sending of the bishops has been prevented by my absence from these kingdoms. But now I have given order to provide what is fitting for their voyage. Their bulls for which I sent are come from Rome, so they may cross over and enter into residence in their sees.[3] You shall inform them of the rentals that will be theirs and the times of their payment. Beyond the rentals, they must be provided with Indians. And let it all be done in that way. I the King. By order of his highness. Miguel Pérez de Almaçán.[4]

From the next royal message to Ovando it may be inferred that fresh difficulties held off the provision for the Hispañola bishops. Ferdinand would have no reason to deceive his representative in the Indies. Hence it seems sensible to find the cause in a shifting of population and growth of economy that led in 1511 to cancellation of the original sees and substitution of the three permanent locations. At the moment, however, the king has evidently been asking for quick papal action on the provision and installation of the prelates. His letter of 1508[5] reaches into a variety of administrative arrangements. Its patronage elements are the following.

> The King: Don Fray Nicolás de Ovando, commander major of the Order of Alcántara, our governor in the islands of the Indies and mainland of the Ocean Sea.
> You should know that Bachelor Anton Serrano and Diego de Nicuesa, procurators in your island, have on their own initiative written

---

[3] The bishoprics were not filled. The reason for this is explained below on p. 119.
   Paragraph taken from *ibid.*, II 5, 119.
[4] For the original Spanish see p. 308.
[5] In *ibid.*, II 5, 125-27. For the original Spanish see pp. 308-10.

to me about several matters. And now, for the great pleasure that I take in advancing the welfare and success of the settlers there, both because it is a patrimony planted by my own hand and nurtured by the efforts I took to foster it, and also because of their firm friendship and fidelity as attested by your report that they are strongly attached to my person, I have authorized for them everything that I could do in favor of this said island.

Their first request reported the fact that the churches built in the island up to this time were erected at the expense of the settlements. Because they were made of thatch, they were many times ruined and had often to be rebuilt, a thing that meant labor to the pueblos and churches always unfinished. They ask me to order that the churches be constructed of durable materials, and that the cost be met by the tithes and first fruits of the island. For the service of God, and to do benefit and largess to this said island, I have ordered that these requests be granted. And I have given a directive to our officials of the Casa de Contratación who reside at Seville to send across professional stone-cutters who will be able to do that work. I have likewise ordered my Gerónimo de Pasamonte, secretary to the most serene queen, my most dear and beloved wife, and our treasurer general in those islands and mainland, to see to it that, as regards the tithes and first fruits collected or to be collected, the prelates when they come are to receive the promised said tithes and first fruits out of the whole sum that you said would be needed for the building of the churches and for the salaries of the ministers, in view of their service in the divine worship, as is completely reasonable. Do you take the said treasurer with you and go and see what he will have to expend in the circumstances, so that I may satisfy my conscience and my duty to God and to [the people of] this island. For what must be spent you will give to the said treasurer a voucher, signed in your own hand, that he may keep the account of what he issues to the deputed two trustworthy citizens of the island who will take charge of the work. Thus through their agency you will allocate what you see has to be spent in accordance with your vouchers, as was noted.

As to the petition of the procurators that the prelates come to this island, I am requesting provision at Rome for their clearance, a matter that they discussed with me some time ago. There is then no need at all for them to await the news from Rome before they take passage. Meanwhile, as they are going for my service, do you give your best attention over there to what touches the service of our Lord, since you see how much we owe for what great mercy He shows us in those lands.[6] . . . Done at Burgos, April 30, 1508. I the King. By order of his highness. Lope Conchillos.

In 1508 with Ferdinand well in control of the regency and able to conduct his diplomatic affairs in peace and security, his Roman ambassador finally won a magnificent victory by obtaining from Rome a bull doing away with restrictions imposed by the *Illius fulciti presidio* and granting full patronage over the church in the Indies. This new document, the celebrated *Universalis ecclesiae regimini*, cut through whatever doubts remained from the large though vague constitutional concession of the 1493 *Inter caetera divinae* and laid a granite foundation under royal government of the American church.

There was a long controversy over the genuinity of the document. In the first place, no original remains today, either in Rome or Madrid. The secret archives of Julius II are missing for the years from 1506 to 1510. Certain things in the text of the bull led Cuevas and others to deny its authenticity; for the term *Nueva España* is used to designate the islands, whereas scholars thought the term was first applied to Mexican land in 1519, and its concessions were held impossible in view of current canon law. The whole question was laid to rest in 1946 by Pedro Leturia in his convincing study, "La bula del patronato de las Indias españoles que falta en el archivo Vaticano."[7] This article offers a reconstructed text based on private documents and early printings, and today the problem may be considered as solved.

In reading this bull it should be realized that the Patronato was not transplanted fully formed, but that it took body as part

---

[6] Paragraphs here omitted are alien to the immediate subject. They do, however, reflect the close touch of Ferdinand with his lands and his generous though shrewd direction of their government.

[7] *Studi e testi*, No. 125 (1946), pp. 402-26.

of the new society that was unfolding. A model had been set in
the Bull of Granada. Alexander VI in 1493 conveyed the powers
implicit in the duty of converting the natives. Then in 1501, as
a reward for the costly enterprise of evangelizing the inhabitants, the pope conceded to the Catholic monarchs all tithes in
the Indies. Three years later, upon royal petition, the three first
episcopal sees were erected. Then in 1508, as the outcome of
negotiations between Ferdinand and Julius II, the king received
the privilege of founding and organizing all churches overseas.
In 1510 and 1511 it was allowed that tithes on metals would not
go to the church but to the crown and that a third of the tithes on
produce of the fields should go to the king. Also in 1511 Seville
was made metropolitan church for all bishops of the Ocean Sea.
Only after 1591 was private foundation permitted for churches,
chapels, and hospitals. Spanish kings considered these grants in-
terdependent and mutually harmonious. No single grant, however, was held equal to the concession of Julius II given in the
following bull.[8]

[*Universalis ecclesiae regimini*]

Julius, bishop, servant of the servants of God, for a perpetual
remembrance.

As we preside by divine disposition, however unmerited, over the
regimen of the universal church, we are happy to concede, especially
to the Catholic monarchs, those favors which bring to them honor and
respect and contribute both to the royal estate of their lands and to
their timely security.

Now but a few years back our most dear son in Christ, Ferdinand,
illustrious king of Aragon and also of Sicily, and Isabella of dear

---

[8] In Hernáez, *Colección*, I, 24-26. It is also in Ribadeneyra, *Manual compendio*,
pp. 408-14; Pacheco y Cárdenas, *Colección de documentos inéditos*, I 34,
25-29; Pedro Frasso, *Tractatus de regio patronatu Indiarum. Questiones
aliquae desumptae et disputatae in alia quinquaginta capita partitae* (Original
edition, 1677-1679. Madrid, 1775), I, 4; Leturia, "Bula dèl patronato," *Studi e
testi* (1946), pp. 421-24; García Gutiérrez, *Bulario*, pp. 27-28. The *Bulario* of
García Gutiérrez unfortunately contains a number of textual errors. For the
original Latin see pp. 310-13.

memory, queen of Castile and Leon, after lifting the agelong yoke of the Moors from Spain, traversed the ocean and brought to lands until then unknown the saving standard of the cross, so that, in as far as they could, they fulfilled the word: "To the whole world their call went forth."

Under an uncharted segment of the heavens they subdued islands and many lands, among them one most rich and populous to which they gave the name of New Spain. In that land, in order that the false and pernicious rites be extirpated and the true religion be planted, at the insistent prayer of the same king and queen we erected one metropolitan church, to wit Ayguaza [sic], and two cathedral sees, Magua and Bayuna, to the highest glory of the name of Christ. Moreover, lest the souls imbued with the new faith, while building churches or holy places in the island, should undertake any pious project in such manner as to bring prejudice upon either the new Christian religion there or upon the temporal dominion of the kings, we agreed with the said King Ferdinand, who was also governor general of Castile and Leon at the time, and with our dear daughter in Christ Juana, queen of those kingdoms and child of King Ferdinand, to this effect, that no church, monastery, or pious place, in the aforesaid islands or regions or in those to be acquired, could be erected or founded without the consent of the same King Ferdinand and Queen Juana, monarchs of Castile and Leon at the time. Now, as it very much concerns the same king that persons of trust, beholden and acceptable, be in charge of the churches and monasteries, they very seriously desire the concession of the right of patronage and of presenting fit persons both to metropolitan and other cathedral churches, already built or in time to be erected, and to any other ecclesiastical benefices, within a year to be computed from the day of their vacancy, while the ordinaries of the places may present to lesser benefices; and that in the event that the said ordinaries for ten days refuse without legitimate reasons to install these persons, any other bishop could at the royal demand in their place freely and licitly install the ones presented.

We are highly conscious of the importance of the Indies and of the aforesaid kingdoms, whose kings have ever been both devoted to the Apostolic See and interested in its honor, credit, and security. Hence we yield to the instant prayer which with great respect the said King Ferdinand and Queen Juana have made and do now make to us. And so, after mature deliberation with our brethren, the cardinals of the holy Roman church, and following their counsel, through our apostolic authority and by these presents we make the following grants to the same King Ferdinand and Queen Juana and to the future kings of Castile and Leon who may be reigning at the time. In the islands and regions of that sea, whether already acquired or later to be acquired, no one may without their express consent construct, build, and erect the greater churches. We grant the right of patronage and the right to present suitable persons to the churches of Ayguaza, Magua, and Bayuna, already mentioned, and to all other metropolitan or cathedral churches, monasteries, and postpontifical dignities, and in collegiate churches to the principal dignities. This right extends to all other ecclesiastical benefices and pious places that are vacant at the time, for a year from the day of their vacancy, in the Indies and regions to which we have referred; that is to say, to cathedral and metropolitan churches and even to churches belonging to religious orders which by law should be subject to consistorial action. We make this grant for those persons presented according to the requirements of the canons to us and our successors as Roman pontiffs, in view of the great expanse of ocean that separates those lands from us.

Regarding benefices below these ranks, we grant this to ordinaries of places, for they are to have the right of installing the persons presented to these benefices. And if the said bishops neglect for ten days to institute the person presented, at once any other bishops of those parts, at the demand of King Ferdinand or Queen Juana or the king living at the time, may in place of the one refusing freely and licitly institute the person named. This we, by our apostolic authority and in virtue of these presents, do concede, notwithstanding other constitutions, apostolic ordinations, or anything else to the contrary.

Therefore let no man take leave to infringe this patent of our concession, nor make rash attempt to do so. If any should presume so to attempt, let him know that he will incur the indignation of the omnipotent God and of His blessed apostles Peter and Paul. Given at Rome, at St. Peter's, the year of the Incarnation of our Lord 1508, July 28, the fifth year of our pontificate.

With this full grant of patronage and presentation now made final, there remained but one question to be settled between Ferdinand and the papacy before the system could go into operation. That was the problem of financing. It is well known that the

king and his wife practiced a most careful economy in administration. Isabella, with her profound respect for her subjects, had
always insisted that tax be assessed by voluntary action of the
cortes and that regular revenues, rather than emergency levies,
should support the nation even in its most extraordinary activities. Though Castile in 1504 enjoyed a crown revenue thirty
times that of 1474, when Isabella ascended the throne, still, as
Prescott writes: "All of this, it will be remembered, was derived
from the customary established taxes, without the imposition of
a single new one."[9] Moreover, the income from the Indies had
not at this early date caught up with their costs to the government. And Ferdinand followed a similar policy throughout
his rule.

To undertake the ecclesiastical enterprise in the western
world called for unusual outlays. Alexander VI had in 1501
made over to the monarchs all the tithes to be collected in that
area. The preceding documents have made clear the intention of
the sovereigns to turn these back to the use of the church, with
some reservations that in the situation were quite understandable. So that these exceptions would have the force of law, the
king now asked Julius II for official recognition of this situation.
The reply was the following bull.[10]

[Eximie devotionis affectus]

Julius, bishop, servant of the servants of God. For a perpetual
remembrance.

The attachment and unique dedication manifested toward us and
the Roman church by our most dear son and daughter in Christ, the
illustrious Ferdinand, king of Aragon and Sicily, and Juana, queen of
Castile and Leon, and the proven constancy of unswerving faith in the
same church and the Apostolic See shown by the same king and queen,
and by Isabella of happy memory, wife of King Ferdinand and mother

---

9 Prescott, *Ferdinand and Isabella*, III, 441-42.
10 In Pacheco y Cárdenas, *Colección de documentos inéditos*, II 5, 205-09. For the
   original Latin see pp. 313-15.

of Queen Juana, and by their other progenitors whose single-minded spirit and untiring cooperation have ever been at our service, eminently deserve that we return their devotion with an equally generous response to their needs and advantage.

We now have the petition of King Ferdinand and Queen Juana to the following effect. A right has been enjoyed by the kings and queens of Castile and Leon for so long a time that its contrary is not found in the memory of man, that when in their kingdoms and dominions they mined gold or silver or other metals, no customary tithe was laid on them for a parochial church or any other religious purpose. The same King Ferdinand, and Isabella his queen while she lived, and after her death Ferdinand alone in his capacity as regent of the same kingdoms and dominions of Castile and Leon, captured and recovered certain maritime islands and other regions to which for ages safe access had been denied to Christians. The Saracens and other infidels had held sway there. But now with strong and energetic leadership, under a propitious heaven the kings won the victory.

It is said that mines of gold and silver and other metals are found in those lands. The kings annexed these recovered islands and regions, and incorporated them into their own kingdoms and dominions. In the islands and regions so recovered, they had a large number of churches and monasteries built. To furnish a stable endowment for these establishments, they assigned the tithes due them from their properties. Moreover, at their own expense they sent out religious and other ecclesiastical persons for the direction and government of the recovered islands and regions. In all the work of recovering these same islands and regions they sustained serious losses and constant peril of material and of persons. They therefore feel that they should not be held to payment of any tithe on mines of gold and silver and metals in the islands and regions now recovered, just as it has been for their mines in their other kingdoms and dominions.

Nevertheless some men question whether King Ferdinand and Queen Juana should not be bound to pay the tithe for this gold and silver and metals which they are having mined in the aforesaid recovered islands and regions. Wherefore, on the part of King Ferdinand and Queen Juana, humble petition is made to us that we deign in our apostolic benignity to concede and to provide opportunely for them and their successors regnant at any time in the kingdoms and dominions of Castile and Leon, to which the recovered islands and regions are annexed or are in future to be annexed. Thus, on the output of the mines of gold and silver and other metals of whatever kind, in the aforesaid islands and regions recovered or to be recovered, where they stand ready to build and endow the churches as needed, they will be in no way held to the payment of a tithe, as has been their custom hitherto in mines of the kingdoms and dominions of the above-named Castile and Leon.

Recalling then with paternal mind the exceptional merits of King Ferdinand and Queen Juana and their said forebears and moved by the urgency of their request, on our apostolic authority, by the tenor of these presents and as a special sign of our favor, we concede and grant to King Ferdinand and Queen Juana and to their successor monarchs of the kingdoms and dominions of Castile and Leon, to which are annexed the islands and regions recovered or at some time to be recovered and annexed, that they be not held to payment of any tithe on the product of the mines of gold and silver and other metals of whatever kind in the islands and regions so recovered, provided that the necessary churches be constructed and endowed by Queen Juana and the aforesaid kings, just as they have up to this time been in no way bound to pay tithes from the gold and silver and other metals obtained from the mines of the said kingdoms and dominions of Castile and Leon. And this notwithstanding the decrees of the Lateran Council and any other constitutions and apostolic ordinations or other things whatsoever to the contrary. Let no man then take leave to infringe this document of our concession and indult, or in temerity dare to do so. But if any should presume to attempt it, let him know that he incurs the indignation of the omnipotent God and His blessed apostles Peter and Paul. Given at Rome, at St. Peter's, the year of the Incarnation of the Lord 1510, April 8, the seventh year of our pontificate.

This prosaic legal letter settled the royal financial situation and cleared the way for what was absolutely necessary to the American church, its economic underpinning. The next chapter completes this story.

CHAPTER IX

Bishops, Tithes, a Patriarch

The Patronato Real de las Indias, like all permanent institutions, came as a response to impelling ideas and situations. Ferdinand and Isabella represented Spanish genius at its point of highest creative potentiality. They saw the need, and the eminent values, in patronage as a dynamic of empire. The papacy, intent on religious interests, realized the emergent opportunity for the spread of the faith in the powerful surge of Iberian ideals under Isabellan leadership—a sweep that continued long after her death because of her salutary government. Columbus, Ovando, Fonseca, and other minds gifted with imagination and insight understood the possibilities present in the lands of the Ocean Sea. Las Casas was now on the scene. Cortés had already joined Velásquez in the Cuban episode, and by 1512 the islands had thrown out lines of communication to the isthmus of Panama and Tierra Firme. As the first Spanish outposts grew into larger and more productive groups and their adventurous members began to run the coasts of both continents, demands in the west coincided with sovereign and pontifical policies to turn what might have been an airy nothing into vigorous corporate operation. Each of the three sectors contributed full force to the organizing process. By the time of Ferdinand's death in 1516, the Patronato stood so firmly founded that it was assured of permanent stability as a fundamental institution in the empire.

In the letter sent by Ferdinand in 1505 to his Roman ambassador, the design was clearly if rather insistently stated. These royal orders should be read with proper softening of magisterial verbs; it was his envoy who received the instructions. Moreover, Julius II looked kindly on Rojas, whose master served the pope so well in thwarting the menace of France to papal independence. Julius too was no novice in estimating his fellow man. If his chancellor made the *Eximie devotionis affectus* of 1510 somewhat overdone in approbation, the pontiff knew that he was dealing with realities. Accordingly, after granting the exception on tithing precious metals, he took considerable time on the larger questions, the fixing of the new bishoprics, and the final settlement of the tithes. He had counted for long on the promise of Ferdinand to cede back to the American hierarchy full support for ecclesiastical enterprise, a promise that was fulfilled to the letter. The king, however, was no Croesus, as his economic record showed. Only later would Charles V and Philip II come into rich overseas revenues. The basic arrangement now to be made had to rest on the actual condition of the treasury of Castile, and any future estimates must be founded on assured and sufficient income.

The first matter attacked was the location of the bishoprics. Although the documentary evidence is meager, it is certain that in 1504 three cathedral churches were definitely instituted. For seven more years they lay unoccupied. There is the merest hint in the instruction of Ferdinand to Ovando on April 30, 1508 that it was not alone Spain that held up the installation of the bishops. He had written: "As to the petition of the procurators that the prelates come to this island, I am requesting provision at Rome for their clearance, a matter that they discussed with me some time ago. There is then no need at all for them to await the news from Rome before they take passage."[1]

---

[1] See above, Chapter 8, p. 108.

When at last the new sees received incumbents, their locations differed from those originally chosen, undoubtedly because further discovery, conquest, and development made a fresh orientation imperative. The case is clarified in this rarely cited bull of Julius II dated 1511.[2]

[*Teniendo en la tierra*]

Bull erecting the cathedral churches of Cuba, Puerto Rico, and Santo Domingo[3]

Julius, bishop, servant of the servants of God, for a perpetual remembrance, the Roman pontiff.

Holding on earth as we do the full authority of the vicar of Him from whom all order comes, who carries His jurisdiction to all portions of the world, with mature counsel we make decisions and dispositions for the greater strength and stability of the Catholic faith, and for the estate and progress of the churches. In particular we provide for metropolitan and other cathedral churches that have been erected, by way of translation, suppression, or new creation, in places whose geography is almost unknown. We take cognizance of all the circumstances and conditions prevailing in these settlements that justify the presence of their venerable prelates. These men grow old and firm in the faith, illumine the churches, and the lowly Christian religion expands and unfolds. And as they advance in temporal affairs, so do they augment the spiritual.

Now the Island of Hispañola, set in the Sea of the Indies, though long oppressed by the infidel yoke was brought back to the Christian religion by the powerful fleet of our zealous dear son in Christ Don Fernando, king of Aragon and Sicily and of Castile and Leon, of

---

[2] In Pacheco y Cárdenas, *Colección de documentos inéditos*, I 34, 29-35. The bull exists, so far as the writer knows, only in its Spanish translation. For the Spanish translation see pp. 316-19.

[3] This title, placing a bishopric in Cuba in 1511, involves Pacheco y Cárdenas in a problem. The redonation-of-tithes document, printed immediately after this one, clearly says of Santo Domingo and Concepción "que son en la Isla de Española." Cuba was first entered in 1511 at Baracoa, and Julius II could not in that year have had knowledge of a developed Cuban location called Concepción. Hernáez, *Colección*, I, 22 places the first Cuban bishopric at Asunción de Baracoa in 1517. Hence Concepción must be here understood as the western bishopric of Santo Domingo. On the death of Pedro Suárez de Deza it was united with that of Santo Domingo.

memory immortal, and by Queen Doña Isabella, then the spouse of the
same king. In this island we erected and instituted cathedral churches,
to wit: Hyaguata the metropolitan church, and Bayuna and Magua. The
same king and queen petitioned us on this subject, and we made the
concession on the advice of our brethren and with the plenitude of our
apostolic authority, as is more fully explained in the letters we dispatched at that time.[4]

However, it has become evident that the sites of the said island
are not appropriate for the permanent life of the said churches, both
because of their location and because of difficulty in obtaining the
necessary supplies. Moreover, there has come to light another island
named San Juan in the same Ocean Sea, and it is now under their
jurisdiction. Beyond that, the regions, towns, and villas in the region
of Santo Domingo in the Island of Hispañola, and also those of Concepción and of Puerto Rico, will furnish excellent accommodations for
cathedral churches and for prelates who will reside there. It has been
our aim to get better knowledge and to provide convenient and opportune remedy for this development, thus to appoint prelates and bring
comfort to the said settlements. We have taken serious deliberation with
our venerable brethren in joint council. Our approbation is greatly
desired by the same King Don Fernando, who is both king of Castile
and Leon and governor general and administrator of those kingdoms
for her serene highness, our dear daughter in Christ Doña Juana, to
whose kingdoms the said islands are subjected and annexed. Petition
also comes from our beloved sons Pedro of Hyaguata, García of Bayuna,
and Alfonso of Magua, preconized for the rule and government of the
said churches of Hyaguata, Bayuna, and Magua, and respectively bearing the titles of these sees.

We, therefore, employing the authority and plenitude of our power,
do suppress and perpetually extinguish the said churches. And for
the exaltation and praise of almighty God and of the Church Militant, we designate and give the title of [episcopal] cities to the regions
and environs of Santo Domingo, of Concepción, and of San Juan.
These erected cities shall be called cathedral sees, the one in Santo
Domingo, the other in Concepción, and the third in Puerto Rico. And
we name their bishops, the first for Santo Domingo, the second for
Concepción, the third for San Juan. These prelates in their said churches

---

[4] The "letters" are the *Illius fulciti presidio.* See Chapter 7, pp. 100-03.

shall worship and do reverence to our God and Lord and to His saints. They shall preach the holy gospel, teach the infidels, and with good conversation convert them to a veneration of the Catholic faith. And they will instruct them, when they are once converted, in the Christian religion and administer to them the holy sacrament of baptism; and this both for the converts and for the other faithful in Christ who live and reside in the said islands. To those who come thither they shall administer and have administered the holy sacraments of confession, of the Eucharist, and the rest. Likewise they shall see that the people of these new islands build for them [churches] of good design, and proper residences. In the same sees, cities, and bishoprics they are to erect parochial churches with their own pastors, dignities, administrators, and officials, and see that these be fit persons. Let them likewise, for the care of souls, provide canonries, prebends, and the other ecclesiastical benefices. And they are empowered to erect and institute regular churches of whatsoever religious orders, as they judge it convenient for the greater increase of the divine service and the need of the faithful. The said bishops will enjoy and use the episcopal insignia, jurisdictions, privileges and immunities, graces and indults, just as other bishops enjoy them by right or custom. These said churches we erect, create, and constitute, for all time, namely: that of Santo Domingo, Concepción, and of Puerto Rico, and we likewise erect and name them as cities; repeating, Santo Domingo, with la Buenaventura, Azua Salvaleón; San Juan de la Alaguana, with Vera-Paz, Villanueva de Yaquinos; Concepción de Santiago, with Puerto de Plata, Puerto Real, la Redena Hava, Salvatierra de la Cabaña, and Santa Cruz. And we concede and assign to all the faithful tenants and inhabitants of the lands, villas, and environs of San Juan, and to its churches, all the said island of San Juan with its districts and its diocese. This is to be interpreted in such wise that each one of the bishops present at the time in the said islands of Santo Domingo, Concepción, and Puerto Rico can exercise and employ in their cities and bishoprics all the jurisdiction, authority, and episcopal power, and they can demand and obtain the tithes, first fruits, and other episcopal rights, just as do the other bishops of the Province of Seville in old Spain. They ask and obtain them by right and law, except those on gold, silver, other metals, and precious stones, which we declare to be exempt and free from tithe.

Moreover we wish that the cited churches of Santo Domingo, of Concepción, and of San Juan be suffragans of the said province and church of Seville and to its archbishopric, which will have for the time metropolitan right. And we concede and reserve to the said king of Castile and Leon forever the right of patronage, and to present to the Roman pontiff fitting persons, for these said churches when vacant, namely, to Santo Domingo, Concepción, and San Juan, so that in filling these posts he will have right to their presentation; that is to say, for bishops and pastors.

Let no one interfere or dare to falsify or pervert the whole content of this patent of our suspension and extinction, erection and creation, institution, concession, assignment, subtraction of decree, and reservation. But if anyone should proclaim intent to do so, he will be known as incurring the indignation of almighty God and of His apostles Saints Peter and Paul. Given at St. Peter's, the year 1511, August 8, the eighth year of our pontificate.

With this decree the three first American bishoprics began to function. Ferdinand then took the step that provided the permanent underpinning for the church in the Indies. Though in full and just possession of all overseas tithes through gift of Alexander VI, he carried out the joint promise he had made with Isabella, and in the famous Concordat of Burgos redonated to the hierarchy in the Indies almost all of what had been freely granted to him, thus setting aside in perpetuity the endowment for the future work of the Patronato. The document throws a powerful light on the essential character of the king. Its solemn prologue indicates the depth of meaning in this unique act of royal generosity.[5]

Redonation of tithes, and concordat between the Catholic monarchs Ferdinand and Juana and the first bishops of the Americas. Burgos, 1512.

In the name of God. Amen. Let it be manifest to all who see the present instrument of capitulation and ordination that in the year of the birth of our Lord Jesus Christ 1512, in the fifteenth indiction, the eighth day of May, the ninth year of the pontificate of our most holy father Julius II, by divine providence pope, in the presence of myself,

---

[5] From Hernáez, Colección, I, 21-25. Also found in García Gutiérrez, Bulario, pp. 31-34 and Frasso, Tractatus, I, cap. 19. Both of the latter omit the first mention of Bishop Manso. For the original Spanish see pp. 319-25.

Francisco de Valencia, canon of Palencia and notary public by the apostolic authority and secretary of the most holy father in Christ bishop of Palencia, the most exalted and powerful princes Don Fernando, king of Aragon and of the Two Sicilies and Jerusalem, Catholic king, and Doña Juana his daughter, queen of Castile and Leon, etc., our lords, on the one part, and each of their highnesses for himself and in his name, because of the portion that belongs to each respectively in the islands, Indies, and mainland of the Ocean Sea, by force of the apostolic bulls conceded to their royal majesties by Pope Alexander VI of happy memory, whose documents are here given word for word after one another so following: [here are inserted the three bulls of earlier times, *Inter caetera divinae* of May 4, 1493, *Dudum siquidem* of September 26, 1493, and *Eximiae devotionis* of May 4, 1493][6] and the reverend fathers in Christ Don Fray García de Padilla, bishop of Santo Domingo, and Don Pedro Suárez de Deza, doctor of decrees,[7] bishop of Concepción, which sees are in the Island of Hispañola, and Don Alonso Manso, licentiate in theology, bishop of the Island of San Juan, bishops-elect[8] by action of our holy father Julius II, in the newly created and erected cathedral churches in the said islands, for themselves and in the name of the bishops their successors who come after them in the said churches, and of the persons to whom pertain the

---

[6] It will be noted that the bulls are not mentioned in the order in which they were issued. Ferdinand may have felt that a change in the order would contribute to clearness and force. He refers first to the bull that gave title to the Indies of the West, then to the one that gave title over islands and lands even in the East Indies if reached by westward sailing, and finally to the one that extended to the Spanish crown the privileges previously given to the master prior of the Orden de Cristo.

[7] Doctor of decrees would today mean doctor of laws.

[8] Hernáez, *Colección*, I, 22 notes that Alonso Manso was presented as bishop of Puerto Rico in 1512 and at Seville formally performed the erection of his church (1512), as his signature there attests. He died in his diocese in 1534. García de Padilla, confessor of Queen Leonore of Portugal, was presented for Santo Domingo in 1512 and erected his church in Seville in 1512, as his signature there in the episcopal palace proves. He accepted the bishopric on the condition that he "should not touch money," and died before consecration. Pedro Suárez was presented for Concepción and erected his church in Seville the same year. Pacheco y Cárdenas, *Colección de documentos inéditos*, I 34, 35 note, says that Fray Xuan de Umite was the first actual bishop in Cuba, named in 1518 for Asunción de Baracoa. In 1523 he moved to Santiago. His provision by Adrian VI of April 28, 1522 is there printed.

aforesaid contents, on the second part, do assent to and make the following agreement:

First: Their highnesses, in order that the bishops with their clergy accept the duty of praying to our Lord for their lives and royal success, for their souls when they depart from this world, for the souls of the kings who will succeed them in their realms, and for the faithful Christians who died in gaining and discovering the same islands, do make gift, grant, and donation to them from this hour and forever, of the tithes pertaining to the said highnesses from these said islands, and the bishops will see to it that they levy them in the form that is approved by their highnesses and as they have levied them according to the concession and donation which Pope Alexander VI of happy memory made to them, as is clear in the bull which his holiness conceded to their highnesses, the contents of which are as follows: [the earlier bull expedited on November 16, 1501 is inserted here].

It is the will of their highnesses that those tithes be divided among the bishops, churches, clergy, buildings, hospitals, and other specified uses.[9] And the said bishops promise, for themselves and their successors and in the name of their churches and clergy, that from this day forward they will observe and fulfill the aforesaid and what is hereinafter contained. And their highnesses make this said gift and donation on the express condition that they will so observe and fulfill, and under no other circumstances.

Item: That the dignities, canonries, prebends, and benefices, just as they were previously created and instituted in the first instance in the said islands of Hispañola and San Juan, conformably with our right in erecting the said churches, cathedral as well as others, so now all others that come to be vacant will depend upon the presentation of their highnesses as a right of the Patronato Real.

Item: That all other benefices that become vacant and are to be assigned to recipients after the first nomination and provision shall be granted to legitimate children of the settlers and inhabitants who have

---

[9] The tithes were to be divided according to the custom of Seville: one fourth to the bishop, one fourth to his cathedral church; of the remainder, two ninths to the crown, four ninths to pastors and curates, three eighteenths to church upkeep, three eighteenths for hospitals. In building new churches the cost was borne one third by the crown, one third by the encomenderos, and the final third by the Indians, who by their labor thus paid tribute to the crown. See Mecham, *Church and State*, p. 29.

come or will come to those kingdoms and take up residence in those parts, and of their descendants, and not to the sons of the natives who were there before the Christians settled. And let this rule stand until their highnesses or their successors determine or provide otherwise in the case. And let the candidates be chosen for excellence, with preceding competition and examination according to the custom of the clergy in the patrimony of the bishopric of Palencia; with the condition that within a year and a half after they are presented, the said sons of the settlers will be obliged to obtain the approval and acceptance of their highnesses and of their successors for such benefices, which same they shall show to the viceroy, governor, and judges of appeal who are or will be in the said islands; and if they do not show their approvals within the said time, the places are *ipso facto* vacant, and their highnesses and their successors can present other persons to these benefices thus vacant, in all things conformably to the aforesaid arrangements.

Item: In virtue of the bull conceded by our holy father Julius II and its declaration regarding the custom that the candidates must wear the tonsure, the said bishops are to make their declaration in this wise: they will wear the crown bare, as large at least as a *real castellano*, and the hair two fingers below the ear and a little lower in the back; and the upper garment will be a mantle or hooded cloak, or the long clerical gown closed or open as one wishes; the vesture will be as long at least as to come within a palm of the instep; and the outer garments and others should not be of red or bright green, nor yellow or any other unseemly shade.

Item: That neither the said bishops nor their successors may give the tonsure to anyone who can neither read nor speak Latin, nor may they make a priest of a father's only son, but must wait until he has two or three sons instead of one only. For it is not to be thought that any person will want all his sons to become clerics. The fact that other sons might be born later does not alter the case. Even so an only son must not be taken from his father.

Item: That in keeping the feasts they observe those ordered by the church and no others, even though promises and vows to do so may have intervened. And in the synods let there be no increasing of the number of feasts beyond what are today kept in the said Island of Hispañola. And if any person should urge an increase in the number now kept in the said Island of Hispañola, let them have only what the church solemnizes and not what other Christians may do, for the Christians there can support themselves in no way other than according to the productivity of the *haciendas* in those said islands.

Item: That the said bishops should levy the tithes in conformity with the bull conceded by our most holy father, and not lay them or any other exaction on gold, silver, or other mineral, nor on pearls or precious stones. They will, according to the same bull, collect them in produce as in Castile, and not in money as they have done for some time. And not for that reason or any other will they remove the Indians, directly or indirectly, from what they have hitherto been doing in the search for gold, but instead they should inspire and direct them to do this service of digging gold better than they have up to now, telling them that this aids in the war against the infidels and in other causes that those can understand who are able to progress toward better work.

Item: That the archbishop of Seville, metropolitan of the churches and bishoprics of the said islands, or his fiscal, may be in and reside in any one of the said bishoprics and exercise those functions that belong to him as metropolitan according to the law, and the said metropolitan may not choose as a substitute any of the prelates of the said islands.

Item: That for those who may have Indians working in the mines, those Indians who go there for the work period cannot be contracted away, or removed, or imprisoned, or summoned to court for any crime other than their own by any judge during that time, lest he induce them to shirk their labor by offer of bread or wine; for this gold is the fruit of the earth and one has to give himself to it in place of something else as is done in Castile.

Item: Those who excuse themselves from suits at civil law because of the tonsure lose their Indians and what they have in the mines, for such an act would appear to show that, whether the cause be lay or ecclesiastical, they could bring it before the ecclesiastical judge without incurring any penalty.

And the said Don Fray García de Padilla, bishop of Santo Domingo, and Don Pedro Suárez de Deza, doctor of decrees, bishop of Concepción, and Don Alonso Manso, licentiate in theology, bishop in the Island of San Juan, after reading and understanding everything contained in this capitulation, and each and every part of it, do authorize and accept it as valid, for themselves and in the name of the bishops who will succeed them in the same churches, and for those who will be provided in the dignities, canonries, prebends, and other benefices, both vacant and not vacant. And they promise and obligate themselves, in what touches or concerns them, to observe and fulfill it completely, and to oblige those other persons whom it covers or concerns, in present and in future, to observe and fulfill it without fail. The said authorization they made in the presence of the most reverend and most honored lord, Don Juan de Fonseca, chaplain major, member of the Council of their highnesses, and gave their hands in promise as loyal and faithful prelates, and knowing and honest men, to keep and comply with all and every part, and neither now nor at any time to contravene anything in all that is here said. And for greater assurance they signed their names, and at the act there were present as witnesses the noble lords Lope de Conchillos, secretary of the queen our lady, the licentiate Zapata, and the doctor Carvajal, of the Council of their highnesses, on their summons and call.

And I, Francisco de Valencia, canon of Palencia, public notary by the apostolic authority, was present for all that is here said and was one of the said witnesses, and I saw the said most reverend bishops sign their names in my register. Because this is a public instrument of capitulation and contract, I had another hand make a faithful copy of it, and with this my customary mark and name I signed and attested. In testimony of the requested and required truth. Francisco de Valencia, apostolic notary.

This state paper, beyond the fundamental redonation of which it is the record, contains the beginnings of basic law for the action of the clergy in the Indies. Almost every paragraph enunciates what was then called a *pragmática*. From the nature of the contract these clauses must of necessity become statutory in their effect, and they will take their place in the code of the Indies compiled by Philip II. Had this legislation been proposed to the Castilians, it would have required the consent of the *cortes*. Though the overseas possessions still belonged to Castile alone, the making of their Patronato law in this case fell to the regent on the one side (with his invalided daughter), and on the other to the representatives of the church, as is explicitly achieved in the compact made. With this document published, it is evident that the Patronato Real de las Indias can now go ahead with its full complement of grant, support, personnel, and enactment of essential law.

In 1513 Ferdinand revealed a most ambitious plan for the development of the Patronato and the church in the Indies. A solid hold had just been won on Tierra Firme and Darién. His men believed that they had found a vast continent. The ruler projected his view with imperial expansiveness, going so far as to envision in the church a wholly new patriarchate, such as that of Constantinople or Alexandria. The proposal here is founded on considerations confined to the spiritual element, for his immediate end is a broad spiritual grant. Behind this direct proposition there were undoubtedly political principles, whose nature it would be interesting to pursue at another time. On July 26, 1513 he instructed his Roman ambassador, Gerónimo de Vich, to have a hierarchy given to Tierra Firme, and to put at its top a patriarch. The king's letter follows.[10]

The King:

Reverend Gerónimo de Vich, of my Council and my ambassador in the court of Rome:

Among the many other gifts and blessings that we have received abundantly from God our Lord, foremost are the victories gained with His help against the pagan enemies of our holy Catholic faith. Many lands and provinces that were missing from her flock are thus subjected and brought back to the obedience of holy mother church. Many souls of the infidel living there are converted by baptism to their Redeemer. And in this holy enterprise our purpose remains firm, as the thing we most desire in the whole world.

Thus far it has pleased Divine Providence that, in gaining possession of the islands and lands discovered in the parts of the Indies of the Ocean Sea, we opened up a large sector of the earth. Because of its tremendous size we were not able to learn the entire extent of Tierra Firme, yet in one single section of the coast more than 1,500 leagues have been discovered. There our men found different kinds of animals

---

[10] In Pacheco y Cárdenas, *Colección de documentos inéditos*, I 39, 264-70. For the original Spanish see pp. 325-29.

that are not found in the other islands, four-footed beasts, and thus they think they are on the continent. It is peopled by a multitude of men. These seem more advanced in reason, capacity, docility, and understanding for the matters of our holy faith than any previously encountered. In this we hope that our Lord will be well served.

In our desire that these numerous souls reach salvation and draw near to the Catholic faith, we do not count the large cost and labor involved. Just now we have sent an armed force imposing both in ships and in personnel. Our intent is that, acting conjointly with the first military body that by our order and at our expense is already in the aforesaid region, they may subject those barbarous nations and bring them under the yoke and obedience of our holy mother church, and in this way remove them from the paganism whose diverse and horrible errors hold them in bondage to the enemy.

It is our purpose, then, to make them Christians. But besides the men of arms, there must be spiritual persons who will teach them the faith and inspire them by their example, and by word and deed lead them to the true knowledge of how to save their souls. Of these persons, some must be ready to go and work in their midst, while others must direct and guide from headquarters.

Our most reverend father in Christ Don Juan de Fonseca, archbishop of Rosano, our chaplain major and member of our Council, is as you know a man of clear lineage and one of the leading nobles of these kingdoms. From the time when the Indies were discovered he has by our command been fully occupied, and he is now occupied, in giving them support and direction. Because of his industry and vigilance, his diligence and care, together with his proven talent and entire lack of interest other than to serve our Lord and fulfill our commands, he has been a most important cause of many of the blessings that have come and do now come in these said Indies. He has not slackened in his care to provide for their needs, nor in the zeal that led to the conversion to our Lord of all those natives. It is his hope that, in view of the great expanse of the land, an entire network of churches with different names will be established there after it has been subdued with the help of our Lord.

You will accordingly approach our most holy father and entreat him, with the help of our certification of credentials that goes with this letter, to give his consent to the following petitions. In consideration of the facts related above and of the signal service to our Lord and the increase of our holy Catholic faith which we may expect will follow from his mediating assistance, may his holiness grant and decree that for the churches that will be erected in future in the said lands of the Indies, those usually referred to as the Province of Castilla del Oro, the said Archbishop Don Juan Rodríguez de Fonseca shall have authority as patriarch of the entire region, on equal terms with the other patriarchs in the church. If he be so appointed, then in view of his merits, doctrine, example, and fidelity, the wide experience he has had in the said Indies, and his notable desire and zeal for converting the nations there found to our holy Catholic faith, we anticipate that our Lord will be well served, our holy Catholic faith spread, and the souls of the great number of people inhabiting that land brought to accept the faith.

Ask, too, that the principal church of that patriarchate be located in the place which the said Don Juan de Fonseca will, with our license and consent, select in the said region. Up to this time, and until there is more knowledge of all the circumstances, no one could choose that location wisely. Emphasize, too, that he will select it with a care for its highest effectiveness. In that land, as has already been said, there are many different provinces. Hence there will have to be many different cathedral churches, if our Lord so wills it. The first province, called the Golden Andalusía, has already been subdued and has a pueblo of Christians and a church named Our Lady of Antigua. It is therefore above all else necessary that we have the holy father appoint and confer authority upon a bishop of the cathedral church of that name, under the said patriarch.

We have in mind the devout Father Fray Juan de Quevedo, brother of the Order of St. Francis of the Observance, who is now preacher of our royal chapel, a man who by his virtuous life and conduct, great prudence, and eminence in letters and all doctrine has ruled in various positions as provincial or guardian for many years in the Province of Andalusía. We believe that, because of his broad experience in such matters, our Lord will be well served if he is appointed to that bishopric. We write to urge that he be given this charge.[11] Much benefit will come from his great service of our Lord—and of us, understandably, if he goes there in the said armada to take over the conversion of this people.

---

[11] Such is the simple form of presentation used by Ferdinand. Quevedo came with Pedrarias as bishop of Darién. On Pedrarias see below, pp. 135, 139.

Lastly, entreat his holiness to concede to us two faculties: the first, for us and the successors in this royal crown of Castile, or for the person who on this matter speaks in our name, that now and for the future I may determine the boundaries of the diocese in the said region [Castilla del Oro] and that I may have the same right for the churches and bishopric of Our Lady of Antigua of the Province of Darién that is today called Golden Andalusía, and which I must presently set up and nurture as those that were earlier instituted and fostered.

The second ought to be the right to divide and allot the tithes of the church of Our Lady of Antigua and the others that will later be developed and instituted, and to assign the revenues of the patriarch, such as the tithes. We request this right on the ground that we are making gift and donation of them by the power conceded by the Apostolic See. Because the prelates go there to instruct and convert that barbaric race, we shall give them tithes in the name of the most serene queen my spouse and my most dear and beloved daughter, as they have been given in creating those said [earlier] churches, excepting the *tercias,* which have to be left for the royal crown of these kingdoms, and perpetually. Since we have made donation of the said tithes, it is reasonable that their division, both those that will be given to the patriarch and those that will be given to the bishops, be left to the person who names their recipient. As for the commission to see to the creation of the church of Our Lady of Darién, see that it comes directed to our most reverend father in Christ, the archbishop of Rosano, our chaplain major. And that, as you see, is the point that will give complete fulfillment to the service of our Lord, the conversion and salvation of the souls of innumerable peoples, and the increase of our holy Catholic faith.

All this is for our service. Do you give it all the care and attention that it deserves, as we expect of you. Entreat and obtain from his holiness and the most reverend cardinals that we secure their approval, so that we can go forward with our plans. And send me your reply to everything here said as quickly as you can. In that you will do me much service. From Valladolid, July 26, 1513. I the King. Authenticated by Secretary Conchillos.

A few words should be devoted to the patriarchs of the Indies and to the matter of royal power to determine or change the boundaries of the dioceses. The other question, the establishment of bishoprics in Tierra Firme and Castilla del Oro, was immediately solved.[12]

At the time of Philip II, Rome became highly interested in substituting the patriarchate for the whole Patronato Real, as will be shown in its place. But there was a continuous succession of patriarchs of the Indies from 1524 to 1852.[13] Fonseca failed to get the post, for reasons not too hard to deduce from the immaturity of the young church. In introducing the list of prelates Hernaéz has some remarks worth quoting:

> Before listing the creation of the archbishoprics and bishoprics of America, it will not be beyond our purpose to speak briefly on the origin and nature of the patriarchate of the Indies. Authors do not agree on the time when it was instituted. Some say that Pius V created it as an honorary office on the petition of Philip II. But the pope rather confirmed than created, . . . for Gil González Dávila notes that Clement VII in 1524 created the first patriarch of the Indies, Don Esteban Gabriel Merino, cardinal archbishop of Jaen.
>
> The dignity is nothing more than a title of honor, for there was no patriarchal church in the Indies, and hence there could be no ecclesiastical installation or presentation for lack of actual jurisdiction in his church. Since the patriarchs of the Indies had no patriarchal church, they were called *episcopi in partibus infidelium*. They were legally said to be, and were held to be, without jurisdiction in both *fora*. Hence in their designated territory they were referred to as *procapellan mayor del rey católico*, and in the armed forces on land or sea were called *vicario general castrense*.[14]

---

[12] Morelli, in *Fasti Novi Orbis*, p. 90, notes that in 1514 "the episcopal see of Darién, Saint Mary of Antigua, is erected," and on p. 96 that this see was translated to Panama in 1521. He cites for this Herrara, *Decades*, Dec. I, Lib. X, cap. 7, which is correct. Hernáez, *Colección*, II, 5-346, provides priceless documentation of the foundation of every diocese in all the Americas, adding much to Gams.

[13] For the list see Hernáez, *Colección*, II, 6-7. In II, 705-06 he prints from the notes of Cardinal Garampi, secretary to Benedict XIV after 1749, the provision, institution, and emolument given the first patriarch, set up in 1524. In II, 6-7, he publishes the entire list, with their dates of election and death and their places of residence.

[14] *Ibid.*, II, 6.

Opinions differ regarding the royal right to readjust or divide diocesan territory without recourse to Rome. García Gutiérrez contends that, although the king obtained the permission to change the boundaries of each diocese whose creation he procured from the Holy See, he possessed no general privilege to alter the limits, but received the concession in each case.[15]

Solórzano Pereira, a militant regalist although highly skilled at law, took the opposite view. In his study *De Indiarum jure* he wrote:

> Antonio de Herrera states firmly that the kings were given this grant by pontifical patent—see his *Historia generalis Indiarum*, Dec. VII, Lib. vi, cap. vii, p. 149—noting that the said document was given to that worthy man, Don Francisco Tello de Sandoval, when he was sent as visitor to the Province of New Spain in 1543, and that he carried the following injunction: That in the Junta of the prelates he was to present the brief that he carried, which had been obtained from his holiness by Juan de Vega, lord of Grajal, ambassador of the king at Rome. [It stated] that on all occasions when it seemed proper to the king and his Council, he might extend or diminish the limits of the bishoprics of the Indies. He was empowered to act in the manner and according to the evidence that would conduce toward the good government and administration of the bishoprics, and to erase grounds of differences between prelates. For when he petitioned his holiness to erect a diocese or to divide it, he could not send exact data on the limits that it should retain, so that his holiness could state and mark off in the bull of creation [its permanent boundaries]. For often it is imperative to make some variation and to change the boundaries for the betterment of the spiritual rule. And after he presented the brief, he was to make an address on what was currently in need of change, and thus to advise the king.[16]

Solórzano then cites a letter of Innocent IV (1243-1254) which authorized the archbishop of Reims to erect a new bishop-

---

[15] García Gutiérrez, *Apuntes*, p. 39.
[16] Joannes de Solórzano Pereira, *Disputationem de Indiarum jure, Tomus Primus sive De justa Indiarum Occidentalium inquisitione, acquisitione et retentione* (Madrid, 1653), Lib. III, cap. 5, nos. 12, 13. But see below, p. 191.

ric in whatever castle he chose, doing it on apostolic authority, but not without the assent of the king. He continues with examples of Spanish kings acting on this power, as in the formation of the episcopates of Arequipa and Guamanga that were carved out of the dismembered Cuzco. Another was Trujillo, formed of parts of the archbishoprics of Lima and of Quito. This argument, of course, proceeds on the assumed principle that the act was juridically correct if it was left unfinished, a not unusual position in seventeenth-century Spain.

From a fairly broad reading of the documents of diocesan creations, it would seem better to follow the opinion held by García Gutiérrez. The Solórzano plea rests on extremely secondary and remote evidence. There is no doubt, however, that in cases regarding conflicting episcopal rights—such as the contest between Michoacán and Mexico in 1536-1544—it was the crown that gave the decision.[17] The papacy, in granting the Patronato, had little prevision of the surrender of jurisdiction that might follow.

[17] On this case see Icazbalceta, *Zumárraga*, pp. 171-73.

CHAPTER X

A Bishop in New Spain

Now that the Patronato Real de las Indias had advanced beyond the trial stage and had become an organized living thing, with its central office in a committee of the Council of Castile (and after 1524 of the Council of the Indies) and with the overseas governors as its subordinate officers, the institution developed with the rapidity—and for a time the mercurial changes—that marked the colonization of the New World. Something of this rush has already been noticed in the first creation, the quick extinction, and the immediate new creation of the dioceses in the islands. If royal plans sometimes ran ahead of feasibility, there was no stopping the onward march, and projected administrative steps came to definite fulfillment. So too in the work of conversion. *Conquistadores* in their lucrative and cruel hunt for gold at first obstructed the noble task by their own sordidness; but when men like Garcés and Zumárraga entered the arena on the side of the natives and the missionaries swung into line, the success was striking. As one surveys the entire field he cannot but admire the buoyant enthusiasm and the imagination displayed in dealing with such *quanta* of time and space as faced the early Hispanic Americans.

A study of the growth of the system is in a sense more rewarding than an investigation of its initial movement. Here, as is always the case, the historian finds the true meaning of a great fact in its development and impact on society. He who is satisfied with causes and beginnings can make no intelligible statement on their significance. Accordingly the documentation hereafter will deal with growth and crisis, both on the front and back at headquarters. Mexico and Peru will claim most attention.

From the West Indies the Spaniards first moved southward to the mainland in the region of Panamá. There Balboa governed until displaced in 1514 by the infamous Pedrarias.[1] The latter chartered expeditions of his adventurous followers up the coasts and overland as far as Nicaragua. One ship bearing the famous Bernal Díaz del Castillo took this warrior to Cuba, in time to join in the 1517 discovery of Yucatán and its Maya culture. In the next year he accompanied Juan de Grijalva, nephew of Governor Velásquez, on the voyage of exploration from Cozumel Island as far as the future San Juan de Ulúa. It was they who first named this land New Spain.[2]

As soon as Velásquez got word of this 1517 discovery, he hurried his chaplain, Don Benito Martín, over to Spain, there to implore the young King Charles to ask Pope Leo X immediately to create a diocese for the newly found land.[3] The optimism of Velásquez (and his chicanery) and the inexperience of Charles V had a most remarkable result in the naming of a new diocese

---

[1] Morelli, in *Fasti Novi Orbis*, p. 110, has this on Pedrarias: "You will wonder what great deed Pedro Arias, or Pedrarias Ávila, had done to bring him the honorable mention in the erection of this first city and church, while nothing is said of Cortés, conqueror of Mexico, whom the pope so praised in another letter, nor of his comrades, nor of the first men to sail the Tyrrhenian Indian Sea before Pedro Arias. He did much in the province of Darién that is outside of Mexico. He suffered much, and was the cause of many injuries to others. Whether he ever saw Mexico I doubt completely. Of him the bishop of Chiapas [Las Casas] wrote: 'The so-called Pedrarias entered like a ravenous wolf. His way was like the wrath of God. He despoiled so many pueblos and homes as to burn a path from Darién to Nicaragua.' Those who wrote the record of his doings lied or exaggerated above the clouds." The myth of Pedrarias recurs twice in documents cited hereafter.

[2] See p. 138.

[3] García Gutiérrez, *Bulario*, p. 527.

and of its bishop, Fray Julián Garcés. The somewhat prolix documentation underlying his story throws much light on the way in which the Patronato evolved in this stirring moment, the initiation of the conquest of Cortés. The materials are here given in order. After the notarial certification by Pedro de la Vega in 1749, the succession of official papers is as follows:

I Introduction to the proclamation of Bishop Garcés to the people of his new diocese

II Presentation of Garcés by Charles V and mandate that he take office at once as authorized by the papal bulls

III Bull of Leo X, January 24, 1518, creating the diocese of Yucatán and Santa María de los Remedios

IV Bull of Clement VII, October 13, 1525, giving the provision of Bishop Garcés for his diocese of Tlaxcala

V Edict of Charles V, September 19, 1526, determining the limits of the diocese of Tlaxcala with reservations about future changes in the boundaries

VI Acceptance of charge by Bishop Garcés and institution of the diocese of Tlaxcala, done in Granada on December 1, 1526

The Appointment of Bishop Julián Garcés[4]

Bulls for the erection of the holy church of Tlaxcala, called Carolina, but today Puebla de los Ángeles. These furnish material for an understanding of the events then transpiring in New Spain and for the holy Caroline church in the peninsula of Yucatán.

Don Pedro de la Vega, of the Council of his majesty, his secretary and chief official of the Secretariate of the Council and of the Committee on the Indies for negotiations with New Spain, certifies that in his same Secretariate he finds the erection done in the following words:

I

Proclamation of Bishop Garcés

Fray Julián Garcés, by the grace of God and of the Apostolic See bishop of Carolina in New Spain. Salvation eternal in the Lord to all and single now and in the future.

---

[4] *Ibid.*, pp. 323-33. For the Spanish and Latin originals see pp. 329-41.

Unconquered Charles and Queen Juana, the same Charles emperor-elect, king of the Romans and of the Spains and of both Sicilies, ever burning with the fire of divine love and zeal for the house of God and intent on the propagation of the orthodox faith, have won from the pagan no few kingdoms and dominions. In the glowing light of truth they had in mind to penetrate islands and continents unknown to us, so that they might bring the dwellers and inhabitants to the true worship of God, our Redeemer, and to the holy faith. In the execution of that purpose Hernando Cortés, a mighty man, with God's assistance crossed over from the Island of Cuba with a ready and well-directed fleet, into a most ample continent which is protected by the region of San Juan de Ulúa. The same Hernando, though under attack, advanced with his army over the mountains and came into the very great Province of Mexico, Tenuxtitlán beside the lake. With enormous labor the enemy was turned back and more than once put to flight. As a result very many of the natives were converted and baptized into the faith. Several churches and monasteries were built for the population. In the city of Tlaxcala, where as yet no bishopric had been set up, our lord Pope Clement VII, with paternal affection wishing to come to the aid of that city and province, decreed the creation and erection of a cathedral church, at the instance of the most powerful King Charles and the queen, Charles being emperor-elect. At the desire of unconquered Charles the city was called Carolina. On the motion of their majesties, the king and queen, the holy father appointed us, Fray Julián Garcés, as bishop and pastor of the said city. He took care that the boundaries of the same diocese should be drawn beforehand, as is seen more fully in the letters of the same pontiff and of their Caesarean and Catholic majesties that express the concession to fix the limits of the diocese. He also granted the faculty of erecting the dignities, canonries, prebends, and other ecclesiastical benefices with or without care of souls, and the other powers committed to us in the aforementioned letters, whose tenor, word for word, follows:

II

Presentation by Charles V

Don Carlos. etc.

Inasmuch as we are in receipt of the record of the good living, merits, and example of the Reverend Father Don Fray Julián Garcés, of the Order of St. Dominic and our preacher, we present him to the bishopric of Yucatán and Holy Mary of Help,[5] in our Indies of the Ocean Sea, the first land discovered in that province to which the Christians who afterward passed on farther gave the name of New Spain. His holiness, upon our prayer and presentation, made grant and appointment to the same bishopric, with the title of Yucatán and Holy Mary of Help, because at that period there lived there the greater number of Christians, and for this he commanded the bulls to be made out. Because the place was afterward left without a population and the men had passed beyond and had established the said lands of New Spain and other provinces, his holiness at our request and that of the said bishop ordered and declared that the said bishopric and its limits should be understood as extended into the confines of New Spain, and that by us it should be marked and bounded. And upon that declaration he directed that the bull and brief be given. The tenor of those said bulls and briefs, one below the other, is as follows:

III

[Sacri apostolatus ministerio]

Bull of Leo X

Leo, bishop, servant of the servants of God. For a perpetual remembrance.

Presiding by heavenly disposition over the ministry of the sacred apostolate, though with little merit, we turn in frequent meditation toward the provinces and regions of the whole earth, and to those especially which by the mercy of the omnipotent God have begun to accept the light of Christian truth in our own day. It is our hope that the cultivation of the orthodox faith may be increased in them; the Christian religion may be propagated; that their inhabitants and dwellers, infused with the doctrine and authority of venerable prelates, may advance in the same faith; and that those same regions, notably the most important, may be ennobled by more worthy titles and greater honors. This we do most of all when the pious petitions of Christian kings ask it, and we understand in the Lord that it will work unto good.

---

[5] Note that this creation of the diocese of Yucatán and Santa María de los Remedios never took effect. The only Spaniards left there in 1517 were dead men or captives. There was no church built by this expedition, contrary to the assertion deriving from the pen of Velásquez. A population built up in Yucatán in mid-century, and it was necessary for Pius IV in 1561 to create the diocese anew. García Gutiérrez has a good note on the facts, ibid., p. 527.

It is recalled that Ferdinand, king of Aragon and Sicily, who during his later life was regent of the kingdoms of Castile and Leon, to the praise and glory of Him to whom belongs the earth and the fullness thereof and all who dwell in it, many years ago organized a strong fleet and sent it out to discover new islands in the Ocean of the Indies. Among other regions subjected to his temporal power he won one called Hispañola Isabella, a remarkable island found by his mariners, and there he brought about the creation of the cathedral churches of St. Dominic and of the Conception of the Blessed Mary. Shortly before he left this earthly life he dispatched a similar fleet carrying some two thousand men to search out other islands in the same area, and he put at its head our dear son Pedro Arias as captain. These men, after sailing many days, came to a certain region called by the natives Yucatán, so large that it is not yet known whether it is an island or a continent. They placed it under the invocation of Blessed Mary of Help, and there near the shore they built a town or settlement with a parochial church under the same name.

Now our most dear son in Christ Charles, illustrious king of Castile, Leon, and the other above-named kingdoms, and he not alone heir and successor of the same King Ferdinand but his follower in truth and courage, learned that the said land or island was traversed by his men through many leagues of latitude and longitude. They reported that it is inhabited by thousands of men, that it enjoys a salubrious climate and fertile soil, that its natives and inhabitants are capable of reason and humane behavior, readily accept our orthodox faith, and quickly embrace its customs and precepts. No small part of that land or island is subject to his rule. In it he has had several towns founded and parochial churches set up. He has hopes that much more of the land will come under his dominion, and that with the darkness of their errors dispelled the people will come to the truth of the light and will recognize Christ, the Redeemer of the whole human race. Therefore he earnestly desires that the said town or settlement, near the seashore as described, be raised to the status of a city, to be called Carolina, and its aforesaid church be made a cathedral church under the invocation of Blessed Mary of Help.

Wherefore, seeing that the said King Charles has humbly besought our favor, taking careful deliberation with our venerable brethren and on their same advice, to the praise and glory of almighty God, the honor of the most blessed and glorious Virgin Mary His Mother, and the joy of the entire celestial family, by the apostolic authority and the tenor of these presents, we erect in perpetuity and institute this town or settlement of the Island of Blessed Mary of Help, wherein now dwell a number of the faithful, and we designate it a city with the name of Carolina. Its cited parochial church is now to become a cathedral church with the same title of Blessed Mary of Help, its bishop to be entitled Carolensis. In this said erected church and its city and diocese he will convert the pagan natives to the cult of the orthodox faith. He will preach and instruct, teach and confirm the converts in the faith, pour out on them the grace of baptism, and he and other ministers will dispense the holy sacraments and other spiritual aids, both to the converts and to those others of the faithful living at the time in or near the said city and diocese. He will enlarge the buildings of the church itself and see to bringing it to the pattern of a cathedral church. In the church and city, and throughout the diocese, he will erect and institute the dignities, canonries, prebends, and other ecclesiastical benefices with or without care of souls, and confer and organize the other spiritual offices as the increase of divine worship and the salvation of the souls of his people demand. He will have the throne and the other insignia and episcopal rights, privileges, immunities, and favors which other cathedral churches and their prelates have in Spain. He will use, possess, and enjoy according to law and custom what they likewise enjoy, and this in future for perpetuity, for the city and territory called Blessed Mary of Help, the limits being drawn by King Charles for the diocese and its dwellers and inhabitants, both clergy and people. This we concede and assign, so that the same bishop of Carolina may at all times in future freely exercise there his episcopal jurisdiction, authority, and power.

Of the gold and silver and other minerals, the gems and precious stones, since we decree them free of tithe, [the king] will not pay tithes and first fruits due according to law. The other episcopal fees the bishop may demand and receive, just as the other bishops in old Spain may do in their cities and dioceses.

The right of patronage is his, and of presenting a worthy person to the said Caroline church within a year, because of the great distance of the place, whenever it becomes vacant—except for the first appointment—and under whatever pope is presently ruling. We concede and forever reserve to the said Charles and to the regnant king of Castile and Leon the presentation of the bishop and pastor of the same church.

Let no man then dare to infringe this patent of our erection, institution, concession, assignment, decree, and reservation, or in temerity dare to do the contrary. But if anyone should presume so to attempt, let him know that he will incur the indignation of almighty God and the blessed apostles Peter and Paul. Given at Rome, at St. Peter's, the year of the Incarnation of the Lord 1518, January 24, the sixth year of our pontificate.

IV

[Devotionis tuae]

Bull of Clement VII

Clement, bishop, servant of the servants of God. To the Venerable Fray Julián Garcés, bishop of Carolina, health and apostolic benediction.

Your proven integrity and the attachment which you are known to have for us and the Apostolic See eminently merit that we hold your person in high regard and reply favorably to your petitions in as far as in God we may. Your concern is for the honor and dignity of your diocese and its surrounding population, especially for the churches standing among the multitude of pagans, where the divine worship is spreading, and the unbelievers, once their blindness is removed and they are converted to the light of the orthodox faith, are imbued with the Christian dogma as the desire of the Catholic princes dictates.

Not long ago Leo X, pope of happy memory and our predecessor, heard the appeal of our most dear son in Christ Charles, illustrious king of the Romans and of the Spains and emperor-elect and king of Castile and Leon. With a well-managed fleet he had won from the pagans the Island of Yucatán on the Indian Sea. Our predecessor erected and gave permanent institution of an important town in that island into a city. He raised the parochial church, built by the Christians immediately after the foundation of the same town under the invocation of Blessed Mary of Help, to the status of a cathedral church for the one Carolinian bishop named, who in the said church and its city and diocese would preach the word of God, carry out the liturgy and other episcopal tasks, employ the throne and insignia and episcopal rights, immunities, and favors which the other cathedral churches and their prelates in the kingdoms of the Spains use, possess, and enjoy by law and custom. And he made provision for that church if vacated by your person after the first erection. He put you in charge as its bishop and pastor, according to the manner more fully laid out in the various letters of the same predecessor.

We now have a petition on your part, to the effect that the limits and confines of the diocese of Carolina are not yet set, for the reason that the Christians of Spain advanced farther under the divine help and acquired another town called Tenuxtitlán in a certain province called New Spain. The same King Charles, emperor-elect, has in mind, for the better position of the same Caroline church and the broadening of its diocesan territory and for your more commodious and becoming holding of your status according to the exigency of the pontifical dignity, to extend the limits and territory of the diocese of Carolina so that the province and town of this Tenuxtitlán itself, or the town Tenuxtitlán and its surrounding district, will come into your territory. Thus both on your part and on that of the same Charles, emperor-elect, we have humble request that we approve and confirm the aforesaid arrangement after it is drawn by the order of King Charles, and to deign opportunely to provide otherwise in the circumstances.

Therefore, completely absolving you and holding you thus absolved from whatever sentence of excommunication, suspension and interdict, and other ecclesiastical sentences, censures, and penalties, if in any way you chance in the present action to be so affected, by the tenor of these presents and yielding to your petitions, by our apostolic authority and without prejudice to anyone whatever, we as a special favor deign to establish, ordain, approve, and confirm the above assignment, even if as is said this move is taken by King Charles after the fact is accomplished as in the premises. We add to our act the strength of perpetual and inviolable firmity, and we supply any deficiencies of law or of fact if any have chanced to intervene in the transaction.

Wherefore you and your aforesaid successors will be empowered there to perform and execute the said acts and the others contained in the letters of our same predecessor and everything else that you were able to perform in the church and city of Blessed Mary in the same island. This same you may perform and execute in the said town of Tenuxtitlán and its environs and other specified territory.[6] And you and the Caroline bishops succeeding you will be known not as the diocesans of Blessed Mary but of Tenuxtitlán or its bounded territory

---

[6] This did not make Garcés the first bishop of Mexico, then called Tenuxtitlán, but of the region after it was delimited by Charles V.

as assigned. And you may and ought to act there in all things just as if, in the erections stated in this and other letters mentioned earlier, the town of Tenuxtitlán with its environs and other named territory had been assigned and applied to the said Caroline church as its diocese. And this notwithstanding any premises of apostolic constitutions and ordinations, or those usually published by provincial or synodal councils, or by previous apostolic confirmation, or by your oath to the same church, or strengthened by whatever firmity, statutes, or customs. Let no man therefore take leave to infringe or in temerity dare to act contrary to this patent of our absolution, approbation, confirmation, supplement, indult, statute, and ordination. But if anyone should presume to attempt it, let him know that he will incur the indignation of almighty God and the blessed apostles Peter and Paul. Given at Rome, at St. Peter's, the year of the Incarnation of our Lord 1525, October 13, the second year of our pontificate.

V

Delimitation of Diocese

Wherefore, employing the said bulls, brief, and declarations of his holiness as they are incorporated above verbatim, and following each one of them as best we can and in duty should, on the request and with the express consent of Bishop Don Fray Julián Garcés we assign and determine the limits of the said bishopric of Yucatán and Holy Mary of Help, as the following provinces and territories: first the entire Province of Tlaxcala; then San Juan de Ulúa from the line of the Agua Vertiente until one comes to Matlata, including the Villa Rica de Vera Cruz and the Villa of Medellín, with all the region of Tabasco and up the Rio de Grijalva as far as Chiápas. Those boundaries and limits and provinces so declared we wish and command, in as far as it is our grant and decision, to be considered, as they have been understood previously and will be in future, as the boundaries, limits, and district of the said bishop of Yucatán and Holy Mary of Help. All of this area and each part of the same shall belong to the said Reverend Father Don Fray Julián and the other bishops who will be there for the duration of our will. There he is empowered to use and exercise his office and jurisdiction as bishop, conformably to the bulls of his holiness. We retain and reserve, as we do now retain and reserve, to ourselves and our successors in the royal crown of Castile, the power and faculty to change, vary, alter, and revoke, shorten, or add to the boundaries and limits and areas as we may desire or find beneficial, in the said bishopric and its provinces, in whole or in part, and as we shall see it accords best with the service of God and our own service. And we order our governor, or judge of residence, who is now or will be in the land, that they declare the selfsame words when, by action of the said bishop or of another person whom we name in his place, markers or boundary stones are placed on the same boundaries and limits and area of the same bishopric, and are recognized as set on the said land for signs of the limits of the said bishopric. Given at Granada, September 19 of the year of the Nativity of our Savior Jesus Christ, 1526. I the King.

I, Francisco de los Covos, secretary to the Caesarean and Catholic majesties, had this written at their command.

Mercurian the chancellor. Fray G., bishop of Osma. Doctor Carvajal, undeserving bishop of the Canaries. Doctor Beltrán G., bishop of Ciudad Rodrigo.

VI

Institution of Diocese of Tlaxcala

After the above apostolic documents had been presented and accepted, we were required by our lord Charles to proceed at once to the execution of the apostolic letters. It is our task to erect and institute, in our said cathedral church of the Most Blessed Virgin of Tlaxcala, the dignities, prebends, portions, and other benefices and ecclesiastical offices, in the city and throughout the diocese. We therefore, Julián, the said bishop and the apostolic commissary, recognizing the aforesaid petition [to change the location of our see] to be consonant with justice and reason, and dutifully ready as a true son of obedience to carry out with all honor the apostolic orders given to us, accept the aforesaid commission. And by the same apostolic authority which we embrace in this first act, we declare, at the instance and command of the aforesaid Caesarean and Catholic majesty, to the honor of God and our Lord Jesus Christ and His Most Blessed Mother, in and under whose name and by the order of our most holy father the church of Tlaxcala is erected into a cathedral church, that we by these presents do erect, create, and institute in the said cathedral church the full range of dignities.[7] . . .

---

[7] The ellipsis contains the enumeration of officials. It was omitted in the notarial copy to obviate listing nonessential data.

All and each of the aforesaid, at the instance, request, and consent of the said lords, King Charles, emperor-elect, and Queen Juana his mother[8] and by the same apostolic authority by which we function in this office, and in the most perfect manner, style, and form of which we are capable and are by duty bound, we erect and constitute, create, make, dispose, and order, with all and each thing necessary and fitting for their performance, notwithstanding anything contrary and those especially that our said most holy lord wished in his apostolic letters not to withstand. And all and each of them, for each and every one now and in the future, or whatever status, grade, order, pre-eminence, or condition he may be, we notify and affirm and bring to the notice of all, and wish by these presents to be so brought to their notice. By the same apostolic authority, in virtue of holy obedience, we command to all and each of the aforementioned that all and single, just as they have been instituted by us, they must observe and make observed. And by the same authority we command and order all the dignities, canons, and integral portionists, since they are obliged respectively to celebrate [Mass] during the week, that at the time of presentation they must be in some sacred order, and at the time of institution or provision they must be priests; and a presentation done otherwise is *ipso facto* by law null, and without any deprivation, exclusion, or declaration, another may be presented and instituted who is constituted in the said orders. Moreover, by the same authority we command that, if any reason arises whence ourselves or our vicar or one in his place must [be absent] beyond the aforesaid time, they are obliged to summon the chapter and be present as capitulars just as on the ordinary days.

In faith and witness of all and each of the aforesaid we have ordered that the present letters be taken as a public instrument, and subscribed and published by a notary public. And we have enforced it with our name, and ordered and made it common knowledge by the attachment of our seal. Given and done at Granada, in our hospice, the year of the Nativity of the Lord 1526.

All in subscription and line is approved by me, the notary signed below. Julián, bishop of Carolina.

And because I, Cristóbal de Peregrino, cleric of Segovia and public notary by apostolic authority, was present at these premises, hence I

---

[8] As is well known, Charles V always included in Spanish state papers his mother's name as (invalided) queen of Castile.

sign the present document, after it was written by the hand of another, with my sign and name, together with the subscription of the Reverend Don Fray Julián, bishop of Carolina, with the said seal appended in testimony of the truth. Demanded and requested, Cristóbal de Peregrino, public notary.

Although in the earlier erections of the bishoprics of the islands and Tierra Firme they suppressed dignities and canonries until the rents became more productive, now, since the said erection was more definite and reliable, there were no suppressions until the Caesarean and Catholic majesties, the king and queen, our lords, determined to annex the dignity of the archdeacon and one canonry to the bishop of Yucatán or Carolina in New Spain, as they had always done to the first bishops. Hence we, the said bishop of Carolina, by the authority of our most holy father, as appears in the bulls of his holiness inserted in the said erection, and with the express will and mandate of their majesties and those of their Council of the Indies, assume and take to our person, and place upon our head the said dignity of archdeacon and one canonry, with its fruits and rents, for our lifetime only, with the understanding that our successor does not inherit this privilege until their majesties make provision after our life, as of the other benefices of this land and bishopric. And as this is truth, we confirm the present document in our name, and it is also confirmed by the secretary of the said Council of the Indies. Done on December 1, 1526. Julián, bishop of Carolina.

This was approved by the lords, the president, and the Council of the Indies in the name of their majesties, in the presence of me, Juan de Sámano, who was called in by the same lords. In testimony of the same I signed it with my own name. In Granada, December 1, 1526. Juan de Sámano.—This accords with the record of erection found in the cited secretariate of New Spain. Madrid, April 30, 1749. Pedro de la Vega.

Possibly the royal statement in Section V above (delimitation of the diocese) contains the most telling portion of the documentation. The words "for the duration of our will" call for no denunciation of a seemingly absolutist proclamation. They cover a situation that was most uncertain in 1526: the possibility of that population's supporting a bishop and furnishing the necessary clergy, and the likelihood of stability in the settlement made by Cortés. One is reminded of the early days of Kentucky and its first bishop of Bardstown. Charles' expression, "we retain and reserve," may appear to stretch the papal grant. Chapter 11 will give it much clarification. So too the condition "as we shall see it accords best with the service of God and our own service." One might call that a typical Habsburg principle and be very much in error. The king was the executive power in Spain from time immemorial, and his authority now covered an immense territory for which he had supreme administrative responsibility. And his constitutional position as interpreter of the grant of patronage included a legislative duty that could not be met by any *cortes,* for the origin of this power did not come from the people but from Rome.

Bishop Garcés reached Tlaxcala early in 1527. His saintly life and zealous leadership accounted for many conversions. As his residential city proved too poor to support a cathedral, the see was transferred on October 3, 1539 to Puebla,[9] where he died in 1542.

---

[9] For the translation, under viceregal approval, see García Gutiérrez, *Bulario,* p. 331. Crown approbation came from Prince Philip in 1543, on which see *ibid.,* p. 332.

CHAPTER XI

The Case of Zumárraga

In the development of the Patronato Real de las Indias there is no more rewarding study than the appointment and administration of that heroic character, Juan de Zumárraga (1468-1548), first bishop and archbishop of Mexico.[1] Here in miniature is the whole story of Spanish colonization: a very rich environment, the structure of pre-Cortesian civilization now in process of union with Hispanic society, and three pillars on which the succeeding centuries will rest—towering Cortés, the able viceroy Antonio de Mendoza, and a bishop unexcelled in the roll of the American hierarchy. Literally catapulted into history "from my corner" of a Franciscan monastery, this man measured up to the highest expectation of his people and his king.

The years 1526-1531 were crucial in New Spain. Cortés, after his overthrow of Aztec hegemony, suddenly revealed a magnificent capacity for creating a new body politic. His work was scarcely solidified when the notorious first *audiencia* arrived to take over rule and to hold his *residencia*. Disaster soon struck. The conduct of Guzmán and Delgadillo undermined the soul of the conquest, the new-won trust and affection of the Indians so thoroughly forwarded by Franciscan ability and dedi-

---

[1] For background see the biography of Icazbalceta, *Zumárraga*.

cation. At this juncture, with unexplainable prescience, Charles V looked about for a churchman to head his projected new diocese embracing the Aztecs and their westerly neighbors. His choice fell upon the comparatively unknown member of the Friars Minor whom he had met casually, but impressively, when in 1517 he made his first entrance into Spain. During Holy Week of 1527 he again visited the same friar, still guardian of Abrojo near Valladolid. His mind made up, he asked Fray Juan to take the assignment, and finding him adamant against so great an honor and public position, he gave what he called an order of obedience which to the lowly religious represented the will of God. Charles immediately sent his presentation to Rome, and quickly dispatched the bishop-elect to his post without provision or consecration. Provision was delayed for two years because of the sack of Rome, only to arrive in Spain with the name "Francisco" instead of "Juan" in the text. In 1530 Zumárraga himself, under threat of violence from the *audiencia,* wrote directly for provision.[2] Not until 1532 did the proper papers reach Spain. Meanwhile the prelate returned to his homeland for consecration, and on his journey back to Mexico he brought priceless cargo: the first American printing press, key personnel, and economic fundaments of prime utility.

For the next fourteen years he was the spearhead of social reorganization and religious development. Relying much on his friend and adviser, Fray Domingo Betanzos, O.P., he coordi-

---

[2] Herrera, *Historia general,* Dec. IV, Lib. VII, cap. 2: "Following upon these events the bishop-elect of Mexico wrote a request for his bulls. For on the one hand the two judges said that without them there was no canonical provision and that they could drive him from the land; and they threatened him at every turn. On the other hand, the information he had sent to court told all that had gone on, and it was the reason for the ample powers given the new *audiencia*—its president and judges—to hold visitation of Nuño de Guzmán, Matienzo, and Delgadillo, to make them face the charges and punish them. It all opened the eyes of the Council of the Indies, and made for better things in after times."

nated seculars and religious into a highly effective clerical force. As protector of the Indians from his first coming, he performed that intricate task with a courage that brought fine success. Five bishoprics were established before his synod of 1546. Two years later he was preconized archbishop, though death took him before installation.

Something must be said as a reasonable explanation of this unusual case. How did Zumárraga come to accept this command of the king as a duty? How could Charles send off a man to organize the clergy and people of a diocese without canonical status as a prelate? How could the bishop-elect excommunicate the members of the *audiencia* and order the clergy to support that sentence? This last act, of course, was nonsacramental, but it implied jurisdiction over the flock. Many more questions lie unanswered, unless one is aware of the special character of the Patronato Real as a constitutional entity and, moreover, as a privilege or favor at law.

To start with this last, Boniface VIII had long ago put into canon law the basic maxim on privilege: *"Odiosa restringi et favores convenit ampliari."*[3] To be more exact: "In case of doubt, rescripts which refer to disputes, or which injure the acquired rights of others, or which favor private persons against the common law, require a strict interpretation; all others are to be interpreted broadly."[4]

The Patronato was a favor beyond the law, but one that would in itself definitely become law for the people enjoying the privilege. If its amplification benefited only its administrator, the donor would certainly add restraint to its enjoyment. This grant, though it did bring much to the administrating crown, in far larger part operated to the benefit of the community, and

---

[3] See *Corpus iuris canonici* (Richter-Friedberg edition. Leipzig, 1879-1881), Reg. 15, R.J. in sexto.
[4] Quoted from John A. Abbo and Jerome D. Hannan, *The Sacred Canons* (St. Louis, 1952), I, 81, under Canon 50.

hence was to be interpreted broadly. Neglecting this distinction may attach to the crown such adjectives as highhanded, autocratic, or even antipapal.

In the nature of things the scope of royal action under the Patronato was bound to broaden. Neither Alexander VI nor Julius II gave away what they did not have as right, nor did they act in frivolity when they delegated the task of conversion to the Spanish crown. Although they assuredly had no clear notion of how far these grants would reach—nor did anyone else in that generation—they just as certainly moved to the center of the problem of religion in the Indies. The assignment was given to a capable hand, and in broad terms. These terms endowed the sovereign with a right which Zumárraga recognized when he was ordered to take the proffered office. Charles, the administrator, at once sent off his man to Mexico with the assurance—barring an act of God, which actually occurred—of certain provision from Rome. Zumárraga in Mexico, before consecration, responded to orders as the presented head of the new diocese which he was to erect. There is another element in his power that need not be discussed here, the Franciscan *Omnimoda*, also a vast privilege, wherein he might discover further authority for his bold and decisive method of dealing with the *audiencia*. At no point will he be found acting as though he had received consecration. His problem was political, not religious. He must have satisfied his commander, as he knew he satisfied his conscience.

These are but a few of the matters in which the case of Zumárraga rounded out the practices of the crown in religious affairs, and custom soon was written down as law. He had a famous nine-year suit with his fellow bishop Quiroga, and he appealed not to Rome but to Madrid for a decision, which incidentally he lost. Suits of laymen against the clergy, of prelates against religious and vice versa, came up frequently in those hectic days of Charles V's Indies, and invariably they found solution under the Patronato. The solutions became law. Few attempted further appeal to Rome, for the reason—if one can be satisfied with contemporary accounts—that Madrid was accepted as in possession of this right as an extension of the patronage. Naturally the king opposed any taking of the case above his head, and a basic *pase regio*—or royal placet—can easily be discerned in these times. The king simply had to take charge. The alternative was chaos and stoppage of operation. Even the most complicated cases were prevented by time-space elements and the slow intervention of agents from a hearing by the pope.

A "good cleric" might have wished that all such troubles as were faced by Garcés and Zumárraga could be taken to the curia. Yet Zumárraga chose to accept royal settlement. None of his later critics were more literate than this master editor of America's first publishing house; none more able in his post, indifferent to the judgments of men, scornful of a threat of removal from office.

What is remarkable here is not that the kings assumed powers beyond the letter of the original grant. In a static society that might have been wrong. In a society as dynamic as that of the early Indies it was unavoidable. The remarkable thing is that they did not resort to violence and tyranny, such as other colonial people suffered (for example, the Virginia nonconformists in the case of the Parsons' Cause for refusal of nonmembers to support the Establishment). And yet it cannot be contended that the system was religiously sound. To quote Icazbalceta:

> In virtue of the *Universalis Ecclesiae* of Julius II dated July 28, 1508, which was interpreted most broadly, and of other concessions later obtained either by custom or by fraud, the kings of Spain acquired such power in the ecclesiastical government of America that—with the exception of the purely spiritual—they exercised an authority that was quasi-pontifical.[5]

---

[5] Icazbalceta, *Zumárraga*, pp. 162-63.

In the material now to be proposed there will be found examples of each step in the process called provision as it was practiced under the Patronato. The discussions held in the Council of the Indies are particularly informative.

To follow the steps in the appointment of Zumárraga it may be useful to offer a skeleton of the main events.

1468   Juan de Zumárraga is born at Durango of Vizcaya, near Bilbao

1527   He is presented to the pope for the bishopric of Mexico by Charles V (December 12)

1527-   Delay in provision occurs at Rome until the Treaty of
1530   Barcelona (June 1529) ends estrangement between pope and king

1528   The elect is named protector of the Indians by Charles (January 10)

The elect sails from Seville for Mexico with the first *audiencia,* unprovided, unconsecrated (end of August)

The elect reaches Mexico City (December 6)

1529   His famous letter is written to the king (August 27)

1530   The elect writes for the dispatch of his bulls of provision (summer)

Clement VII signs the preconizing bulls (September 2)

1531   The elect is summoned to court for advice to the Council of the Indies and for consecration (January 25), though the latter could have been done in Mexico according to the tenor of the bulls, "one bishop and two dignitaries assisting"

1532   The corrected bull is sent to Spain with the name "Juan" (April 15)

Zumárraga leaves Mexico for Spain (April 30)

He has already been present at court (November)

1533   He is consecrated in the Convent of San Francisco, Valladolid, by the bishop of Segovia (April 27)

Charles V sends the executorial letters to the second *audiencia* (August 2)

These letters are presented to the *audiencia* (December 27)

1534 Zumárraga proclaims the erection of his diocese in Toledo (early in year)

He leaves Seville (June), reaching Mexico City in October

The documents relative to the institution of Zumárraga[6] are presented in the following order:

I Consistorial act, August 12, 1530[7]

II Papal provision for Zumárraga, September 2, 1530

III Erection of the church of Mexico, Toledo, 1534

    a. Beginning of allocution of Bishop Zumárraga

    b. Bull of Clement VII establishing the Mexican church

    c. Conclusion of the allocution

IV Erection of the archbishopric of Mexico, 1546

    a. Consultation of Council of the Indies, January 25, 1536

    b. Consultation of Council of the Indies, September 8, 1544

    c. Consistorial relation of Cardinal Álvarez de Toledo on erecting the metropolitans of Mexico, Lima, Santo Domingo, February 12, 1546

---

[6] This series of documents, with the exception of the provision, is taken from García Gutiérrez, *Bulario*, pp. 257-77. The provision is in Icazbalceta, *Zumárraga*, Appendix II, pp. 68-69. For the documents in Latin or Spanish see pp. 341-56.

[7] Actually, on September 2, 1530 Clement VII expedited six bulls for the creation of the church of Mexico. They were, in order: (1) erection of the church of Mexico; (2) provision of Zumárraga as its bishop; (3) an order to the archbishop of Seville to participate in the creation of the new diocese, which would belong to the province of this metropolitan until further action was taken; (4) notice of the above facts to the ecclesiastical chapter of Mexico;

I

Consistorial act erecting the cathedral of Mexico, August 12, 1530

Upon the exposition of the Most Reverend Cardinal de Valle the church begun and in progress in the city of Mexico in India was erected into a cathedral: and next that the bishop or others deputed may extinguish the number of canons and dignities: and, from this time, that whole region was assigned as a diocese until other churches are erected there. The church was erected under the name of the Assumption of the Blessed Virgin Mary. To it was provided the person of Fray Francisco, of the Order of Minims.—A.C.R.R., fol. 207 v. 2, 187.

II

Papal provision for Zumárraga

This particular public instrument is taken from certain apostolic letters that are verified by their lead seal upon fluted cords, and their exact tenor is as follows:

Clement, bishop, servant of the servants of God. To our dear son Francisco de Zumárraga, elect of Mexico, health and apostolic benediction.

Our apostolic office, laid on us by heaven though with little merit in ourselves, bids us direct the regimen of all the churches. In fulfilling that task of the divine commission we must act with both love and caution, so that when the question of appointment arises, we study to place in the pastoral charge such shepherds as will know how to embrace the flock of the Lord confided to their care, to instruct them by the word of truth and much more by the example of holy living, and with confidence in God give them sound direction and effective government and maintain them in health and peace.

The church of Mexico, previously parochial, we have this day raised and instituted as a cathedral church. And we have reserved and conceded to Charles, our most dear son in Christ, ever august emperor of the Romans and their king, and to the regnant king and queen of

---

(5) notice of the same to the city of Mexico; (6) notice of the same to the clergy of Mexico. On September 3, 1530 a special bull was sent permitting his consecration in Mexico, for it provided that "one bishop and two dignitaries" be sufficient for the sacrament (Icazbalceta, *Zumárraga*, p. 96, note 3). Icazbalceta prints this bull in the appendix to *ibid.*, Doc. num. 15, following the text of the above bulls. To avoid prolixity these bulls are omitted here except for (1) and (2).

Castile and Leon, with the advice and assent of our brethren, by our other letters as is seen contained more fully in them, the patronage and the right of presenting a fit person for the said erected church, both on the first occasion and as often as it is vacant after the first erection.

Now, looking with paternal care and solicitude toward the rapid and felicitous provision for the Mexican church, lest it be long exposed to difficulties, we have held thorough discussion with the same brethren on the point of presenting to it a useful and productive person. At last we directed the eye of our mind upon you, professed of the Order of Friars Minor, a man of probity and of legitimate age, of whose religion, zeal, knowledge of letters, integrity of life, soundness of moral judgments, wisdom in spiritual matters and skill in temporal affairs, and gifts of many virtues trustworthy evidence is apparent. After considering all these facts we gave due thought and reflection to your person, whose merits command our acceptance and that of our brethren and of the Mexican church. On their same advice and with the consent of the said Emperor Charles, we provided for you as bishop and pastor and put you in charge of the management, rule, and direction of the same church of Mexico. We committed to you fully the spiritualities and temporalities of that church, trusting in Him who gives all gifts and bestows all rewards that under God your actions will bring to the said Mexican church, in your happy rule and with the aid of divine grace, a useful governance, benevolent direction, and encouraging increase in the same spiritual and temporal interests. Take, then, this divine burden laid on your shoulders with a ready spirit. Strive to carry on the aforesaid office and administration with such devotion, confidence, and tact that the same Mexican church will, under a provident and fruitful stewardship, rejoice that it is in your hands and that you will deserve to obtain, beside the reward of eternal bliss, the blessing of ourselves and the Apostolic See and endless graces therefrom. Done at Rome, at St. Peter's, the year of our Lord 1530, September 2, the seventh year of our pontificate. D. de Viterbo — A. de Santa Cruz — Jo. della Chiesa — P. Lambert — Jo. Molluer — N. de Ariza — Fr. Branconi Spalluzeli — A. de Villareal.

And I, Diego de Arana, notary public by apostolic authority in the diocese of Córdova, took this present copy with my own hand from the said original apostolic documents, in the town of Madrid, diocese of Toledo, the year of the birth of our Lord 1533, May 29, the tenth year of the pontificate of the same lord our pope, in the sixth indiction. And I compared it with the original in the presence of the same Reverend Fathers Fray Pedro de Nieva, Fray González de Medina, of the Friars Minor, the layman Martín de Laris, of the diocese of Calahorra, both called and summoned for this. I therefore put it into official form, and signed it with my usual sign, and strengthened it with my name. In faith to all and each, called and summoned. Diego de Arana, notary apostolic.

III

Erection of the church of Mexico which embraces all others of the same province

Allocution of Bishop Zumárraga

Juan de Zumárraga, bishop by the mandate of God and the Apostolic See and servant of the church of Mexico under the eternal militant gospel of the divine Christ: grace and peace from God the Father and His consubstantial only-begotten Son, the author of peace, who by the pouring out of the blood of His divine body brought this to us, wiping out all sin. For the handwriting against us meant our doom, but He took it from us, affixing it to the cross and bringing peace by the blood of His holy cross to all on earth and in heaven.[8] . . .

And to give effect to the action they brought me half-buried from the corner of my Franciscan institute, useless that I am and altogether unequal to the execution of so great a charge. For among them there were not lacking many who in my judgment could well have filled the post with their most holy and dedicated talents. They named and chose me as the first bishop of Mexico, and our most holy lord, Pope Clement, the seventh of that name, with the becoming condescension of paternal affection, sent his apostolic letters through the royal hands and directed them to me with regardful care. These letters came written on vellum in the Roman style, with the apostolic lead in threads of red and saffron silk pendant, complete, entire, not modified or written over but void of all tampering and suspect dealing. They were presented to us by him who acted as the king's agent before a great crowd in the principal holy place of the church and during the invocation of the blessing of

---

[8] Here seventy-five lines of the allocution have been omitted by the author. These lines include eulogies of the rulers and the early missionaries in the Indies. They explain the royal decree ordering the institution of the cathedral with all its officials and dignitaries. While the language is ornate and majestic, it is more abundant than pertinent to the present purpose and its ideas are repeated in the other documents here presented.

the Holy Spirit. We received them with due reverence and submission. And we now read them word for word, as follows:

[Sacri apostolatus ministerio]

Clement, bishop, servant of the servants of God. For a perpetual remembrance.

Presiding by heavenly disposition over the ministry of the holy apostolate, though surely with less than sufficient merit, we turn in frequent meditation toward the provinces of the whole world and especially to those which by the mercy of the omnipotent God have in our very time begun to accept the light of Christian truth. Our desire is that in them the cultivation of the orthodox faith be increased, the Christian religion be spread, the citizens and inhabitants, replenished by the instruction and rule of their venerable shepherds, advance in that same faith, and their homelands, particularly the more notable, be honored and decorated with greater distinctions. This is most welcome when the trusting appeals of Catholic kings and his Caesarean majesty call upon us, and when we realize that in our Lord such action will redound to good.

The town of Mexico lies in the Indies of the so-called Tyrrhenian Sea. Some time back, under the auspices of the well-remembered Ferdinand, king of Aragon, and Isabella, queen of the kingdoms of Castile and Leon, through the agency of our beloved son, the noble Don Pedro de Arias, soldier of Segovia and captain general of their military forces destined for the same Indies, these newly discovered islands were captured from the power of the infidel there resident and brought under the sway and temporal dominion of those kings and their successor kings of the same kingdoms. This Mexico is now in the obedience and domain of our dear son in Christ, Charles, ever august emperor of the Romans, the heir and successor of the said kings and their emulator in his will to exalt the orthodox faith everywhere in the same kingdoms. The said captain and governor has held them continuously since their recovery. The region is a most noble land, broad and extensive, sharply differing from the territory surrounding it. Within it are more than twenty thousand householders and residents, of whom many are of the faith. Others, both new converts and barbarians, have come there from various places and there make their homes. Among other buildings they have many churches, monasteries, and pious places, constructed by the zeal of their royal majesties and the said captain.

They have one parochial church dedicated to the Blessed Virgin Mary, with useful structures adjacent. Thither all these faithful come, as to their own parish church, for Masses and the hearing of the Divine Office and the reception of the sacraments of the church. The said Emperor Charles earnestly wishes that the same parish church be erected and instituted into a cathedral and its town given city status.

We have taken full deliberation on this matter with our venerable brethren, the cardinals of the holy Roman church. Wherefore, upon the humble petition made to us by the same Charles, to the praise and glory of the omnipotent God and the same heavenly Blessed Mary and the exaltation of the same faith, by the apostolic authority and the tenor of these presents, we yield to the prayer of Emperor Charles. And with the joint counsel and assent of our said brethren, we erect this town of Mexico and its parochial church of the Blessed Mary into the cathedral city of Mexico, to be invoked under the same name of the Blessed Mary, for one bishop of Mexico who will in that city and diocese preach the word of God and convert the infidel to the same faith. He will instruct, teach, and confirm in the same faith those thus converted and others of the faithful, administer the sacraments to them and have them administered, and the said parish church and its appendages he shall remake into a cathedral. He is to erect and institute, in the aforesaid city and diocese respectively, the collegiate and parish and other churches, monasteries, chapels, hospitals, oratories, and other holy places, and in these the respective dignities, in the number assigned to him and with the endowments and proper appurtenances as specified, for the greater, principal, conventual, and other dignities, personnel, administrations, and offices even with the cure of souls, and those elective; likewise the canonries, prebends, integral and partial portions, chaplaincies, vicarages, other ecclesiastical benefices with or without care and chapters, also those capitular abbatial and others conventual. And he is to erect other livings and institute them respectively, and the other temporal, spiritual, jurisdictional, and pontifical offices and all and each of the other posts that other bishops of the same kingdoms are entitled and accustomed to employ and use as they see it expedient for the exaltation of the holy faith and the saving of the souls of the faithful. And he may freely use, possess, and enjoy all and each of the other privileges, prerogatives, pre-eminences, and graces which the other mentioned bishops do by law and custom employ, retain, and exercise.

In the same Mexican church we erect and institute the chapter of canons, and the persons, the episcopal and capitular table, the seal, insignia, jurisdictions, privileges, and episcopal and capitular preeminences. And the citizens and householders we honor with the name of city. And we grant to the same erected church the erected city for its own city, and for its diocesan territory the lands, islands, country places, and towns which the said Emperor Charles or his Council, called of the Indies, shall order legalized and assigned, after they specify and ordain the necessary boundaries and limits. And we appoint for its clergy and people the citizens and householders as said. For its endowment and the more decent sustenance of the pontifical dignity and its extant bishop we assign the tithes, first fruits, and other rights episcopal and spiritual, and the temporal rights to the goods, properties, and revenues, which Emperor Charles or his Council shall designate and ordain. And so the bishop of Mexico, by our appropriation and application, may in his said city and diocese exercise the episcopal jurisdiction, authority, and power, and freely enjoy the tithes, first fruits, and such rights. Moreover we affirm the right of patronage, so that [the king] may himself or through another or other procurators, deputed for the case even before vacancies, present fit persons within a year, because of the distance of the region, both this first time and as often as the places are vacant, for the Mexican church, to us and to whatever pontiff is ruling at the time, so that through us or them respectively they may become bishop and pastor of the same church. And we, by the counsel and assent of the same [brethren] reserve, concede, and assign to the aforesaid Emperor Charles, by reason of [the right of] the same kings of Castile and Leon, and to the extant king or queen of the same, all and each of the dignities, persons, administrations and offices, canonries, prebends, portions, chaplaincies, vicarages, monasteries, priories, and all other like benefices for the extant bishop of Mexico and his vicar, notwithstanding apostolic ordinations and constitutions or anything else to the contrary. Let no man, then, take leave to infringe this patent of our erection, institution, decoration, application, appropriation, reservation, concession, and assignment, nor in temerity attempt to oppose it. But if any should so attempt, let him know that he will incur the indignation of the omnipotent God and the blessed apostles Peter and Paul. Given at Rome, at St. Peter's, the year of the Incarnation of the Lord 1530, September 2, the seventh year of our pontificate.

Conclusion of allocution

After the presentation of these apostolic letters and their reception by us, as premised, we were with proper urging required on the part of the most serene Lady Juana, and the ever-august Charles her son, monarchs of Spain, to proceed to the fulfillment of the apostolic letters and their contents, so that we might erect and institute, in our aforesaid cathedral church, dedicated to the honor of the most glorious Assumption of the Virgin Mary and built in the said New Spain, the dignities, canonries, prebends, portions, and other benefices and all other ecclesiastical offices, as we deemed it most expedient for the city and the entire diocese. We, therefore, the said Juan de Zumárraga, bishop and commissary apostolic, understanding that the petition and requisition mentioned are right and consonant with reason and wishing as a true and obedient son to carry out reverently the orders directed to us, as we are bound to do, have beforehand accepted the commission. And by the same apostolic authority by which we act in this office, at the instance and request of the said majesty, we do by the tenor of these presents erect, create, and institute the aforesaid cathedral church of the city of Mexico in the said New Spain, to the honor of God and our Lord Jesus Christ and the most Blessed Virgin His Mother, with whom and under whose title the cathedral church is erected, through the same our most holy Lord.[9] . . .

XXIV. We desire, moreover, and by the agreement and good pleasure of his most serene majesty we establish, decree, and order that the fruits, revenues, and income of all the tithes of the cathedral as of the other churches of the said city and diocese be divided into four equal parts. One part we shall have for ourselves and our successor bishops in the future for all time, to sustain the expense of the pontifical office, so that we may preserve our estate with decent regard for the needs of the pontifical charge without any diminution of our special provision. The dean and chapter and the remaining ministers of the church, whom we have already assigned, will have another fourth, to be divided among them as previously arranged. As to the remainder, though by approved apostolic norms and the usage of long years, practice, and custom, the same Catholic majesty is accustomed to receive and possess the third part (in Spanish, *tercias*) integrally, still he

---

[9] Thirty-six chapters establishing personnel and duties are here omitted. Chapters 24 and 38 are included because of their unique significance.

wishes to extend to us the hand of liberality as he has extended it to others and for the dignities already named, and so he further makes us and our said bishop successors and the chapter his debtors. Whereby, refreshed by his gift, we are bound to pray for him and the successors of his same royal majesty, since he gives us freedom and exemption in this fourth part, for ourselves and our said church. The two remaining fourths, then, we decree shall be divided into nine shares, of which two will belong to the same most serene majesty, in token of his superiority and his right of patronage and by reason of his having acquired the said land. This we apply, to be taken and possessed, for all future time. . . .

XXXVIII. And because newly emergent institutions need new support, therefore in virtue of the aforesaid letters we reserve to ourselves and our successors the most ample power of amending, enlarging, and in what is necessary instituting and ordaining in future, as we may with the consent and at the request and instancy of his royal majesty, in the following matters: both on the question of the perpetual or temporary taxation of our endowment, on the limits of our bishopric, and on all its benefices; and on the retention of the tithes or their division according to the tenor of the bull of Alexander [VI], through which there was made to the same kings of Spain the donation of the tithes (though at present they are through the same royal majesty donated to us for our sustenance, although donated under the specified qualifications). All of which and single, at the instance and request of the said my lords the queen and king, and by the same apostolic authority upon which we on our part do act, we erect, institute, create, make, dispose, and ordain, with all and each element necessary and opportune. And this notwithstanding anything whatever to the contrary and those facts particularly that our aforesaid most holy lord [pope] in his pre-inserted apostolic letters wishes not to withstand. And all and each of these points, for all and each of those present and future of whatever state, grade, order, pre-eminence or condition they may be, we intimate, announce, bring to the notice of all, and wish to be so brought. And we command by these presents, by the aforesaid authority and in virtue of holy obedience, to all and each of the above-mentioned, that they observe and cause to be observed all and each as they are by us instituted. In virtue of these, all and each, for a testimony of the premises, we have seen to it that the present letters become herewith a public instrument, put down in writing by a public notary and published; and we have made them now common knowledge by the appending of our seal. Done at Toledo, the year of the Incarnation of our Lord 1534.[10]

IV

Erection of the archbishopric of Mexico

Consultation of the Council of the Indies, 1536

Résumé of a consultation of the Council of the Indies for Charles V. They propose favorable response to appeals for creating archbishoprics in Mexico and Santo Domingo. Madrid, 26-I-1536.

Also, now that the islands and provinces of Tierra Firme are populated, a matter of congratulation for your majesty, there are in those lands sixteen prelates provided by the presentation of your majesty; and yet among the many other provinces, though they have governors, there were and are no prelates appointed, as is true of Nueva Galicia, Veragua, Paria, Nueva Toledo, and Río de la Plata. [At the margin: Consult the *cabildo* of Seville (cross out "Toledo") so that it can send its opinion.]

Previous appeals in this matter have had to come to the archbishop of Seville as to their metropolitan, nor has one been named in all the said islands and Tierra Firme. From this follow serious inconveniences, for some of the bishoprics lie two thousand leagues beyond, the least being one thousand; and the spiritual government of these dioceses, with their metropolitan so far away, cannot be what it ought to be nor what it could be. The Council, discussing this subject, thinks that it is a just and necessary consideration, and that, as there are such large dioceses in those lands and they are so remote and so distant from each other, we should obtain from our most holy father, at the supplication of your majesty, that he create two metropolitans for all the Indies. One should be in the city of Mexico in New Spain, and the other in the city of Santo Domingo in the Island of Hispañola, raising the bishops there to archbishops, and they should have for suffragans such bishops as your majesty will declare.

And the bull for that provision must come with a derogation of any other concession made to the archbishops of Seville, to end the

---

[10] This date of 1534 conflicts with the statement of Icazbalceta that this function took place on December 28, 1533. He adds that immediately after this taking of possession Zumárraga addressed a moving letter to the mendicant orders of Spain begging them to cross over with him to New Spain and take part in the harvest of souls.

headship that they have in the matter. The need for what is asked is very evident, and this change will remedy all evils and mistakes that have arisen, and the daily appeals awaited by the archbishop of Seville. As this touches very closely the discharge of the royal conscience, we beg your majesty to order that it be done soon. [At the margin: Write to the *conde*.]

Moreover, because many other letters are being sent to the ambassador of your majesty resident in Rome, touching the service of God and the welfare of those regions, we ask your majesty to order him to give careful and immediate attention to the settling of this matter, and that he write to this Council what he has done on the subject, sending us the bulls or briefs that will expedite the arrangement.

May our Lord increase the life and imperial estate of your majesty with more *reinos* and *señorios*. From Madrid, January 25, 1536. Signed: Cardinal García de Loaisa, bishop of Siguenza; Doctor Diego Beltrán; Doctor Juan Bernal Díaz de Lugo; Licentiate Gutierre Velázquez de Lugo. [Outside: For reply.]

Consultation of the Council of the Indies, 1544

Résumé of a consultation of the Council of the Indies for Charles V. A memorandum of the petition from the procurators of the city of Mexico proposes that they have an archbishop in Mexico, and asks that their appeal meet favorable action. Valladolid, 8-IX-1544.

Among other matters in which the city of Mexico has appealed to your majesty by a petition on important points that have been seen in this Council, there is one that relates that the city grows each day more populous and expands; and it is, and they hope it will always be, the capital of all New Spain, for the city is so distinguished and is in such a fine territory. In that province there are many bishops, and to keep pace with the improvement of the land there is need to erect more cathedral churches. The people of that region are increasing in wealth. Their prelates find many negotiations held up, and appeals therefrom may follow between them and the officials in Seville where resides the archiepiscopal *audiencia* and, up to now, the metropolitan. And indeed, it becomes a grave situation if any person be under penalty from an ecclesiastical judge in the said New Spain, or in duress or excommunication or other kind of hardship, and he has to travel four thousand leagues back and forth to find a remedy, meantime suffering many vexations. They have implored of your majesty that he erect the cathedral church of Mexico into an archiepiscopal and metropolitan church for the other churches, and that forthwith and soon they have it in New Spain.

We have discussed this in the Council with the most reverend cardinal of Seville, president of the Council and, as we have noted, metropolitan of those territories, and with the bishop of Cuenca, president of the chancellery of this town. To the most reverend cardinal and those of the Council it appears that there is justice in the reasons given by the city of Mexico for its petition, as it is not right for that new church in the new world to lack the order which the universal church has given to all Christianity for its better spiritual government, though the bishop of Cuenca thinks that for the present we can defer this provision. May your majesty order in this affair how he will be served. Signed: Cardinal García de Loaiza [sic], archbishop of Seville, Doctor Juan Bernal Díaz de Lugo, Licentiate Gutierre Velázquez de Lugo, Licentiate Gregorio López.

Consistorial report

Consistorial report of Cardinal Juan Álvarez de Toledo, upon the erection of the metropolitans of Mexico, Lima, and Santo Domingo. Rome, St. Peter's, 12-II-1546. [At the margin: A.M.: Of Mexico, Santo Domingo in the Island of Hispañola, the City of the Kings, cathedral churches. February 12, 1546.]

Your most blessed paternity. On other occasions, for the praise and glory of almighty God and the propagation and increase of the Christian republic, at the petition of the unconquered kings of the Spains, of Ferdinand and Isabella of glorious memory, and then afterwards of Charles V, ever-august emperor of the Romans and their grandson, your holiness has erected, instituted, and re-erected very many cathedral churches in their kingdoms, islands, lands, and dominions situated in the great western Ocean Sea. And their bishops and dioceses, as seemed at the time most expedient, you subjected and attached to the metropolitan church of Seville and its extant archbishop, so that they became its suffragans and recognized and followed it as their mother church.

But in the passing of time experience has taught that the peoples of the aforesaid islands and territories, because of the extent of lands and seas and the numberless thousands of leagues between them, found themselves unable to cross over and obtain recourse in prosecuting their appeals and in carrying on negotiations with the said city of

Seville without serious danger and even risk of life. If, however, your holiness would erect and elevate some cathedral churches of those parts into metropolitans, and their bishops to archbishops, the rest of the churches and their bishops with their dioceses could depend upon and follow them.

On this matter his Caesarean and Catholic majesty, within whose right of patronage are included the kingdoms, lands, islands, and dominions aforesaid, desires on his part to consult the advantage of his subjects. With the simultaneous express consent of the devoted servant of your holiness, García de Loaysa, titular of Santa Susanna, cardinal priest and archbishop of Seville, who comes forward as the legal spokesman for himself and his successors, his majesty makes humble supplication to your holiness that you deign to erect and institute cathedral metropolitan churches, three in number, and to raise their bishops to archbishops with the archiepiscopal dignity, jurisdiction, and superiority, and that you dispatch the pallium, the cross, and other metropolitan insignia, without enacting anew the provisions or requirements for their persons or churches. The three are these: the cathedral church of Mexico in New Spain, the cathedral of Santo Domingo in the Island of Hispañola, and the cathedral of the City of the Kings in the Province of Peru: Juan de Zumárraga in Mexico, Alfonso de Fuentemayor in Santo Domingo, and Gerónimo de Loaysa in the City of the Kings. And it should be declared that the future metropolitan of Mexico has as suffragan cathedrals that of Antequera, of Michoacán, of Tlaxcala, of Guatemala, and Ciudad Real de las Llanos de Chiapa; and cathedral churches of Mexico are to be instituted in future with the boundaries and limits if, as, and when it shall seem most expedient to his Caesarean majesty and his successors.[11]

And for the churches in the premises erected into metropolitans, and all the others given and assigned as their suffragans, may your holiness deign to order them forever severed and dismembered from the province of the metropolitan church of Seville; and the prelates of the same thus dismembered churches, together with the clergy and people of their cities and dioceses, to be altogether removed and totally free from the dominion, superiority, and visitation of the same devoted

---

[11] The new extension of the Patronato grant guaranteed papal institution of whatever new diocese the king found necessary for Mexico. It did not give general power to the king to reallocate ecclesiastical boundaries.

servant of your holiness, García, cardinal and now archbishop of Seville. In this your holiness will perform an act first of all pleasing to God, and worthy of your clemency and doubtless highly necessary for the Christian republic. To be stated with the proper customary clauses employed in similar business. (A.M.) Friday, February 12, Rome, at St. Peter's, 1546. The relator, Carl Burgen.

On that same February 12, 1546 Paul III dispatched the bull *Super universas orbis ecclesias* to the crown and to the pertinent ordinaries and metropolitans. As the tenor of that document coincides completely with the recommendations in the above three consultations of the Council of the Indies, its text is not printed here. It can be found in García Gutiérrez immediately after the foregoing materials.[12] The three metropolitans of Mexico, Santo Domingo, and Lima are erected and made independent of Seville, henceforth to depend directly on the Holy See and to enjoy the full prerogatives of the archiepiscopal rule. For one reason it might have been useful to supply the full text of the bull, because a clause is inserted that could have special significance. The clause is this: "in the kingdoms, islands, lands, and dominions situated in the great sea of the Western Ocean and subject to our dear son in Christ Charles, ever-august emperor of the Romans who is also king of the kingdoms of Castile and Leon, which lands are recognized as under the right of patronage of the aforesaid Charles, emperor and king, because of the apostolic privilege, against which there has to this day been no derogation."[13] One might suspect because of the language used that there was thought in the mind of the curia of limiting the privilege. No such plan is divulged in the correspondence available, though the succeeding chapters will show that the grounds for later complaint arose during the reign of Charles.

---

[12] The bull is in García Gutiérrez, *Bulario*, pp. 277-78.

[13] The particular clause in this second paragraph of the bull is "cui non est hactenus in aliquo derogatum."

In the foregoing materials the reader has found the Patronato Real de las Indias operating in the pattern that it would
hold down to the latter Bourbons. Though Philip II in 1568-
1570 weathered a great storm and therefore is sometimes said
to have given the final form to the system, that judgment might
well be challenged in view of the foregoing documents. When
Charles V handed over the crown to his son every facet of the
Patronato had been cut, so far as the positive elements of the
institution are concerned. The following pages will examine
some few of its negative characteristics and some of the tensions
that came near to causing an explosion from within.

CHAPTER XII

The *Pase Regio*

W hen the three archbishoprics of Mexico, Lima, and Santo Domingo were instituted in 1546, with concomitant separation of the American hierarchy from the parent metropolitan of Seville, the church in the Indies stood established in the fullest estate of royal patronage. The model fashioned in the process remained fixed for the next three centuries. There would be no deviation from the manner of appointing the ecclesiastical staff, guiding and reviewing their action, redefining the boundaries of each diocese as the times demanded,[1] providing man power and material support for their work, and adapting them to whatever fresh policy the crown might devise. The king-patron managed his huge "benefice" with such thorough attention and fruitful development that the words of Ribadeneyra— "the most precious pearl in the royal diadem"—might well have been accepted at face value. For so the king looked upon his unique and prosperous institution.

One further gain would round out the entire enterprise. In the homeland the *reino* of Granada, first area under a royal pa-

---

[1] The bulls of establishment for each subsequent diocese prove that the king got papal permission to redefine boundaries whenever a new instituting took place. These bulls are reproduced in Hernáez, *Colección*, II. García Gutiérrez, *Bulario*, adds to the materials given in Hernáez several pertinent documents with valuable editorial comment.

tronage, had on all counts brought benefit to people and regime. Ever after that fundamental year of 1486 the crown persevered in the hope of incorporating the whole of peninsular Spain within its patronal control. Rome on the other hand persistently held back, for reasons both spiritual and temporal, until at last in the critical Bourbon period Benedict XIV, remarkable canonist and scholarly pope, made the grant in 1753. This concession forms the matter of Chapter 14.

It is now in place to examine several points that stand out sharply in the practice of the system. For it was, with all its grandeur, a very human institution. And no matter how clear and permanent its title, how broad its direct achievement and its indirect contribution to the life of the empire, there were what moderns call certain "built-in" tensions ingrained in the very nature and character of the Patronato Real de las Indias. Foremost among these, and active from beginning to end, was the *pase regio*.

This simple term, which reminds one of the sentry's "pass," indicates more exactly the royal consent, permit, or license for appointees and official documents to pass to and from the papacy to kingly subjects in the patronage. Just as no person might pass over the Atlantic without crown permission, so no action that altered the appointive and directive power of the patron was admitted by the Spanish court. As a right the *pase* never obtained the explicit approval of Rome. Yet throughout the empire it drove its roots so deeply as to become embedded in the general law.[2]

An early but significant instance of the royal assumption of this prerogative arose in New Spain when in the 1530's Clement VII conferred upon Cortés the patronage for his district of

---

[2] One should not confuse the empirical evidence of this "built-in" situation with the philosophical theory underlying the dicta of regalism, a fault found constantly in the writing of Ribadeneyra on the Patronato.

Oaxaca. The event occasioned this later succinct comment by
Morelli (Muriel) in his *Fasti Novi Orbis:*

No issue in the regalia of the Indies is so sacred as that this right
[of patronage] be held secure *in solidum* for the king. And when about
1533 the pope conceded to Hernando Cortés the right of patronage over
the churches of his marquisate of the Valley, the Catholic king forbade
its use. He ordered the apostolic letters remitted to the Council of the
Indies, as a grant obtained on false premises, and not one that could be
conceded by the sovereign pontiff if he were informed by the petitioner
of the prejudice thus brought upon the royal prerogative.[3]

At law the point would seem well argued by Charles V.
Although in the canon law of rescripts the particular, if granted
after the general, is considered as an exception to the latter in
what is particular,[4] there is here the overriding view that the
crown by formal and perpetual grant held the entire overseas
patronage, within which any private patronage would not only
be deleterious at this early date but would also expect the con-
currence of the patron in view of the totality of his obligations.
Not until 1591 did the crown admit the establishment of private
patronage,[5] and then only after the public law had been so well
grounded that a private grant would not detract from the general welfare of the institution. By that time no challenge could
upset the royal jurisdiction, and the claim of the Patronato had
become axiomatic.

This *pase regio* might be seen as implicit in the great grant
of the Patronato de las Indias. Under that grant the papacy
transferred to the king its authority to control the allocation of

---

[3] Morelli, *Fasti Novi Orbis*, p. 86, discussing the 1508 grant of Julius II. The order
was conveyed to Cortés by the *audiencia* of New Spain on March 20, 1532,
for which see Pacheco y Cárdenas, *Colección de documentos inéditos*, I 13,
237-50.

[4] See in *Codex iuris canonici*, Canon 48 with its historical citations.

[5] The law approving this new practice is found in *Recopilación de leyes de los
reinos de las Indias* (Madrid, 1681), Lib. I, tit. 6, ley 43.

tithes and to set up the hierarchy, down to the lowest ranks of "dignities." That charge gave grave responsibilities to the royal patron: to observe and direct the clergy, to supervise their policies and work, to see in short that the ecclesiastical life was sound and that the church could broaden to fit the needs of the flock. This right was in a way purely religious. But from another standpoint it contained political connotations of the first rank. A king to whom all his people looked for their religious welfare, and who channeled so many means to that end, had a grip on his subjects' thoughts, affections, and respect beyond anything imaginable today. Should either a subject or the Roman curia attempt to bypass him, as happened on occasion, the act was in his eyes constitutionally unintelligible and politically of such weighty significance that it seemed to shake the pillars of state. The curia and papal ambassadors in Madrid, with only their outsiders' knowledge, usually had no insight into the shock that such a view might give to the monarchy. It is to the credit of Pius V and Benedict XIV, as will be seen, that they truly understood this fact. They were, on their part, faced with the tremendous *fait accompli* that originated in the first days of European expansion, and they both withdrew from the effort to reverse it.

The king ruled in the Patronato according to the canon law of the church as modified by his charter as patron and by his patronal legislation. Being supreme patron, he took cognizance of any cause affecting the "benefice" over which his patronage, as El Sabio said,[6] had the right to "watch." In administration he placed in charge whatever person he chose over a work that he as patron had inaugurated, and according to the conditions which he set down for its proper functioning. He met all human needs of his incumbents as well as he could, protected them against all attack, expected of them regard for his patronal office and its responsibilities.

----

[6] See Chapter 2, p. 22.

That subjects could challenge his power as patron would have been unthinkable. To sue against his beneficial regulations was allowed, but he was the final judge. Severe chastisement awaited anyone who rashly challenged royal rights.[7] The holy father, indeed, always retained the power to quash the Patronato, and the lesser power to advise the patron on his stewardship; but he would not interfere with the normal rule of the patron any more than a reasonable administrator would undercut his subordinate and still leave him in office.

This situation certainly justified in the king's mind a practice such as the *pase regio*. The inherent difficulty was that the patronage involved a grant too dynamic to be contained within older concepts of small geographical areas and of customary delegated jurisdictions. This was something larger than was ever before set in motion, and quite likely the popes had no realization of the potential ramifications of the grant which they made in a moment of exuberant generosity.

Julius II in 1508 had written his *Universalis ecclesiae regimini* for the known Caribbean islands. His words, however, echoed the ambitious thought of Ferdinand, and they were addressed beyond the three sees of Hyaguata, Magua, and Bayuna, to *"alias quascumque Metropolitanas . . . in dictis Insulis et locis,"* which he had previously described in the bull as "the aforesaid islands or regions or in those to be acquired." Over all this land in the Ocean Sea he conceded the right of patronage to the kings of Castile and Leon and to their successors for all time. His guiding document had been the Bull of Granada, a fulsome grant yet hedged round with that fine phrase, *"nullum aliud ius."* Julius employed no such limiting word,

---

[7] Mecham, *Church and State*, p. 26, cites the case of a lawyer of Charcas arguing in a mid-seventeenth-century court that the crown had no right to take cognizance of a purely ecclesiastical judicial proceeding. For this he was heavily fined and warned against any public repetition of his statement.

nor indeed would it have been of much effect if he had done so, in view of his transference of an administrative control embodying the entire material support and appointment of personnel. Moreover, this was not the ancient and tight little *reino* of Granada, but two vast and previously unknown continents. Under the impact of Spanish penetration that grant was destined to include an indefinite expansion. The task assigned to the kings was hemispheric in scope: the conversion of all the natives and the preservation of faith in the Hispanic immigrants. This immense labor supposed on the part of the crown an entire dedication, with its crucial charge the maintenance of a missionary force in good condition for the campaign. This they accepted frankly as a delegation of full authority and they proceeded to act on it.

Historians not infrequently have burdened the kings-patron with epithets of a pejorative character for the firm stand taken in defense of this authority. It seems unfair to treat their forthright conduct with so little understanding. Their royal duties were inextricably tied in with the royal interests: to avoid unnecessary diminution of revenues, to uphold the morale and efficiency of the team at work in the field, to cement the segments of empire, to preserve reverence for the crown and respect for its rule, and especially to forward the uplifting of the native until his lot would fit the ideal of the law—that he come to live as did the *paysano de Castilla*. Straightforward action, even mistakes in judgment or in discharge of the duty, deserve in this tumultuous era patience and consideration. Perfect performance in the face of the unusual geography, surface and subsoil resources, navigational factors, native races, reliability of distant officials, and the temptation toward extravagant personal behavior on that remote frontier, demanded such a ruler as never lived.

All of this, too, is asking the wrong question. Granted that the Spanish kings may have acted as paragons of virtue, what business did they have in a quasi-pontifical position? How can the civil regime expect to supply the motivation of religion? Political government has as its proper aim to provide the atmosphere in which human beings may reach their best human goals. It cannot provide all the means of reaching these goals, especially the highest, the service of God. To think otherwise is to endow sovereignty with universal control, including the right to establish its own religion and the power to furnish all impulse and thought toward practicing divine worship and decent behavior. Henry IV of France is said to have advised that a king be of the religion of his people, not that he fasten his religion on them—or, he might have added, to try to take the place of their sovereign pontiff. Politics should be an aid to religion.

The state cannot attempt to initiate religious doctrine or the spiritual helps, or to direct the religious conduct of individual and group. There lay the radical fallacy in the Patronato as practiced. Patrons are a useful institution, but a royal patronage tends toward "overpatronizing." And in a situation where the patron operated with no check other than his own conscience, he quite naturally went on to attempt a positive influence on the whole system. The outlook was too purely administrative. It was as though a university president thought of himself as the teaching staff, the really educative factor in the organization. Administration is a high art, but its art is not to teach. So in the Patronato, there was a splendid organization, but it was meant for the external life. It could not produce the spiritual power back of religious living, and it kept far removed the influence of the pope as chief pastor in the church. With the many successes of the patronage there came over the Spanish people the notion that, as they had accomplished so much, they were therefore unexceptionable in their methods. In this they weakened the core of religion and left it more form than substance. All the protective patronal legislation could not shape the soul. That required direct contact with the uplifting force, divine help or grace, where politics is of necessity bound to be sterile of viable productivity.

The use of the *pase regio* must be distinguished in origin from another practice employed by kings in their dealings with Rome, although in Spain both came to blend into a common attitude. This earlier usage was the *placet* and its partner the *exequatur*. The former expressed royal pleasure or agreement in a specific proposal of Rome. The latter gave permission for its performance. Their most notable manifestation appeared in the "acceptance" of a papal election, or more stridently in the frequent Hohenstaufen custom of stating "nonacceptance." Both were constantly referred to as "rights," though in general they had no more juridical validity than the assertion of an absolutist, than the use of *force majeure* and unilateral conclusion, with no foundation in law or privilege. Men of might simply flaunted battalions before the pontiff pledged to mercy and spiritual assistance. In medieval Spain, where executives felt compelling restraint, such as Enrique IV, brother of Isabella, found in his *cortes* at Burgos,[8] kings rarely ventured on such a course. In the rest of Europe the exercise of kingly power underwent great development during the fourteenth century. Marsiglio of Padua, William of Ockham, and other advocates of the conciliar theory furnished impressive exhortation for kings to fish in these muddy waters, and the Schism furthered the effort. At the same time there appeared in Naples the thorny official proclamation called the *Monarchia Sicula*.[9] The latter descendants of the Normans, either for enlargement of revenues or the simple assertion of independence in action, insisted that no communication from Rome, no matter how small it might be, should be circulated without previous censorship and acceptance by government. This

---

[8] See above, p. 40.

[9] For its pretended origin in an actual grant of Urban II to Count Roger see Pastor, *History of the Popes*, XVIII, 66. This was a personal grant to Roger.

Neapolitan practice proved highly contagious, in the direction of Spain. When the Great Captain, Gonzalo de Córdova, performed heroic deeds in the conquest of that kingdom, without any plan of his own he saw this fantastic concept introduced among his usually logical countrymen. Later kings, particularly Philip II, would fight tenaciously to prevent papal stoppage of the convenient ukase.

In the *Recopilación de leyes de los reinos de las Indias* one may find the formal statutes on the *pase regio* in numerous titles. Thus in Libro I, título 7, ley 15 there is the requirement for prelates to remit to the Council of the Indies all briefs and bulls not given the *pase* by the Council. It dates from a *cédula* of Philip IV in 1643.

> We entreat and charge the archbishops and bishops of our Indies, whenever the case arises, to collect all the briefs in their territories from his holiness or the apostolic nuncios and from there brought into those provinces, if they have not been passed by our royal Council of the Indies. And they may not approve or allow the use of these in any way. When gathered, they are to remit them to our said Council at their first opportunity, and they must give orders that all this be done and carried into execution with the necessary care.

In Libro I, título 9, ley 1 the same Philip orders his Council to take in hand the fulfillment and execution of the apostolic bulls and briefs, in as far as they do not prejudice the right and regalia conceded by the Holy See in the Patronato.

> We order and command the president and members of our royal Council of the Indies to watch over, fulfill, and execute all the letters, bulls, and briefs from the Apostolic See that are dispatched by our most holy father in negotiations and problems, in conformity with the disposition of the sacred canons, provided that there be no derogation or prejudice to our royal patronage and the apostolic privileges and concessions which the lords kings our predecessors and ourselves hold from the Holy See and pertain to us by right and custom. They are to suspend the execution of those letters, bulls, and briefs that are dispatched in contravention of these rights and our royal pre-eminence

and patronage. And they are to give us account of such, so that, interposing the necessary and legitimate remedies, we may petition his holiness after he is better informed. They are to give no place to or permit bringing prejudice or novelty in that which has belonged to us and our predecessors and is ours by law, apostolic favor, and custom. Thus all will work better for the service of God our Lord and the ecclesiastical and temporal government and peace of the Indies. And they shall likewise take, fulfill, and execute whatever letters and patents the superiors of religious orders bring into the realm, as has been done and is now done and observed.

Libro I, título 9, ley 2, from a *cédula* of Charles V in 1538, orders the *audiencias* of the Indies to gather the originals of the bulls and briefs that have not received the *pase* of the Council and send them to the same Council for renewed supplication to his holiness, and meantime not execute them.

Libro I, título 9, ley 3 of Philip IV in 1640, repeats that the officials are to collect, without executing, the briefs and other dispatches that have not been passed by the Council, and send them here.

Libro I, título 9, ley 7, from a *cédula* of Philip II in 1571, commands that the *audiencias* send to the Council the bulls and briefs conceded in favor of the religious, lest they give rise to difficulty with the bishops.

It appears that, since the *pase regio* blocked off the natural exchange between the papacy and the church in the Spanish empire, such acts were replete with emotional stress, and not only between the principals in the case, Rome and Spanish officialdom. The effects went further. Within the kingdoms of his majesty lived a race nurtured on the tradition of popular expression of opinion and of will, and on the pursuit of high designs. They were a vocal people. Habsburg centralization did of course remove the teeth of protest in many such administrative changes as the gradual decline of the *cabildo* as a local power, in denuding the strength of provincial bodies, and sometimes in the transfer of residence, as in the relocation of native groups in

New Spain. And after the early conquest of America frontier opportunities and discoveries furnished other outlets for energy and expression, broadening the horizons and lessening the strains of society. The omnipresence of royal rule likewise hampered complaint. Nevertheless, the thought of *el santísimo padre* on one side and of *justicia* on the other could quickly rouse the strongest feeling, especially in lowly individuals and among far-off bishops and their clerics. The crown was particularly solicitous of the one most independent sector—the religious orders—and it was in this sector, as will appear in the following chapter, that the greatest contest arose over the Patronato.

The national conviction back of the *pase regio* was given utterance in stark language shortly before the election of Pius V in 1566. Figueroa, president of the Council of State, affirmed in a public session of the Council that in Spain there was no pope![10] He did not mean to dissociate himself or his country from the universal ecclesiastical jurisdiction of the papacy. Spaniards if anything prided themselves on the highest orthodoxy. His thought was that the power of the Patronato was complete, and that in matters under its concern the pope left abundant authority to the crown. As long as doctrine and canon law were preserved, the same law conferred on the patron through his grants of privilege the management of his entire patronal domain. Until this grant were withdrawn—and the crown read in its terms that it was perpetual—it would remain secure *in solidum*, safe from any competitor. The word "perpetual" written into the various bulls was probably accepted more categorically than in any privilege otherwise given to Spain. Surely none embraced an area of greater import. And although the kings well knew that sovereigns often restricted earlier universal grants through con-

---

[10] Cited in *ibid.*, XVIII, 1, quoting D. L. Serrano, *Correspondencia diplomática entre España y la Santa Sede durante el pontificado de S. Pio V* (Rome, 1914), I, 444, n. 23.

cessions given outsiders at later dates, yet the enormous investment that Spain had put into its Patronato Real de las Indias came in its course to lead public opinion, the clergy, and officialdom to take a wholly positive view of perpetuity. As an aside for future reference, the same thinking drew from subordinates in church and government an almost unquestioning alignment with the will and policy of the royal person. King-country-religion as one became a monolithic ideal, and opposing critics or counterforces would come off bad seconds in conflict.

In this dramatic situation no one will miss the fact of emergent tension, for there are visible clear signs of a psychological arrogance that could readily become pathological. Figueroa, speaking to and for the Council of State, forgot what manner of man he was as he transferred undoubted success into the assertion of royal omnicompetence. Religious exaltation intensified the emotional state, for Pius V himself said in 1568 that "the king of Spain was the only Catholic sovereign who protected the Church."[11] Philip II was so convinced of the utter righteousness of his position that he burst into tears of rage when Castagna, the papal nuncio, brought admonition from the pope that the *pase regio* was out of character in a Catholic king.[12]

There is pathos in this picture of Philip II. He seems to have believed sincerely that a stoppage of the *pase regio* would undermine his authority in the Patronato and the whole system of the church in the Indies, and with that his kingly position. He could point to a magnificent achievement. Under the guidance of the crown of Castile and Leon the seventy years after 1508 brought a historic proliferation of thirty dioceses in America, from Guadalajara to Santiago de Chile. The dioceses and their first bishops,[13] in order of foundation, were:

---

[11] Quoted in Pastor, *History of the Popes*, XVIII, 29.
[12] *Ibid.*, XVIII, 40, 57.
[13] See Hernáez, *Colección*, II, *passim*, for this documented list and the bulls of institution.

1512	Santo Domingo	García de Padilla
1512	San Juan de Puerto Rico	Alonso Manso
1514	Santa María del Antigua-Panamá	Juan de Quevedo
1518	Yucatán-Mérida	Julián Garcés
1518	Asunción de Baracoa-Santiago de Cuba	Juan de Vinte
1526	Tlaxcala-Puebla	Julián Garcés
1531	Santa Marta	Tomás de Órtiz
1532	Caracas	Rodrigo Bastidas
1534	México	Juan de Zumárraga
1534	Nicaragua	Pedro de Zúñiga
1534	Cartagena	Gerónimo de Loaysa
1535	Antequera-Oaxaca	Juan López de Zárate
1536	Michoacán	Vasco de Quiroga
1537	Cuzco	Fernando de Luque y Olivera
1537	Guatemala	Francisco de Marroquín
1538	Chiapas	Juan de Arteaga y Avendaño
1539	Comayagua-Honduras	Juan de Talayera
1540	Compostela-Guadalajara	Antonio de Ciudad-Rodrigo
1542	Lima	Gerónimo de Loaysa
1545	Quito	Garci Díaz Arias
1547	Popoyán	Juan del Valle
1548	Asunción de Paraguay	Juan de Barrios
1551	Charcas	Tomás de San Martín
1556	Vera Paz (Costa Rica)	Pedro de Ángulo
1561	Santiago de Chile	Rodrigo González Marmolejo
1562	Bogotá	Martín de Calatayud
1567	Imperial-Concepción	Antonio de San Miguel y Vergara
1570	Tucumán	Gerónimo de Villa Carrillo
1577	Arequipa	Antonio Ervas
1577	Trujillo	Alonzo Guzmán de Talavera

Working under these bishops were hundreds of clerics, hundreds of thousands of Christians, and a mission system that had already organized large native groups up and down two continents and was now moving steadily ahead with solid development. The earlier need for crown expenditure, in point of tithes and subsidies, had reversed itself, so that now the royal treasury counted on receiving its portion of these imposts to supply its own requirements. In all the Hispanic regions a diocesan clergy was active. Religious orders contributed generously to work in city and town, and they had full charge of conversion of the border tribes. The size and complexity of this task had called into being a highly competent *cámara* (central office) in the Council of the Indies that paralleled in some way the Roman congregations. These officers were engaged in continuing examination of the broad front, charting desirable new movements, providing a constant flow of men to replace those no longer able to labor, and judging in the endless conflicts of interests arising in the all-too-human make-up of society. In the scheme Philip II occupied the central position. Overly administrative, he had little time for thought on basic principles, such as the obvious fact that the sovereign pontiff may not abdicate his supervision over all parts of the church; and he clung stubbornly to his *pase regio* in a sort of neurotic anxiety. Although he was known for slow and careful decision, aside from his English marriage he rarely made a strategic retreat.

Philip II had been king ten years when in 1566 Pius V was elected. It fell to this pope to achieve the widest practical application of the reforming canons of the Council of Trent. The council, despite all its doctrinal and disciplinary measures, had been unable through force of circumstances to attack the foremost obstacle to any permanent reform, the grip of Catholic princes on church life and action. Pius V understood this problem, and his reign shows a tenacious determination to insure that the church be recognized as a free and independent society in its own sphere of faith and morals.[14] In Spain he saw the historical paradox of a most earnest religious regime putting a blockade against communication with the necessary center of its religion. And he went to great lengths to find a solution that could remedy this unhappy situation.

Toward Philip II personally the pope felt and showed the highest regard, but his ecclesiastical policy underwent thorough review. That policy was predicated on entire subordination of the clergy to the royal will. The policy may be traced from the earliest days of Spain in the Indies. Ferdinand in 1493 began the practice when, in a *cédula* to the Padre Custodio, he named those Franciscans who were chosen to go out with Columbus on his second voyage.[15] In 1522 the bishop of Cuba pleaded in a memorial to Charles V that the king restore to his diocese the territory of the island of Jamaica which the crown had assigned elsewhere.[16] Two years later Charles V ordered the same bishop to send a delegated cleric to hurry the consecration of several churches in his diocese and to confirm the neophytes.[17] In 1526 Charles forbade the inquisitor general, the archbishop of Seville, to give asylum to two swindlers lately returned from the Indies, and ordered him instead to put them in prison.[18] In 1529 he called for and received depositions of witnesses on the purported misconduct of Bishop-elect Zumárraga in his dealings with the first *audiencia*.[19] That same year Empress Juana signed an order for Zumárraga to see to it that the Indians used no

---

[14] See Hughes, *Popular History*, pp. 180-85, for a pungent view of Trent's failure to face this problem. His little volume is distinctly not "popular," for its reading requires intellectual training above the average and its frequent ascents above the level of mere data introduce views that will certainly not please the populace. It is a masterly compendium of interpretative history.

[15] Pacheco y Cárdenas, *Colección de documentos inéditos*, I 21, 516.

[16] *Ibid.*, II 6, 15.

[17] *Ibid.*, II 1, 129.

[18] *Ibid.*, II 9, 237-39.

[19] *Ibid.*, I 40, 468-560.

pulque.[20] Queen Isabel in 1531 sent notice to the priors of several Dominican houses in New Spain to reprimand what she termed the "pulpit excesses" of certain preachers.[21] Next year the *cabildo* of Santiago de Cuba complained to the crown about the "partiality" of their bishop toward various persons.[22] In 1533 Queen Isabel dispatched a mandate "ordering" the bishop of Cuba to absolve from blame the licentiate Vadillo whom he had recently excommunicated.[23] And in 1573 Philip II directed Francisco de Toledo, viceroy of Peru, to exercise general supervision over the use of the *bula cruzada* just conceded by Gregory XIII.[24] If one add to these few examples the significant orders contained in the redonation of tithes of 1512,[25] there appears quite clearly the quasi-pontifical character in the kingly station. This utter subjection of clerics to the royal will indicates a frame of mind which would readily make a custom of the *pase regio.* Men of the cloth, under the dual pressure of royal orders and royal bounty, gave full compliance to a crown whose proclaimed policy and constant effort strove to rebuild religion throughout the world.

Such attitudes as these explain a rather shocking instance of the intrusion of royalty in ecclesiastical matters. It was an effort to block the papal right to review an attack on one of the Spanish hierarchy.

In December of 1557 Bartolomé Carranza was raised to the primatial see as archbishop of Toledo. A highly revered scholar, he had been employed as diplomat and arbiter of religious difficulties in the Low Countries, and he came to his post with every promise of success. Yet before the next summer had passed he found himself charged by the Inquisition with expressing dangerous views in his sermons and writings, and he was arrested

---

[20] *Ibid.*, II 9, 433.
[21] *Ibid.*, II 10, 60.
[22] *Ibid.*, II 4, 253.

[23] *Ibid.*, II 4, 309.
[24] *Ibid.*, I 18, 397-99.
[25] See above, pp. 121-26.

and jailed.[26] This posed a problem for the sovereign pontiff, in that one of his highest officers could be put in jeopardy by Spanish powers and made into a sign of scandal. At once the papal envoy to Spain lodged the protest of Pius V and demanded that the prelate be brought to Rome for investigation and, if need be, for trial. Philip II and his ministers demurred, for they saw in the Inquisition the strongest bulwark of orthodoxy and of the Patronato, and they refused to allow the Holy Office to become subject to an outside or superior court. In this they were ready to forget completely that Sixtus IV had instituted the Inquisition, for usage had in their minds transferred its character into that of a totally national institution. In this hazy thinking one may readily find the cause for the deviation of the Inquisition in earlier days. The case might be dubbed a matter of hypnotic mendacity.

To blacken the cause of the archbishop it was remarked that he had been close to Charles V during the last days of the emperor, and rumor had it that for this reason their former king had died a heretic—a morbid word in public opinion. Shorn of his good name, his metropolitan powers, his personal and literary possessions, Carranza languished in prison for nine years while the investigators tried to reach a verdict, and that mostly without any taking of testimony from the accused. At last in 1567 the hapless man was allowed to be taken under guard to Rome, for Philip II saw that he was facing a very determined person in the Vatican, one who would die rather than neglect his duty toward his archbishop. Carranza never returned to his homeland or his see. Tension between king and pope, and the endless process of Spanish charges and supposedly new evidence kept the trial going until long after Pius V died. At last in 1576 the plaintiff was declared innocent of heresy. Within a year he died.

---

[26] This case is thoroughly treated in Pastor, *History of the Popes*, XVII, Chapter 8 and XVIII, Chapter 2, with all its basic documentation.

The episode was a sad reflection on the *pase regio*, because of which, in this instance, a prelate was not allowed to pass from the royal jurisdiction into the proper tribunal at Rome.

Pius V encountered this unchurchly attitude of Spain on another front. It was the use of the *pase* to block the publication of the celebrated bull *In coena Domini*. Ever since the year 1364 it had been customary in Rome to read this bull in solemn ceremony on Maundy Thursday, and then to send it out to all bishops for promulgation in their dioceses.[27] Its principal content was a list of twelve censures for attacks on the faith or on the constitution of the church, and the penalties could be absolved only by the pope himself.

In the promulgation of 1566 an event occurred that presaged trouble. For in that year the Spanish bishops refused to publish the bull unless they had the permission of the royal council.[28] In good time Philip II realized that the communication differed in no respect from previous editions, and he quickly ordered the hierarchy to make it public. This situation prompted the pope to reconsider the scope of the bull in future editions, and hence it was that the 1568 issue contained five new clauses pointed directly against caesaropapalism. They were the following: (1) Excommunication is automatic for those who, at the risk of their souls, presume to withdraw themselves from obedience to the pope, present or future, or in any way to recede from it. (2) The same penalty applied to those who appealed from the pope to a future general council or who gave counsel, aid, or favor to the same. (3) Like censure fell on those who drove out of their kingdoms the patriarchs, archbishops, or bishops. (4) Similar action would befall those who entered into capital or criminal processes against ecclesiastics. (5) The last was a

---

[27] This bull continued in annual publication until 1770. Its provisions are now part of canon law.

[28] Pastor, *History of the Popes*, XVIII, 36.

mandate from the pope, in virtue of holy obedience, to every patriarch, archbishop, and bishop, and all others exercising the care of souls, including secular and regular priests deputed to hear confessions, not to make pretense of ignorance of these censures, but to take care that they have a copy of this document and read it carefully.[29]

In Spain these five points had considerable application. Every archbishop and bishop, upon entrance into office, was bound by law to swear fealty and obedience to the crown and observance of the royal patronage of the Indies.[30] Exile had been made the penalty for rejection of the king's entire jurisdiction as practiced in the Patronato system. The bull, then, created an uproar. Philip II, backed by most of his bishops, refused to let it be read, and thus threw down the gauntlet to the papacy. In the ensuing conflict Spanish diplomats did no good to the king by their unrealistic appraisal of the saintly pope. Requesens, ambassador at the Vatican, wrote to Madrid that curial officials in Rome were attempting to turn away the pope from necessary reforms by involving him in quarrels with the princes.[31] His colleague Tiepolo, the Venetian ambassador, spread the opinion that Pius V intended not only to control spiritual affairs but also those purely civil. From Madrid, Castagna reported to the pope that he could account for the excitement of the king only by the insistence of his ministers that the publication of the bull would cause a revolution in the Spanish dominions.

In it all the pope kept his head, and his heart. Philip II on his part complained that the bull had been published in his dominion of Naples without the *exequatur*, and he appealed for his argument to the validity of the *Monarchia Sicula*. Then on

---

29 *Ibid.*, XVIII, Appendices 2-3, pp. 463-66.
30 The prelate swore not to oppose the royal patronage at any time or in any act, not to impede or obstruct the use of the royal jurisdiction. See *Recopilación*, Lib. I, tit. 7, ley 1 and p. 293.
31 Pastor, *History of the Popes*, XVIII, 38, and the same for Tiepolo's acts.

August 30, 1568 he issued a royal *pragmática* that forbade under grave penalty the publication of any papal rescript, brief, or
other ordinance, without the usual *exequatur*. At the same time
he stated that, in the papal warning to confessors not to absolve
those guilty of violating the injunctions of the bull without previous retraction, the holy father was abusing the sacrament of
penance. To this Pius replied without mincing his words: "Such
language befits the new heretics. The king should use his sound
common sense." Moreover, to assuage the grief of the king in
this trouble, to which was added his own personal sorrow occasioned by the unhappy death of his son Don Carlos, Pius wrote
him in compassionate terms, while urging him to be careful of
counselors who put into his mind thoughts that could cause him
untold anxiety. And a special congregation of cardinals was convoked to discuss the objections raised against the bull.[32]

Despite all these difficulties the bull was published un-
changed, but not through the royal channels, for the secular
clergy were thoroughly entangled in the meshes of royal control.
It was done through confessors of religious orders to whom it
was sent by their generals in Rome, on orders of the pope. Philip
II finally dropped his opposition, for he was involved in a more
portentous issue, the investigation of the whole regime of the Patronato that is to be examined in the following chapter.

Two centuries later an unusual instance of the use of the
pase regio occurred under Philip V. It was the refusal to admit
a pontifical favor, the Benedictine privilege, into any part of the
Spanish empire.

On November 4, 1741 Benedict XIV issued a document that
carried important social overtones, both for Catholic countries
and for those now under other religious organization. It was a
change in marriage law. In 1563 the Council of Trent, in its
twenty-fourth session, had laid down the discipline for the sacra-

---

[32] This paragraph closely follows the account in *ibid.*, XVIII, 49-51.

ment of marriage in the famous article *Tametsi*.[33] Marriages were declared invalid unless performed before a priest and two witnesses, and this in unions between two Catholics, a Protestant and a Catholic, or two Protestants. There is no point here in discussing the origin of the legislation or its utility; but as time went on it led to many hardships. Deep-seated social antipathies grew out of the enforcement of the law. More seriously, the validity of all kinds of marriages was called into question. In numerous localities the legitimacy of offspring under this rule depended on religious prescription. Inheritance of title to land or rank, fitness for holy orders and for numerous lesser offices and contractual arrangements, especially the intimate ties of love and duty in the home, lay under a duress that was unbreakable. The difficulties were widespread wherever the formula *"Cujus regio eius et religio,"* had been fixed after 1555.

To meet the facts of the "mixed marriage" and the Protestant marriage, Benedict XIV devised a new formula for the extrinsic part of the ceremony. Marriages between Catholics continued to require for validity the presence of the priest and two witnesses. For the other two cases the church withdrew its demands, and these marriages were henceforth to be considered valid regardless of what is called the Catholic "form." The social benefits deriving from this change would form an impressive chapter in history.

The Benedictine privilege was originally extended to the Low Countries.[34] Within a comparatively short time it was applied to whatever region sought to enjoy it, and almost every part of Europe, Asia, Africa, and America accepted it wherever Catholic law was concerned. In Spain, however, and throughout the Spanish empire, as likewise in the Portuguese dominions,

---

[33] The full text of the decree is given in Denzinger, *Enchiridion symbolorum,* pp. 344-45.
[34] *Ibid.,* pp. 398-402.

this remedial legislation failed to receive royal approbation and thus to become the law of the land. In parts of the United States formerly under the Spanish flag Tridentine rigidity surrounded the law of marriage down to the twentieth century. This meant that in all that time Catholics and non-Catholics, whenever they came under the inheritance of Patronato law, were bound by the ancient rule in the Caribbean islands and in continental territory throughout the extensive ecclesiastical province of Santa Fe. That comprised the archdiocese of Santa Fe in New Mexico; the diocese of Gallup, including parts of New Mexico and Arizona; the diocese of El Paso in its New Mexican section; the present diocese of Tucson; and the large province of Los Angeles. All of Hispanic Central and South America and the Philippine Islands maintained the same severe legislation. There is no estimating the range of the restriction brought upon all these people by this crippling use of the *pase regio*.

There was apparently no limit to the application of the *pase* to clerical activities. The royal permission was necessary for introducing into the empire the celebration of new feasts of the church. In 1664, when Rome allowed the observance of solemnities for the Immaculate Conception, a royal *cédula* approved the Mass and Office of the day and gave permission for the printing of the texts to be used throught the Spanish realm.[35] There is a royal order directing the celebration of the recently instituted feast of the Patronage of St. Joseph in 1777 and a royal printing was commanded for the appropriate liturgical forms.[36] In 1816 a similar *cédula*, full of regal permissions, extended to the imperial clergy the liturgy for the Office and Mass of the Sacred Heart.[37] In 1773 a general *cédula* forbade the bishops to use the formula "Imprimatur" or any other that indicated independent authority to permit publication.[38] In 1768 Charles III

---

[35] Hernáez, *Colección*, II, 524.   [37] *Ibid.*, II, 544.
[36] *Ibid.*, II, 538.   [38] Herr, *Revolution*, p. 202.

by royal decree blocked the circulation in Spain of any Roman decision referring to books listed in the Index.[39]

The exaggerated importance attached by the kings to the *pase* is seen in documents authorizing the creation of new dioceses and the simultaneous action, always with Roman permission, to establish new boundaries for the contiguous bishoprics. In 1779 Charles III obtained the bulls for the organization of the diocese of Nuevo Leon. His *cédula* implementing the Roman institution contains the following words:

> I have been informed that various towns in the colony of Nuevo Reino y León, and Coahuila and Texas, subject to the bishop of Guadalajara, and others under the bishop of Michoacán and the archbishop of Mexico, are unable to receive episcopal visitation because of the great distances involved and for other reasons. Hence I resolved after hearing these complaints that it would be fitting to erect a diocese with the title of Nuevo Reino y León, so as to bring proper remedy to one and other parties concerned. To this effect I ordered that the necessary bulls be obtained from his holiness. With that accomplished, and my *pase* given in the ordinary form, my Council of the Cámara of the Indies, in a consultation of December 19 of the past year, pointed out to me that to fulfill my praiseworthy intentions all that was needed was to name the secular person who would, according to custom, make the assignment and division of the territory of the said new diocese. Accordingly Fray Antonio de Jesús Sacedón, provost of the bishop of the new diocese, is given the task of erecting this church as the elected prelate desires.[40]

A final example of royal meddling with strictly pontifical business occurred in the year 1794 in connection with the famous Synod of Pistoia. Eight years previously the bishop of that see convoked his clergy and a number of outside theologians of Gallican bent to consider "reform." The upshot was a quite heretical set of *acta* signed by 233 members of the group. Pius VI, in his *Auctorem fidei*, called upon Catholic prelates to reject the

---

[39] *Ibid.*, p. 207.
[40] See the full document in García Gutiérrez, *Bulario*, pp. 246-49.

proposals of the synod. Charles IV, under the influence of his Jansenist advisers, refused the *pase* of this papal bull into Spain.[41] It should be added that in 1800, when contrary advice gave the king a more realistic view of what he had done, he reversed his opposition and with his *pase* permitted its free circulation.

When the use of this power is seen in full perspective, one cannot but conclude that a system which produced the *pase regio* contained within itself a basic antagonism toward the very thing it was meant to support, and doubt arises as to the candor and integrity of the royal outlook on religion. The *pase* epitomized the entirely oppressive tendency of the Patronato, and it dealt a shattering blow to the independent administrative machinery of the universal church. In fact, it made the Spanish church a state church. A strait jacket was laced round the clergy, who should have been free to follow the policy and decision of their own leaders and who instead succumbed to the mandates of a—perhaps well-meaning—civil potentate. The removal of appointive and directive power from the father of the clergy, the pope, wrecked any family spirit and trusting union with their head. In the assumption of complete power over temporalities and finances there was a fundamental threat against the existence of that liberty and independence of mind that members of the church expect in their spiritual guides. From the papacy was taken the right to be supreme judge of the pope's own men and the final court of appeal. The stopping of free communication was the rankest tyranny over priest and bishop. In this refusal of passage to papal directives, unless the *pase* was granted, the king made himself equivalently superior to the ruler of the church.

In 1566 the holy father spoke the plain truth about the system. When in that year Philip II pleaded his right, under the

[41] Herr, *Revolution*, pp. 405, 429-30.

Monarchia Sicula, to block from Naples and Spain the official Roman documents, Pius V instructed Camiana, his nuncio at Madrid, to tell Philip that the monarch was simply using that claim as a tool "to make the Catholic king a pope."[42] For he exercised direct veto over papal administration of the church in Spain.

The fundamental statute written into the Patronato Real by the crown is contained in the severe *cédula* issued by Philip II from San Lorenzo on June 1, 1574. It is found in Libro I, título 4, ley 1 of the *Recopilación.* The statute is as follows.

Inasmuch as the right of ecclesiastical patronage belongs to us in the whole commonwealth of the Indies from the fact that we discovered and acquired the new world and built and endowed the churches and monasteries there at our own expense and that of the noble Catholic kings, our predecessors, and from the further fact of the bulls by which the sovereign pontiffs on their own motion conceded this power for the preservation of religion and justice to which we are obliged, therefore we command and ordain that this right of patronage in the Indies must forever be held undivided and complete for ourselves and our royal crown. There can be no departure from this right either in whole or in part, whether by gift, grant, privilege, or any other disposition which we or the kings our successors make or concede. Let it not be thought that we will give over this right of patronage to any person, church, or monastery, or that we in any way will prejudice the right of patronage. Nor may anyone plead against it a custom, prescription, or other title, whether this person or persons be a clerical community, a secular church, or a monastery, unless the person do this in our name and with our authority and power. Let no secular person, nor cleric, order, convent, congregation, or community of whatever standing, condition, quality, or pre-eminence, whether by plea in court or extra-judicially, for whatever reason or cause, dare to intrude into matters touching this patronage, nor prejudice us in this subject. No one may

---

[42] Pastor, *History of the Popes,* XVIII, 11. The *pase regio* as it touched the related roles of bishop, king, and pope forms the central theme in Vicente Rodríguez Valencia, *El Patronato regio de Indias y la santa sede en Santo Toribio de Mogrovejo (1581-1606)* (Roma, 1957).

present to a church, benefice, or other ecclesiastical office, nor receive such a presentation, throughout all our Indies, except by our own presentation or that of a person to whom we by law or patent of provision delegate the right. And the person who does otherwise, if he be a secular, incurs the loss of title to all rights that he holds from us throughout the entire Indies, and he will be unable to hold or obtain any other such title; he will moreover be exiled perpetually from all our kingdoms. If he be an ecclesiastic, he will be considered exiled from all our kingdoms, nor can he either hold or receive a benefice or ecclesiastical office in all our kingdoms. And the one and the other incur the other penalties established by the laws of these kingdoms. And our viceroys, *audiencias*, and royal justices are to proceed with all rigor against those who disregard the enforcement and power of our right of patronage. They are to take action on their own official right, or at the petition of our public prosecutor or any other person who shall sue, and in the execution of the process they are to use the promptness that is demanded by the case.

In actual practice its force depended upon the oath taken by all prelates at their institution, an oath contained in the edict of Philip IV proclaimed in 1629 and found—in indirect discourse —in Libro I, título 7, ley 1.

Before entering into office all archbishops, bishops, and visitors ecclesiastic must take solemn oath before a notary public and witnesses that they will not oppose the royal patronage at any time or in any act, that they will protect it and comply fully with its obligations in all and through all acts that are required by it without placing any hindrance whatsoever against its processes. They will not impede or obstruct the use of the royal jurisdiction, will stand up publicly for the royal rights and the royal revenues that belong to the king from any source, in particular the two ninths of the tithes of the church in the Indies that are reserved to the kings, and they will assist the ministers of the state in whatever concerns the Patronato, fully and without any opposition whatsoever. They will carry out the nominations, institutions, and collations to which they are obliged under the same patronage . . .

CHAPTER XIII

Religious Orders and
the Patronato

In the administration of the Patronato Real there was a clearly marked pyramid of jurisdiction. At the bottom the field workers comprised bishops, the secular clergy, religious orders, and a number of professional laymen engaged as assistants of various superior officers. Next in order came the vice patrons. These men acted as qualified and fully empowered agents of the central controlling body, the Council of the Indies. The Council formed the supreme executive, legislative, and judicial commission, charged with keeping a sharp outlook on the progress of religion in the Indies and an even sharper eye on whatever external or internal agency might attempt to induce "derogation" of the royal prerogative in the patronage. Finally there was the king, the patron himself.

Two items mentioned briefly and somewhat obliquely in the previous chapter reveal under direct examination a deep focus of tension in the patronal administration. In connection with the 1568 issue of the bull *In coena Domini* it was remarked that the secular clergy of the country found themselves too tightly enmeshed in the net of patronal organization to dare take part in the circulation of the bull, for fear of royal displeasure. The pope accordingly bypassed them and secured its publication through the channel of confessors of the religious orders. Then

in 1571 Philip II issued an order to the effect that his American
audiencias should pick up all copies of papal bulls and briefs
conceding favors to the religious and forward them to the Council of the Indies, thus to forestall difficulties that might arise between bishops and regulars.

These clues suggest the possibility of unhealthy divergence
between the two clergies, as they likewise indicate the struggle
of the royal patron to fit religious orders into his concept of a
state-directed church. The stresses ensuing from this situation
produced strains of highest moment, and on more than one occasion approached the breaking point where ancient and venerable
orders debated leaving the Spanish Indies for work in other
lands. This tension arose from no general ill will or insubordi-
nation on the side of the orders, but rather from the historical
development and the peculiar administrative character of the
patronage-in-action. While its point of climax coincided with the
1568 trouble over the *In coena Domini,* the problem always constituted a critical area for the royal concern.

As in the case of the *pase regio,* so in dealing with the orders
the crown plunged into a position that was as needless as it was
harmful. In using the *pase* successive kings presumed the right
to sit in judgment on papal direction of the hierarchy and thus
of the whole Spanish church. With the orders the crown followed
a similarly contradictory policy. To convert America it gladly
accepted the aid of these corporations that were immediately
subject to and empowered to act by the holy father, and then
proceeded to treat this segment of the clerical army as though it
took its origin from the Council of the Indies and recognized no
direct dependence on the papacy. As Icazbalceta noted in regard
to the bishops of New Spain, so it could be said of the kings that
"they wanted the religious, but without their privileges."[1] Deprived of their charters, the latter would no longer have been

---

[1] Icazbalceta, *Zumárraga,* p. 153.

those bold forces that had manned every missionary expedition since the fifth century. The administrative mind tended to turn these men into machines, forgetful of person, dealing only with works, though with the best of good will and large expenditure of resources for the person because of the work.[2]

A clear indication of this kingly outlook is found in the *cédula*, already cited, sent by Philip II in 1571 to the *audiencias* of the Indies. The ruling entered into the *Recopilación* and is found in Libro I, título 9, ley 7. In translation it reads:

> That the *audiencias* send to the Council the bulls and briefs con-
> ceded in favor of religious, if these should lead to any differences with
> the bishops:
> Correspondents from the cathedral churches of New Spain have
> related to us certain differences that arose between bishops and regu-
> lars, to the harm and prejudice of the welfare and salvation of the
> natives. These evils can be avoided if all follow the dispositions of the
> holy Council of Trent in regard to proper order and relations between
> bishops and regulars, so necessary in each diocese as it is in other parts
> of Christendom. We, desiring to provide what is most conducive to the
> service of God our Lord and our own service, as also to the peace and
> conformity between ecclesiastics and the welfare of the natives, do
> order and command the *presidentes* and *oidores* of all our royal *audi-*
> *encias* in Peru and New Spain that encounter such difficulties to send
> to our Council of the Indies by the first ships the briefs and bulls of his
> holiness that he has conceded on the petition and for the favor of the
> religious of those provinces, or an authorized translation of the same,
> removing those documents from the power of the superiors and re-
> ligious who possess them, and doing this with all speed and care. And
> we charge them to hand over and surrender the same for the said
> cause, and to place no hindrance whatsoever in the way. We declare
> that, if the bulls and briefs already have the *pase* of our royal Council
> of the Indies, it will be sufficient to send authorized translations of

---

[2] Throughout this discussion it will help to maintain balance of judgment if one
recalls the generous though careful view of Pastor, *History of the Popes*,
XVIII, 335: "On the whole, therefore, owing to the deeply religious feeling
of the Spanish people, the royal right of superintendence was favorable to
the church."

them. If they have not had the *pase*, they must send the originals, for the purpose stated in the laws of this title.

The key words in this *cédula* lie in the royal assertion: "We, desiring to provide what is most conducive to the service of God our Lord." Though Philip II would certainly have demurred at the charge, his statement is on its face preposterous, and it indicates a megalomania that could lead to the most absurd as well as to the most radical of solutions. Implied in those words is the fullest claim to religious prerogative: he will decide whether the papal commissions provide what is most conducive to the service of God our Lord. His, too, is the final judgment as to the appropriateness of papal grants to the pope's own men, and he can nullify those grants without answering to any man.

This stand demanded of religious a subjection of the intelligence and an obedience far more blind that anyone was ever asked to offer in the keeping of his vows. It blandly accepted the principle of an absolute papal vicariate that could never be delegated by a pope because such delegation is intrinsically impossible. Moreover, no religious vows to obey anybody but his religious superiors; a layman has no claim on his fulfillment of those vows. Since this dictum made law for a most enthusiastic, active, closely organized, and determined type of human beings, it was certain to lead to a sea full of troubles. And when the lay king pretended to speak for the silenced holy father—whose personal charter or privilege was here under question—one could wonder at the incalculable assumptions of power claimed by a civil ruler. Wisely had Pius V counseled Philip II to look twice at the advice of his ministers.[3]

This policy toward the orders was undoubtedly an outgrowth of the concept of patronage as it developed in the ruling minds of the Council during the first Spanish century in the Indies. The patron overlooked his dependence upon the grantor of his pat-

---

[3] *Ibid.*, XVIII, 37, 41.

ent, and he went on to act as if the grant were not rescindable. In fact, he took definite steps to see that it would not be rescinded. This is well borne out by the *cédula* of Philip II issued at San Lorenzo on June 1, 1574 and appended to the previous chapter.

Philip II, who himself initiated the legislation on religious orders that is found in the *Recopilación*, may well have been influenced by the action taken at the contemporary Council of Trent which he cites in the law of 1571. The council sat intermittently through the years 1545-1563, and much of its attention went to the reform of the orders, for there was much to reform. In its twenty-fourth session bishops were declared to have full power in their own dioceses and to have the right in ordinary circumstances to direct all matters of religion with their own hands.[4] Out of this statement of principle a multitude of problems soon arose. After the council ended many bishops refused any longer to recognize the existing privileges of the so-called mendicant orders. Some claimed for their own cathedral treasuries the inheritances of religious from their families or from generous benefactors. Others canceled rights to hear confessions, preach, distribute Communion, and even to exist within their dioceses. These prelates wanted the order men under the same regime as their own diocesans.

Now, the whole organization of religious orders rests on the idea that their membership and tasks are world wide, and their rights as corporations at law are given them directly by the Holy See upon its confirmation of their fundamental constitutions. To bodies such as the Dominicans, the Franciscans, the Jesuits, and the Augustinians it would have been fatal if they were separated into as many units as there were dioceses. Pius V, when he took up the problem of confirming the decrees of the council, was able, as a former member of the Dominican order, to amplify

---

[4] *Sacrosancti et oecumenici concilii Tridentini canones et decreta* (Parisiis, 1910), Sessio XXIV, *passim*.

and adjust the conciliar language to fit the historical perspective. His bull on the subject is dated August 16, 1567, and it became established law.[5] The letter took account of the recent arbitrary episcopal dealings with the orders. Those prelates, the pope said, labored in every way to make the mendicants subject to themselves and proclaimed that the care of souls was not the affair of the religious but only of the secular clergy. He clarified twenty-six passages in the words of the council that had previously been interpreted to the prejudice of religious.

Philip II, after he had "approved" the conciliar decrees, used the extreme interpretation of blanket powers for bishops over regulars as an argument for nationalizing the orders within his realm, and he took measures to make them independent of their higher superiors residing abroad. For each group he sought to institute a Spanish commissary with complete charge over all its members in his empire. All the Franciscans in the Indies had to accept a commissary general. In the long document instituting this office that was sent to all houses of the Friars Minor on November 6, 1571 the reason for this new departure is given in palatable form. It is said that this special official must be set up for the Indies because his field is too far off from the minister general at Rome for effective government. Moreover, the area over which he has charge is larger than the area in which all the rest of their order labors, while their work there, in comparison with the totality of Franciscan world interests and enterprises, is so much more diversified and difficult as to demand the creation of this special office.[6]

---

[5] On the situation see Pastor, *History of the Popes*, XVII, 268-73. Hernáez, *Colección*, I, 469-519, presents important papal bulls that lay down pertinent restrictions to the actions of religious in organized dioceses.

[6] See the directive in Joaquín García Icazbalceta, *Nueva colección de documentos para la historia de México* (México, 1886), I, 132-37. Pastor, *History of the Popes*, XVII, 249, credits Philip II with the motive of religious zeal as part cause of his general attitude: that he wanted to separate his Spaniards from foreign decadence in religious orders!

It is clear that orders which were capitular in structure found greater difficulty in resisting this demand than did the more centralized institutions. The Jesuits too had a procurator for the Indies, but his function was much more limited, as is seen in the following orders inaugurating the office:

Instruction for the Procurator of the Indies of the West,
by Edward Mercurian, general. Done at Rome,
September 28, 1574

The office of the procurator of the Indies of the West will deal principally with two things. The first is that it will provide the necessities for the provinces of Peru and of Mexico, in conformity with what will be decided by the general and by superiors of those parts of the Indies. It will at the appropriate time obtain the materials needed for the use of the colleges in those countries, for the equipment of the men whom they will send to those provinces, and when necessary will serve as a warehouse to keep the stores that it provides.

The second function will be diligent and faithful care in wrapping and sending the letters and other reports which come from Rome or from any other place for those provinces, and likewise those that come from those provinces for the general or for other persons. And they will not open the papers that come to the general, but send them sealed as they arrive.

Serving as assistant to the procurator will be the one whom Father Visitor Doctor Plaza and the father provincial of Andalusia will appoint, and he will give such help as will be required; but in all else he shall be under the obedience of the superiors of the colleges to which he may be attached.

The procurator will have a chest locked with two keys, one of which he will himself retain and his assistant the other. There he will keep the money and the books of the sums that he receives, and of the expenses. Thus he will write in the said book what he puts into the chest and what he withdraws. Each year, at the time of the departure of the fleet, they will send the statements for that year in duplicate on different ships, written in clear and distinct form and signed by their own hands, to the provinces of Peru and Mexico. They will likewise send identical copies to Rome.

The said procurator will keep the following five books: (1) in the first he will write the orders for goods that he sends and receives;

(2) in the second he will write the records of the foundations of the colleges or the affairs of the said provinces, and these he will forward to Rome, written in Latin; (3) in the third book are written the revenues of each college and of each province; (4) in the fourth book he will keep record of the directives he receives from Rome touching on his office; (5) in the fifth he will write the decisions of the consultations held in the Province of Andalusia regarding the business affairs of the said provinces of the Indies. If it becomes urgent to deal with the king and his officials on any point regarding the forwarding of some provisions, or matters of this character, and there is no time to write to Rome and wait for a reply, let the procurator propose this immediately to the father provincial of Andalusia so that he may call a consultation on the subject, with the procurator present if he can be there.

He will understand that in the house or college where he lives he must obey the superior in matters pertaining to the regulations and government of that house or college.

He will take care of the guest quarters in Seville for ours who are going to the Indies, in accordance with what the king has given for that purpose, and see to it that the money provided by the king, the real and a half [three sixteenths of a peso or dollar] a day to cover the expense of those on the way to the Indies, goes for their upkeep and the use of the said province.

The procurator will do all in his power to bring comfort to ours in the Indies, and send them the annual letters and the edifying letters, as well as the bulls and other documents that are issued at Rome. From Rome, September 28, 1574.[7]

The Spanish Jesuits did maintain a procurator at Madrid, but only for the purpose of representing the order before the crown and its councils when some movement arose to jeopardize

---

[7] This document was copied and translated from Film Roll 134, entitled *I, Mex.*, *1-2*, in the Jesuitica Collection at St. Louis University. The procurator resided in Seville. The last two lines in the instruction were later to cause much concern because of royal interference with the principle and the official opening of the mail. Consequently, about 1620, the use of cipher came to be employed generally for important correspondence. The first cipher was apparently broken about 1640, but the second lasted down into the eighteenth century. Copies of these two ciphers are in the Jesuitica Collection at Loyola University in Chicago.

their constitutional rights. A typical case came in 1572 in connection with their exemption from paying tithes that was granted
by Paul III in 1549. Three Spanish bishops demanded the payment. Father Porres succeeded in having the demand revoked,
defending the cause in a long and painful trial.[8]

It was not easy for them to escape the general ruling that the
Spanish provinces of the religious orders accept a commissary
to rule over their Hispanic membership and work. From 1554 to
1560 they had employed somewhat the same setup when St.
Francis Borgia was sent there by St. Ignatius Loyola and Father
Laýnez, the two first generals. This move, however, had no con-
notation of permanence nor of giving one-man rule to all the
provinces of the country. It was done to achieve uniformity of
practice under the Constitutions of the order, and it was never
repeated after 1560. In the next year Father Jerome Nadal came
with the title of commissary and visitor universal of all Jesuits
in Europe, and in 1562, with his work of visiting done, he
moved on to France. Perhaps the critical reason why this order
was able to avoid the general regulation lay in the fact that
Philip II and St. Francis Borgia were on terms of the warmest
friendship and regard. When Laýnez in 1562 obtained royal exemption from three serious demands—the estopping of the visitation by Father Nadal, the prohibition against sending Spanish
Jesuits to other European nations, and the restriction against the
exporting of monies collected in Spain for the support of the
Gregorian University—his first argument was the respect Philip
II had for Borgia and Loyola and the worth of the work done by
their fellow religious.[9] As a new order they could more easily
make their own terms with authorities in Spain, and this will be
found true also in the Indies.

---

[8] Antonio Astráin, *Historia de la Compañía de Jesús en la Asistencia de España*
  (Madrid, 1928), III, 68-73.
[9] See in regard to this episode the letter of Laýnez to Philip II, in *ibid.*, II, 617-19.

This policy of separating Spanish members of the orders from their universal organization was but one of the many vexations caused them by the system of the Patronato. Though for the most part the officials tried to show appreciation for their services, yet they labored under heavy disabilities—and that despite the continual pleading of the religious with their European fellows to cross over and join them in the great missionary adventure. Patron, vice patrons, and the members of the Council of the Indies, civilians for the most part, found it difficult to understand why the Patronato in its ultranationalism and laicism failed to meet the needs of the religious.

In the *Recopilación* some ninety-seven statutes dealt directly with the orders and another thirty-four regulated them in the *doctrinas* for the Indians and the missions.[10] Philip III in 1608 was the author of Libro I, título 15, ley 13, which provided that "the viceroys and *presidentes* may for just causes remove one order from its *doctrinas* and substitute another." This would appear to be a reasonable deduction of interpretation under the patronal power. However, it was not a civil but an ecclesiastical act, and as such it took from the proper ecclesiastical authority his freedom to maintain his assigned position and to direct his subordinates, while at the same time it opened the way to arbitrary decisions against which he could do nothing but protest.

Ley 15 of the same title, made by Philip II in 1570, ruled that "when bishops ask for religious to man the *doctrinas*, the religious prelate will provide them, with no excuse or objection." This is a direct invasion of the rights of superiors, not to speak of their special privileges such as the *Omnimoda* of Adrian VI to be presented below; and no canonical statute could support it in court. Another intrusion by an alien command is

---

[10] See "De los religiosos" in *Recopilación*, Lib. I, tit. 14, leyes 1-97. Tit. 15 of the same book treats "De los religiosos doctrineros." A *doctrina* was technically a parish made up of Indians.

the law of Philip II in 1571, ley 19 in título 15. It orders the Franciscans on the missions to have at least three men reside with the *doctrinero* in a *vicaría*,[11] to save him from undue loneliness. While this rule imposed an extra burden of support on the order, its more serious intervention consisted in the very giving of the command rather than making an amicable effort to obtain consent from the order for a generally desirable arrangement.

Ley 20 of Libro I, título 15, enacted by Philip IV in 1634, insisted on the fullest recognition of the patronage in every act of the religious. Each religious superior on taking office had to swear, as did every bishop on his installation in his diocese, to uphold the Patronato at all times. Now, in this law the point is directly enforced:

It is our will that in the choosing and proposing of men for the *doctrinas* and curacies, the provincial and his chapter will nominate three men for each post, as is proper. Of these three our viceroy, *presidente*, or governor, who is the agent of our *Real Patronazgo*, will choose one.

It would be difficult to find an attack more direct than this on the constitutional right of appointment in an order chartered by the papacy. The superior, who has the duty to sustain his men, must appoint them, yet any effort to make the direct appointment would have met stout resistance from a Council of the Indies charged to see that no "prejudice" was done to the royal patronal rights.

Philip II in 1587 made the provision that became Libro I, título 15, ley 14: "The religious prelate is to furnish the means of sustenance for his *doctrineros* because they are mendicants." As such they had no right to the royal funds owed from a true presentation. Ley 23 explains correctly that one with a vow of

---

[11] A *vicaría* was technically the domicile of a vicar, here of a *doctrina*. A *doctrina* should be distinguished from a *misión* in that the latter was not a unit of a diocese but of the more primitive and introductory organization for converting the Indian.

poverty may not take title to an established diocesan "living." Philip II in 1593 put it into the *Recopilación* of the future as Libro I, título 15, ley 25 in this form: "Their stipend is free-will gifts." Nevertheless the administration had found a way around this principle quite early. In 1594 Viceroy Velasco of New Spain granted an annual subsidy of three hundred pesos to the missionary Gonzalo de Tapia in Sinaloa. From that year until 1608 the grant was two hundred and fifty pesos annually, and after 1608 three hundred pesos of silver to each man engaged on the missions. If in *doctrinas*, the priests received the salary common to *doctrineros*, but it was given entirely to the support of the actual workers and could be applied to no other purpose.[12]

This matter of royal support led to another extravagant judicial assumption on the part of the crown, wherein it clearly appropriated the churchly right of decision. The case presented itself to Francisco de Toledo, viceroy of Peru, as early as 1569, when he told the Jesuits to take over care of the Indian parishes or *doctrinas* as a regular policy. They demurred for two reasons: they were unwilling to be pinned down to town and village parishes, for they had come to work immediately in the missions, among the *infideles* or heathen; moreover, their rule forbade—and still forbids—them to accept a fixed stipend for any religious action that they might perform. Their provincial, Portillo, asked Toledo to wait until he could hear from Rome on the point. The viceroy, though a constant admirer of their order, nevertheless wrote about the situation to the king and told him that the Jesuits would be practically useless if they did not undertake work with the Indians in the established towns; otherwise they might as well go back to Europe.

---

[12] For these data see W. Eugene Shiels, *Gonzalo de Tapia* (New York, 1934), p. 134, and also Astráin, *Historia*, IV, 432. The crown actually provided a constant minimal supply for its workers.

The reply of Philip II was typical of a man under the illusion that he was a papal vicar. It is found in Libro I, título 15, ley 27:

Since doubt has arisen over whether it is permissible for religious of the Company to undertake work among the Indians in their *doctrinas*, and it appears clear from the bull of his holiness Pope Adrian [VI] that they are entitled to do as the other religious do, we order that they obey and comply.

Thus Philip II commanded in 1573. The king who had so sought the help of the order because of his professed regard for its work and who had offered them every means to continue their operations, now that he had them in his system decreed obedience to what his canonical conscience discovered in a papal bull. Naturally the case did not end there.[13]

To grasp more clearly the nature of the tension between Patronato law and the religious orders in the empire, it is necessary to state certain fundamental concepts that escaped the official view of the place properly occupied by the orders in the large body of the Spanish clergy. The concepts may be summarized in the remark of Pius V to Philip II's ambassador in Rome, Requesens. They were discussing the changes demanded in religious life by the decrees of the Council of Trent. The holy father said that he opposed placing the reform of the orders in the hands of bishops who were not themselves religious and who had had no experience in monastic affairs.[14] To a novice in the matter this opinion may appear trivial. But when one considers that the orders had performed the major work in expanding the American church, and that from time immemorial they constituted a unique though extensive section of the sacerdotal class, a judicious treatment of their place in that ecclesiastical sphere

---

13 This case is treated summarily in Astráin, *Historia*, II, 312-14 and more fully in III, 151-76, where its wider impact is carefully studied.

14 See the note on Requesens in Pastor, *History of the Popes*, XVII, 251. The statement was made on September 13, 1566.

was imperative. Without such treatment they would remain in the picture as an impersonal group of whirling atoms.

The judgment of Pius V could throw light upon many highly laudatory histories and biographies of particularly notable missionaries.[15] These heroes are personalities of unsurpassed quality; yet a religious knows that this is not half the story. From daily living he realizes a fact that is unnoticed by many onlookers: the greater part of his success is due far less to his individual powers than to the order of which he is a member. It is undoubtedly difficult for those who live no corporate life to comprehend this point, though it is elemental to one bound up in the large human organism of an order. Men of the world are accustomed to make their single ways up from the raw strife of youth through trial and failure to final victory and success, and they often say of themselves that they are self-made men. Their ambitions are their own, the creations of their individual souls. Help may come to them from scattered friends or interested builders of great projects, but in the last analysis they are alone in the quest that forms the ideal of their lives.

With a religious things are otherwise. Here too is a man, an individual, but he is something more. He is part of a corporation with a purpose larger than his own, with means that surpass his single powers, and with a bond of union that puts in close conjunction the abilities of many men. His outlook overreaches his own limitations. For him the first consideration is always the order, that moral being that holds him and his brothers as one, young and old, great and small, timid and bold, wise or callow, productive or only standing and waiting. He has the mind of a companion, and an *esprit de corps* as a private in a company that is linked in its component parts by unique regard, prayer,

---

[15] See, for example, Francis Parkman, *The Jesuits of North America in the Seventeenth Century* (Boston, 1867), a work that is often the only useful piece of baggage in the hands of such writers.

and a common governance. This last vital force of command and obedience runs up and down the whole gamut of the structure in that special authority which is communicated to his command by the holy father. One, then, who reads his story should look beyond the talents and moral qualities of the individuals to the cohesive and directive force implicit in all their activity. Each person must reach his own best development; but the planning, the initial movements, the regime, the constant assistance, the encouragement in success and the care in hardship, all flow from what he calls with sincere regard *his* order.

It is not remarkable that the popes should make of these bodies what are called exempt orders, that is to say, orders largely exempt from episcopal rule. They are meant to retain their own characteristic tools of work, the fields wherein these may be used, their daily order of life, their special manner of prayer, close union with their superiors, and complete dedication to the tasks assigned by the holy father. In a sense they are expendable; but by the pope, not by his subordinates. They do not have a local diocesan outlook; their first interest is in their own particular task which they are to fulfill in some restricted assignment that they can do well. They are in a way historical rather than contemporary, and their history best shows what they are.

Since the days of Basil and Benedict inspired leaders have come upon unique ideas of religious service and at the same time have known how to win followers and construct permanent societies of men and women who vow to pursue these ideas and ways of life. The popes, recognizing their contribution to the totality of Christianity, have given sovereign approval to their institutes and placed them in strategic positions where their special abilities and labors would contribute to the general purposes of the church. All of their right, accordingly, rests on the papal charter. On the other hand, they constantly turn for their protection to the holy father, just as they look on him with gratitude and defend him with all their energies. This immediate connection with Rome brings a universality to their outlook; they are world wide in membership as they are in interest. Nonetheless in their local situations they bend every effort for the local duty; and only such men can be called upon to enter the raw mission fields, where the qualities mentioned give them particular competence.

Thus it fell out that when Ferdinand and Isabella extended their patronage to the Indies, they singled out the orders to initiate the work. It became an immense field, and the record of the orders is clear to students of that field. They furnished not only the missionaries; for when the missions were ripe for conversion into dioceses, many men chosen to be bishops were members of the orders. And in the crucial point of replacement of personnel, they long had the only ready supply. Then, too, by the example of their lives they inspired many generous persons to give them monetary support. The story of Latin American church building exhibits many notable examples of this fact. They led the way in writing the many books that informed other missionaries and the general public of primitive conditions, languages, geography, natural resources, ethnography, and even paleontology and medicine. Knowledge of these things was necessary for their work, and it poured naturally from their efforts. And they had a seemingly inexhaustible train of younger men to take their places when they were worn out with labor. These facts must be kept in mind if one wishes to understand how mission fields could be manned for centuries rather than for years, how a self-sustaining body could preserve its material structure and its moral being and thus be ready for any call from the hierarchy.

Most of the hierarchy saw these things clearly. Some few who had missionary lands within their large dioceses found trouble and misunderstanding when dealing with the orders. Yet if a bishop's clergy were drawn from one order, it was the order and not he who provided the absolutely essential factor of success; that is, the maintenance of the force in the field. Their funds were not tithes nor endowed revenues but alms. In their personal problems they confided in their superior rather than in the bishop, and he alone could make a wise choice in the reassignment of duties and men. The superior too would be the natural spokesman in the choice of policies, though he presented them for episcopal inspection if they appeared to clash with ideas of the bishop. In point of the defense of his subjects, he had an ineluctable obligation to them and to his order that could not be transferred to any other person.[16] This final matter was the crux of the whole debate.

To men of the orders, because of their very difficult assignments, the pope for ages has given special privileges particularly fitted to the needs of the various orders. One of significance in this story is the famous *Omnimoda,* the bull granted to the Franciscans in 1522 by Adrian VI. Because of its pertinence to what follows it is here given in full translation. As may be seen in its conclusion, it was written by the pope in Spain. He was performing the duties of regent for the absent king and emperor, Charles V, when he was surprised by the news that the unanimous vote of the electoral college had chosen him to succeed Leo X on January 9, 1522. Before he sailed for Rome from Tarragona on August 4 he issued as pontiff-elect a number of important pronouncements, among them this response to the king,[17] whose captain Cortés had but lately petitioned the crown to obtain members of this order to aid in the spiritual conquest of the Aztecs.

----

[16] On this general subject some illuminating examples will be found in Carlos E. Castaneda, *Our Catholic Heritage in Texas* (Austin, 1936-1942), the best history of colonial Texas, and in *Bishop Tamaron's Visitation of New Mexico in 1760,* translated and edited by Eleanor B. Adams (Albuquerque, 1954).

[17] It is found in García Gutiérrez, *Bulario,* pp. 35-37. According to Morelli, *Fasti Novi Orbis,* p. 101, the *Omnimoda* was revoked by Gregory XIII.

[*Omnimoda*]

Adrian VI to Charles V

May 10, 1522

To our dear son in Christ, health and apostolic benediction.

You have shown us your ardent desire to increase the Christian religion and to convert the infidel, in particular those whom the Lord Christ has brought under your rule in the lands of the Indies. And now you send us your earnest prayer that we provide the means to obtain this increase and conversion and to extend a proper guidance to those souls that our Redeemer won by the offering of His precious blood. You ask that you have our authority to choose select men from the mendicant orders, especially from the Friars Minor of the Regular Observance, and to send them across to your Indies with the particular faculties that are mentioned in your recently proposed request.

The pastoral charge enjoins on us that we weigh above all else what concerns the salvation of souls. From our first years [in your service] we have known full well the very fervent zeal of your Caesarean majesty in augmenting the Christian commonwealth, and we commended this holy and laudable work in the Lord. It is our wish to grant your petition and to provide, as we do by these presents provide; namely, that members of all the mendicant orders and particularly of the Order of Friars Minor of the Regular Observance who are nominated by their superiors and are led by the Holy Spirit to offer themselves can and may freely and lawfully go out to the above-mentioned Indies, for the conversion of the natives and the upbuilding of their faith. Let these men be of such maturity in virtue and in doctrine as to satisfy your Caesarean majesty or your royal council, and be fitted for the enterprise. We lay this burden of judgment on the conscience of their superiors, who are to nominate and license them.

And now, that there be no lack of the merit of obedience in so holy a task for those who are in that manner nominated and who freely offer themselves, we prescribe for this merit of obedience that they conduct themselves in their journeys and labors as did the disciples of Christ our Lord, with the certain hope that, as they imitate them in the labor, so they will share with them in the reward. And from this moment we gladly give the friars our apostolic benediction.

But to prevent the number of Friars Minor from becoming so large as to cause confusion, we wish that your august majesty or your royal council fix and assign the number of those who are to be sent. After these religious are nominated and licensed by their superiors, we order strictly under pain of excommunication incurred *ipso facto* that no person in an inferior position dare in any way to impede them, even though these religious be at the time engaged in the hearing of confessions, preaching, teaching, or acting as guardian, custodian, minister, provincial, or commissary general. Despite the holding of any such office, they may and should go.

However, in order that the said friars may not want for a shepherd in those lands, we establish and provide that they choose from among their number two or three or more who will rule them, in the manner that to the group or its majority may seem proper. Those so elected, for a three-year period or more or less according to their Constitutions as their Spanish custom has it, are to have the prelacy for that term and no longer. All will remain constantly in obedience to their minister general and general chapter, so long as the latter enact nothing prejudicial to their journeying and the conversion of the infidel. Any decision whatsoever made against our express mandate and consent is to be of no effect. And because the lands of the Indies are so far from the usual residence or visitation of the minister general, and this will make difficult any referring to him of cases within his competence, we desire and by these presents grant that the prelates who *pro tempore* undertake the ruling of their brethren in the aforesaid Indies shall have complete authority and faculties over the friars under them in *utroque foro*, just as the minister general has these faculties. However, in this matter the minister general, under whose obedience they should remain, may limit and circumscribe this said authority as he sees it to be necessary.

Now, to ensure the greater success of conversion among the infidel and the salvation of all the souls living in the same Indies, we wish and by these presents do make a further grant. The aforesaid prelates of the friars, and others whom they choose as superiors while living in the Indies, in the localities where as yet no dioceses are created—or if they have been created, they or their vicars would be distant a two-days journey[18]—will have our own full power [*omnimodam auctoritatem nostram*][19] both toward their brethren and the others [clergy] of

---

[18] The *dieta* or day's journey was taken as twenty miles.
[19] The full power included far more than sacramental power and embraced much of what came under administrative law.

either class [regular or secular] delegated in that location for the
work [of conversion] and also over the Indians converted to the faith,
just as over their Christian companions working in the conversion.
This full power in both external and internal forums is conceded to
their prelates and to those friars delegated by them, when they judge
it opportune or expedient for the conversion of the said Indians and
for their guidance and progress, and over any others of the Catholic
faith under obedience to the holy Roman church. And this said power
extends to every act that a bishop may perform, except those demanding episcopal orders, until such time as the Holy See shall judge
otherwise.

Inasmuch as our predecessors have granted, as we know, several
indults to the friars whom in their day they allotted for service in the
said Indies, we confirm them in these indults, and in as far as there is
need we reaffirm them. It is our will that the said prelates of the friars
now in service there, and those to whom they wish to extend the faculties, shall have in general and in particular all the aforesaid indults
thus far conceded and in future to be conceded, so that in freedom and
justice they may possess and enjoy them. Let all these indults be taken
here as sufficiently expressed, and as though they were transferred word
by word from their originals. And this notwithstanding the apostolic
constitutions, particularly that of Sixtus IV beginning *Etsi Dominici
gregis* and the bull *In coena Domini,* and any other however contrary
to this grant. Given at Saragossa under the ring of the fisherman,
May 10, 1522.[20]

Of similar character yet more restrained was the grant made
to the Jesuits by Paul III on June 6, 1546.[21] They were per-

---

[20] Bernal Díaz del Castillo, in *Verdadera historia de los sucesos de la conquista de
la Nueva España* (México, 1904), printed many times in original and translation since its first appearance in Madrid in 1632, writes in Chapter 167:
"Adrian VI sent bulls to New Spain with many indulgences for the hospitals
and churches. He wrote a letter in support of Cortés and all of us conquerors
who were his companions. In it he encouraged us to take a great interest in the
holy conversion of the natives, not to kill or rob from them but to live with
them peacefully as far as possible. He enjoined on us to forbid and stop their
human sacrifices, sodomy, and other inhuman practices, . . . and he sent other
holy bulls to absolve us [from any penalties we had incurred]."
[21] *Monumenta historica Societatis Jesu: Epistolae et instructiones Sancti Ignatii*
(Madrid, 1903-1911), I, 397. This grant was unusual in that its powers could

mitted: (1) the recitation of the canonical hours according to the form of the new Breviary; (2) the faculty of preaching the word of God everywhere, with no license required from anyone to do so; (3) the power of hearing confessions of any one of the faithful of either sex; (4) the faculty of absolving from all reserved cases in the forum of conscience; (5) the power of commuting vows reserved to the Apostolic See, except those reserved in the bull *In coena Domini;* (6) the right to administer the Eucharist and the other sacraments not requiring episcopal consecration, so long as this did not go contrary to the right of others, and no license of another person was necessary for this; (7) the faculty to celebrate Mass and administer the Eucharist after noon if one were occupied before noon either in hearing confessions or in other pious works.

These faculties were communicated to the father general, to be delegated by him to those for whom he judged it proper. The privilege to preach and hear confessions anywhere was granted until the Holy See should judge otherwise.

Mention has been made of these unusual grants to clarify the idea of a religious order, its universality, its exemptions, and its identity as a specific group destined to go at the call of the papacy wherever it was needed. There is no particular necessity to point out a possible result of opposition to the orders deriving from these privileges. That could happen wherever there was little of understanding of the nature of an order. The grants throw light on the meaning of the Patronato laws regarding the pontifical briefs or bulls. The Patronato wanted a uniformity everywhere for easy administration. In the situation such uniformity could not prevail, and contradiction was to be expected if one were to be true to his membership in an order. Back of

---

be delegated to diocesan priests. A form used for this delegation is found in *ibid.,* I, 398-99, as of June 5, 1546, and limited at first to twenty priests at a time.

all this there is the question of priestly vocation and its variety, a discussion that in this volume would have no useful place. It is due to Philip II to note that he authorized departure from normal practice when he saw it was called for. In 1572 he modified the supervisory powers of the vice patron in regard to local movements of the Jesuits. Earlier he had demanded that they receive permission for any change of residence. Now he wrote:

To our viceroys, presidents, and auditors of our royal courts of our Indies, islands and mainland of the Ocean Sea, and our governors and justices therein, to whom this our royal order shall be shown: . . . We command you all and singly that when henceforth anyone of the said religious of the Company who has gone thither from these kingdoms with permission shall wish to pass from one college to another, or from one province to another, after getting due authorization from his superiors, you shall permit and consent to it without demur, and you shall give and cause to be given all possible aid and assistance for his journey to his mission.[22]

Such was the law. But a historical study based merely on law has its difficulties. In time some statutes, though preserved in successive issues of the *Recopilación,* fell out of usage.[23] More common in history is failure to execute the law, and on this point the early Franciscans in the Indies had much to suffer. Their first years of work in New Spain, and to a lesser extent in Peru and other lands, brought such remarkable conversions and received so general an approval from public opinion and official report that the *padres* were unprepared—as was the ordinary public—for what the second twenty years would bring. Down to the end of the 1530's they consolidated initial victories gained shortly after the conquest. Soon after that an altogether new

---

[22] Quoted from Michael Kenny, *Romance of the Floridas* (Milwaukee, 1934), p. 260. The same point is treated in J. Fred Rippy and Jean Thomas Nelson, *Crusaders of the Jungle* (Chapel Hill, 1936), p. 24.

[23] Compare the case cited in note 7, p. 173 above with the penalties laid down by Philip II on pp. 193-94.

phase of Spanish experience was thrust upon the entire immi-
grant group.

The first inklings of conflict appeared in a letter sent to
Charles V by the earliest synod of bishops held in Mexico in
1537.[24] This letter dealt with affairs in New Spain. Icazbalceta
wonders why it was signed by Zumárraga, who knew how erro-
neous were its strictures on the religious, and he concludes that
the bishop condescended to approve the right of his colleagues
to speak their minds rather than obstruct them at this time when
the hierarchy was in its infant stages. The writer, or writers, of
the hostile lines declared that the order men publicly spoke
ill of the bishops, depreciated their office, threatened their appointed visitors, deceived the Indians as to episcopal motives
and accomplishments, and counseled the Indians not to admit
them into the pueblos. Although the passage began with the statement that this was to be a eulogy of the religious, it ended by
asserting that, as the *padres* had fought the first *audiencia,* so
now they were in competition with the bishops. There was no
good word for the many fine Franciscans who had done such
notable work in that region. The hand that concocted this mischief is not identifiable, but the hurt done to its victims when the
word got out was deep. The chief point of attack lay in the exemption of the order; the letter called for a removal of this
privilege, although it asked that no harm be done to the order
or any of its members. It goes without saying that what irri-
tated this episcopal hand was the *Omnimoda,*[25] but above that
was a callow ignorance of what the religious had accomplished,
not to speak of an uninformed dislike for the very concept of
their way of life.

---

[24] On this letter see Icazbalceta, *Zumárraga,* pp. 149-54. It is found in the appendix
to the biography as item 21.

[25] On the vicissitudes of the *Omnimoda* and its ultimate disappearance under the
Patronato regime see the thoughtful article of Robert Charles Padden, "The
Ordenanza del Patronazgo, 1574," *The Americas,* XII (April 1956), 333-54.

But a far greater trial awaited the *padres*. By 1540 the Aztec confederacy was firmly settled in Christianity, though continuous contact with much of the native populace demanded that the religious go to them in their mountain homes and sparse settlements in the rough northern section of the province. Despite official demand that they be moved away from their farms and homes into newly created pueblos near the monasteries, and the consequent ill-feeling among this poor people, in general the relations between Spaniards and Indians were smooth. The influence of the great Zumárraga increased this harmony. From abroad immigration increased. Agriculture, industry, and trade began in earnest.

Then suddenly a sense of satisfaction with past victories was swept away in an unforeseen development. Great explorations to the north brought back much geographical knowledge and tales of hidden riches, of many unknown peoples, and even of golden cities. Soon frontier governors began to issue patents to prospect for precious metals. Down in Bolivia an Indian herder had in 1545 found the fabulous deposits of Potosí. Now in the next year the remarkable strike at Zacatecas some 440 miles northwest of Mexico opened the way for gold and silver hunters. At once the rush was on, but this time the Spaniards on the border of New Spain found more than their match. Natives whose lands were invaded on this sector put up stout and tenacious resistance. These were the Chichimeca, the Spanish expression for uncivilized Indians, and for forty years their fighting so taxed the civil and military powers of the newcomers that the viceroy warned Philip II of imminent danger to the whole province.[26] They might all have to leave the country unless he provided some defense better than guns and swords and horses, for the Chichi-

---

[26] Philip Wayne Powell, *Soldiers, Indians, and Silver: The Northward Advance of New Spain, 1550-1600* (Berkeley, 1952), has a first-rate study of this Chichimeca war and its social results.

meca captured all three and used them better than their invading enemy. That new defensive policy, the use of missions, would come in 1573.

For the moment the feverish search for gold and silver, and the concomitant disregard for the rights of Indians who stood in their way, seemed to contaminate this venturesome element; and the results were harmful for the *padres*. This had a special impact on the *doctrineros*, those in direct contact with the converts and catechumens who because of their inferior position were forced to play their menial part in the exploitation of the mines. The religious now found the Indians had suddenly become distrustful. The Spaniards thwarted the friars as they tried to protect the native. When they continued to carry on their functions as they had done from the beginning, officials complained about their exempt position and their use of the *Omnimoda*. The very Spaniards who should have seen in the success of the friars their own best insurance for retaining possession of the Indies and building a sound empire, attacked their reputations and belittled their work. *Encomenderos*, men influential in higher circles, were particularly critical of the religious. The result of this turn of events was a disheartened group who, though they performed a large part of the ministry, found themselves to some extent checked on every side. That the king himself espoused these views appears in a *cédula* of 1557, in which he warns the prelates of New Spain to guard against religious "novelties"; the orders of St. Dominic, St. Francis, and St. Augustine must be watched carefully in the matter of marriages that they allow the Indians, and the use of the *Omnimoda* must be brought under sharper control.[27]

---

[27] See Vasco de Puga, *Provisiones, cédulas, instrucciones de su magestad: ordenanzas de oiditores y audiencia, para la buena expedición de los negocios, y administración de justicia: y governación desta Nueva España: para el bueno tratamiento y observación de los Indios, dende el año 1525 hasta este presente de '63* (México, 1563), p. 194.

In 1562 Fray Jerónimo de Mendieta wrote to his commissary general in Mexico, Fray Francisco de Bustamante, a brilliantly pessimistic view of the whole Franciscan situation. The *audiencia*, he said, was hunting gold; its agents rob and burn; the king's men forget their triple duty to honor God, save their souls and those of others, and assist the royal conscience. The friars have sought these ends, but his majesty is badly served in his officials. He continues:

But now if our service is no longer acceptable, and they do not wish us to work with evangelical liberty and authority, for they impugn our work with charges that we seek only our own interests and power and possessions; then his majesty can discharge his royal conscience through other pastors and chaplains who may be more faithful to him than we are. And we can get licenses to go back to Spain. For we do not have to administer the holy sacraments with opprobrium and ridicule on the priestly office and the doctrine of Jesus Christ. For among these people, such as they are, the friars receive no more credit and respect than the populace has for the officials. There is no reason why we must be willing witnesses of the destruction of this harvest that has cost us so much labor and sweat, while the devil laughs in our faces and sees himself winning more from this war between ourselves than he got in his peaceful dominion over the Indian republic.[28]

A joint letter of the higher Franciscan superiors of New Spain went to Philip II in 1567. They told him how his subordinates with their diversity of policy and predatory tactics upset the whole government of the province. Philip's reply amounts to a rebuke: he thanks them for their writing, asks them to tell him whatever they think needs attention, and answers none of their requests or complaints.[29]

At the very time, however, Madrid came under heavier fire. Fray Pedro de Azuaga, O.F.M., sent a memorandum to the Council on the "evils that are destroying the Indies, for lack of

---

[28] Icazbalceta, *Nueva colección*, I, 4. The report is found on pp. 1-34.
[29] *Ibid.*, I, 53.

proper treatment of the natives and of their instruction in the faith."[30] And Fray Alonso Maldonado of the same order brought the controversy to a head by going as the official spokesman of his fellows in New Spain to present their views to the king and to the holy father. To Philip II he sent word that many Franciscans were begging to be sent back to Spain, for they were unable to preach or hear confessions because of the turmoil in the Indies. The officials were destroying their reputation as they were abusing the Indians, and deceived the king as to the true state of affairs back of such a move as the conspiracy of Martín Cortés and his fellow *encomenderos* who wanted to be free of Spain. Moreover the friars could not get any more recruits from Spain, so bad was the name of the Indies. The pope had to give some of them special indulgences to get them to volunteer for the missionary work. Unless things were changed, all the friars would abandon the Indies.[31]

These words of Maldonado echoed letters sent to Madrid and Rome by prelates and public-minded citizens from many parts of the Indies, and they gave rise to the meetings of 1568. Thence arose the one supreme challenge to the Patronato Real. In Madrid the king and the Council of the Indies realized the danger and summoned civil and religious leaders to a long conference on how to adopt ways and means to cure the upset conditions across the sea. This *junta* in turn found that Rome was now determined to give the church in that area a thorough investigation. Pius V set up a special commission of cardinals—Amulio, Caraffa, Cervini, and Sirleto—to hear the complaints of the American spokesmen and to draft a plan for remedying the ecclesiastical troubles. Meanwhile the pope sent vigorous instructions to his ambassador in Madrid to make sure that the king understood the gravity of the situation and held himself

---

[30] See in Pacheco y Cárdenas, *Colección de documentos inéditos*, I 11, 170-78.
[31] Sor Mónica, *La gran controversia del XVI siglo* (Madrid, 1952), pp. 174 ff.

ready to accept the decision of the papacy on its solution. In order to have good liaison between the two courts, Pius V asked St. Francis Borgia to join his commission. The saint begged off from so onerous a duty, for he was both general of the Jesuits and on excellent terms with the king. He did, however, offer a point of view that was ultimately accepted. The commission advised the holy father to appoint a nuncio in the Indies, who would report directly to him and from him carry orders to the overseas hierarchy. Borgia urged instead that he attempt to work things out with the bishops on the spot, as the only feasible way to accomplish the results desired in Rome. To help these bishops Borgia recommended sending members of religious orders who had had the experience of similar difficulties in the missions of the East.[32]

The same problems were threshed out in both capitals. There was the sphere of the *encomenderos*, offering a threat to break from Spain if the crown would not grant longer tenure than one generation, and generally hostile to the *doctrineros*. Some bishops demanded that the religious be reduced to a strictly diocesan condition. Others called upon the holy father for the institution of one or more personal representatives who could act in reserved cases and give sentence in matters of trial without waiting for months and years to get a reply through the slow transit of

---

[32] *Ibid.*, pp. 154, 169-72, 173-78. Borgia recommended that no reversal of the role of the crown be attempted: it would run counter to the whole trend of rule in the Indies and upset many usages that had become traditional; it would cause utmost confusion in titles, in authority, and in Indian allegiance; it would be asking a superhuman sacrifice of the royal will after seventy-five years of laborious effort to carry out the mandate of Alexander VI; it would involve the creation of a wholly new institutional setup in the church; better to trust the existing mechanism when it is shored up by papal advice and direction in its most sensitive and power-laden areas. Pacheco y Cárdenas, *Colección de documentos inéditos*, I 11, 154-62, has an instruction from Philip II to Ambassador Zúñiga at Rome in 1572, asking for a full patriarchate of the Indies, increase of faculties for the prelates there, and concession of the right to establish commissaries for the orders.

the mails. The miserable plight of the natives in Peru and New Spain worried the civil power of Spain and the religious mind of the papacy. In 1568 a proposal for the establishment of a Congregation of Propaganda, which would assign and direct all missions in the entire world from its Roman center, plagued the royal patron and caused concern in Rome itself, where again Borgia became a pivotal adviser.[33] And to the north Elizabeth of England claimed the interest of both parties.

Philip II maintained an open mind and a slow hand throughout the investigation. On most points he was ready for reform. In 1573 he would give distinct orders that henceforth soldiers should have no part in frontier expansion, that the missionary should take his place, and that in dealing with the Indian only measures of peace and justice should be tolerated. His instructions to his new viceroy of Peru, Francisco de Toledo, gave special emphasis to this manner of dealing with the native. On sending missionaries he departed from the long-time rule that only three orders might exist in the Indies, and he opened the way for several new contingents of religious to enter those broad lands. As to the creation of a nuncio, he would have none of it unless that officer resided in Madrid.

The holy father heard his commission in several meetings. One of his men, whose name is unknown, suggested that he tell Philip II that as the patronage had been granted by the pope, so it could be retracted if there were a demonstrated need of such a move. From other angles previously discussed in these pages, it is clear that Pius V took a strong position on protecting the liberty of the church. However, after long consideration he decided that no good could come from the precipitate quashing of the Patronato. Instead he sent to the king through his ambassador a letter that, while it commended his majesty, nevertheless

---

[33] On the Congregation of Propaganda proposal and its result, see Shiels, *Tapia*, pp. 17-18.

made pointed criticism of his subordinates and encouraged the royal conscience to a line of conduct that would bring blessing both on the royal estate and the religious life of his subjects in the new world. The pope's letter offers a convenient summary of the present discussion. It is in the form of an instruction of his secretary of state, Alexandrini, to Castagna, his representative in Madrid. Together with the instruction the pope sent a brief message directly to Philip II. It is dated August 17, 1568,[34] and its pertinent lines read as follows:

Our predecessors conceded that that part of the earth [the Indies] should be subject to you and your successor princes. You, Philip, deserve rather praise than exhortation, for as a Catholic prince you have striven hard for the propagation of the faith. It was for that reason that your crown was given the charge to see that the subjects would be well governed, given a good example, and receive from your hand a constant outpouring of charity and prudence. We beg you to command and order your governors there to use their abilities and proceed with greater zeal in spreading the faith, so that under their regime the natives never feel oppression or grief.

The instruction, to be delivered personally by Castagna to Philip II, runs thus:

It is your task, most reverend nuncio, to explain to his majesty with great tact, that in these matters dealing with necessary changes in the conquest of the Indies, the ideas dominant in the mind of the holy father proceed from no thought other than his zeal and concern for his pastoral mission and the spiritual help of those races. With his zeal there is united a holy affection becoming the loving and kindly father of all. He cherishes a burning desire for the progress of the Christian religion in all parts of the world, most of all in those regions where the planting of the Catholic faith has already been begun. It would ill become him merely to look on while the hearts of those people grow lukewarm, as does a new plant that lacks tending. On the contrary, he

---

[34] This letter of Pius V to Philip II is found in Sor Mónica, *Gran controversia*, p. 180. The instruction follows on pp. 181-86. Both were drawn from the Vatican archives by that omnivorous investigator.

must lead it on with all care and effort to its ultimate perfection, teaching the people to observe all that the Lord commanded.

Moreover, so that all those races, and those others who already walk the road of truth, may come to the knowledge of God, whose infinite mercy exceeds even the hopes of his majesty (as is clear), it is proper for the service of God and likewise for the concern of his majesty toward those races who trust in him and thus help satisfy the royal conscience, that his majesty offer them every reason for being thankful to the blessed God that they find themselves under his protection and care. All this, most reverend nuncio, you should express in such a manner that his majesty, in his orders to the officials through whom he has to act in these affairs, must harbor no least doubt that in the reforms to which I allude, the holy father speaks with the deepest sincerity and solely for the greater honor of God. Certainly our holy father has this purity of intention, and he has dedicated his life to promoting the welfare of this enterprise. On his part he expects that his majesty will further the reform of the officials mentioned with the same pure intention and in no other sentiment.

After explaining the mind and aims of our holy father as to this great task, you may also make clear to his majesty that the choice of persons recently sent to Peru, New Spain, and Florida has been well received here. His holiness hopes, moreover, that as a consequence of the good reports about them they now find themselves in the best frame of mind and will to comply faithfully and diligently with the orders given for religious work in the name of the glorious memory of Charles V and of his majesty, orders that up to this time have not been fulfilled by the officials in spite of the good will of him who sent them. From now on there should come a more fruitful result in what is so generally desired, the glory of God and the service of those provinces.

One of the chief things to keep in mind is that we are dealing directly with the conversion of the infidel, for that is the purpose for which the Catholic kings of Spain were authorized to conquer those lands. It is imperative that they at once prepare and send priests and teachers able to preach the gospel and give instructions in the holy faith. These should be men of zeal for the good of souls, who are ready to offer shining evidence of our Christian religion as much by their lives as by their doctrine. To maintain and sustain these priests and teachers in becoming and reasonable manner, the officials who have charge of those provinces should provide the necessary support, taking from the current revenues what is indispensable for this purpose and making sure that through no default of proper and due support there be a lack of the clerics needed for this work. It is essential to see that no lay persons who are scarcely able to explain the Sunday services should have charge over these matters.

Care should also be taken in regard to admitting catechumens to holy baptism. They should be well disposed for its reception and taught about the holy sacrament. Those already baptized, particularly the younger people, should be instructed in religion and in what has to do with political life and Christian conduct, and their teachers should not break down by example what they command by their word. To facilitate these instructions the officials should choose places convenient both to the neophytes and to the teachers who are occupied in this conversion and education, so that those who live far away do not have the extra burden of making long journeys to meet their disciples. In the same vein, when the Indians do not live in one community but are scattered through the distant mountains, it might be better to bring them together in one place if that can be done without injustice, and those unwilling to move may receive some punishment, though it should be done gently in keeping with the spirit of these new foundations. When pagans and Christians live together, the former are not to be allowed to have places for practicing their idolatry. It is better to destroy such places so that the baptized will not suffer relapse. Pagans may not be permitted to keep the Christians from grasping and holding to our religion.

In those localities where the old Christians and the new live together, precautions are to be taken that the old give a good example to the new and not come to be the reason for these to blaspheme the name of God. The behavior of the old should be such that the neophytes, looking on their elders, are confirmed in their faith and try to copy their way of life. The pagans, too, when they compare their evil habits, will feel confusion and be drawn to embrace the faith of Christ. If old Christians lead bad lives, they should be chastised in public and not allowed the repeated tolerance of their misdeeds, to the harm and scandal of the young and the gentiles. In summary, the new and the old should dwell together in peace and the fear of God. Everything should be shunned that might induce a slackening of virtuous living and cause disturbances and excesses that abet the vices and grave evils common among those peoples. But if accustomed to sobriety and self-control, they will withstand the temptations connected with presence at pagan meetings and carousals. It will deserve all praise if the officials oblige the pagans in these groups to keep the laws of marriage and stop the custom of each woman having several husbands.

His holiness feels sure that those officials, following the orders of his majesty and their own sense of responsibility, will be instant in the administration of justice. Nevertheless, it is in point to urge special watchfulness so that no one, neither individuals nor the officials nor the converts, make use of Indians as slaves, in their homes or on the land, but that they be treated in the assignment of work and employed only as servants who accept the work of their own choice. They must be paid the wage agreed at the time of hiring, and a becoming wage, as the apostle teaches in his letter to Philemon. Nor should they be subjected to capricious or damaging taxes. Justice should be shown them impartially, between each other and in their relations with the *patrones*, and in such a way that if on occasion these weaker ones are oppressed by their masters or other persons, they may with confidence come before a just court and feel satisfied that their verdict is as fair as what is given to the old Christians.

On another matter, if his holiness understands correctly, among the chief ordinances of his majesty there is this injunction, that both the religious among these people who preach the gospel and those other persons sent to convert them and keep them in the faith are to be well received by all the officials and revered by them and the others living in each pueblo. They must be held in honor especially by all military officers and soldiers. Let these latter remember to be exact in this matter, for it is necessary if the priests and catechists are to enjoy authority and work for the honor of God.

Let all officials keep before their minds, and we understand that this is emphatically imposed on them by order of your majesty, that the Christians in those parts who are not clerics, whatever be their station, must keep to a truly Christian life as is due to our holy religion. It is of the first importance that, while they carry out their duties and work to save their souls, they assist the converts and to the best of their power draw on the pagan to conversion, according to the word of the prince of the apostles: "I exhort you as strangers and pilgrims to abstain from carnal desires which war against the soul. Behave yourselves honorably among the pagans; that, whereas they slander you as evildoers, they may, through observing you, by reason of your good works glorify God in the day of visitation." Hence their lives must be upright, to prevent the Christians from growing indifferent or going back to their old ways, and the pagans from holding to their old errors, in the face of such evils as adultery, concubinage, and the excessive and covetous pursuit of the conquest of treasure. To do away with these evils (which his holiness beholds with much concern), we rely confidently on the authentic Christian piety of his majesty and on his selection, as a strong and salutary remedy, of persons of integrity who will be in charge of the justices, and of the other functionaries and secular officials of those regions; and that after he has reviewed the merits and demerits of each, his majesty will reward the good and correct the bad, with punishment for those whom he finds guilty in those points. And he will not fail to condemn the oppression of the poor, "lest from their cries God rise up [in vengeance]," for that would cause great harm to the Christian religion in those lands.

Observe the greatest care in taking up arms against those gentiles, and do not declare war unless the situation fulfills those conditions needed for it to be held just. Let there be no cruelty, as the Gospel exhorts. Surely his holiness feels satisfied with the way the case was met in Florida, and he desires that similar conduct be applied in other places.

It should be recognized in those lands that a line of behavior contrary to what is here indicated has provoked great harm to the honor of God and His holy religion, and to the general good of the people and their progress, and, without a doubt, to his majesty also, injuring his conscience and his good name. The careful observance of these points will serve in future to undo the harm of the past, and with the help of God it will bring good results.

Finally his holiness never ceases to offer to his majesty all spiritual helps and the aids necessary for the honor of God and the salvation of these people.

Thus terminated the famous challenge to the Patronato. Philip II made serious efforts to assist the Franciscans and the other orders, and his new mission policy of 1573 completely rid the frontier of the dangers of border war as it opened the way for refreshingly successful conversion by the missionaries. The entire case, however, illustrates one of the great tensions built into the patronage by the chief patron.

CHAPTER XIV

The Patronato Real Universal

In 1753 Ferdinand VI obtained from Benedict XIV the long-sought patronage over the Spanish mainland. Ever since the famous bulls of Innocent VIII and Julius II the kings had been royal patrons of Granada and of the Indies. Now they held universal patronage throughout the empire.

Royal patronage was originally conferred in view of crusade and conversion. Both *Orthodoxe fidei propagationem* and *Universalis ecclesiae regimini* presented definitely religious obligations, restricted to lands to be brought into the church. The kings repeatedly asked for the same power in the homeland, but no cogent reason could be found for the grant until the fateful 1750's brought threat to the whole front of the church. At this point a combination of forces urged the pope to make a concession as much misunderstood as it was significant of serious change in the European theater. No external danger moved the scholarly and amiable pontiff. Now, in the words of Pastor, he had to "steer the bark of Peter between the Scylla of state absolutism and the Charybdis of 'enlightenment' and rationalism."[1] In Spain, as he wrote confidentially to his friend Cardinal Ten-

---

[1] Pastor, *History of the Popes*, XXXV, 47. The remarks on the concordat rely much on the treatment given the subject by the same author, *ibid.*, XXXV, 57-75, an excellent summary of the making and the meaning of the treaty.

cin, he had seen the flashing of the sword over his head.[2] To avoid losing everything and save what could be saved he concluded the famous concordat. In France the contesting and perversion of papal decisions by the Jansenists led many people to doubt if there were any truth at all. In that atmosphere the deists preached contentment with the simple truths of natural religion, and with much success, abetted of course by the "republicans" of the Paris Parlement[3] who used the religious issue to open the great attack on the crown. Meanwhile the encyclopedists began their campaign, *écrasez l'infame*. Facing this picture, the holy father worked untiringly for peace with the Catholic governments. Such was the background for the concordat of 1753. Ferdinand himself acted in the negotiations with a sharp eye for finance, and undoubtedly with a royal sense of pride in rounding out his universal patronage. Yet the concessions of Rome, and they were most unusual, cannot be explained without taking account of what went on in the political circles of Lisbon, Paris, and Madrid and in the intellectual offensive of Diderot, d'Alembert, Rousseau, and Voltaire.

In its immediate effects this remarkable convention opened to the Spanish crown a rich new field for enlarging its power and its revenues. The Spanish hierarchy had long been closely entwined in the Patronato system. They would now be far more intimately united to the royal will, and yet the crown took on no new obligations toward the church but gained much in the transfer of monetary arrangements. The future was dubious.

For Rome the concordat with all its surrenders still brought to an end a burdensome set of financial transactions and replaced a multitude of petty revenues with one large monetary

---

[2] *Ibid.*, XXXV, 69.

[3] For this early use of the word "republicans" see *ibid.*, XXXV, 249. Pastor has an exceptionally fine treatment of the Jansenist and Parlement attack on the crown heralding the Revolution. This is found in XXXV, 239-87 and XXXVI, 376-415.

sum. The immediate loss was heavy, but the long-term gain in esteem and regard might well be argued as a worthwhile change. And in the purely religious sphere it drew the poison for the time from one large threat of Spanish separatism. This last purpose moved the pope strongly. In the curia his act met much disfavor, yet he held to his point of view in profound conviction that the treaty was a necessity. Men still debate his wisdom in this action, but not his integrity.

As the document attests, his holiness cut through the meshes of long diplomatic wrangling and chose a quick and sure way of reaching the agreement that was so imperative. He found Ferdinand willing to entrust Figueroa, auditor for Castile on the Rota, with power to conduct secret negotiations with the pope. His own secretary of state, Cardinal Valenti, enjoyed his complete confidence. For two and a half years they worked at the monumental problems until on January 11, 1753 the two signed the concordat as plenipotentiaries. On January 31 the king ratified it, and the pope followed on February 20.

The treaty was written and signed in both Italian and Spanish, with a brief introduction and conclusion in Latin. The translation is here made from the Spanish. Ribadeneyra printed the entire document.[4] Hernáez and Mercati omitted the Latin sections.[5] Ribadeneyra added to the concordat its two subsequent explanatory bulls, the *confirmatoria* of June 9, 1753, and the *finalis* of the following September 10.[6] These are simply restatements, and they changed nothing. As will be seen, the concordat and the transfer of capital funds sealed the transaction. More-

---

[4] Ribadeneyra, *Manual compendio*, pp. 318-43.
[5] Hernáez prints the concordat alone, in *Colección*, II, 642-47. The best text for the concordat is in G. Mercati, *Raccolta de concordati in materia ecclesiastiche tra la Santa Sede e la autoritá civili* (Roma, 1919), pp. 422-37, both in Italian and in Spanish, with a good introductory note.
[6] In his transcription Ribadeneyra has a number of lesser errors. The two supplementary bulls are added immediately after the treaty.

over, it contains all the statistical data and the actual reasoning underlying the contract.[7] It follows at once.

[Concordat of 1753]

Benedict XIV, pope, for a perpetual remembrance.

Some time back, that is, on January 11 just passed, certain proposals and discussions still awaiting settlement at the beginning of the month and touching particularly on ecclesiastical discipline, royal patronage, and other matters wanting proper completion and agreement in the treaty that had been approved, established, and confirmed between this Apostolic See and Philip V, who during his life was Catholic king of the Spains, were brought to conclusion and subscribed by our dear son Silvius Valenti, cardinal priest of the holy Roman church and plenipotentiary of ourselves and this see, and our equally beloved son Master Manuel Ventura Figueroa, our chaplain and auditor of petitions at the apostolic palace, plenipotentiary for our most dear son in Christ Ferdinand, Catholic king of the same Spains. The treaty contained eight articles and its tenor is as follows:

1. As his holiness, our most holy father Pope Benedict XIV, happily reigning, is always anxious to maintain the most sincere and cordial relations between the Holy See and the nations, princes, and Catholic kings, he has let no opportunity pass to show the most substantial and definite proofs of this ready good will toward the renowned, devoted, and pious Spanish people and toward their monarchs, who are by title and constant religious practice the Catholic kings, ever attached to the Apostolic See and to the vicar of Christ on this earth.

2. In the first years of his pontificate his holiness observed that the concordat, concluded on October 18, 1737 between Pope Clement XII of happy memory and the glorious King Philip V, contained an agreement to the effect that the pope and the king should appoint deputies charged to review in friendly spirit the reasoning of one and the other party, with reference to the old controversy over universal royal patronage that had been claimed on the one side but whose establishment remained undecided. With that in view he took care to approach the two cardinals, Belluga and Acquaviva, now deceased, so that they might obtain from the court of Spain the naming of persons with whom he

---

[7] Mercati's Spanish text was used for this translation. For the original Spanish see pp. 357-69.

could treat in this nettling question, and he gave the two cardinals his personal memorandum to facilitate their study and to keep before their minds the intentions and the rights of the Holy See.

3. However, he soon recognized that in actual practice this was not the way to reach the desired goal and that letters and replies took them far away from ending the dispute and rather multiplied and stirred a controversy that he had thought settled. This went so far that he began to fear an unhappy rupture, disastrous and fatal to one or the other side. At that point, as he felt sure of the truly religious spirit of King Ferdinand VI, happily reigning, and of his equable and just attitude in wishing to remove the differences that were constantly recurring, and also of his generous understanding of the wishes of his holiness, the holy father thought it unwise to pass over so favorable an opportunity for reaching the agreement set forth in the following chapters. These they afterward reduced to final form and signed through the procurators and plenipotentiaries of both sides in the same manner as similar conventions are normally reached.

4. His majesty King Ferdinand VI explained to his holiness, our holy father, the necessity for reformation of certain arrangements in the discipline of the secular and regular clergy of the Spains. For this his holiness agreed to provide the necessary powers in specific chapters. These he would prepare in accord with the sacred canons, the apostolic constitutions, and the decrees of the holy Council of Trent. His holiness desired earnestly to complete this work during the time of his pontificate. Despite the press of other affairs and his own advancing age that was now great, he promised to take personal responsibility for the quick dispatch of those many fatiguing problems in the minor points of the question that had multiplied through the years of his predecessors while they were discussing the bull *Apostolici ministerii*,[8] the founding of the University of Cervera, the establishment of the famous College of San Ildefonso, and the other relevant matters brought up by the kings of the Spains.

5. No objection was made against the kings of the Spains having the royal patronage throughout the *reinos* of the Spains, or the right to nominate for the archbishoprics, bishoprics, monasteries, and consistorial benefices vouched for in writing and recorded in the books of

---

[8] *Apostolici ministerii*, regulating church discipline in Spain, was sent to Philip V by Innocent XIII on May 23, 1724. See *Catholic Encyclopedia*, I, 647.

the *Cámara*. For the right was argued from bulls, apostolic privileges, and other adduced titles. Nor did their discussion touch on nomination by the Catholic kings for the archbishoprics, bishoprics, and benefices vacant in Granada and in the Indies and for certain other particular benefices. His holiness declared that the royal crown should retain in peaceful possession this nomination in the event of vacancies as it had done hitherto, and each side agreed that those nominated for the archbishoprics, bishoprics, monasteries, and consistorial benefices should in future continue the expediting of the respective bulls in Rome, in the same manner and form as hitherto practiced, with no innovation.

6. Since there was serious disagreement over the nomination of simple residential benefices by the kings of the Spains, excepting as said those of the *reinos* of Granada and the Indies, and as the Catholic kings urged the propriety and right of this nominating by virtue of the universal patronage, while the Holy See did not fail to expose the reasons that to its mind demanded freedom for these benefices and their collation in the apostolic months,[9] and for the cases of their reservations, and the same see likewise presented the need for free nomination of the ordinaries in those months, after long opposition there at last emerged common consent in the following tenor.

7. The holiness of our blessed father Pope Benedict XIV reserves to his private free collation and that of his successors forever in the Apostolic See fifty-two benefices (whose titles are named below), for which his holiness and his successors hold the right of freedom to provide, thus to reward those Spanish ecclesiastics who deserve special recognition for their probity, good reputation, unusual talent, and services toward the Holy See. And the collation of these fifty-two benefices will belong forever and directly to the Holy See in whatever month and by whatever means they become vacant, even though it be

---

[9] Ordinary months were those in which the bishops might confer benefices; namely, March, June, September, December. The remaining eight were apostolic months reserved to the popes for special collation. An ancient ruling of Rome had provided that benefices vacant for eight months might be filled by the pope. See Rule 9, "de mensibus papalibus," in Franz Xavier Wernz, *Jus canonicum*, edited by Pietro Vidal (Roma, 1927), II, tit. 4, no. 229. Alternative months meant those in which, by special privilege, bishops might collate; they ran every other month beginning with February. In a practice of long duration bishops had used these months to assign benefices that would be vacant in the future.

by royal action or if in some manner one of them be associated with those belonging to the royal patronage of the crown or be situated in a diocese where some cardinal may have the indult to confer benefices. In none of these situations may prejudice be done to the Holy See. And the bulls for these fifty-two benefices must always be expedited in Rome according to the present schedule of taxation, with the customary emoluments paid to the dataria and the apostolic chancery. And all this will be done with no imposition of other dues and without exacting the bank notes, as will be said below.

8. The names, then, of the fifty-two benefices are the following:
In the Cathedral of Ávila — Archdeaconate of Arevalo
Cathedral of Orense — Archdeaconate of Bubal
Barcelona — Priorate, once regular, now secular, of the collegiate church of Santa Ana
Cathedral of Burgos — Mastership of the school
Burgos — Archdeaconate of Valenzuela
Cathedral of Calahorra — Archdeaconate of Naxera
Calahorra — Treasureship
Cathedral of Cartaxena — Mastership of the school
Cartajena — Simple, of Alvacete
Cathedral of Zaragoza — Archpriestship of Daroca
Zaragoza — Archpriestship of Belchite
Cathedral of Ziudad Rodrigo — Mastership of the school
Cathedral of Santiago — Archdeaconate of la Reyna
Santiago — Archdeaconate of Santa Thesia
Santiago — Treasureship
Cathedral of Cuenca — Archdeaconate of Alarcón
Cuenca — Treasureship
Cathedral of Córdova — Archdeaconate of Castro
Córdova — Simple, of Villalcazar
Córdova — Loan-fund of Castro y Espejo
Cathedral of Tolosa — Sacristyship
Tolosa — Hospital
Cathedral of Gerona — Archdeaconate of Ampueda
Cathedral of Jaén — Archdeaconate of Baeza
Jaén — Simple, of Arzonilla
Cathedral of Lérida — Preceptorship
Cathedral of Seville — Archdeaconate of Jérez
Seville — Simple, of the Puebla de Guzmán

Seville — Loan-fund in the church of Santa Cruz de Ezixa
Cathedral of Mallorca — Preceptorship
Mallorca — Provostship of San Antonio of San Antonio de Vienn.
Of no Province in Toledo — Simple, of Santa Maria de Alcalá-Real
Orihuela — Simple, of Santa Maria de Elche
Cathedral of Huesca — Cantorship
Cathedral of Oviedo — Cantorship
Cathedral of Osma — Mastership of the school
Cathedral of Osma — Abbacy of San Bartolomé
Pamplona — Hospital, previously religious, now an encomienda
Pamplona — Preceptorship general of the place of Olite
Cathedral of Plasencia — Archdeaconate of Medellín
Cathedral of Plasencia — Archdeaconate of Truxillo
Cathedral of Salamanca — Archdeaconate of Monleón
Cathedral of Siguenza — Treasureship
Cathedral of Siguenza — Abbacy of Santa Coloma
Cathedral of Tarragona — Priorate
Cathedral of Tarazona — Treasureship
Cathedral of Toledo — Treasureship
Toledo — Simple, of Vallejas
Tuy — Simple, of San Martín de Rosal
Cathedral of Valencia — Major sacristyship
Cathedral of Urgell — Archdeaconate of Andora
Cathedral of Zamora — Archdeaconate of Toro

9. So that in future there may be regularity in the collations, presentations, nominations, and institutions of the benefices that become vacant in the said *reinos* of Spain, it is agreed in the first place that archbishops, bishops, and inferior collators should from now on continue to provide those benefices as they have always done in the past when they fell vacant in their ordinary months, of March, June, September, and December, even though the Apostolic See be vacant at the time. Moreover, it is agreed that the ecclesiastical patrons will in the same months and in the proper manner continue to present the benefices of their patronage, with the exception of the alternative months when they conferred them antecedently, presentations which in future they shall never confer.

10. Secondly, the prebends *ex officio*, which will actually be provided by opposition and open competition, will in the future be conferred and expedited in the canonical manner and with the same

ceremony that has been used previously without innovation in anything, and not in the form used for the lay patronage over particular situations.

11. Thirdly, they will not only confer the parishes and benefices
with care of souls in future as they have in the past, by opposition and
competition when they are vacant in the ordinary months, but even
when they fall vacant in the months and cases reserved, for this presentation belongs to the king. In all those cases they should present to the
ordinary [the person whom] the patron believes most worthy among
the three chosen by the synodal examiners as fit and approved for the
care of souls.

12. Fourthly, now that agreement has been reached to leave untouched the right of ecclesiastical patrons to present the benefices of
their patronages in the four ordinary months, and to continue the old
custom whereby some *cabildos*, rectors, abbots, and societies endowed
with ecclesiastical authority have recourse to the Holy See for confirmation of their elections by apostolic bull, there is no intention of
introducing any change in these practices. All these usages remain as
they are and as they have been followed.

13. Fifthly, saving forever henceforth the reservation of the fifty-
two benefices assigned for free collation by the Holy See and the
declaration made in the list set out above, in order to reach amicable
agreement on the great controversy over the universal patronage, his
holiness compacts with his majesty the Catholic king and his successor
kings that they have forever the universal right to nominate and present
without exception to all the metropolitan churches, cathedrals, collegiate churches, and dioceses of the *reinos* of the Spains as possessed
today, and to the major postpontifical dignities and other dignities of
the collegiate churches, as also to the canonries, portions, prebends,
secular and regular ecclesiastical offices and benefices, both with and
without care of souls and of whatever character that are at present or
may in future be founded (nor may the founders reserve to themselves
and their successors the right to present), in the dominions and *reinos*
of the Spains which the Catholic king actually possesses, with the whole
generality of rights that they find comprehended in the apostolic months
and the cases of general and special reservation; and the same to hold
true in the case of vacancies of benefices in the ordinary months when
the archiepiscopal and episcopal sees are found vacant or are for any
other reason unoccupied.

14. And for a greater benevolence his holiness surrogates to the Catholic kings the right, now held by the Holy See because of its reservations, to confer the benefices in the *reinos* of the Spains either by itself or through the channels of the dataria, apostolic chancery, nuncios of Spain, and persons having indults, giving to their majesties the universal right to present to the said benefices in the *reinos* of the Spains as now constituted, with the faculty of using this right in the same way as is now used and exercised in the rest of the patronage pertaining to the royal crown. For the future there will be no move to concede to any apostolic nuncio of Spain or cardinal or bishop of Spain an indult to confer benefices in the apostolic months without the express permission of his majesty and his successors.

15. Sixthly, to make sure that in future all these actions will proceed in due order and to maintain unbroken the authority of the bishops as far as possible, it is agreed that all those presented and nominated by his Catholic majesty and his successors, even though the places become vacant as a result of royal process, are to receive without exception the institution and canonical collation from their respective ordinaries with no expediting of apostolic bulls aside from the confirming of elections as herein indicated, and aside from the individual cases of provision or nomination wherein, because of defect of age or other canonical impediment, some dispensation is needed or an apostolic concession or an act that otherwise requires authority higher than the ordinary power of the bishops. In all such cases and those like to them there must always be recourse to the Holy See, as has been done in past time when similar favors or dispensations were required, and with payment of the nominal fees to the dataria and apostolic chancery, without imposing pensions or exacting the bank notes, as will be said hereafter.[10]

16. Seventhly, for the same purpose of maintaining unimpaired the ordinary episcopal authority it is agreed and declared that by the

---

[10] These bank notes that caused so much disturbance were thus described by Benedict XIV in a letter to Tencin: "For a long time it has been a custom that in collations and provisions made by the Holy See certain annual pensions were reserved from the fruits and income of those benefices; and for their more certain payment, checks or notes drawn on public bankers were demanded from the beneficiaries provided" (quoted in Pastor, *History of the Popes,* XXXV, 71). Their usage caused such loss at Rome that the king felt obligated to pay a large lump sum to extinguish all claims for damages.

cession and surrogation of the stated rights of nomination, presentation, and patronage there is not to be understood as conferred on the Catholic king or on his successors any ecclesiastical jurisdiction over the churches comprehended in the expression of their rights or over the persons whom they present or name for the said churches and benefices. These no less than the others (upon whom the Holy See will confer the fifty-two reserved benefices) remain subject to their respective ordinaries, nor may they claim exemption from that jurisdiction, saving always the supreme authority which the Roman pontiff, as pastor of the universal church, holds over all the churches and ecclesiastical persons, and likewise protecting always the royal prerogatives that belong to the crown in virtue of the royal duty of giving particular care to the churches of the royal patronage.

17. Eighthly, his majesty realizes that, by reason of the cession of the royal patronage and its rights to him and his successors, the dataria and apostolic chancery will be left without the assistance of the expeditings and the annates, and that thus a notable loss will come upon the pontifical treasury. He accordingly takes on himself the obligation to consign in Rome under title of recompense for this one only occasion, and to put at the disposition of his holiness the capital sum of 310,000 Roman *scudi*, which at the rate of three per cent will produce annually 9,300 *scudi* in the same money, a sum that represents the product of the agreed ceded rights.

18. In times past some differences arose over certain arrangements made by the Holy See in regard to the cathedrals of Palencia and Mondoñedo. In this matter his majesty the Catholic king agrees that with the ratification of the present concordat the persons concerned will now enter into possession of those disputed rights. To go to another situation, the continuing claim to the universal patronage has brought about the recrudescence of the old controversy on the imposing of various charges and the demand for bank notes. In an effort to put a complete stop to all the complaints that have been made on this point from time to time, the holiness of our blessed father has shown himself prepared and resolved to abolish the employment of additional exactions and of the bank notes. The use of these imposts occasioned most unhappy consequences and forced the pontifical treasury against its will to accept new devices for revenue, because the receipts from those bank notes went for the most part into salaries and fees for the ministers who serve the Holy See in the universal government of the church.

19. On his side the majesty of the Catholic king, no less for his inherited devotion toward the Holy See than for the particular affection in which he holds the sacred person of his holiness, has decided to hand over on this one occasion an aid that, if it does not match the whole sum due, still will give part relief to the expense imposed on the pontifical treasury for maintaining the official staff. Consequently the king accepts the obligations of transferring to Rome 600,000 Roman *scudi* which at three per cent produce annually 18,000 *scudi* of the same currency. With this transfer there is abolished forever the usage of imposing charges and demanding bank notes, not alone in the matter of collating the fifty-two benefices reserved to the Holy See, but in the above-named confirmations and in recourse to the same Holy See for obtaining dispensations connected with the collation of the benefices. This will mark the end of these imposts, in such wise that for all future time the requirements of charges and bank notes will be abandoned, but without prejudice to taxes due up to the present moment.

20. There has been another area of controversy, not over the right of the apostolic *cámara* and the nunciature of Spain in regard to the perquisites and fruits of the diocesan churches vacant in the *reinos* of the Spains, but in the use, exercise, and effects of the said right, and on this it has been thought necessary to come to some settlement and composition of differences. To end these arguments the holiness of our blessed father derogates, annuls, and leaves as having no effect all the pertinent apostolic constitutions of earlier times and all the concordats and conventions previously made between the apostolic *cámara* and the bishops, *cabildos*, and dioceses, and whatever other arrangements were made to the contrary. From this day of ratification of this concordat all those gratuities and fruits exacted or not exacted of the vacant churches go to the religious purposes prescribed by the sacred canons, with the promise that for the future there will be no obligation from any source whatever to give to any ecclesiastical person, though he have special or most specially named faculties to claim them, the fruits and gratuities of these episcopal churches, seeing that they will be applied to religious uses, except those here expressly singled out as having their agreed destination. There is conceded for the future to the majesty of the Catholic king and his successors the electing of the fiscal agents and collectors (provided that they be ecclesiastical persons), with all the proper and necessary faculties for the said effects. Under the royal protection they are to be administered and directed faithfully to their stated purpose.

21. And his majesty, in reverence for the Holy See, obligates him-self to deposit in Rome at the disposition of his holiness, for this one occasion only, a capital sum of 233,333 Roman *scudi*, which at three per cent produces annually 7,000 *scudi* of the same currency. Beyond that, his majesty agrees to assign in Madrid, at the disposition of his holiness, from the revenues of the *cruzada* 5,000 *escudos* a year for the maintenance and subsistence of the apostolic nuncios. That whole sum is in consideration and recompense for the revenues given up by the pontifical treasury in the expressed cession of the gratuities and fruits of the vacant churches, and with the accepted understanding that in future there will be no concession of similar faculties.

22. His holiness on the faith of the Holy See and his majesty on the word of the Catholic king promise mutually for themselves and in the name of their successors unalterable firmness and perpetual en-durance of all and each of the preceding articles. They desire and declare that neither the Holy See nor the Catholic king will claim more than what is here expressed and comprehended in the said articles, and that they will consider as void and of no effect whatever action may be taken against all or any of them at any time whatsoever.

23. For the validation and fulfillment of what is here agreed the concordat will be attested in the customary form and it will go into full effect and have entire force as soon as the capital sums of recom-pense expressed above are consigned, the fact of which shall consti-tute its ratification.

In proof of which we the undersigned, in virtue of the respective powers of his holiness and his Catholic majesty, have endorsed the present concordat and sealed it with our own proper seal in the apos-tolic palace of the Quirinal this eleventh day of January of 1753.

Cardinal Valenti

Manuel Ventura Figueroa

Now that the said King Ferdinand in his turn has approved, con-firmed, and held ratified this treaty with its modifications as they are fully contained in the above document, whose words we by these presents wish to be taken exactly and as they are here inserted, we therefore will to consider the treaty herein embodied as ratified, en-during in perpetual stability, and to be kept unbroken. Hence, acting on our own decision, with certain knowledge and after careful con-sideration, in the plenitude of our apostolic power, we by the tenor of these presents ratify forever the treaty inserted above as it was approved, confirmed, and ratified as premised by the same King Ferdinand. We hold it ratified and we promise on the word of the Roman pontiff that the stipulations made in the said treaty by the said Silvius, our cardinal and plenipotentiary of the said see, will be seriously and inviolably fulfilled and performed.[11] We declare that the present document may at no future time be attacked or held to contain any vice or fraud or deceit or nullity caused either by our own intent or by any imagined defect however great. It is to stand forever as perpetually genuine, valid, and effective, and it obtains and gains by right its plenary and integral effects and is to be observed in its totality. And this notwithstanding any apostolic letters whatsoever, or general edicts of universal, provincial, or synodal councils, or special constitutions and ordinations, or any need for us or our chancery to act on the rule of not taking away an acquired right, or anything else to the contrary. Our meaning is that we specially and expressly derogate for this one case from all and each of these inhibitions as clearly and exactly stated, leaving them otherwise permanent in their force, everything to the contrary notwithstanding. Given at Rome at St. Mary Major under the ring of the fisherman, February 20, 1753, the thirteenth year of our pontificate. D. Cardinalis Passioneus. Place (   ) for the ring of the fisherman.

---

[11] This extraordinary iteration of promise to fulfill stemmed from the worried mind of a king plagued by his impetuous counselors.

CHAPTER XV

Perversion of the Patronato

It is customary to say that the Patronato Real perished when the nineteenth century brought the disappearance of the Spanish empire. This dictum, while true, is superficial and it neglects two capital points. The Patronato experienced fundamental change forty years before that great independence movement created twenty-one successor republics. Moreover, the perversion of the system exercised a truly causal influence on the revolt. This statement, however, belongs rather to general history than to the immediate substantial question.

As the eighteenth century entered its third quarter, the dynamic power in royal patronage passed its zenith and fell into a decline that presaged oblivion. It was still a vigorous institution during the reign of Ferdinand VI, a fact amply evidenced by reports from the Indies and official approbation at home.[1] For the past two hundred and fifty years it had fulfilled the purpose that brought it into life, the expansion of religion and empire. Then with apparent suddenness the center reversed its function and made that vast beneficent organization into an instrument directly subservient to crown exaltation and enlightened despotism. Unhappily the well-intentioned Bourbons became victims of

---

[1] On this subject see Pastor, *History of the Popes*, XXXV, 414-18 and 426-28. See also Rippy and Nelson, *Crusaders of the Jungle*, *passim*.

a fear and trepidation inspired by counselors whose aims were far from help to either church or king. These latter experts in political maneuver made a good man, Charles III, into *el beato pernicioso* (the holy scoundrel). The regalism that they fostered was but a passing phase of kingship designed to prepare for the enlightened new age. Spanish kings submitted to the process. They formed the Family Compact, signed despotic decrees, abolished age-old rights and corporations, and destroyed the independence and authority of the Spanish church.[2] Within no distant time Charles IV would publish a ukase for confiscation of all *obras pias* or church-affiliated investments, to gain funds for supporting the Francophile policies of 1804. Quite understandably does Vanconselos charge them with treason to Spain.[3] Through it all "the most precious pearl in the royal diadem" lost its meaning and assumed the new role of enhancing the royalty rather than the *reinos* of the king.

In the historical course of the Patronato there is much to remind one of the government of imperial Rome. In the two a

---

[2] Herr, *Revolution*, p. 36, expresses the opinion that "the regalist policy of the Spanish Bourbons and the rise of men of Jansenist views to leading posts in the hierarchy after the middle of the eighteenth century destroyed the independence and authority of the Spanish church." And he adds: "The most immediate effect of Spanish regalism and Jansenism was to establish in Spain a royalist absolutism equal to that of Louis XIV." For a firsthand account of this regalism see Giménez Fernández, *Concilio*, Capítulo I, "El regalismo jansenista español en el siglo XVIII."

[3] José Vasconselos, *Historia de México* (México, 1956), outlines his charge in treating the *siglo dieciocho*. He adds that the kings militarized and introduced an alien culture into the Indies and undermined the loyalty of their people to traditional Spanish ideals by accepting the legalisms of Campomanes, such as the concept that associations and groups have no rights unless a government grants charters to them. See also Francisco Antonio Encina, *Historia de Chile desde prehistoria hasta 1891* (Santiago, 1940-1954), IV, 407: "El concepto Borbónico fue 'Todo para el pueblo, pero sin el pueblo,' " quoting Altamira and, while noting useful reforms, sketching with accuracy the despotism of their enlightenment: "El estado, yo soy." He cites Cabarrus to the effect that the Bourbons tried to remove the ambiguities of twenty centuries in the belief that twenty years would suffice to regenerate the empire (p. 419).

magnificent world outlook operated from simple central administration. Both institutions exhibited breadth of imagination and
finality of decision. Both clung conservatively to original patterns while adapting these same patterns throughout enormous
territorial and demographic areas. Both made unique codes of
law whose spirit persevered long after the parental authority
had departed. In its heyday each system was superior to its human directors, whether they were models of statesmanship or
weaklings supported by the momentum of the institution itself,
and each left a permanent mark on the minds of successor nations which in new life attempted to carry on the cultural character of their progenitors. Finally, like Rome, the Patronato fell
from the top. The capital patron ceased to perform his proper
function of support for the immense religious charge that was
bequeathed to him. Crown control metamorphosed from an earlier forthright zeal, if overbearing yet not fraudulent, into a
self-centered absolutism. Its signs are multiform, but in essence
it went so far beyond the *pase regio* as to embrace hostility to
the Holy See and achieve a purely autonomous church. It became Jansenistic, in the then current meaning of the term, not
of followers of Quesnel but frankly antipapal. And to stabilize
this new attitude it executed three travesties of patronal right:
the acceptance of the Ribadeneyra doctrine on the patronage, the
extinction of one of its chief auxiliaries in the field, and the calling of the famous Fourth Provincial Council of Mexico.

The primary document of this chapter deals with the second
of these three acts. It is treated first, not directly for its own interest but as a perfectly clear illustration of the regalism then
rampant. It is the royal *Pragmática* issued on April 2, 1767, and
it speaks for itself.[4]

---

[4] This document is copied and translated from a film reproduction of the original
preserved in the Roman archives of the Jesuits. Its citation is *Hist. Soc.
Centr. Arch. S.J.*, Vol. 185, folios 22-33. The brochure measures 29 x 21 cms.
and is in a state of perfect preservation. For the original see pp. 370-77.

[*Pragmática sanción*]
PRAGMATIC SANCTION of his majesty
having the force of law for the expulsion from these kingdoms of the
religious of the Company of Jesus, occupation of their temporalities,
prohibition of their re-establishment at any time, with the additional
regulations herein expressed
The year 1767, in Madrid
The Royal Press of the Gazette for the dispatches of the fourth
month
Fourth seal   Year of 1767

Don Carlos, by the grace of God king of Castile, Leon, Aragon,
the Two Sicilies, Jerusalem, Navarre, Granada, Toledo, Valencia, Cor-
sica, Murcia, Jaén, the Algarves, Algeciras, Gibraltar, the Canary Islands, the East and West Indies, the islands and mainland of the Ocean
Sea: archduke of Austria, duke of Burgundy, of Brabant, of Milan,
count of Habsburg, of Flanders, of Tyrol and Barcelona, lord of
Vizcaya and Molina and the rest: to the most serene prince Don Carlos,
my very dear and beloved son; to my children, prelates, dukes, mar-
quises, counts, grandees, priors of the orders and commanders and
subcommanders, alcaldes of castles, strong points and plains, and to
the members of my council, the president and auditors of my *audiencias*, the *alcaldes* and *alguacils* of my palace, court, and chanceries;
and to all *corregidors*, intendants, assistant, governors, *alcaldes* major and ordinary, and all other judges and justices of my *reinos* and
of the king's land, lords' lands, abbey lands, military orders of whatever estate, condition, quality, or pre-eminence they be, those of today
and those to come, and each and whichever of you: KNOW that in
consonance with the decision of the members of my royal council,
meeting in extraordinary session on last January 29 to consider the
effects of the recent disturbances,[5] and in conformity with the opinions

---

[5] The Hat and Cloak Riots of March 23-25, 1766 and the so-called Rising in
Azpeitia shortly afterward. See Pastor, *History of the Popes*, XXXVII, 100,
note 2 for a summary account of these commotions. They were stirred by
hatred of the Italian minister Squillace but imputed by interested parties to
the Company.
   José Bravo Ugarte in his *Historia de México* (México, 1941), II, 282
compresses the best historical judgment on this suppression in his statement
that Aranda, Moniño, and Campomanes persuaded Charles III that the

expressed to me by persons of reliable character and experience whom I summoned to meet and give their judgment on the above decision;[6] and moved by weighty reasons bearing on my duty to maintain my people in subordination, tranquillity and justice, and other urgent, just, and compelling motives that I keep hidden in my royal breast; using the supreme administrative power that the All-Powerful has put into my hand[7] for the protection of my vassals and respect for my crown;

Jesuits were conspiring to overthrow him and that his life was in danger. Neither this charge nor any other implied in the indictment has ever been proved, nor has proof been attempted. The central reason for ministerial attack lay in the close attachment of the Company to the pope, who was the chief object of Jansenist and Voltairean opposition, and this not only for the dogmatic religion but because the papacy supposedly blocked such social and economic betterment as was desired by the Enlightenment. Beyond this the ministerial group could find support in an unofficial but vocal anti-Jesuit party, whose dislike for the order lay in a multitude of events and attitudes that offended various sectors of the imperial community. These latter causes ranged from the order's attachment to educational principles and practices at variance with certain views of the Enlightenment and on through a whole gamut of envy and hostility connected with the economy of the reductions of Paraguay and other highly successful missions, the dispute on the Chinese and Malabar rites, Jesuit semi-independence of episcopal rule and even of the Patronato, rivalries between religious orders, and a number of cases where men of the Company showed themselves less than tolerant in the face of justifiable criticism. However, the final impasse was the definite creation of a determined group of men who now controlled the mind of Charles III and aimed at revolution in the Spanish constitutional life. Cloaking themselves under the absolute rule of the king and utilizing the subservience of lay and ecclesiastical leaders, they were at the moment in complete charge.

6 These were Roda, Muniáin, Múzquiz, Grimaldi, the Duke of Alba, Masones, and Father Eleta. See Pastor, *History of the Popes*, XXXVII, 97, where he calls the father confessor Osma rather than Eleta.

7 This phrase was used to avoid possible conflict with church authority on grounds of competence, for the Jesuits as clerics were protected by the *forum ecclesiasticum*. The dodge was suggested by the council, though obviously Charles III had no right in the situation unless it lay in his patronage. Ribadeneyra, however, had written that this entire jurisdiction came from sovereignty, and it was so held by the regalists. That the king used *arrière pensée* is attested by his orders to the Fourth Provincial Council of Mexico of 1771 and his insistence on their discovering whether any spokesman there opposed his *regalia* or his Patronato Real. The final business of this council was to petition the pope for total suppression of the Company. See Gerardo Decorme, *Historia de la Compañía de Jesús en la República Mexicana* (Guadalajara, 1914), I, 13, 14, 20.

I have come to order the expulsion from all my dominions of Spain, the Indies, the Philippine Islands and adjacent lands, of the religious of the Company of Jesus, priests as well as coadjutors or lay brothers who have made their first profession, and those novices who choose to follow them; and the sequestration of the temporalities of the Company in my dominions; and for the uniform execution of all these matters I have given full private commission and authority by my royal decree of February 27 to the Count of Aranda, president of my council, with the power to proceed henceforward and apply the means necessary to enforce the said law.[8]

I. I have accordingly ordered my council to publicize this said royal decision throughout all my *reinos*.[9] They are to assure the rest of the religious orders of the confidence, satisfaction, and appreciation they merit of me because of their loyalty, sound doctrine, observance of monastic discipline, exemplary service to the church, solid knowledge of their proper studies, sufficiency of members to aid the bishops in spiritual shepherding of souls, and their noninterference in affairs of governmental business that is so alien to monastic and ascetical life.

II. The council will likewise notify the reverend diocesan prelates, the municipal governments, ecclesiastical *cabildos*, and other estates or political bodies of the realm, that the just and grave motives which forced me to this measure, despite the pain it causes, remain hidden in my royal person, and I am employing the purely administrative right without resorting to other powers. In that I follow the impulse of my royal clemency as father and protector of my people.

III. It is my will that the sequestration of the temporalities of the Company include all their goods and effects, the chattels and fixed properties or ecclesiastical revenues that they hold legitimately throughout the kingdom, without neglecting their debts, the intentions of founders, or the pensions of the individual members who will during the remainder of their lives receive one hundred pesos a year if priests, and ninety if lay brothers, payable from the general accumulation that represents the properties of the Company.

IV. Not to be counted among those who receive this pension are foreign Jesuits who live improperly within my dominions, in their colleges

---

[8] On the suppression as a whole the finest work ever written is the account of Pastor, *History of the Popes*, running through Volumes 35-38.

[9] This was done simultaneously everywhere in the empire on April 2, 1767.

or outside of them or in private homes, wearing the cassock or in the garb of abbés, and in whatever business they may be occupied. They must all leave my *reinos* with no exception.

V. In no way do these pensions extend to novices who choose freely to follow the rest, for they are not bound by profession and they are at liberty to withdraw.

VI. It is my will that if any Jesuit abandons the ecclesiastical state, to which all are hereby remitted, or if by his works or writings he gives just cause of displeasure to the crown, the pension assigned to him will lapse forthwith. And he may not presume that the body of the Company, so much at fault in the broadest and highest duties, intends or permits any of its members to write against the reverence and submission due to my order under any guise or color of apology or defense likely to disturb the peace of my *reinos,* or by using secret emissaries to conspire to that end. In this unlooked-for event the pension of all will be stopped.

VII. Every six months the Bank of Circulation will deliver the semi-annual pension to the Jesuits, under the supervision of my minister at Rome who is to take special care to find the names of those who have died or who by their own fault have lost right to the pension, and he will therefore cancel that obligation.

VIII. As to the administration and equitable application of the properties of the Company to religious causes, such as the endowment of poor parishes, of conciliar seminaries, houses of mercy, and other pious purposes, in which situations I shall ask the judgment of ecclesiastical ordinaries regarding what is needful and proper, I reserve the right to take independent action to prevent any defrauding of true religion or prejudice to the general good or to the claims of any third party.

IX. By my law and general order I prohibit any individual of the Company or any corporate community from returning to any of my *reinos* under whatever pretext or color of right. On the contrary, the justices will take exact care to prevent such a thing and use most rigorous measures against those who break this law, their helpers, and those who deliberately cooperate with them, punishing them as enemies of the public welfare.

X. No truly professed Jesuit, even though he leave the order with the permission of the pope and become a secular cleric or pass to another order, may return to these *reinos* without obtaining my special permission.

XI. Should such a person obtain that permission, and it will be given only after careful inquiry, he must take an oath of fidelity in the hands of the president of my council. He must promise in good faith that he will not deal in public or in secret with members of the Company or with their general, and that he will not engage in their affairs or make any move or contact either directly or indirectly in favor of the Company, under penalty of being treated as an enemy of the state, and privileged evidence may be validly used against him.

XII. By no means may he teach, preach, or hear confessions in these *reinos*, even though he has cut himself off as one says from the order and from the obedience of the general. He may, however, enjoy ecclesiastical support, as that does not require him to be employed in such occupations.

XIII. No vassal of mine, though he be secular cleric or religious, may ask for letters of admission from the general of the Company nor from another in his name, under penalty of being held an enemy of the state, and against him the privileged evidence will be similarly valid.

XIV. All those vassals who at present possess such letters of admission must surrender them to the president of the council, or to the corregidors or justices of the realm who will forward them to the official archives so they may be filed, and no one will make use of them in the future. But past possession will incur no process if one complies punctually with the duty of turning them in. And the justices will keep secret the names of those who have surrendered them, to avoid causing unfavorable publicity for those so cooperating with the law.

XV. Every person who carries on correspondence with the Jesuits will, since this act lies under general and absolute prohibition, receive severe punishment in proportion to his guilt.

XVI. I expressly forbid anyone to write, declaim, or air his views on this whole subject either for or against the case. I impose immediate silence on all my vassals in this matter and command that those who do otherwise be punished as guilty of attack on the sovereign.

XVII. To prevent angry disputes and the spread of false reports among the people, who have no right to judge or interpret the orders of the ruler, I give express command that no one produce, publish, or sell brochures or books dealing with the expulsion of the Jesuits from my dominions without special license of the government. And I forbid the press censor and his subdelegates, and all the justices of my *reinos*, to grant any such permits or licenses, for this whole matter must be handled under the orders of the president and ministers of my council, and it will be carefully watched by my prosecutor.

XVIII. I most seriously charge the reverend diocesan prelates, and the superiors of the religious orders, not to allow their subjects to write, publish, or speak in public about this affair, and they will be held responsible for such an unlooked-for fault on the part of any of them. This I declare to be covered by the law of the sovereign lord John the First, and by the royal *cédula* circularized by my council on September 18 of the past year ordering its prompt execution. All must co-operate to carry out this injunction, for it highly concerns the public order and the good name of the same persons, lest they feel the effect of my royal displeasure.

XIX. In keeping with what is here expressed, I have ordered my council that they see to expediting and publishing the royal *Pragmática* so that it come to the attention of all my subjects and be observed without fail and come to be widely known. The justices and territorial courts are to carry out the penalties declared against those who violate its clauses with exact, prompt, and unvarying execution. To this end the council will, before transacting any other business, give the necessary directives, because this is what most concerns my royal service. Know that I have ordered the councils of the Inquisition, of the Indies, of the Orders, and of the Interior to be sent copies of my royal decree for their respective information and compliance. To obtain punctual and uniform enforcement in all my dominions, the full council, after it had heard published the royal decree of March 27 containing the previous resolution[10] and had ordered complete and exact fulfillment and compliance with what was therein expressed, gave their consent to the expedition of these presents with the force of law and Pragmatic Sanction, just as if voted and promulgated in the *cortes*. Wherefore it is my will that this order be accepted and received as though done in the *cortes*, with no objection raised on any point of law, and for this if it be necessary I derogate from and annul all legislation that may

---

[10] Pastor, *History of the Popes*, XXXVII, 107, gives the date as March 20, though the number 27 is clear in the original. This referred to a circular letter sent to civil authorities on that day, with instructions not to open the enclosed packet before Thursday, April 2, and then at once to carry out the order. The packet contained the decree of expulsion of February 27, 1767 and the instruction of Count Aranda. Fuller citations from the original documents are given in that place.

be or is to the contrary. Hence I charge the very reverend archbishops, bishops, superiors of all religious orders both mendicant and monastic, visitors, provisors, vicars, and other prelates and ecclesiastical judges in these my *reinos* to obey the expressed law and *Pragmática* according to its letter, and not to permit under any pretext that it be violated in any way in as far as is commanded. I order the members of my council, the president and auditors, the *alcaldes* of my palace and court, and my *audiencias*, chanceries, assistant, governors, *alcaldes* major and ordinary, and finally the judges and justices of all my dominions, to protect, fulfill, and execute the cited law and Pragmatic Sanction, and to see that it is kept and observed in all and through all, taking for this the steps that are required, with no need of further declaration on the subject. It must be punctually carried out from the day of its publication in Madrid and in the cities, villages, and country places of these my *reinos*, in the customary form. Thus all will contribute to my royal service and to the peace, prosperity, and assurance of the public welfare of my vassals. As this is my will, and as these presents are a true copy of my decree as testified by my scribe of longest service in the *Cámara*, Don Ignacio Esteban de Higareda, and by the government of my council, do you give it the same faith and credit as the original. Given in the Prado, April 2, 1767.

I THE KING.

I, Don Joseph Ignacio de Goyeneche, secretary of our lord king, have had it written by his order.

The Count of Aranda. Don Francisco Cepeda. Don Jacinto de Tudó. Don Francisco de Salazar y Aguero. Don Joseph Manuel Domínguez. Registered: Don Nicolás Berdugo, assistant to the chief chancellor. Don Nicolás Berdugo.

In the villa of Madrid, on the second day of the month of April in 1767, at the gates of the royal palace before the principal balcony of the king our lord, and at the gate of Guadalajara where there is the public concourse and the market of the merchants and the public offices, Don Juan Estevan de Salaverri, Don Juan Antonio de Peñaredonda, Don Benito Antonio de Barreda, Don Pedro Ximénez de Mesa, and the alcaldes of the residence and court of his majesty being present, the above Pragmatic Sanction was announced for publication to the accompaniment of trumpets and drums by the voice of the public crier, in company with several bailiffs of the said royal residence and court and many other persons.

This is certified by me, Don Francisco López Navamuel, scribe of the *Cámara* of the king our lord, for those who are in his council. Don Francisco López Navamuel. And I certify that what I attest is a copy of the royal Pragmatic Sanction and its publication.

Here is a full picture of the regalism that subverted the independence and authority of the Spanish church. Its prime principle read: "I am the state." An enlightened despot would do all things for the people, but without the consent of the people. Their business was not to discuss his acts, but to obey and comply with them. Refusal became an attack on the state and would be so punished. That the ruler violated the constitution, derogating from any law or custom contrary to his *Pragmática*, presented no difficulty, for his word justified any deed. Summarily he sentenced a large body of men with no discrimination between good or bad. No trial, no bill of particulars or proof of misdeeds was necessary beyond the royal assertion. In assembling the culprits, no distinction of sick, old, or dying prevented mass condemnation. As to guilt, no reference was made to an investigation held but twenty-four years previously, and its resultant royal approval of both their doctrine and their conduct. Sequestration of their immense properties required no judicial process nor remuneration beyond the scanty hundred pesos per annum. And if one of them spoke against the edict, all would be deprived of their pensions. Death awaited any member who came back to Spain, and his cooperators. Every other religious person or corporation was commanded to uphold the decree under heavy penalty, and bishops and superiors were made personally responsible for their compliance. The royal prerogative was taken to enable the king to make a secular priest of every ordained member of the expelled order, and to forbid under fearsome threat any attempt to enter the order elsewhere. Religious obligations of the dispersed group were by the royal will to be transferred to any other desired personalities, or simply dropped, as happened to many of the missions in the

Indies. Papal establishment of the order offered no hindrance to their disestablishment by the crown. Regalism embraced religious headship.

This was a far cry from the centralist behavior of Philip II. The *cortes* of Castile sometimes kept him waiting for years to receive his *subsidio*, and on one occasion roundly censored him for extravagance in wardrobe and reduced his budget in that item.[11] And his response to Pius V on reform in the Indies has already been observed in Chapter 13.

It is interesting to note how the hierarchy fell in line with this new direction of affairs. Two years later, in 1769, Pope Clement XIV polled their membership on their approval of the expulsion. Of the fifty-six Spanish prelates forty-two approved, six opposed, and eight gave no opinion. Herr comments on the vote: "Because of the growth of so-called Jansenism among its members, the Spanish hierarchy was divided on the expulsion. . . . The episcopacy on the whole defended the measure."[12] There is more to it than that, as Giménez Fernández finds in his study of the Fourth Provincial Council of Mexico. They surrendered their freedom and followed the dictation of peace or of opportunity,[13] copying the lines of Febronius and Van Espen to justify the unjustifiable.

Twelve years before the publication of this *Pragmática* there appeared in Madrid the treatise on the Patronato Real that has

---

[11] See Edward W. Kearney, *Philip II and the Castilian Cortes: A Study in Sixteenth Century Absolutism* (unpublished thesis, Loyola University [Chicago], 1955), pp. 86 ff. Philip made great use of the *cortes* to find out what the people wanted done. Kearney holds that they loved and trusted him.

[12] Herr, *Revolution*, pp. 22-23. It is interesting to contrast this episcopal reaction with a letter written in 1584 by Bishop Salazar of Manila to the hierarchy assembled in the Third Provincial Council of Mexico, wherein he warned them to beware of the threat to freedom of religion latent in the Patronato. The letter is found in the Bancroft Library, University of California, M-M 268, folios 204-219v. It is dated July 1, 1584 and is indexed as coming from "El S.ʳ Obpo de la China."

[13] Giménez Fernández, *Concilio*, p. 10.

been so frequently cited in these pages. Dedicated to Ferdinand
VI, who did not follow it, the work offered a legalistic basis for
the regalism practiced by his successors. The author Ribadeneyra
was a strange person. Born in Puebla, New Spain, in 1710, he
received a good education and became a member of the royal
audiencia of Guadalajara, whence he passed to the rank of criminal prosecutor in the *audiencia* of Mexico. About 1750 he went
to Spain and, among other productions, published the famous
Manual compendio de el regio patronato Indiano in 1755. Returned to Mexico, he was a close follower of Viceroy Croix, who
had him made royal assistant to the future provincial council.
There he so exasperated the fathers with his arrogance, ped-
antry, and pride as to lose all respect and influence. His written
observations on that council sent him into obscurity, and his
only known later date is that of his death in the first half of
the year 1773.

Giménez Fernández speaks of his *Manual* as fawning, regalist, and absurd. Its flattering dedication to Ferdinand VI wearies
the reader. The chapters succeed one another in orthodox fashion, with the authority of the legist but the history and logic of
a child. And yet he was the type of the time-serving bureaucracy
in that age of the Bourbons, not so canny as Campomanes and
surely not Voltairean as were Aranda and Roda. His concepts
are purely a defense of the regalia. His learned citations and
quotations of authorities remind one of the playing of Cervantes.
The alphabetical index looks, for all its masquerade, like a
row of buttons: Adam, Seth, Enos, Ascanius, Caligula, produce
the law of nations; Pliny, King Roderick, and Justinian encum-
ber his pages. He finds the origin of the patronage in the temple
of Solomon, the ark of Noah, the birth of Eve, and the whole
Old Testament; jumping then to Recared, Alfonso I, and the
concordat of 1753. To him the Patronato Real de las Indias owes
nothing to the pontifical grant, and he considers other writers
foolish in their allusions to Alexander VI and Julius II. And yet

this man was appointed chief royal observer at the Provincial Council of 1771.

The *Manual* gives a clear-cut view of regalism as it affected the patronage. "The right of patronage is innate in their majesties because of their dominion in the Indies."[14] Its fountains are the conquest itself, their lordship over the land, donation of ground, building and endowment of churches, redeeming of the territory from the pagans.[15] Hence he adds: "the papal grants were superabundant, for the king had the right to direct his special church from the start, and papal grant could not add to the fact of patronage for this is essentially *laical,* that is, it arises from the purely political position of the sovereign."[16] Accordingly, "men should now consider it useless to take the pains that they do to find its origins in apostolic privileges." In consequence "the Patronato is not renounceable because the right is inseparable from the crown." And he runs back the practice of patronage to the first Christians. Its usage among the Visigothic kings he approves as good law. In Capítulo VIII, No. I, he gives to the king the right to take first cognizance of offenses within the patronage because his is the primary juridical possession,[17] for his power is lay and secular, and the pope in his grant merely honored the king, who already held the right. In such cases it is necessary only that the royal prosecutor *de facto* cite the defendant. The canon law is thus subjected to the crown.

There should at this point be no doubt that the exercise of patronage also derives from titles other than the grant of a pope. The definition of El Sabio clearly states those titles. But this temporal right which depends fundamentally on the spiritual right annexed to it has no meaning if the spirituality is given second place. To be a patron demands before all else the powers

---

[14] Ribadeneyra, *Manual compendio,* p. 57.
[15] *Ibid.,* pp. 54-55.
[16] *Ibid.,* pp. 45, 51, 82.
[17] *Ibid.,* pp. 150-51.

granted in an ecclesiastical privilege, and no one could properly exercise that right in the church without such concession. And yet Ribadeneyra's handsome book had much influence at the time. Even Hubert Howe Bancroft later considered it the best summary of the patronal power. In the hands of such men as formed the council of Charles III, "enlightened" and "philosophic," it proved most useful in upholding the regalist doctrine and presenting a front to awe those too ill-informed to question its assumptions. It likewise served the anti-Rome faction of both bishops and ministers to persuade the king in his otherwise shaky position. Ferdinand and Isabella, who began the Patronato Real, would not have recognized their future child.

A striking exhibition of how this regalism undermined the ideals of the chief patron and destroyed the independence and authority of the clergy is seen in the calling and the deliberations of the Fourth Provincial Council of Mexico, held in that viceregal capital in 1771. The very purpose and summons of the council fell into line with the ministerial designs, which were to bring a kind of enlightenment into the overseas dominions, and with which the king complied entirely. And the manner of its sessions, the matter the members were permitted to discuss, the incidental petition they were ordered to propose to Rome—total extinction of the order recently expelled from Spain—and the final royal review and rewriting of their decrees betray the reversal now come on the role of patron of the Indies.

Manuel Giménez Fernández, on whose scholarly little book these remarks draw so heavily, obtained such intimate familiarity with the actors behind the scenes of the council that his judgments, based on their letters and announced joint efforts, throw brilliant light on the subject here under discussion.[18] The circle began with the king's confessor, Fray Joaquín Eleta, later

---

[18] Giménez Fernández, *Concilio*, Capítulo I. "El regalismo jansenista español en el siglo XVIII," pp. 9-36, is devoted to this topic.

bishop of Osma and archbishop of Thebes, the guide and directive influence in the whole gamut of heterodox regalistic politics.
Round him were grouped more able but not more passionate or
convincing men, for though he is characterized as an ignorant
and fanatic Romanophobe with little knowledge of history, with
his pen he held the group united in their course of action as his
persuasive voice led the king to follow their counsel. He was at
his post before the fatal *Pragmática* of April 2, 1767, of which
he was a coauthor; he fronted in the condemnation of the bishop
of Cuenca who spoke out against that decree; he took part in
prohibiting the publication of the monitory of Parma and in
driving through the papal suppression of the Company of Jesus.
He is credited with the fall from power of Wall, as he likewise
had a chief part in the appointment of every bishop during his
tenure of office. He led the party of *Golillas*, or men of the little
ruff, who followed the policies of Carvalho of Portugal and
sought to annul the papal power in favor of the regalia of the
crown. There was no crisis of conscience in the people but a for-
getting of duty and a corruption in the ruling classes: nobles,
educated men, higher clergy, intellectuals, grandees, bishops,
generals of religious orders, ministers, and writers without deep
national religious sentiment. Foremost among them were Aranda,
Roda, Arriaga, Jose de Gálvez, Grimaldi, Cavallero, Azara,
Labrador, Croix, Bucareli, Lorenzana, and their mentors Moniño
and Campomanes. Under cover of emancipation from Rome they
deprived the Spanish church of its liberty, and they began it
with an attack against all the orders.

In New Spain a local flurry in Puebla led its bishop, Fabián
y Fuero, to circulate general charges against the orders. The
primate, Lorenzana, took it up with the whole circle, and Eleta
soon had the council of the king choose a sounding board for
action in a set of overseas provincial councils. Mexico led off.
The royal council fixed the procedure: 1) the viceroy and metropolitan should summon the convocation; 2) the *Tomo regio*, or

royal guidebook, would lay down the agenda; 3) all reference
to church immunity and jurisdiction must be avoided; 4) the
council should re-establish ecclesiastical discipline among the
clergy, regulate its ministries and the administration of spiritual
assistance, provide sound doctrine for the pueblos, and let the
royal council review the proceedings, subject to the approval of
the king; 5) they must reverence the *regalia* of the king and
maintain due respect for it; 6) after meeting they must send the
acta in authentic copy to his majesty for his inspection and confirmation.[19] The king accepted this ministerial arrangement and
ordered it carried out.

The council, which began on January 13, 1771, opened with
praise of the king, the "conserver of the Catholic faith, the universal father who has divine right, natural, and political, and is
to be obeyed more than natural parents." Lament was expressed
for the setback in the spiritual conquest of the Indies "due to
recent events," and that the missions built with such labor were
in many cases abandoned and their natives returned to the hills.
Religious were ordered to be subject to their bishops, and these
latter might combine or disperse groups that had lost their use-
fulness or fervor. But the overriding enthusiasm was for the
regalia, and thus the late expulsion of a great order received fulsome eulogy. On October 23, 1771, in secret session, the council
addressed a petition to the Holy See to suppress the entire order,
and three days later the council, assisted (!) by the viceroy,
came to a close. Its acts were dutifully sent to the king, who as
ruler and royal patron chose to assure himself and his *reinos* of
the merits of its declarations and to seek its final approval at
Rome through the work of his minister Roda, and later Moniño.
That approval never came, for the entire proceedings were un-
canonical and had no more ecclesiastical standing than a meeting of royal ministers. What is clear throughout is the blatant

---

[19] *Ibid.*, p. 45, is a breakdown of the heads of agenda.

regalism, disregard for papal upholding of religious orders, and sycophancy of the hierarchy. These provincial councils were deliberately organized to achieve such results, and in that they were successful. The irony of the situation lay in the fact that the very Eleta who inspired the movement by his own blunders blocked the publication of the *acta* and the success of its appeal to Rome.

These three episodes illustrate the reversal in the position of the royal patron over his patronage. Throughout the previous chapters other similar actions of the Bourbons have been noted. A final case may be found in the royal decree at the death of Pius VI in 1799.[20] As a long conclave was anticipated, and Napoleon might prevent the election of a new pope, the church in Spain would employ the following procedure until the king "recognized" the new pope: the ecclesiastical courts would continue their normal functions; bishops would grant all matrimonial dispensations; consecrations of new bishops would be decided by a tribunal named by the king; the bishops should not let their inferiors "worry the consciences of his majesty's subjects" by discussing the death of the pope or the terms of the decree. This Jansenist promulgation was written by the court preacher, Josef Espiga.

How far all these things reacted on public opinion is difficult to gauge. One sole bishop in Spain, Carvajal y Lancaster, bishop of Cuenca, dared to protest in public, and he suffered public condemnation.[21] The law made it extremely dangerous for others to follow his example, and there is little record of such a trend until the movements for independence began. One other bishop, Abad y Queipo of Michoacán, spoke out strongly against the deterioration of the lower clergy, their lack of education and of the means of proper subsistence. American-born priests, he said,

---

[20] Herr, *Revolution*, pp. 425-26.
[21] Giménez Fernández, *Concilio*, p. 39.

should be raised to the episcopacy. He described the damage done to layman and clerk by the 1804 decree confiscating to the crown the properties of the *Obras Pias*. And his reward was confinement by the Inquisition till his death in 1824.[22]

History wrote the external dissolution of the Patronato in the severance of overseas provinces from the Spanish empire. One section after another went its own way after Napoleon took over the peninsula in 1810. These independent peoples refused to accept appointments of the hierarchy from Madrid, and crown funds for the support of all phases of religion, from seminaries to metropolitan sees, ceased to be forthcoming. Accordingly the entire machinery of the institution came to a full and final stop. In Spain itself the deeds of anticlerical forces in nineteenth-century government led the papacy to a definitive termination of patronal rule in the concordat of 1851. Though the king might still nominate the higher clergy and provide their support, no longer could any canonical case be heard except in the tribunals of the holy father. Finally the church, taught by bitter experience, legislated in its new Code of Canon Law of 1918 that: "No right of patronage can in the future be validly acquired under any title."[23] And the Code went on to state: "If the Apostolic See has conceded either in concordats or aside from them the indult of presenting to a vacant church or even to a vacant benefice, there is not in this a source of the right of patronage, and the privilege of presenting must be given strict interpretation by the tenor of the indult."[24]

In the various seceding nations there was for a time clamor to regain the patronage. Venezuela still operates under a self-constructed patronage. In Mexico the struggle became complicated and bitter until Juárez and his revolution put a definite

---

[22] Lillian Fisher, *Champion of Reform* (New York, 1955), is full of interesting material on the Patronato in the early 1800's.

[23] *Codex iuris canonici*, Canon 1450.

[24] *Ibid.*, Canon 1471.

end to it.[25] Nevertheless the three hundred years of traditional thinking still inclines governments to meddle with religion, and the past century has seen some sharp conflicts over the issue. For all practical purposes, however, the power has passed forever.

---

[25] See on the Mexican struggle over the patronage after independence W. Eugene Shiels, "Francisco Pablo Vásquez and the Independence of Mexico," *Mid-America*, XXX (July 1948), 177-86.

PART TWO

The Originals

T his section presents the texts of the original bulls, decrees, and instructions that underlay the actual development of the Patronato Real. Every effort was made to give them in faithful translation where they occurred in the narrative of Part 1. But for the scholar the originals speak with an integrity that is incomparably greater than a modern English version. They are the true foundations of the study, and they will open up many avenues overlooked in the previous pages. They alone really show the soul of the times and of the men who made the system. Their nuances, color, and tone enrich the understanding of motive and circumstance. In them one can read between the lines, much better than in any translation, the shifting positions and attitudes of the interested parties, even the changes in chancery method and performance. Most of all, the personalities of the authors stand out clearly in their style of composition and this offers much aid to one who wishes to interpret their acts.

The principles governing the selection of these documents have already been stated and explained. They form a simple scaffolding for the answer to the direct question: what was the Patronato Real? On the same premise the editorial comment is purposely restricted to variant readings in the printed sources. Textual criticism, too, is kept to a minimum that seems necessary for the demands of the inquiry.

*Romanus pontifex**
(Nicholas V, 1454)

Nicholas Episcopus, Servus Servorum Dei. Ad perpetuam rei memoriam.

Romanus Pontifex coelestis Clavigeri successor et Vicarius Jesu Christi cuncta mundi climata omniumque Nationum in illis degentium qualitates paterna consideratione discutiens, ac salutem quaerens[1] et appetens singulorum, illa perpensa deliberatione, salubriter ordinat et disponit, quae grata Divinae Majestati fore conspicit, et per quae oves sibi divinitus creditas ad unum ovile Dominicum reducat, et adquirat eis felicitatis aeternae praemium, ac veniam impetret animabus, quae eo certius, auctore Domino, provenire credimus, si condignis favoribus, specialibus gratiis eos Catholicos prosequamur Reges et Principes, quos veluti Christianae Fidei athletas et intrepidos, non modo Sacracenorum caeterorumque Infidelium Christi nominis inimicorum feritatem reprimere, sed etiam ipsos eorumque Regna, ac loca etiam in longissimis nobisque incognitis partibus consistentia pro defensione et augmento Fidei debellare, suoque temporali dominio subdere, nullis parcendo laboribus et expensis, facti evidentia cognoscimus, ut Reges et Principes ipsi, sublatis quibusvis dispendiis, ad tam saluberrimum opus peramplius animentur.

Ad nostrum siquidem nuper, non sine ingenti gaudio et nostrae mentis laetitia, pervenit auditum quod dilectus Filius nobilis Vir Henricus, Infans Portugalliae Charissimi in Christo Filii Nostri Alphonsi, Portugalliae et Algarbii Regnorum Regis

---

* Hernáez, *Colección*, II, 824-30; García Gutiérrez, *Bulario*, pp. 11-12. For the translation see pp. 50-55.

[1] All spelling and punctuation in Part 2 follows that of the sources cited. Hernáez uses the modern spelling, the diphthong *ae* in place of the old form *e*. A diphthong was not employed in papal documents until the middle of the sixteenth century.

illustris, patriis inhaerens vestigiis, clarae memoriae Joannis, dictorum regnorum Regis, ejus genitoris, ac zelo salutis animarum et Fidei ardore plurimum succensus, tamquam Catholicus et omnium Creatoris Christi miles, ipsiusque Fidei acerrimus et fortissimus defensor et intrepidus pugil, ejusdem Creatoris gloriosissimum nomen per universum terrarum orbem etiam in remotissimis et incognitis locis divulgari, extolli et venerari, necnon illius ac vivificae, qua redempti sumus, Crucis inimicos perfidos Saracenos videlicet, ac quoscumque alios Infideles ad ipsius Fidei gremium reduci, ab ejus ineunte aetate, totis adspirat viribus, post Ceptensem Civitatem in Africa consistentem, per dictum Joannem Regem ejus subactam dominio, et post multa per ipsum Infantem nomine dicti Regis contra hostes et Infideles praedictos, quam etiam in propria persona, non absque maximis laboribus et expensis ac rerum et personarum periculis et jactura, plurimorumque naturalium suorum code [caede?] gesta bella, ex tot tantisque laboribus, periculis, et damnis non fractus neque territur, sed ad hujusmodi laudabilis et pii propositi sui prosecutionem in dies magis atque magis exardescens in Oceano Mari quasdam solitarias Insulas Fidelibus propalavit, ac fundari et construi inibi fecit Ecclesias et alia pia loca, in quibus Divina celebrantur Officia, et dicti quoque Infantis laudabili opera et industria quamplures diversarum in dicto Mari existentium Insularum incolae seu habitatores ad veri Dei cognitionem venientes, sacrum Baptisma susceperunt, ad ipsius laudem et gloriam, ac plurimarum animarum salutem [et] Orthodoxae Fidei propagationem ad Divini cultus augmentum.

Praeterea, cum olim ad ipsius Infantis pervenisset notitiam, quam nunquam vel saltem a memoria hominum non consuevisset per hujusmodi Oceanum Mare versus meridionales et orientales plagas navigari, illudque nobis Occiduis adeo foret incognitum, ut nullam de partium illarum gentibus certam notitiam haberemus, credens se maxime in hoc Deo praestare obsequium, si ejus opera et industria mare usque ad Indos, qui Christi nomen colere dicuntur, navigabile fieret, sicque cum eis participare, et illos in Christianorum auxilium adversus Saracenos et alios hujusmodi Fidei hostes commovere posset, ac nonnullos Gentiles seu paganos nefandissimi Mahometi secta minima [minime] infectos populos inibi medio existentes continuo debellare, eisque incognitum sacratissimum Christi nomen praedicare ac facere praedicari. Regia tamen super auctoritate munitus, a viginti quinque annis citra exercitum ex dictorum Regnorum gentibus, maxime cum laboribus, periculis et expensis, in velocissimis navibus, Carabellis nuncupatis, ad perquirendum mare et Provincias maritimas versus meridionales partes, et polum antarticum annis singulis fere mittere non cessavit; sicque factum est ut cum nave hujusmodi quamplures portus, Insulas, et maria perlustrassent, ad Ghineam Provinciam tandem pervenirent; occupatisque nonnullis Insulis, portubus ac mari, ejusdem Provinciae adjacentibus, ulterius navigantes, ad ostium cujusdam magni fluminis, Nili communiter reputati, pervenerunt, et contra illarum partium populos, nomine ipsorum, Alphonsi Regis et Infantis, per aliquos annos guerra habita exstitit, et in illa quamplures inibi vicinae Insulae debellatae ac pacifice possessae fuerunt, prout adhuc cum adjacenti mari possidentur.

Exinde quoque multi Ghinei et alii Nigri vi capti, quidam etiam non prohibitarum rerum permutatione, seu alio legitimo contractu emptionis ad dicta sunt Regna transmissi; quorum inibi copioso numero ad Catholicam Fidem conversi exstiterunt, speraturque, Divina favente clementia, quod si hujusmodi cum eis continuetur progressus, vel populi ipsi ad Fidem convertentur, vel saltem multorum ex eis animae Christo lucrifient.

Cum autem, sicut accepimus, licet Rex et Infans praedicti, qui cum tot tantisque periculis, laboribus et expensis, necnon perditione tot naturalium Regnorum hujusmodi, quorum inibi quamplures perierunt ipsorum naturalium, dumtaxat freti auxilio Provincias illas perlustrari fecerunt, ac portus, Insulas, et maria hujusmodi acquisiverunt et possederunt, ut praefertur, ut illorum veri Domini, timentes ne aliqui cupiditate ducti ad partes illas navigarent, et operis hujusmodi perfectionem, fructum et laudem sibi usurpare vel saltem impedire cupientes, propterea, seu lucri commodo aut malitia ferrum arma lignamina aliasque res et bona ad Infideles deferri prohibita portarent vel transmitterent, aut ipsos Infideles navigandi modum edocerent, propter quae eis hostes fortiores ac duriores fierent, et hujusmodi prosecutio vel impediretur vel forsan penitus cessaret, non absque offensa magni Dei et ingenti totius Christianitatis opprobrio, ad obviandum praemissis, ac pro suorum juris et possessionis conservatione, sub certis tunc expressis gravissimis poenis prohibuerint, et generaliter statuerint, quod nullus nisi cum suis nautis ac navibus et certi tributi solutione, obtentaque prius desuper expressa ab eodem Rege vel Infante licentia, ad dictas Provincias navigare, aut in earum portubus contractare, seu in mari piscari praesumeret; tamen successu temporis evenire posset, quod aliorum Regnorum seu Nationum personae, invidia, malitia aut cupiditate ducti contra prohibitionem praedictam, absque tributi solutione hujusmodi ad dictas Provincias accedere, et in sic adquisitis Provinciis, Portubus et Insulis ac mari navigare, contractare et piscari praesumerent, et exinde inter Alphonsum Regem et Infantem, qui nullatenus se in iis sic deludi paterentur, et praesumentes praedictos quamplura odia, rancores, dissensiones, guerrae et scandala in maximam Dei offensam et animarum periculum verisimiliter subsequi possent et subsequerentur.

Nos, praemissa omnia et singula debita meditatione attendentes, quod cum olim praefato Alphonso Regi quoscumque Saracenos ac Paganos aliosque Christi inimicos ubicumque constitutos, ac Regna, Ducatus, Principatus, Dominia, possessiones et mobilia et immobilia bona quaecumque per eos detenta ac possessa invadendi, conquirendi, expugnandi, debellandi et subjugandi, illorumque personas in perpetuam servitutem redi-

gendi, ac Regna, Ducatus, Comitatus, Principatus, Dominia,
possessiones et bona sibi et successoribus suis applicandi, appro-
priandi, ac in suos successorumque suorum usus utilitatemque
convertendi, aliis nostris Litteris plenam et liberam inter caetera
concessimus facultatem: dictae facultatis obtentu idem Alphonsus Rex, seu quis auctoritate praedictus Infans juste et legitime
terras, portus et maria hujusmodi adquisivit ac possidet, illaque
ad eundem Alphonsum Regem et ipsius Successores de jure
spectant et pertinent, neque quivis alius ex Christifidelibus absque ipsorum Alphonsi Regis et Successorum suorum licentia
speciali de illis se hactenus intromittere licite potuit nec potest
quoquomodo, ut ipse Alphonsus Rex ejusque Successores et
Infans eo sincerius huic tam piissimo ac praeclaro et omni aevo
memoratu dignissimo operi, in quo cum animarum salus, Fidei
augmentum et illius hostium depressio procurentur, Dei ipsiusque Fidei, ac Reipublicae universalis Ecclesiae rem agi con-
spicimus, insistere valeant et insistant, quos, sublatis quibusvis
dispendiis amplioribus, seu per Nos et Sedem Apostolicam
favoribus et gratiis munitos fore conspexerint.

De praemissis omnibus et singulis plenissime informati,
Motu proprio, non ad ipsorum Alphonsi Regis et Infantis, vel
alterius pro eis nobis super hoc oblatae petitionis instantiam,
maturaque prius desuper deliberatione praehabita, auctoritate
Apostolica et ex certa scientia, de Apostolicae potestatis plenitudine, Litteras facultatis praefatas, quarum tenores de verbo
ad verbum praesentibus haberi volumus pro insertis, cum omnibus et singulis in eis contentis clausulis ad Ceptensem et praedicta et quaecumque alia etiam ante datam dictarum facultatem
Litterarum acquisita, ea, quae in posterum nomine dictorum
Alphonsi Regis suorumque Successorum et Infantis in ipsis ac
illis circumvicinis et ulterioribus ac remotioribus partibus de
Infidelium seu Paganorum manibus adquiri potuerunt, Provincias, Insulas, Portus et maria quaecumque extendi, et illa sub
ejusdem facultatis Litteris comprehendi, ipsarumque facultatis

et praesentiarum Litterarum vigore jam acquisita et quae in futurum acquiri contigerit, postquam adquisita fuerint, ad praefatum Regem et Successores suos ac infantem, ipsamque conquestam, quam a Capitibus de Boxador et de Nam [Nun] usque per totam Ghineam, videlicet versus illam meridionalem plagam extendi, harum serie declaramus, etiam ad ipsos Alphonsum Regem et Successores suos et Infantem, et non ad aliquos alios, spectasse et pertinuisse, ac in perpetuum spectare et pertinere de jure; necnon Alphonsum Regem et Successores suos ac Infantem praedictos in illis, et circa quaecumque prohibitiones, statuta, et mandata etiam poenalia et cum cuiusvis tributi impositione facere, et de ipsis et de rebus propriis et aliis ipsorum Dominiis disponere et ordinare potuisse, ac nunc et in futurum posse libere et licite, tenorum praesentium, decernimus et declaramus, ac pro potioris juris et cautela suffragio, jam acquisita et quae in posterum acquiri contigerit, Provincias, Insulas, Portus, loca et maria quaecumque, quotcumque et qualiacumque fuerint, ipsam conquestam a Capitibus de Boxador et de Nam [Nun] praedictis, Alphonso Regi et Successoribus suis Regibus dictorum Regnorum ac Infantis praefatis, perpetuo donamus, concedimus et appropriamus per praesentes.

Praeterea, cum ad perficiendum opus hujusmodi multipliciter sit opportunum, quod Alphonsus Rex et Successores ac Infans praedicti, necnon personae quibus hoc duxerint, seu aliquis ipsorum duxerit committendum, illius dicto Joanni Regi per felicis recordationis Martinum V, et alterius indultorum etiam inclytae memoriae Eduardo, eorundem Regnorum Regi, ejusdem Alphonsi Regis Genitori, per piae memoriae Eugenium IV, Romanos Pontifices, Praedecessores nostros, concessorum versus dictas partes cum quibusdam Saracenis et Infidelibus de quibuscumque re et bonis et victualibus, emptiones et venditiones, prout congruit facere, necnon quoscumque contractus inire, transigere, pascisci, mercari ac negotiari, et merces quascumque ad ipsorum Saracenorum et Infidelium loca, dummodo

ferramenta, lignamina, funes, naves seu armaturarum genera
non sint, deferre; et ea dictis Saracenis et Infidelibus vendere,
omnia quoque alia et singula in praemissis, et circa ea oppor-
tuna vel necessaria facere, gerere et exercere, ipsique Alphonsus
Rex, Successores et Infans in jam adquisitis et per eum adqui-
rendis Provinciis, Insulis ac locis quaecumque Ecclesias, Monasteria et alia pia loca fundare ac fundari et construi: necnon
quascumque personas Ecclesiasticas, saeculares et quorumvis
etiam Mendicantium Ordinum Regulares (de Superiorum tamen
licentia) ad illa transmittere, ipsaeque personae inibi etiam,
quae advenerint, commorari, ac quorumcumque in dictis partibus existentium vel accedentium Confessiones audire, illisque
auditis, in omnibus praeterquam Sedi praedictae reservatis casi-
bus debitam absolutionem impendere ac poenitentiam salutiferam injungere, necnon Ecclesiastica Sacramenta valeant libere
ac licite decernimus; ipsique Alphonso et Successoribus suis,
Regibus Portugalliae, qui erunt in posterum, et Infanti praefato
concedimus et indulgemus. . . . Datum Romae, apud S. Petrum,
anno Incarnationis Dominicae millesimo quadringentesimo qui-
quagesimo quarto, VI Idus Januarii, Pontificatus nostri anno
octavo.

*Inter caetera quae**
(Calixtus III, 1456)

Calixtus, Episcopus, Servus Servorum Dei. Ad perpetuam
rei memoriam.

Inter caetera quae Nobis, Divina disponente clementia, in-
cumbunt peragenda, ad id nimirum solliciti corde reddimur, ut
singulis locis, et praesertim quae Saracenis sunt finitima, Divinus cultus ad laudem et gloriam Omnipotentis Dei, et Fidei
Christianae exaltationem vigeat, et continuum suscipiat incre-

---

* Hernáez, *Colección*, II, 824-30; García Gutiérrez, *Bulario*, pp. 13-15. For the
translation see pp. 55-57.

mentum; et quae Regibus et Principibus per Praedecessores nostros, Romanos Pontifices, benemeritis concessa sunt, et causis legitimis emanarunt, ut omnibus sublatis dubitationibus robur perpetuae firmitatis obtineant, Apostolico munimine solidemus. Dudum siquidem felicis recordationis Nicholas Papa V, Praedecessor noster, litteras concessit tenoris subsequentis: . . . Cum autem, sicut pro parte Alphonsi Regis et Henrici Infantis praedictorum ipsi supra modum affectent, quod spiritualitas in eisdem solitariis Insulis, terris, portubus et locis, et Mari Oceano versus meridionalem plagam in Guinea consistentibus, quas idem Infans de manibus Saracenorum manu armata extraxit, et Christianae Religioni, ut praefertur, conquisivit, praefatae Militiae Jesu Christi, cujus reddituum suffragio idem Infans hujusmodi conquistam fecisse perhibetur, per Sedem Apostolicam perpetuo concedatur; et declaratio, constitutio, donatio, concessio, appropriatio, decretum, obsecratio, exhortatio, munitio, inhibitio, mandatum et voluntas, necnon Litterae Nicholai Praedecessoris hujusmodi, ac omnia et singula in eis contenta confirmentur. Quare pro parte Regis et Infantis praedictorum nobis fuit humiliter supplicatum, ut declarationi, constitutioni, concessioni, appropriationi, decreto, obsecrationi, exhortationi, injunctioni, inhibitioni, mandato vel voluntati, ac Litteris hujusmodi, et in eis contentis pro illorum substantia firmiori, robur Apostolicae confirmationis addicere: Necnon spiritualitates ac omnimodam jurisdictionem ordinariam, tam in praedictis acquisitis, quam aliis Insulis, terris et locis per eosdem Regem et Infantem, seu eorum successores, in partibus dictorum Saracenorum in futurum acquirendis, praefatae Militiae et Ordini hujusmodi perpetuo concedere, aliasque, in praemissis, opportune providere de benignitate Apostolica dignaremur.

Nos igitur attendentes Religionem dictae Militiae in eisdem insulis, et in terris et locis fructus afferre posse in Domino salutares, hujusmodi supplicationibus inclinati, declarationem, constitutionem, donationem, appropriationem, decretum, obse-

crationem, exhortationem, munitionem, injunctionem, sequuta
quaecumque, rata et grata habentes, illa omnia et singula actori-
tate Apostolica, tenore praesentium, et certa scientia confirmamus et approbamus, ac robur perpetuae firmitatis subsistere
decernimus: Supplentes omnes defectus, si qui forsitan intervenerint in eisdem; et nihilominus auctoritate et scientia praedictis perpetuo decernimus, statuimus, et ordinamus, quod spiritualitas et omnimoda jurisdictio ordinaria, dominium et potestas
in spiritualibus dumtaxat, Insulis, villis, portubus, terris et locis
a Capitibus de Boxador et de Nam [Nun] usque per totam
Guineam, et ultra illam Meridionalem plagam usque ad Indios,
acquisitis et acquirendis, quorum situm, numerum, qualitatem,
vocabula, designationes, confines et loca praesentibus pro expressis haberi volumus, ad Militiam et Ordinem hujusmodi perpetuis futuris temporibus spectent atque pertineant, illaque eis
ex nunc tenore, auctoritate et scientia praedictis concedimus et
elargimur.

Ita quod Prior Major pro tempore existens Ordinis dictae
Militiae et omnia et singula Beneficia Ecclesiastica, cum cura et
sine cura, saecularia et Ordinum quorumcumque Regularium in
Insulis et terris et locis praedictis fundata et instituta, seu fun-
danda et instituenda, cujuscumque qualitatis et valoris existant
seu fuerint, quoties illa in futurum vacare contigerit, conferre, et
de illis providere. Necnon Excommunicationis, suspensionis, et
interdicti aliasque Ecclesiasticas sententias, censuras et poenas,
quoties opus fuerit, ac rerum et negotiorum pro tempore in-
gruentium qualitas id exegerit, proferre, omniaque et singula,
quae locorum Ordinariis in locis, in quibus spiritualitatem habere censentur, de jure vel consuetudine facere, disponere et
exequi possint et consueverunt, pariformiter absque ulla dif-
ferentia facere, disponere, ordinare et exequi possit et debeat;
super quibus omnibus et singulis ei plenam et liberam [jurisdic-
tionem] tenore praesentium concedimus, decernentes Insulas,
terras et loca acquisita et acquirenda hujusmodi, nullius Dio-

cesis existere: ac irritum et inane, si secus super his a quoquam, quavis auctoritate, scienter vel ignoranter, contigerit attentari.

Non obstantibus Constitutionibus et Ordinationibus Apostolicis, necnon statutis, consuetudinibus, privilegiis, usibus et naturis, dictae Militiae juramento, confirmatione Apostolica vel quavis alia firmitate roboratis, caeterisque contrariis quibuscumque. Nulli ergo omnino hominum liceat hanc paginam nostrorum confirmationis, approbationis, constitutionis, suppletionis, decreti, statuti, ordinationis, voluntatis, concessionis, elargitionis, infringere vel ausu temerario contraire. Si quis autem. . . .

Datum Romae, apud S. Petrum, anno Incarnationis Dominicae millesimo quadringentesimo quinquagesimo sexto. Idibus Martii, Pontificatus nostri anno primo.

Laudibus et honore*
(Eugene IV, 1436)

Eugenius Episcopus Servus Servorum Dei ad perpetuam rei memoriam.

Laudibus et honore dignissima carissimi in Xto filii Nostri Joannis Castelle et Legionis Regis illustris actus et opera quibus ipse strenue vel uti pugil et athleta prout celebris *[1] descendit adversus Saracenos perfidos Xrianique nominis inimicos etiam proprio corpore non indulgens aciem dirigere dictorum Saracenorum terras et loca Xti fidelium dictioni subjugare non tepescit ac preclare illud erga Nos et Romanam ecclesiam splendere dignoscitur integritatem devotionis intra nostre mentis archana revolventes digne ducimur ut ipsius Regis illas presertim quibus etiam ad salutiferam similium actuum operumque continuationem Johannes prefatus ac ejus successores pro tempore exis-

---

* In the archive of Simancas, Sección Patronato Real, legajo 69, 1. For the translation see pp. 64-65.

[1] In these bulls an asterisk always indicates a missing or illegible word or words.

tentes Castelle et Legionis Reges ferventius animari possint
petitiones et auditiones ipsas favorabiliter admittamus hinc est
quod Nos etiam recensentes quod felicis recordationis Urbanus
Papa II predecessor Noster devotionis et reverentie quas reco-
lende memorie Rex Hispaniarum tunc existens ad eandem ecclesiam gerebat magnitudinem digne perstringens ipsi Regi Hispaniarum necnon ejus successoribus illorumque militibus Ecclesias et Capellas quas ipsi in predictorum terris Saracenorum
caperent ac in Regno inibi edificari facerent per suas litteras
concessit necnon ejusdem Joannis Regis qui ut asserit ipsius
vigore concessionis a suis progenitoribus qui sicuti Catholice
Zelatores fidei multas ab ipsis Sarnecenis non sine magnis periculis dispendiis laboribus * et expensis terras recuperarunt et
conquisiverunt jus desuper complectendo plurimorum dignitatum aliorumque bonorum ecclesiasticorum disponere necnon in
diversis ecclesiis locis et Capellis ius patronatus habere digne
super his hac parte supplicationibus inclinati concessionem pre-
dictam et quevis inde secuta rata et grata habentes illa auctoritate Apostolica ex certa sciencia confirmamus et insuper ius
patronatus omnium et singularum etiam quas in terris ab eorundem Sarnacenorum manibus per ipsos Joannem Regem et ejus
successores acquirendis et Mesquitis locisque dictorum Sarnacenorum fieri et ad laudem divini nominis adaptari contigerit necnon aliarum quas predicti Joannes Rex et ejus successores in
Castelle et Legionis Regnis ac prefatis acquirendis terris de suis
bonis fundaverunt atque doitaverunt ecclesiarum et presentandi
locorum ordinariis personas idoneas ad ipsas quotiens vacaverint eisdem Johanni Regi ac ipsius successoribus auctoritate predicta perpetuo reservamus iure tamen omnislibet alterius in
omnibus alias semper salvo Nulli ergo omnino hominum liceat
hanc paginam nostre confirmationis approbationis communi-
tionis et reservationis infringere vel ei ausu temerario contrahire
si quis autem hoc attemptare presumpserit indignationem omnipotentis Dei ac beatorum Petri et Pauli Apostolorum Ejus se

noverit incursurum datum Bononie anno Incarnationis dominice Millesimo quadringentesimo trigesimo sexto Nono Kalendas Augusti Pontificatus nostri anno sexto.

*Orthodoxe fidei propagationem**
(Innocent VIII, 1486)[1]

Innocentius, Episcopus, Servus Servorum Dei. Ad perpetuam rei memoriam.

Orthodoxe fidei propagationem nostre cure celitus commissam et Christiane religionis augmentum et animarum salutem barbararum quoque nationum et aliorum infidelium quorumlibet depresionem et ad fidem conversionem supremis desiderantes affectibus Catholicos reges et principes ad id navantes Christi athletas et propugnatores acerrimos Apostolicis gratiis et favoribus prosequi continuo non cessamus ut tam pro necessario tam qualis Immortali Deo cujus causa agitur accepto operi eo diligentiori et solerciori cura insistant quo exinde cognoverint se preter animarum suarum salutem Apostolice Sedis benevolentiam uberrime quesivisse et illa eis libenter concedimus per que expugnatorum per eos pro tempore locorum et incolarum earundem sub eorum ditioni manutentioni et conservationi

---

* In the archive of Simancas, Sección Patronato Real, legajos 38, 4 and 69, 1. For the translation see pp. 66-70.

[1] This original of 1486 and its copy of 1488 (respectively legajos 38, 4 and 69, 1 in Sección Patronato Real of Simancas) when compared present an interesting study in the reliability of transcriptions. The copy employs abbreviations over forty times when its original spells completely. Words are altered: *consuetudo* to *asuetudo* and *consistencia* to *asistencia*, apparently at whim. *Spiritualibus* occurs as *Spanalibus*; *opida* disappears entirely, as do *eo* and *ei* and *ac* several times, and *applicati* appears as *alocati*. *Contingeret* fares badly. *Prioratuum* vanishes once, while *obtinentium* becomes *obtentis*, and *consensu* is *assensu*. *Concedimus* is once written *ac dicimus*. *Dote* and *dotari* are frenchified to *doite* and *doitari*. The vital *contradictores* somehow becomes *a tradictores*. The 38, 4 is a wonderfully preserved parchment, and when compared with the 69, 1 indicates the world of difference between cultured Rome and crusading Spain in the days of Granada.

ac in illis constituimus Ecclesiasiarum monasteriorum et aliorum beneficiorum ecclesiasticorum votive devotioni et bonorum
eorundem occupatorum recuperationi et conservationi utiliter et
salubriter valeat provideri.

Sane carissimus in Christo filius Noster Fernandus Rex et
carissima in Christo filia Nostra Helisabeth Regina Castelle et
Legionis illustres inter alios Christianorum reges et reginas
Sumi rerum omnium Opificis et Conditoris cunctorum bonorum
Auctoris Dei Omnipotentis gratia amplissimorum regnorum dif-
fusissimo imperio et aliarum diversarum provinciarum Domino
subditorum obediencia devotione et observantia facultatum quoque omnium que sumis regibus necessaria fore noscuntur af-
fluencia et ubertate etate florida et animo ad omnia preclara
facinora parato in consiliis providencia et in administranda
iusticia constancia ac multarum preclarissimarum rerum ab eis
gestarum gloria et in re militari pericia fortitudine et audacia
decorati ut tantorum bonorum Auctori gratias referrent et ali-
quid preclarum ad Ejusdem Omnipotentis Dei honorem et imperii Christianorum propagationem aggrederentur non solum
coeptum opus expugnationis infidelium insularum Canarie prosequi et continuare curarunt.

Sed etiam regnum Granate ante eorum oculos consistens pro-
sapie regnum Hispaniarum debitum aspurcissimis Saracenis
Christiani nominis hostibus detentum superioribus annis oppug-
nare et eorum ditioni subiicere ac in locis ab eisdem Sarracenis
acquisitis et acquirendis ecclesias monasteria et beneficia ecclesiastica erigi eisdem certam partem decimarum ac fructuum et
redituum et proventuum ecclesiasticorum dictorum locorum
applicari et eo eis dotari facere devenerunt. Et non in propria
sed Eiusdem Omnipotentis Dei fortitudine et providencia confidentes opus ipsum omni ex parte dificilimum prosequendo illius
civitates castra opida et alia loca plurima fere tertiam eiusdem
regni Granate partem uti accepimus constituencia Divina favente dementia eorum ditioni subiugaverunt. Et tam in regno

Granate quam insulis predictis prosperitatis votivis successibus subiugare non cessant in dies ad quorum civitatum locorum et castrorum acquisitorum et que acquiri contigerit in futurum per eos et eorum successores Castelle et Legionis Reges conservationem sub eorum imperio et manutentione fidei prefate in eisdem, ut dilectus filius nobilis vir Enecus López de Mendoza Comes de Tendilla ipsorum Fernandi Regis et Helisabeth Regine Capitaneus pro eorum parte orator ad Nos et Sedem Apostolicam destinatus Nobis eorum nomine exposuit. Plurimum conferre arbitrantur quod Cathedralibus ecclesiis monasteriis et conventualibus prioritatibus pro tempore in locis per eos in eisdem insulis et regno Granate hactenus acquisitis ac villa Portus Regalis Gadicen Dioc ac aliis locis in regno Granate et insulis noviter populandis in futurum preficiantur persone ecclesiastice probe et diligentes orthodoxe fidei zelatrices vite munditia et morum honestate decore in spiritualibus provide et temporalibus circumspecte ac eisdem Regibus pro tempore grate et accepte et per similes obtineantur canonicatus et prebende et dignitates quecumque eorundem Cathedralium et Collegiatarum ecclesiarum acquisitorum et que acquirerentur et popularentur in posterum locorum predictorum, quarum laudabili vita et conversatione Divinorum assidua et devota celebratione ac ad benevivendum persuasione et exhortatione incole locorum eorundem pro tempore existentes a vitiis abstinere et virtutibus navare et suarum animarum salutem indefesso studio querere et eorundem Regum statum sincere devotionis affectu prosequi procurarent ab omni rebellione prorsus abstinerent.

Nos igitur qui nuper per alias Nostras litteras ad supplicationem Regis et Regine predictorum certis prelatis erigendi quecumque ecclesias monasteria et alia beneficia ecclesiastica in locis predictis illisque pro eorum dote fructus reditus et proventus ecclesiasticos applicandi facultatem concessimus sperantes quod si predictis Fernando Regi et Helisabeth Regine et pro tempore existentibus Castelle et Legionis Regibus concederetur Ius Patronatus ecclesiarum monasteriorum dignitatum prioratuum canonicatuum et prebendarum ac portionum huiusmodi profecto conservationi et manutentioni incolarum locorum eorundem acquisitorum et que acquiri contingeret in futurum sub eorundem Regum devotione sincera et in fide Catholica perseverancia opportune consulerentur persone quoque eisdem ecclesiis et monasteriis ac prioratibus presidentes ac dignitates canonicatus et prebendas et portiones huiusmodi obtinentes pro tempore eorundem Regum patronorum protectione auxilio et favore adiute occupata bona ecclesiarum monasteriorum prioratuum dignitatum canonicatuum et prebendarum recuperare et conservare facilius possent et ab omni oppressione defenderentur sustinerentque in singulis eorum opportunitatibus relevamen ac volentes conservationi fidei et status eorundem Regum in eisdem locis necnon ecclesiarum monasteriorum dignitatum prioratuum canonicatuum et prebendarum ac portionum huiusmodi necnon personarum illa obtinentium commoditatibus consulerent tenemur.

Habita super his cum fratribus Nostris deliberatione matura, de illorum consilio et expresso consensu plenum Ius Patronatus et presentandi personas idoneas Sedi Apostolice ad Cathedrales ecclesias necnon quorum fructus reditus et proventus ducentorum florenorum auri de Camara secundum extimationem communem valorem annuum excedant monasteria et prioratus conventuales in eisdem locis regni Granate et insularum Canarie per eosdem Fernandum Regem et Helisabeth Reginam hactenus acquisitis et que tam per eos quam eorum successores Hispaniarum Reges qui pro tempore erunt acquiri populari de novo quandocumque contigerit in futurum, et in predicta villa Portus Regalis consistentes et consistencia, necnon maiores post Pontificales in eisdem Cathedralibus et principales in Collegiatis, et locorum ordinarii ad alia monasteria et non maiores post Pontificales dignitates canonicatus et prebendas eorundem integras vel dimidias portiones Cathedralium et Collegiatarum in

eisdem locis jam erectarum et aliarum que in eis erigi contingeret postquam erecta et fructus reditus et proventus rite eis ut
prefertur applicati fuerint etiam ab eorum primeva erectione
vacantia perpetuis futuris temporibus Fernando Regi et Helisabeth Regine eorumque successoribus in perpetuum dictorum
Regnorum Regibus qui pro tempore erunt auctoritate Apostolica
tenore presentium concedimus et volumus ad eos de cetero
plenarie et libere pertinere et quod ad presentationes huiusmodi
quas per eosdem Fernandum Regem et Helisabeth Reginam eorumque successores pro tempore fieri continget sedes ipsas personas pro tempore ei presentatas ad Cathedrales ecclesias et
monasteria eisdem ecclesiis et monasteriis in presules et abbates
respective preficere, et tam sedes ipsas ad prioratus conventuales
ac majores et principales dignitates in Cathedralibus et Collegiatis Apostolica quam locorum ordinarii ad alias dignitates
canonicatus prebendas integras vel dimidias portiones huiusmodi presentatas pro tempore personas instituere in eisdem
ordinaria auctoritatibus teneantur et debeant et pro tempore
facte per sedem Apostolicam et Eius legatos speciales et generales reservationes ecclesiarum monasteriorum prioratuum dignitatum canonicatuum et prebendarum ac portionum et quevis
alie gratie et littere in quibus beneficia ecclesiastica Iuris Patronatus Laicorum de iure non includuntur ad ecclesias monasteria
prioratus conventuales dignitates canonicatus et prebendas ac
portiones que Iuris Patronatus huiusmodi fuerint.

Nullatenus si extendant provisionesque et perfectiones ab
eadem Sede et ordinariis aliter quam ad huiusmodi presenta-
tionem pro tempore nullas et invalidas fore de eorum fratrum
consilio prefata Auctoritate statuimus et ordinamus decernentes
irritum et inane quicquid secus super his a quoquam quavis auctoritate scienter vel ignoranter contigerit attemptari.

Et nichilominus venerabilibus fratribus Archiepiscopo Tol-
lete et Palencie et Conchen Episcopis per Apostolica scripta
mandamus quatenus ipsi vel duo aut unus eorum per se vel per

alium seu alios premissa ubi quando et quotiens expedire cognoverint fuerintque pro parte Fernandi Regis et Helisabeth Regine eorumque successorum predictorum legitime requisiti solemniter publicantes faciant eosdem Fernandum Regem et Helisabeth Reginam ac successores pacifica quasi possessione Iuris Patronatus et presentandi perpetuo potiri et gaudere, et personas per eos pro tempore presentatas recipi et admitti et ad presentationes ipsas si canonice facte fuerint prefici et institui juxta statuti predicti tenorem Contradictores auctoritate Nostra appellatione postposita compescendo. Non obstantibus Constitutionibus et ordinationibus Apostolicis ac juramento confirmatione Apostolica vel quavis alia firmitate roboratis ecclesiarum et monasteriorum huiusmodi ordinumque eorundem statutis et consuetudinibus ceterisque contrariis quibuscumque seu si locorum ordinariis prefatis vel quibusvis aliis communiter vel divisive a Sede predicta indultum existat quod interdici suspendi vel excommunicari non possint per litteras Apostolicas non facientes plenam et expressam ac de verbo ad verbum de indulto huiusmodi mentionem per hoc autem Regibus prefatis in eisdem monasteriis prioratibus dignitatibus canonicatibus et prebendis ac portionibus et beneficiis ecclesiasticis.

Nullum aliud Ius quam Patronatus et presentandi huiusmodi acquiri volumus nec alias quomodolibet Apostolice Sedis et aliarum ecclesiarum libertati superioritati ac iurisdictioni in eisdem preiudicari intendimus nulli ergo omnino hominum liceat hanc paginam Nostre concessionis statuti ordinationis decreti mandati et voluntatis infringere vel ei ausu temerario contraire si quis autem hoc attemptare presumpserit indignationem Omnipotentis Dei ac beatorum Petri et Pauli Apostolorum Eius se noverit incursurum. Datum Rome apud Sanctum Petrum anno Incarnationis Dominice millesimo quadringentesimo octuagesimo sexto Idus Decembris Pontificatus Nostri Anno Tercio.

Inter caetera divinae*
(Alexander VI, 1493)

Alexander, Episcopus, Servus Servorum Dei. Charissimo in Christo filio Ferdinando Regi et charissimae in Christo filiae Elizabeth, reginae, Castellae, Legionis, Aragonum, Siciliae et Granatae illustribus, salutem et Apostolicam benedictionem.

Inter caetera divinae majestati beneplacita opera et cordis nostri desiderabilia illud profecto potissimum existit ut fides catholica et christiana religio nostris praesertim temporibus exaltetur, ac ubilibet amplietur et dilatetur, animarumque salus procuretur, ac barbarae nationes deprimantur et ad fiden ipsam reducantur. Unde cum ad hanc sacram Petri sedem, divina favente clementia (meritis licet imparibus,) evocati fuerimus, cognoscentes vos tamquam veros catholicos Reges et Principes, quales semper fuisse novimus et a vobis praeclare gesta toti pene jam orbi notissima demonstrant, nedum id exoptare sed omni conatu, studio et diligentia, nullis laboribus, nullis impensis, nullisque parcendo periculis etiam proprium sanguinem effundendo, efficere ac omnem animum vestrum omnesque conatus ad hoc iamdudum dedicasse, quemadmodum recuperatio regni Granatae a tyrannide Saracenorum hodiernis temporibus per vos cum tanta divini nominis gloria facta testatur, digne ducimus non immerito et debemus illa vobis etiam sponte et favorabiliter concedere, per quae huiusmodi sanctum et laudabile ac immortali Deo acceptum propositum in dies ferventiori animo ad ipsius Dei honorem et imperii christiani propagationem prosequi valeatis. Sane accepimus quod vos qui dudum animum proposueratis aliquas insulas et terras firmas remotas et incognitas, ac per alios hactenus non repertas, quaerere et invenire ut illarum incolas et habitatores ad colendum Redemptorem nostrum et fidem catholicam profitendum reduceretis, hac-

---

* Hernáez, *Colección*, I, 12-14. For the translation see pp. 78-81.

tenus in expugnatione et recuperatione ipsius regni Granatae plurimum occupati, huiusmodi sanctum et laudabile propositum vestrum ad optatum finem perducere nequivistis, sed tandem, sicut Domino placuit regno praedicto recuperato, volentes desiderium adimplere vestrum, dilectum filium Christopherum Colon, virum utique dignum et plurimum commendandum ac tanto negotio aptum, cum navigiis et hominibus ad similia instructis, non sine maximis laboribus et periculis ac expensis destinastis, ut terras firmas et insulas remotas et incognitas huiusmodi per mare ubi hactenus navigatum non fuerat, diligenter inquireret. Qui tandem divino auxilio facta extrema diligencia in mare oceano navigantes, certas insulas remotissimas et etiam terras firmas quae per alios hactenus repertae non fuerant invenerunt, in quibus quamplurimae gentes pacifice viventes et ut asseritur nudi incedentes nec carnibus vescentes inhabitant, et ut praefati nuncii vestri possunt opinari, gentes ipsae in insulis et terris praedictis habitantes credunt unum Deum creatorem in coelis esse ac ad fidem catholicam amplexandum et bonis moribus imbuendum satis apti videntur spesque habetur quod si erudirentur nomen salvatoris Domini nostri Jesu Christi in terris et insulis praedictis facile induceretur, ac praefatus Christophorus in una ex principalibus insulis praedictis jam unam turrim satis munitam, in qua certos Christianos qui secum iverant in custodiam et ut alias insulas ac terras firmas remotas et incognitas inquirerent posuit, construit et aedificari fecit. In quibus quidem insulis et terris jam repertis aurum, aromata et aliae quamplurimae res pretiosae diversi generis et diversae qualitatis reperiuntur. Unde omnibus diligenter et praesertim fidei catholicae exaltatione et dilatatione (prout decet catholicos Reges et principes) consideratis, more progenitorum vestrorum clarae memoriae regum, terras firmas et insulas praedictas illarumque incolas et habitatores vobis divina favente clementia subjicere et ad fidem catholicam reducere proposuistis.

Nos igitur huiusmodi vestrum sanctum et laudabile propositum plurimum in Domino commendantes, ac cupientes ut illud
ad debitum finem perducatur, et ipsum nomen Salvatoris nostri
in partibus illis inducatur, hortamur vos quamplurimum in
Domino et per sacri lavacri susceptionem qua mandatis apostolicis obligati estis et viscera misericordiae Domini nostri
Jesu Christi attente requirimus, ut cum expeditionem huiusmodi
omnino prosequi, et assumere prona mente orthodoxae fidei zelo
intendatis populos, in huiusmodi insulis et terris degentes ad
christianam religionem suscipiendum inducere velitis et debeatis, nec pericula nec labores ullo unquam tempore vos deterreant
firma spe fiduciaque conceptis quod Deus omnipotens conatus
vestros foeliciter prosequetur. Et ut tanti negotii provinciam
apostolicae gratiae largitate donati liberius et audatius assu-
matis, moto proprio, non ad vestram vel alterius pro vobis super
hoc nobis oblatae petitionis instantiam, sed de nostra mera libe-
ralitate et ex certa scientia ac de apostolicae potestatis plenitudine, omnes insulas et terras firmas inventas et inveniendas, detectas et detegendas, versus occidentem et meridiem, fabricando
et construendo unam lineam a polo artico, scilicet Septentrione,
ad polum antarticum, scilicet Meridiem, sive terrae firmae et
insulae inventae et inveniendae sint versus Indiam aut versus
aliam quamcumque partem, quae linea distet a qualibet insularum quae vulgariter nuncupantur de los Azores et Cabo Verde
centum leucis versus occidentem et meridiem. Itaque omnes insulae et terrae firmae, repertae et reperiendae, detectae et dete-
gendae, a praefata linea versus occidentem et meridiem, [quae]
per alium regem aut principem christianum non fuerint actualiter possessae usque ad diem Nativitatis Domini nostri Jesu
Christi proxime praeteritum, a quo incipit annus praesens mille-
simus quadringentesimus nonagesimus tertius, quando fuerunt
per Nuncios et Capitaneos vestros inventae aliquae praedictorum insularum, auctoritate omnipotentis Dei nobis in beato
Petro concessa, ac vicariatus Jesu Christi qua fungimur in terris,

cum omnibus illarum dominiis, civitatibus, castris, locis, villis, juribusque et jurisdictionibus ac pertinentiis universis, vobis haeredibusque et successoribus vestris Castellae et Legionis in perpetuum tenore praesentium donamus, concedimus et assignamus, vosque et haeredes ac successores praefatos illarum dominos cum plena, libera et omnimoda potestate, auctoritate et jurisdictione facimus, constituimus et deputamus. Decernentes nihilominus per huiusmodi donationem, concessionem et assignationem nostram nulli christiano principi qui actualiter praefatas insulas et terras firmas possiderit usque ad praedictum diem Nativitatis Domini nostri Jesu Christi jus quaesitum sublatum intelligi posse aut auferri debere. Et insuper mandamus vobis in virtute sanctae obedientiae ut (sicut etiam pollicemini, et non dubitamus pro vestra maxima devotione et regia magnanimitate vos esse facturos) ad terras firmas et insulas praedictas viros probos et Deum timentes, doctos, peritos et expertos, ad instruendum incolas et habitatores praefatos in fide catholica et bonis moribus imbuendum destinare debeatis, omnem debitam diligentiam in praemissis adhibentes. Ac quibuscumque personis, cujuscumque dignitatis etiam imperialis et regalis status, gradus, ordinis vel conditionis, sub excommunicationis latae sententiae poena, quam eo ipso si contra fecerint incurrant, districtius inhibemus ne ad insulas et terra firmas, inventas et inveniendas, detectas et detegendas, versus occidentem et meridiem, fabricando et construendo lineam a polo artico ad polum antarticum, sive terrae firmae et insulae inventae et inveniendae sint versus Indiam aut versus aliam quamcumque partem, quae linea distet a qualibet insularum quae vulgariter nuncupantur de los Azores et Cabo Verde centum leucis versus occidentem et meridiem, ut praefertur, pro mercibus habendis vel quavis alia de causa accedere praesumant, absque vestra ac haeredum et successorum vestrorum praedictorum licentia speciali.

Non obstantibus constitutionibus et ordinationibus apostolicis caeterisque contrariis quibuscumque. In illo a quo imperia et dominationes ac bona cuncta procedunt confidentes, quod dirigente Domino actus vestros si huiusmodi sanctum et laudabile propositum prosequamini, brevi tempore cum foelicitate et gloria totius populi Christiani vestri labores et conatus exitum foelicissimum consequentur. Verum quia difficile foret praesentes litteras ad singula quaeque loca in quibus expediens fuerit deferri, volumus ac motu et scientia similibus decernimus quod illarum transumptis manu publici notarii inderogati subscriptis, et sigillo alicuius personae in ecclesiastica dignitate constitutae seu curiae ecclesiasticae munitis, ea prorsus fides in judicio et extra ac alias ubilibet adhibeatur, quae praesentibus adhiberetur, si essent exhibitae vel ostensae. Nulli ergo omnino hominum liceat hanc paginam nostrae commendationis, hortationis, requisitionis, donationis, concessionis, assignationis, constitutionis, deputationis, decreti, mandati, inhibitionis et voluntatis infringere vel ei ausu temerario contraire. Si quis autem hoc attemptare praesumpserit, indignationem omnipotentis Dei ac beatorum Petri et Pauli apostolorum ejus se noverit incursurum. Datum Romae apud sanctum Petrum anno Incarnationis Dominicae millesimo quadringentesimo nonagesimo tertio, quarto nonas maji, pontificatus nostri anno primo.

Eximiae devotionis*
(Alexander VI, 1493)

Alexander, Episcopus, Servus Servorum Dei. Charissimo in Christo filio Ferdinando Regi, et Charissimae in Christo filiae Elisabeth Reginae, Castellae, Legionis, Aragonum et Granatae illustribus, salutem et Apostolicam benedictionem.

Eximiae devotionis sinceritas et integra Fides quibus Nos et Romanam reveremini Ecclesiam non indigne merentur ut illa vobis favorabiliter concedamus, per quae Sanctum et laudabile propositum vestrum et opus incoeptum in quaerendis terris et

---

* García Gutiérrez, *Bulario*, pp. 21-22. For the translation see pp. 82-84.

insulis remotis ac incognitis in dies melius et facilius ad honorem Omnipotentis Dei et Imperii Christiani propagationem ac
Fidei Catholicae exaltationem prosequi valeatis. Hodie siquidem omnes et singular terras firmas et insulas remotas et incognitas versus partes Occidentales et Mare Oceanum, per Vos seu
Nuntios vestros ad id propterea non sine magnis laboribus periculis et impensis destinatos repertas et reperiendas inposterum,
quae sub actuali dominio temporali aliquorum dominorum
Christianorum constitutae non essent, cum omnibus illarum
Dominiis, Civitatibus, Castris, Locis, Villis, Jurisdictionibus universis, vobis haeredibusque et successoribus vestris Castellae et
Legionis Regibus in perpetuum, motu proprio et ex certa scientia ac de Apostolicae potestatis plenitudine donavimus, concessimus, et assignavimus prout in nostris inde consectis litteris plenius continentur.

Cum autem alias nonnullis Portugalliae Regibus qui in partibus Africae, Guineae et Minae auri alias insulas etiam ex
similibus concessione et donatione Apostolica eis acta repere-
runt et acquisiverunt, per Sedem Apostolicam diversa privilegia,
gratiae, libertates, immunitates, exemptiones, facultates, litterae, et indulta concessa fuerint, Nos volentes etiam (prout dignum et conveniens exsistit) Vos, haeredesque et successores
vestros praedictos non minoribus gratiis, praerogativis et favoribus prosequi: motu simili, non ad vestram vel alterius pro vobis
super hoc oblatae petitionis instantiam, sed de nostra mera libe-
ralitate, ac eisdem scientia et Apostolicae potestatis plenitudine,
vobis et haeredibus et successoribus vestris praedictis, ut in insulis et terris per vos seu nomine vestro hactenus repertis huiusmodi et reperiendis in posterum, omnibus et singulis gratiis, et
privilegiis, exemptionibus, libertatibus, facultatibus, immunitatibus, litteris et indultis Regibus Portugalliae concessis huiusmodi, quarum omnium tenores ac si de verbis ad verbum praesentibus insererentur, haberi volumus pro sufficienter expressis
et insertis, uti, potiri, et gaudere libere et licite possitis, et de-

beatis in omnibus et per omnia perinde ac si illa omnia vobis ac haeredibus et successoribus vestris praefatis specialiter concessa auctoritate Apostolica; tenore praesentium de speciali dono gratiae indulgemus, illaque in omnibus et per omnia ad vos haeredesque ac successores vestros praedictos extendimus pariter, et ampliamus ac eisdem modo et forma perpetuo concedimus.

Non obstantibus Constitutionibus et Ordinationibus Apostolicis, necnon omnibus illis quae in litteris Portugalli de Regibus concessio[-s] huiusmodi concessa sunt non obstare, caeterisque contrariis quibuscumque. Verum quia difficile foret praesentes litteras ad singula quaeque loca in quibus expediens foret deferri, volumus, ac motu et scientia similibus decernimus, quod illarum trassumptis manu publici Notarii inde rogati subscriptis et sigillo alicuius personae in Ecclesiastica dignitate constitutae seu Curiae Ecclesiasticae munitis, ea prorsus fides indubia, in judicio, et extra, ac alias ubilibet adhibeatur, quae praesentibus adhiberetur si essent exhibitae vel ostensae. Nulli ergo omnino hominum liceat, hanc paginam nostrorum indulti, extensionis, ampliationis, concessionis, voluntatis, et decreti infringere vel ei ausu temerario contraire. Si quis autem hoc attentare praesumpserit, indignationem Omnipotentis Dei ac Beatorum Petri et Pauli Apostolorum ejus se noverit incursurum. Dat. Romae apud Sanctum Petrum, anno Incarnationis Dominicae millesimo quadringentesimo nonagesimo tertio, et quarto nonas Maii, Pontificatus nostri anno primo.

Dudum siquidem*
(Alexander VI, 1493)

Alexander, Episcopus, Servus Servorum Dei. Carissimo in Christo filio Ferdinando Regi, et Carissimae in Christo filiae Elisabeth, Reginae, Castellae Legionis Aragonum et Granatae illustribus, salutem et Apostolicam benedictionem.

---

* García Gutiérrez, *Bulario*, pp. 23-24. For the translation see pp. 85-87.

Dudum siquidem omnes et singulas insulas et terras firmas inventas et inveniendas versus Occidentem et Meridiem quae sub actuali dominio temporali aliquorum dominorum Christianorum constitutae non essent vobis haeredibusque et successoribus vestris Castellae et Legionis Regibus, in perpetuum, motu proprio et de certa scientia ac de Apostolicae potestatis plenitudine donavimus, concessimus et assignavimus, vosque ac haeredes et successores praefatos de illis investivimus, illarumque dominos cum plena, libera, et omnimoda potestate, auctoritate, et jurisdictione constituimus et deputavimus prout nostris inde confectis litteris, quarum tenorem ac si de verbo ad verbum praesentibus insererentur haberi volumus pro sufficienter expressis, plenius continetur.

Cum autem contingere posset quod Nuntii et Capitanei aut vasalli vestri versus Occidentem et Meridiem navigantes ad partes Orientales applicarent, ac insulas et terras firmas quae inde fuissent vel essent reperirent, Nos volentes etiam vos favoribus prosequi gratiosis, motu et scientia ac potestatis Apostolicae plenitudine similibus, donationem, concessionem, assignationem et litteras praedictas, cum omnibus, et singulas insulas et terras firmas inventas et inveniendas ac detectas et detegendas quae navigando aut itinerando versus Occidentem aut Meridiem huiusmodi sint vel fuerint aut apparuerint, sive in partibus Occidentalibus vel Meridionalibus et Orientalibus et Indiae existant, auctoritate Apostolica tenore praesentium in omnibus et per omnia perinde ac si in litteris praedictis de eis plena et expressa mentio facta fuisset extendimus pariter et ampliamus. Vobis ac haeredibus et successoribus vestris praedictis per vos vel alium seu alios corporalem insularum ac terrarum praedictarum possessionem propria auctoritate libere apprehendendi, ac perpetuo retinendi, illasque adversus quoscumque impedientes etiam defendendi, plenam et liberam facultatem concedentes, ac quibuscumque personis etiam cuiuscumque dignitatis, status, gradus, ordinis, vel conditionis, sub excommunicationis latae sententiae poena, quam contra facientes eo ipso incurrant, districtius inhibentes ne ad partes praedictas ad navigandum, piscandum vel inquirendum insulas vel terras firmas aut quovis alio respectu seu colore ire vel mittere quoquomodo praesumant, absque expressa vel speciali vestra ac haeredum et successorum praedictorum licentia.

Non obstantibus constitutionibus, facultatibus, assignationibus, per Nos vel praedecessores nostros, quibuscumque Regibus vel Principibus, infantibus, aut quibusvis aliis personis aut Ordinibus et Militiis de praedictis partibus, maribus, insulis atque terris, vel aliqua eorum parte, ex quibusvis causis etiam pietatis, vel fidei aut redemptionis captivorum et aliis quantumcumque urgentissimis, et cum quibusvis clausulis etiam derogatoriarum derogatoriis, fortioribus, efficacioribus et insolitis, etiam quascumque sententias, censuras, et poenas in se continentibus, quae suum per actualem et realem possessionem non essent sortitae effectum, licet forsan aliquando illi quibus donationes et concessiones huiusmodi factae fuissent aut eorum Nuntii ibidem navigassent. Quas, tenores illarum etiam praesentibus pro sufficienter expressis et insertis habentes, motu, scientia et potestatis plenitudine similibus omnino revocamus, ac quoad terras et insulas per eos actualiter non possessas pro insertis habere volumus; necnon omnibus illis quae in litteris praedictis voluimus non obstare coeterisque contrariis quibuscumque. Datum Romae apud Sanctum Petrum anno Incarnationis Dominicae millesimo quadringentesimo nonagesimo tertio 6 Kalend. Octobris Pontificatus Nostri anno 2.

*Eximie devotionis**
(Alexander VI, 1499)

Alexander episcopus servus servorum Dei. Carissimo in Christo filio Ferdinando Regi et Carissime in Christo filie Helisabeth Regine Hispaniarum catholicis salutem et apostolicam benedictionem.

Eximie devotionis sinceritas et integra fides quibus Nos et Romanam reveremini ecclesiam non indigne merentur ut honestis petitionibus vestris illis presertim per quas reipublice christiane necessitatibus pro tempore occurentibus valeat subveniri quantum cum Deo possumus favorabiliter annuamus. Cum itaque sicut ex litteris vestris et etiam vestri apud vos oratoris relatione accepimus vos inteligentes mala et damna que superiori anno perfidissimi Turchi Christi nominis hostes Christianum sanguinem continue sitientes Christianis intulerunt, et adhuc inferre non cessant maxima[m] classem maritimam nec minorem terrestrem exercitum ad invadendum Christianorum terras et dominia, parantes more Catholicorum Regum et Principum pro nostra singulari erga ipsam rempublicam Christianam affectione proposueratis pro viribus vestris ipsis perfidis Turchis resistere et jam magnam classem parare coeperitis. Et quia ad premissa peragenda maximas et intolerabiles expensas subire oportet necesse sit vobis in Regnis, Insulis, Terris et Dominiis vestris aliquas exactiones aut subsidia velut in partibus loquuntur Sisam regnicolis et habitatoribus Regnorum Insularum et Dominiorum praedictorum super victualibus imponere prout alias occurrentibus similibus necessitatibus facere consuevistis pro parte vestra nobis fuit humiliter supplicatum ut si contigerit ad dicte Sise impositionem devenire illam a secularibus et ecclesiasticis personis Regnorum Insularum Terrarum et Dominio-

---

* Pacheco y Cárdenas, *Colección de documentos inéditos*, II 5, 4-7. For the translation see pp. 88-89.

rum predictorum sponte solvere volentibus exigere valeatis licentiam concedere aliasque in praemissis oportune providere de benignitate Apostolica dignaremur.

Nos igitur attendentes conveniens esse ut occurente fidei catholice et ipsius reipublice Christiane defensione persone ecclesiastice et seculares id sponte facere volentes etiam sua suffragia per novas impositiones libere prestare possint huiusmodi, supplicationibus inclinati vobis, ut si contigerit in Regnis, Insulis, Terris et dominiis vestris predictis dictam Sisam pro huiusmodi defensionis necessitate imponere illas a saecularibus et ecclesiasticis ac religiosis personis utriusque sexus Regnorum Insularum Terrarum et Dominiorum predictorum cuiuscumque dignitatis status gradus ordinis et conditionis fuerint sponte solvere volentibus, pro uno anno duntaxat et non ultra in premissum defensionis opus et non in alios usus omnino convertendam, exigere et levare libere et licite valeatis auctoritate Apostolica tenore presentium de specialis dono gratie indulgemus non obstantibus constitutionibus et ordinationibus apostolicis ac statutis et consuetudinibus ecclesiarum, monasteriorum et aliorum religiosorum locorum ac ordinum quorumcumque juramento confirmatione apostolica et quavis firmitate alia roboratis ceterisque contrariis quibuscumque. Nulli ergo omnino hominum liceat hanc paginam nostre concessionis infringere vel ei ausu temerario contraire. Si quis auten hoc attemptare praesumpserit indignationem omnipotentis Dei ac beatorum Petri et Pauli Apostolorum ejus se noverit incursurum. Datum Rome apud Sanctum Petrum anno Incarnationis dominice milessimo quadringentesimo nono, duodecimo Kalendas Aprilis pontificatus nostri anno octavo.

*Eximiae devotionis**
(Alexander VI, 1501)

Alexander Episcopus, Servus Servorum Dei. Charissimo in Christo filio Ferdinando Regi, et charissimae in Christo filiae Elisabethae Reginae Hispaniarum Catholicis, salutem et Apostolicam Benedictionem.

Eximiae devotionis sinceritas, et integra fides quibus Nos et Romanam reveremini Ecclesiam non indigne merentur ut votis vestris, illis praesertim per quae circa Catholicae Fidei exaltationem ac infidelium et barbararum Nationum depressionem libentius et promptius intendere valeatis. Sane pro parte vestra Nobis nuper exhibita petitio continebat quod Vos pia ducti devotione pro Fidei Catholicae exaltatione summopere desideratis (prout jam a certo tempore citra, non sine magna impensa vestra ac laboribus, facere coepistis, et in dies magis facere non cessatis) Insulas et partes Indiarum acquirerere et recuperare, ut in illis quacumque damnata secta abjecta, colatur et veneretur Altissimus. Et quia pro recuperatione Insularum et partium praedictarum vobis necesse erit graves subire impensas et grandia pericula perferre, expedit ut pro conservatione et manutentione dictarum Insularum postquam per Vos acquisitae et recuperatae fuerint, ac perferendis impensis ad conservationem et manutentionem praedictarum partium necessariis, ab illarum incolis et habitatoribus pro tempore existentibus decimas exigere et levare possit. Quare pro parte vestra nobis fuit humillime supplicatum ut in praemissis vobis statuique vestro opportune providere de benignitate Apostolica dignaremur. Nos igitur qui eiusdem Fidei exaltationem et augmentum nostris potissime temporibus supremis desideramus affectibus, pium et laudabile propositum vestrum plurimum in Domino commendantes, huiusmodi supplicationibus inclinati, Vobis et successoribus vestris pro tem-

---

* García Gutiérrez, *Bulario*, pp. 25-26. For the translation see pp. 90-91.

pore existentibus, ut in Insulis praedictis ab illarum Incolis et habitatoribus etiam pro tempore existentibus, postquam illae acquisitae et recuperatae fuerint (ut praefertur), assignata prius realiter et cum effectu juxta ordinationem tunc Diocesanorum locorum, quorum conscientias super hoc oneramus, Ecclesiis in dictis Insulis erigendis per Vos et successores vestros praefatos, de vestris et eorum bonis dote sufficienti, ex qua illis Praesidentes earumque Rectores se commode sustentare, et onera dictis Ecclesiis pro tempore incumbentia perferre, ac cultum Divinum ad laudem Omnipotentis Dei commode exercere, juraque Episcopalia persolvere possint, Decimam hujusmodi percipere ac licite et libere levare valeatis, auctoritate Apostolica, tenore praesentium de speciali dono gratiae indulgemus. Non obstantibus Lateranensis Concilii ac aliis Constitutionibus et Ordinationibus Apostolicis caeterisque contrariis quibuscumque. Nulli ergo omnino liceat hanc paginam nostrae concessionis infringere, vel ei ausu temerario contraire. Si quis autem hoc attentare praesumpserit, indignationem Omnipotentis Dei ac Beatorum Petri et Pauli Apostolorum ejus se noverit incursurum. Datis Romae apud Sanctum Petrum, anno Incarnationis Domini millesimo quingentesimo primo, sextodecimo Kalendas Decembris, Pontificatus nostri anno decimo.

INSTRUCTIONS TO COLUMBUS*

(Ferdinand—Isabella, 1493)

Instruccion del Rey é de la Reina nuestros Señores para D. Cristóbal Colón, Almirante de sus Altezas de las islas é tierra-firme descubiertas é por descubrir en el mar Océano á la parte de las Indias, é su Visorey e Gobernador dellas; é otrosi Capitán general de esta armada que agora sus Altezas envian á las dichas islas é tierra-firme, para la forma que se ha de tener en este viage que agora face por mandado de sus Altezas, asi en

---

* Navarrete, *Colección*, II, 77-83. For the translation see pp. 93-94.

su partida é del armada que lleva, como en su camino, y después que allá sea llegado, Dios queriendo, en esta que se sigue:

Primameramente pues á Dios nuestro Señor plugo por su alta misericordia descobrir las dichas islas é tierra-firme al Rey é á la Reina nuestros Señores por industria de dicho D. Cristóbal Colon su Almirante, Visorey é Gobernador dellas, el cual ha fecho relacion á sus Altezas que las gentes que en ellas falló pobladas, conoció dellas ser gentes muy aparejadas para se convertir á nuestra Santa Fe Católica, porque no tienen nungena ley ni seta; de lo cual ha placido y place mucho á sus Altezas, porque en todo es razon que se tenga principalmente respeto al servicio de Dios nuestro Señor, é ensalzamiento de nuestra Santa Fe Cathólica; por ende sus Altezas deseando que nuestra Santa Fe Católica sea aumentada é acrescentada, mandan é encargan al dicho Almirante, Visorey é Gobernador, que por todas las vias é maneras que pudiere procure é trabaje atraer á los moradores de las dichas islas é tierra-firme á que se conviertan á nuestra Santa Fe Católica; y para ayuda á ello sus Altezas envian allá al docto P. Fr. Buil, juntamente con otros Religiosos quel dicho Almirante consigo ha de llevar, los cuales por mano é industria de los Indios que acá venieron, procure que sean bien informados de las cosas de nuestra Santa Fe, pues ellos sabrán e entenderán y mucho de nuestra lengua, ó procurando de los instruir en ella lo mejor que ser pueda; y porque esto mejor se pueda poner en obra despues que en buen hora sea llegada alla el armada, procure é haga el dicho Almirante que todos los que en ella van, e los que mas fueren de aqui adelante, traten muy bien é amorosamente á los dichos indios, sin que les fagan enojo alguno, procurando que tengan los unos con los otros mucha conversacion é familiaridad, haciéndose las mejores obras que ser pueda; é asimismo, el dicho Almirante des dé algunas dádivas graciosamente de las cosas de mercaradías de sus Altezas que lleva para el resgate, é los honre mucho; é si caso fuera que alguna ó algunas personas trataren mal á los dichos indios en cualquier manera que sea, el Almirante, como Visorey é Gobernador de sus Altezas, lo castigue mucho por virtud de los poderes de sus Altezas que para ello lleva; y porque las cosas espirituales sin las temporales no pueden luengamente durar, terná el dicho Almirante é Gobernador a las otras cosas la orden siguente. . . . Fecha en la Ciudad de Barcelona veinte é nueve dias del mes de Mayo, ano del Nacimiento de Nuestro Señor Jesu-Cristo de mil é cuatrocientos noventa y tres años. Yo el Rey—Yo la Reina. Por mandado del Rey e la Reina. Fernand Álvares.

INSTRUCTIONS TO OVANDO*

(Ferdinand—Isabella, 1501)

El Rey e La Reina: Granada, Setiembre 16 de 1501

Lo que vos Fray Niculás Dovando. Comendador de Láres, de la orden de Alcántara, abeys de facer en las Islas é Tierrafirme del Mar Océano, donde abeys de ser Nuestro Gobernador, es lo siguiente:

Primeramente, procurareis con muncha deligencia las cosas del servicio de Dios, e que los officios devinos se fagan con muncha estimacion e órden e rreverencia como conviene.

Item: porque Nos deseamos que los Yndios se conviertan a Nuestra Fée Cathólica e sus ánimas se salven, porque este es el mejor bien que les podemos desear, para lo qual es menester que sean ynformados en las cosas de Nuestra Fée, para que vengan en conoscimiento della, ternays muncho cuidado de procurar, sin les facer fuerza alguna, como los rreligiosos que allá estan, los ynformen e amonesten para ello con muncho amor, de manera que lo más presto que se pueda se conviertan; e para ello daréys todo el favor y ayuda que menester sea.

---

* Pacheco y Cárdenas, *Colección de documentos inéditos,* I 31, 13-25. For the translation see pp. 95-97.

Item: con Nuestras provisiones que llevays, procuraréis
como todos los vecinos e moradores de las dichas Islas e Tierra-
firme, se conformen con vos con sus personas e gentes, e vos
obedezcan como a Nuestro Gobernador en todas las cosas que
vos, de Nuestra parte le mandades; e ternáys muncho cuidado
como todos estén siempre en toda paz e concordia e xusticia, e
faciéndola administrar a todos, igualmente sin excepcion de
personas; e poniendo para ello buenos e suficientes menistros e
oficiales, castigando todo lo que se daba castigar en xusticia.

Item: procurareys como los yndios sean bien tratados e
puedan andar syguramente por toda la tierra, e nunguno los
faga fuerza nin los rroben, nin fagan otro mal nin dapño,
poniendo para ello las penas que vieredes ser menester, e execu-
tándolas en las personas quen ella fueren culpantes, e faciendo
sobrelo los pregones e defendimientos nescesarios.

Item: debéys de Nuestra parte a los Caciques e a los otros
principales que Nos, queremos que los Yndios sean bien tratados como Nuestros buenos súbditos e vasallos, e que nenguno
sea osado de les facer mal nin dapño; e ansi lo abeys de mandar
de Nuestra parte pregonar; e si dende aquí adelante alguno les
ficiere algun mal o dapño, o les thomasen por fuerza algo de
lo fagan saber, porque vos lo castigareys en tal manera, que
dende aquí adelante nenguno sea osado de les facer mal nin
dapño a otro.

Item: porque somos ynformados que algunos cristhianos de
las dichas Islas especialmente de La española, thienen thomadas
a los dichos yndios sus muxeres e fixas e otras cosas contra su
voluntad; luego como llegaredes, dereys órden como se los
vuelvan todo lo que les thienen thomado contra su voluntad, e
defendereys so graves penas, que de aquí adelante nenguno sea
osado de facer lo semexante, e si con las Yndias se quysieren
casar, sea de voluntad de las partes e no por fuerza.

Item: porque Nuestra merced e voluntad es, que los yndias
Nos paguen Nosotros tributos e derechos que Nos an de pagar

como Nos lo pagan Nuestros súditos vecinos de Nuestros Reynos e Señorios; pero porque la forma como acá se pagan e cobran a ellos sygund la calidad de la Tierra; hablareis de Nuestra parte con los caciques e con las otras personas prencipales e los yndios que vieredes son menester, e de su voluntad concordareis con ellos lo que Nos ayan de pagar cada uno, cada año, de tributos; e dichos de manera quellos conozcan que non se les face ynxusticia. . . .

Item: porque Nuestra merced es que los Cristhianos quen la dicha Isla Española viven e vivieren de aquí adelante, non vivan derramados; e que nenguno viva fuera de las poblaciones quen la dicha Isla se ficieren, e que cada uno puede traer en su heredad una chosa o casilla en que se acoxa quando fuere a ver o a habrar su heredad. . . .

Item: por quanto Nos thenemos merced de Nuestro Muy Santo Padre, de los diezmos e premycias de las dichas islas e Tierra-firme, daréys orden como todos ansí cristhianos como Yndios diezmen e paguen premycias de lo que obreren e trataren e debieren de maíz e paguen premycias conforme al arancel que lleváys, ques el más avenible quen Nuestros Reynos de a podidi facer.

INSTRUCTIONS TO OVANDO*
(Ferdinand, 1503)

El Rey   Zaragoza, Marzo 29, 1503
        Fray Nycolas de Ovando, governador de la Isla de Española. . . .

En quanto al salario que desis que se ha de dar a los clerigos que en ellas estan por quel servicio que hazen en confesar e bautizar e dar los Santos Sacramentos por quel Comendador Bovadilla avia señalado á cada uno dellos ciento e cinquenta

---

* Pacheco y Cárdenas, *Colección de documentos inéditos*, II 5, 45-46. For the translation see pp. 97-98.

pesos de oro en cada un año e questo se les facia poco, e que
después vos les aviades facer pagar a respeto de sesenta pesos
de oro cada un año y los frayles tornen lo que llevaron demas,
mandamos que de aquí adelante fasta tanto que nos mandemos
proveer lo que sobre esto se faga cada uno de los dichos clérigos
tengan de salario en cada un año cient pesos de oro e quen lo
pasado que hayan servido les sea pagado a este respeto sobre
lo que ovieren recevido.

En quanto al capitulo que dezis que seria bien que el papa
concediese Bulas plenarias de composycion para los vezinos de
estas Islas, a vesto nos paresce que por aora no es necesario.

En quanto al capitulo que dezis que fray Juan de Robles
traía memorial de los hornamentos que se previene ser para las
yglesias de alla, ya lo mandamos proveer como vereys por las
cosas que se envian para ello.

En quanto al capitulo que dezis que se concedan algunas
indulgencias para los que dieren limosnas a las yglesias e ospi-
tales, en esto nos escriviremos a nuestro muy santo padre e se
procurare como asy se fagan. . . .

En quanto al otro capitulo que nos ovimos mandalo que de
las cosas de algodon e otras cosas que se oviesen de los yndios
e de otras partes fuera del termino de las poblaciones, se pagase
a nos el diezmo, e por que las liberdades que ovimos concedido
a los yndios no se puede aver cosa dellos sino es conprada, e
que en esto resciven agravio los vezinos de las dichas yslas, nos
vos mandamos que en quanto a esto nos fagays saber lo que vos
pareciere que debemos mandar proveer, y entre tanto moderadlo
vos como vierdes que mas cumple a nuestro servicio e al bien
de los vezinos de las dichas yslas.

FROM THE WILL OF QUEEN ISABELLA*

(1504)

Otrosi por quanto yo tuve deseo siempre de mandar reducir
las Leyes de el Fuero, e Ordenamientos, y Pragmaticas en un
cuerpo, donde estobiesen mas brevemente, et mejor ordenadas,
declarando las dubdas, e algunas contrariedades que cerca de
ellas ocurren, e los gastos que de ello se siguen á mis Súbditos,
et Naturales; lo qual á capsa de mis enfermedades e otras
ocupaciones no se ha puesto por obra; Por ende suplicamos al
Rey mi Señor e Marido, e mando e encargo á la dicha Princesa
mi fija e al dicho Principe su marido e mando á los otros mis
Testamentarios que luego hagan juntar un Prelado de sciencia
e consciencia con personas doctas e sabias e experimentadas
en los Derechos, e vean todas las dichas Leyes del Fuero e
Ordenamientos e Pragmaticas, e las pongan, e reduzcan todas á
un cuerpo, de esten mas breves e compendiosamente complidas.

SECOND CODICIL TO THE WILL†

Item por quanto al tiempo que nos fueron concedidas por la
Santa Sede Apostolica las yslas y tierra firme del mar oceano
descubiertas y por descubrir, nuestra principal intencion fue al
tiempo que lo suplicamos al Papa sexto Alejandro de buena
memoria que nos hizo la dicha concesion de procurar e de yndu-
cir y traer los pueblos dellas y los convertir á nuestra santa fé
católica y enviar á las dichas islas y tierra firme prelados religiosos y clerigos y otras personas doctas y temerosas de Dios,
para instruir los vecinos y moradores de ella en la fé católica,
y los enseñar y dotar de buenas costumbres y poner en ellos la
diligencia debida segun las mas largamente en las letras de la

---

* Jordan de Asso y Miguel de Manuel, *Ordenamiento*, p. xv. For the translation
see pp. 98-99.
† Pacheco y Cárdenas, *Colección de documentos inéditos*, II 5, 92-93. For the translation see p. 99.

dicha concesion se contiene, por ende suplico al Rey mi Señor
muy efectuosamente y encargo y mando á la dicha Princesa mi
hija y al dicho Principe su marido que así lo hagan y cunplan y
que esto sea su principal fin, y que en ello pongan mucha diligencia y no consientan ni den lugar que los indios vecinos y
moradores de las dichas yndias y tierra firme ganadas y por
ganar reciban agravio alguno en sus personas ni bienes, mas
manden que sean bien y justamente tratados, y si algun agravio
an recebido lo remedien y provean por manera que no escedan
cosa alguna lo que por las letras apostólicas de la dicha concesion nos es injungido y mandado.

*Illius fulciti presidio**
(Julius II, 1504)

Julius episcopus servus servorum Dei. Ad perpetuam rei
memoriam.

Illius fulciti presidio cujus sunt terre cardines et cui cogita-
tiones hominum preparantur. Quique actus mortalium superat
et dirigit ac cujus providentia ordinationem suscipiunt universe
partes officii nobis concessi ad ea libenter exponimus per que
singulis in tenebris constitutis et ad verum lumen quod est
Christus accedere cupientibus lucis. Rady resplendeant unde
in singulis locis prout illorum necessitas et alie rationabiles
cause id exigunt novas Archiepiscopales et Episcopales sedes
ecclesiasque pro excellenti Sedis Apostolice preeminentia plan-
tamus ut per novas plantationes nova populorum adhesio militanti ecclesie accrescat religionisque Christiane et catholice fidei
professio ubique consurgat dilatetur et floreat ac loca etiam
humilia illustrentur ut eorundem locorum incole et habitatores
novarum sedium et honorabilium Presulum cum decenti numero
ministrorum assistentia circumfulti auctore domino felicitatis

---

* Pacheco y Cárdenas, *Colección de documentos inéditos*, II 5, 86-91. For the translation see pp. 100-03.

eterne premia facilius valeant adipisci. Sane cum carissimus in
Christo filius noster Ferdinandus Rex et Carissima in Christo
filia nostra Elisabeth Regina Castelle Legionis ac Sicilie illustres
pro augmento ejusdem religionis Christiane et ad Dei laudem
necnon dicte fidei catholice exaltationem pro viribus hactenus
non cessaverint neque cessant in dies non solum in Europa sed
etiam in Africa et in partibus Asie loca et dominia infidelium
ab eorundem infidelium servitute et tirannide eripere, ut inibi
eadem fides catholica plantetur et planta dilatetur. Et inter
cetera regna et dominia a mauris et saracenis ac aliis infidelibus
recuperata Nuper quamdam notabilem insulam in insulis indiarum nuncupatis consistentem seu eisdem insulis adjacentem
eorum valido et potenti exercitu ac classe maritima adversus
dictos infideles preparatis, ab eisdem infidelibus deo auxiliante
eripiendo ipsorum Regis et Regine dominio subjecerint. Et post
hujusmodi recuperationem et subjectionem non contenti dominio
temporali, sed volentes magis quantum eis liceret in eadem
insula sic recuperata et acquisita quam insulam Spagniolam de
cetero nuncupari voluerunt etiam spiritualiter ad exaltationem
ejusdem fidei catholice edificare non destiterint religiosos et
doctos viros ad dictam insulam transmittere ut inibi verbum Dei
predicarent ipsosque infideles eorum predicationibus ad fidem
Christianam converterent. Sed quia dicti religiosi et alie persone
ad hoc destinate inibi eorum mansionem firmam non faciunt
neque habent idem fructus ex hoc non pervenit qui proveniret
si in dicta insula deputarentur persone idonee qui inibi mansionem perpetuam haberent ac verbo et exemplo proficerent.
    Nos habita super iis cum venerabilibus fratribus nostris
deliberatione matura de illorum consilio rege et regina prefatis
hoc etiam summe cupientibus et super hoc nobis supplicantibus
ad ipsius Dei laudem et gloriam ac venerationem Beate gloriose
Virginis Marie totiusque coelestis curie jubilationem Hyaguata
et Magua ac Bayuna provintias, terras sive oppida in dicta
insula consistentia civitatum titulo de fratrum eorundem consilio

et apostolice potestatis plenitudine Auctoritate apostolica tenore presentium insignimus illaque in civitates et in provintia in qua est Portus Dominici nuncupatus ac eandem Hyaguatensem unam Metropolitanam Hyaguatensem nuncupandam sub invocatione Anuntiationis seu Incarnationis ejusdem Beate Virginis pro uno Archiepiscopo et in Magua unam Maguensem ac in Bayuna civitatibus sic ex oppidis sive terris civitatum titulis insignitis et decoratis unam aliam Bayunensem nuncupandas Cathedrales ecclesias pro uno Maguensi et altero Bayunensi episcopis qui in dicta insula verbum Dei predicent dictosque infideles et gentes barbaras ad fidem Christi convertant et conversos in eadem fide instruant et doceant eisque baptismi gratiam impendant et sacramenta ecclesiastica ac alia spiritualia eisdem ac omnibus aliis Christianis in illis pro tempore degentibus ministrent ambitumque et formam tam Metropolitane quam cathedralium ecclesiarum predicatarum et cujuslibet earum designent et edificari faciant ac in eis illarumque civitatibus et diocesibus ecclesiasticas dignitates canonicatus et prebendas aliasque beneficia ecclesiastica cum cura et sine cura prout pro divini cultus augmento et alias pro animarum salute expedire cognoverint respective erigant et instituant ac alia spiritualia conservent et seminent cum Archiepiscopali et Episcopalibus insigniis jurisdictionibus privilegiis immunitatibus et gratiis quibus alii Archiepiscopi et Episcopi de jure vel de consuetudine potiuntur et gaudent seu uti potiri et gaudere poterunt quo modo libet in futurum de similibus consilio et potestatis plenitudine auctoritate et tenore predictis erigimus et instituimus ipsamque totam insulam Spagniolam pro provintia Archiepiscopali eidem ecclesie Hyaguatensi et illius Archiepiscopo pro tempore existenti pro illius vero diocesi terras loca et oppida videlicet dictum portum Santi Dominici ac-Ceni ayucubet, guayagua Azua Iguanama Higuei Nicao Aramana Aycagua Magaren Canobocoa, Camuti Elbonao et Elmanie. Easdem vero Maguensem et Bayunensem ecclesias Cathedrales dicte ecclesie Hyaguatensi pro ejus suffraganeis. Et Maguensi pro ejus civitate civitatem Maguensem ac pro diocesi et districtu terras oppida et loca videlicet Marien Macorix et terras de Huatiguana Abaraco Cauxina, terram de Himataonex, de Manguato Caono terram de Hyavaroex Coaxec Cibao, terram de Himataonex Cubao Lostiguaos Elma-corix Elcotrix, Bayunensi vero ecclesiis predictis similiter pro ejus civitati civitatem Bayunensem et pro diocesi et districtu terras oppida et loca videlicet de la Maguana Jabonico Xinabuer, Jacahuer, Iguanuco Atryco Cleahax guacaci Xurugua Taxguanuo Camaye Elcahayseto Elbaoruco Jaquimo, Laxaguana Guahyqua et Haniguayagua perpetuo assignamus. Ita ut Archiepiscopus metropolitica et tam ipse in sua metropolitana quam singuli ex Maguensi et Bayunensi episcopis predictis in suis provintiis civitatibus et diocesibus respective metropoliticam et episcopalem jurisdictionem auctoritatem et potestatem exerceant et decimas primicias ac alia jura episcopalia percipiant et exigant prout Archiepiscopi et Episcopi Regnorum et dominiorum eorundem Regis et Regine in suis Archiepiscopatibus et Episcopatibus civitatibus et diocesibus de jure vel consuetudine seu ex privilegiis eis concessis percipiunt et percipere possunt. Nulli ergo omnino hominum liceat hanc paginam nostre insignitionis erectionis institutionis et assignationis infringere vel ei ausu temerario contraire. Si quis autem hoc attemptare presumerit indignationem Omnipotentis Dei ac beatorum Petri et Pauli Apostolorum ejus se noverit incursurum. Datum Rome apud Sanctum Petrum anno Incarnationis dominice millesimo quingentessimo quarto decimo septimo Kalendas Decembris Pontificatus nostri anno primo.

TO AMBASSADOR FRANCISCO DE ROJAS*

(Ferdinand, 1505)

El Rey

Comendador francisco de Rojas, del mi consejo e mi ambaxador de Roma, yo mande ver las bullas que se expedieron para la creacion e provicion del arçobispado e obispados de la Española, en las quales no se nos concede el patronadgo de los dichos arçobispado e obispados ni de las dignidades e calongias, Raciones e beneficios con cura e sin cura en la dicha ysla Española se an de helijir, es menester que su santidad conceda el dicho patronadgo de todo ello perpetualmente a mi e a los Reyes que en estos Reynos de castilla e de leon suscedieren, aunque en las dichoas Bullas no aya seydo fecha mincion dello como hizo en los del Reyno de Granada.

Otro si la ereccion de las dichoas dinidades, calongias, Raciones e oficios eclesiasticos de la dichoa ysla viene cometida a los dichos arçobispo et obispos, no hasyendo minsion de la presentacion; es menester que en la dichoa bulla del patronadgo mande el papa que no pueden ser eregidas las dichoas dignidades e calongias e otros beneficios sy no de mi consentimiento como patron, e que la dicha ereccion venga cometida al arçobispo de sevilla para que a mi consentimiento la haga, e que no se puede proveer ny ynstituir asy desta primera vacacion de la prima erecion como cada e quando del dicho arçobispo de sevilla e sus subcesores arçobispos de sevilla pueden compeler e apremiar al dicho arçobispo e obispos de las personas que por mi e por mis subcesores Reyes destos Reynos fueren presentados, e no a otros algunos, e sy dichos arçobispo e obispos o qual quier dellos seyendo Requiridos por las personas presentatas a sus procuradores legitimos no los quisieren ynstituir, el dicho arçobispo de sevilla que por tienpo fuere los ynstituya

---

* Pacheco y Cárdenas, *Colección de documentos inéditos*, II 5, 80-83. For the translation see pp. 105-06.

e por que por la mucha distancia que hay destos Reynos a la dicha ysla Española, yo e los Reyes dellos que despues fueren no podriamos presentar dentro del termino de los quatros meses quel derecho dispone, aveys de procurar que los dichos quatro meses se alarguen a diez o ocho meses.

ya sabeys como yo e la serenisima Reyna my muger, que aya santa gloria, teniamos por donacion apostolica todos los diezmos, premicias, de las yndias e tierra firme del mar oceano al tiempo que acordamos de facer en la dicha ysla Española los dichos arçobispado e obispados, asy mesmo de fazer donacion a los dichos arçobispos e obispos e yglesias e beneficiados de los dichos diezmos e primicias, Reservando para nos los dichos diezmos que en estos Reynos se dicen tercias, e todos los diezmos del oro, plata e metales, e brazil e piedras preciosas, e perlas, e aljofar, e aveys de procurar que su santidad mande que los dichos arçobispo e obispos e yglesias e beneficiados en la dicha Española e en las otras yslas e tierra firme del mar oceano que son e fueren heregidas e no gozar de mas parte de los dichos diezmos de lo contenido en la dicha colacion que dello les hesimos e que todo lo otro que por ello Reservamos a nos e a nuestros subcesores en estos Reynos, nos quede perpetuamente Reservado, no enbargante lo contenido en las letras apostolicas de la colacion de los dichos arçobispo e obispos se contiene que aya de gozar de los dichos diezmos e de otra manera, como vereys por las dichas letras apostolicas.

Otro si por las dichas letras apostolicas e la provisyon de los dichos arçobispado e obispados e biene cometido a los dichos arçobispo e obispos que pueden señalar e dividir el anbito de los dichos arçobispado e obispados, e porque podria ser que ellos no se concordasen sobre ello o unos o otros sienpre yndicasen, es menester que su santidad mande que yo e la persona o personas a quien yo lo comitiere faga la dicha divisyon e apartamiento e el dicho arçobispado e cada uno de los dichos obispados ayan de gozar de anbito e territorio que asy les fuere

señalado; por ende, yo vos encargo e mando que luego fableys
de mi parte a su santidad e les supliqueys quiera conceder todo
lo suso dicho; en la espedicion de todo ello poned mucha diligencia lo mas presto que ser podiere, e me lo embiad despachado con correo cierto, porque las Bullas de los arçobispado
e obispados no se an de dar a los proveydos hasta que a questo
venga despachado; en ello me fareys mucho plazer e servicio.
De la cibdad de segovia a trece dias del mes de setiembre de
MDV anos. Yo el Rey. Por mandado del Rey mi señor, gaspar
de grizyo. señalada del doctor angulo e licenciado çapata.

INSTRUCTIONS TO OVANDO*

(Ferdinand, 1507)

El despacho de los obispos se ha detenido por mi absencia
destos reynos, pero agora yo mando proveer lo que conviene
para el despacho de ellos, y en syeido venidas sus bullas de
Roma, por las quales yo enbio agora, se despacheron para que
vayan a Resydir alla y vos escrivire que son las Rentas de que
han de gozar y de que tienpo y sy no enbargante que tengan sus
Rentos han de ser proveydos de Indios; y como o no. . . . Yo El
Rey, por mandado de su alteza. Miguel Perez de Almaçan.

INSTRUCTIONS TO OVANDO†

(Ferdinand, 1508)

El Rey: Don fray nycolas de ovando, comendador major de
la horden de Alcantara, nuestro governador de las yslas indias
e tierra firme de mar oceano.

sabed quel bachillor anton serrano y diego de nycuesa,
procuradores desa ysla, me han escrito de supparte algunas
cosas e por la mucha gana que tengo de hacen bien e merced a

---

* Pacheco y Cárdenas, *Colección de documentos inéditos*, II 5, 119. For the translation see p. 107.
† *Ibid.*, II 5, 125-27. For the translation see pp. 107-09.

los pobladores della, asi por ser heredad plantada de mi mano, por le que he trabajadado en criarla e a un tanbien por el grande amor e fidelidad que vos me escrivis que tienen contyno a mi persona les he otorgado todo lo que buenamente he podido en favor desa dicha ysla.

Primeramente que por quanto las Yglesias que se han fecho en esta ysla hasta agora an seido fechas a costa de los pueblos e como han seido de paja hanse perdido muchas veces e tantas se han tornado a edificar, de que los pueblos han rrecibido trabajo e las yglesias estan todavia por hacer, suplicaronme mandase haver las dichas yglesias de obra durable a costa de los diezmos e primicias desa ysla, e yo por servicio de nuestro señor e por hazer bien e merced a esa dicha ysla, lo he mandado asi proveer e he enbiado a mandar a los nuestros oficiales de la casa de contratacion que Residen en la cibdad de Sevilla que envien oficiales canteros los que fueren menester para ello, e asy mismo ha mandado a mi geronimo de pasamonte, secretario de la serenisima Reyna, mi muy cara e muy amada muger, nuestro thesorero general desas yslas e tierra firme que de los diezmos e primicias que hallaren cogidos ee los que cogieron hasta que los prelados que han de yr alla ayan de Recibir los dichos diezmos e primicias que a ellos prometieren de todo el dinero que vos le dixerdes ser necessario para la fabrica de las dichas yglesias, asi mismo para pagar los salarios a los minis-tros della porque el culto divino se haga como es Razon. por ende tomad con vos al dicho thesorero e ved lo que sera nece-sario que se gaste en lo suso dicho para que yo cunpla conmi consciencia e con dios e con los desa dicha ysla, e para lo que fuere necessario que se gaste dareys cedula firmada de vuestro nonbre para el dicho thesorero, para que se le Recibe en cuenta lo que diere a diputados personas buenas vicinos desa ysla para que tengan cargo de la dicha obra por cuya mano se aya de gastas lo que se oviere ee gastar con vuestras cedulas como dicho es. asy mismo luego que los dichos procuradores que

fuesen los prelados a esa ysla mande proveer a Roma por el
despacho dellos el qual me traxeron ya otra vez e no como hera
necesario de manera que para su yda se espera el despacho de
Roma, entretanto que ellos van por servicio mio que vos tengays
mucho cuydado de las cosas que alla tocaren a servicio de nuestro senor pues veded quanta Razon es segund la mucha merced
que nos hace en todas partes. . . . Fecha en Burgos Abril 30
1508 Yo el Rey por mandado de su Alteza lope conchillos.

*Universalis ecclesiae regimini**
(Julius II, 1508)

Julius, Episcopus, Servus Servorum Dei. Ad perpetuam
rei memoriam.

Universalis ecclesiae regimini, Divina dispositione licet im-
meriti praesidentes, illa praesertim Catholicis regibus libenter
concedimus, per quae eis decus et honor accrescat, ac earumdem
terrarum Regum statui et securitati opportune consulatur; sane
cum paucis ante temporibus charissimus in Christo filius noster
Ferdinandus Aragonum etiam et Siciliae Rex illustris, et clarae
memoriae Elisabeth, Castellae et Legionis Regina, diutino
Maurorum jugo ex Hispania ejecto, in Occeanum penetrantes,
ignotis etiam terris salutiferum Crucis vexillum intulissent, ut
scilicet, quantum in se fuit, verbum illud ratum facerent, *In
Omnem terram exivit sonus eorum;* subjugassentque sub axe
ignoto et insulas et loca plurima, et inter caeteras maximi praetii
et populantissimam unam, illique Novam Hispaniam nomen
imposuissent: Nos in ea, ut falsis et perniciosis ritibus extirpatis
vera Religio plantetur, ad eorumdem Regis et Reginae preces
instantissimas, unam Metropolitanam Ayguacensem et duas
Cathedrales, videlicet Maguenensem, et Bajunensem, Ecclesias
cum summa Christiani nominis gloria ereximus; et ne animi
nova Fide imbuti, si pium aliquod opus aggrederenter in in-

---

* Hernáez, *Colección,* I, 24-26. For the translation see pp. 110-12.

struendis Ecclesiis aut locis piis, illud in tali parte Insulae hujusmodi facerent, unde aut Religioni Christianae ibidem recenti, aut temporali Regum dominio praejudicium aliquod afferri posset, accepimusque quod praefatus Ferdinandus Rex,[1] qui etiam Castellae et Legionis Regnorum hujusmodi Gubernator Generalis existit, ac charissima in Christo filia nostra Joanna eorumdem Regnorum Regina ac ipsius Ferdinandi Regis nata, eis quod nulla Ecclesia, Monasteria, aut locus pius, tam in praedictis jam acquisitis, quam aliis acquirendis insulis et locis, absque eorumdem Ferdinandi Regis et Joannae Reginae ac Regum Castellae et Legionis pro tempore existentium consensu, erigi aut fundari possint; et cum expediat eidem Regi, Ecclesiis et Monasteriis praefatis, personas fidas et gratas et acceptas praeesse, jus Patronatus et praesentandi personas idoneas tam ad Metropolitanas quam alias Cathedrales Ecclesias erectas et pro tempore erigendas, et alia quaecumque Beneficia Ecclesiastica infra annum a die illorum vacantia computandum, et ad inferiora Beneficia Ordinariis locorum, et in eventu quod praefati Ordinarii infra decem dies absque legitima causa instituere recusaverint, quicumque alius Episcopus ad eorum requisitionem praesentatum hujusmodi instituere possit, concedi summopere cupiunt.

Nos attendentes praemissae Insulae et praedictorum Regnorum, cujus Reges Apostolicae Sedi devoti et fideles semper fuerunt, decori et venustati ac securitati cedere, ad magnam

---

[1] The clause beginning "quod praefatus Ferdinandus Rex" strikes one immediately as an anacolouthon, for its verb is lacking. In the texts printed by Hernáez, Frasso, García Gutiérrez, Leturia, Pacheco y Cárdenas, and Ribadeneyra the wording is identically faulty. None but Leturia indicates needed correction, though Ribadeneyra in his accompanying Spanish translation introduces what ought to be there by adding (without comment), after "Juana Reyna," the following: "quo lo es del mismo Rey Fernando, tienen gran deseo de que se les conceda, que sin su consentimiento. . . ." Again, eight lines later, he glosses: "con vivas ansias desean se les conceda el derecho de Patronato" (Ribadeneyra, *Manual compendio*, p. 411). Though this corrects the sense, it does not minimize the difficulty of establishing an exact textual reading.

instantiam quam super hoc fecerunt ac faciunt apud Nos praefati Ferdinandus Rex et Joanna Regina, debitum habentes res-
pectum, habita super his cum fratribus nostris Sanctae Romanae Ecclesiae Cardinalibus deliberatione matura, de illorum
consilio, eisdem Ferdinando Regi et Joannae Reginae, ac Castellae et Legionis Regi pro tempore existenti, quod nullus in
praedictis acquisitis et aliis acquirendis Insulis et locis maris
hujusmodi, Ecclesias magnas, alias quam Ferdinandi Regis et
Joannae Reginae ac Regis Castellae et Legionis pro tempore
existentis expresso consensu construi, aedificari, et erigi facere
possit, ac jus Patronatus et praesentandi personas idoneas ad
Ayguaçen et Maguen et Bajunen praedictas, et alias quascumque
Metropolitanas ac Cathedrales Ecclesias et Monasteria ac Dignitates in eisdem Cathedralibus etiam Metropolitanis post Pontificales majores, et in Collegiatis Ecclesiis principales, ac
quaecumque alia Beneficia Ecclesiastica et pia loca in dictis
Insulis et locis pro tempore vacantia; videlicet, ad Cathedrales
etiam Metropolitanas ac etiam Regulares Ecclesias ac Monasteria, de quibus consistorialiter disponi debeat, infra annum
a die vacationis, et eorumdem propter longam maris distantiam
nobis et successoribus nostris Romanis Pontificibus canonice
intrantibus; ad inferiora vero Beneficia hujusmodi locorum
Ordinariis, jus vero instituendi personas praesentas ad inferiora
Beneficia hujusmodi eisdem Ordinariis, et si Ordinarii praefati
personam praesentatam infra decem dies instituere neglexerint,
ex tunc quilibet alius Episcopus illarum partium, ad requisitionem Ferdinandi Regis seu Joannae Reginae, aut Regis pro
tempore existentis, hujusmodi praefatam personam ea vice instituere libere et licite valeat, auctoritate Apostolica tenore
praesentium concedimus; non obstantibus praemissis, et aliis
Constitutionibus et Ordinationibus Apostolicis caeterisque contrariis quibuscumque.

Nulli ergo omnino hominum liceat hanc paginam nostrae
concessionis infringere, vel ausu temerario contraire; si quis

autem hoc attentare praesumpserit, indignationem Omnipotentis Dei et Beatorum Petri et Pauli Apostolorum ejus se noverit incursurum.

Datis Romae, apud Sanctum Petrum, anno Incarnationis Dominicae millesimo quingentesimo octavo, quinto Kalendas Augusti, Pontificatus nostri anno quinto.

P. de Comitibus. Registrata apud me, Sigismondum.

Eximie devotionis affectus*
(Julius II, 1510)

Julius, episcopus, servus servorum Dei. Ad perpetuam rei memoriam.

Eximie devotionis affectus quem carissimus in Christo filius noster Ferdinandus Aragonie et Sicilie Rex Catholicus ac carissima in Christo filia nostra Johanna Castelle et Legionis Regina Illustres ad nos et Romanam gerunt ecclesiam nec non inconcusse fidei probata constantia qua eandem Ecclesiam et sedem apostolicam tam ipsi Rex et Regina quam clare memorie Elisabeth Ferdinandi Regis conjunx et Johanne Regine genetrix ac alii progenitores eorum sinceris animis et indefessis obsequiorum studiis continue coluerunt non indigne merentur ut votis eorum illis presertim per que eorum utilitati et comoditati oportune consulatur condignis favoribus annuamus. Sane pro parte Ferdinandi Regis et Johanne Regine nobis nuper exhibita petitio continebat quod licet Regis et Regine Castelle et Legionis qui fuerunt pro tempore a tanto tempore cujus contrarii hominum memoria non existit dum in eorum Regnis et Dominiis aurum vel argentum aut alia metalla fodi fecerunt ex auro et argento et aliis metallis ex hujusmodi fodinis pro tempore extractis et habitis nullam decimam alicui ecclesie parochiali vel alio loco

---

* Pacheco y Cárdenas, *Colección de documentos inéditos*, II 5, 205-09. For the translation see pp. 113-15.

religioso persolvere consueverint ipseque Ferdinandus Rex et
Elisabeth Regina dum in humanis ageret et ea vita functa idem
Ferdinandus Rex qui eorumdem Castelle et Legionis Regnorum
et dominiorum Administrator existit certas insulas maritimas
et alia loca ad que antea per longissima tempora Christianis non
patebat tutus accessus a Sarracenis et aliis infidelibus tunc
occupata manu forti potenti cum eorum exercitu ad id preparato
deo auxiliante a manibus et occupatione dictorum Saracenorum
et infidelium eripuerunt et recuperarunt in quibus ut dicitur
etiam fodines auri et argenti et aliorum metallorum existunt
ipsasque insulas et loca sic recuperata aliis eorum Regnis et
dominiis annexuerunt et incorporarunt ac in insulis et locis
predictis sic recuperatis quamplures ecclesias et monasteria
construi et edificari fecerunt ad sufficientem dotem ex bonis ex
quibus decimam debetur assignaverunt et pro illorum regimine
et gubernatione religiosas et alias personas ecclesiasticas ad
insulas et loca predicta sic recuperata eorum propriis sumptibus
et expensis transmiserunt et in ipsarum insularum et locorum
recuperatione gravia damna et pericula tam rerum quam personarum sustinuerunt et propterea credant de fodinis auri et
argenti ac metallorum in insulis et locis recuperatis hujusmodi
sicut de aliis fodinis in Regnis et dominiis eorum existentibus
ad aliquam decime solutionem non teneri nichilominus a nonnullis dubitatur an Ferdinandus Rex et Johanna Regina prefati
ad solutionem decime hujusmodi auri et argenti ac metallorum
que insulis et locis recuperatis predictis effodi facient teneantur.
Quare pro parte Ferdinandi Regis et Johanne Regine predictorum nobis fuit humiliter supplicatum ut eis eorumque successoribus Regibus Castelle et Legionis Regnorum et dominiorum quibus insule ac loca recuperata applicata sunt seu alia
recuperanda applicabuntur pro tempore existentibus quod de
fodinis auri et argenti et aliorum metallorum cujuscumque
generisque in insulis et locis predictis sic recuperatis et recuperandis in quibus ecclesias necessarias construi facere et suffi-

cienter dotari parati existunt pro tempore effodi facient, ad
solutionem alicujus decime minime tenentur prout de auro et
argento ac aliis metallis que in fodinis Regnorum et dominiorum
Castelle et Legionis predictorum hactenus solvere non consueverunt concedere ac alias in premissis oportune providere de
benignitate apostolica dignaremur. Nos itaque Ferdinandi Regis
et Johanne Regine et progenitorum predictorum preclara merita
paterna consideratione pensantes, hujusmodi supplicationibus
inclinati, Ferdinando Regi et Johanne Regine prefatis eorumque
successoribus Regibus Castelle et Legionis Regnorum et dominiorum quibus insule et loca recuperata applicata sunt seu alia
recuperanda applicabuntur pro tempore existentibus, quod de
fodinis auri et argenti et aliorum metallorum cujuscumque
generisque in insulis et locis predictis sic recuperatis et dummodo per Johannam Reginam et Reges prefatos ecclesie neces-
sarie construantur et sufficienter dotentur in recuperandis pro
tempore effodi facient ad solutionem alicujus decime non teneantur, prout de auro et argento ac aliis metallis que in fodinis
Regnorum et dominiorum Castelle ac Legionis predictorum
hactenus solvere minime consueverunt auctoritate apostolica
tenore presentium de specialis dono gratie concedimus et indulgemus. Non obstantibus Lateranensis Concilii et quibusvis
aliis Constitutionibus et ordinationibus apostolicis ceterisque
contrariis quibuscumque. Nulli ergo omnino hominum liceat
hanc paginam nostre concessionis et induli infringere vel ei
ausu temerario contraire. Siquis autem hoc attemptare presumerit indignationem Omnipotentis Dei ac Beatorum Petri et
Pauli Apostolorum ejus se noverit incursurum. Datum Rome
apud Sanctum Petrum anno Incarnationis dominice millessimo
quingentesimo decimo, sexto idus Aprilis,[1] Pontificatus nostri
anno septimo.

---

[1] In Pacheco y Cárdenas the date is miscopied as "millesimo quingentesimo sexto
idus Aprilis."

*Teniendo en la tierra**

(Julius II, 1511)

Bula erigendo las cathedrales de Cuba, Puerto Rico y Santo Domingo

Xulio Obispo siervo de los siervos de Dios, para perpétua memoria Pontífice Romano

Teniendo en la tierra todas las veces de aquel de quien reciban el órden, extendiendo la potestad de su xuresdeccion á todos los climas del Mundo; Ordenamos e disponemos con maduro consexo para major firmeza e fundamento de la Fé católica del Estado e progreso de las iglesias, en particular de las metropolitanas e de otras cathedrales que se han erixido por via de translacion ó de supresion, ó nueva creacion, en lugares casi non conoscidos; e reconoscidas todas las circumstancias e cualidades de dichos pueblos, abtorizados con la presencia de sus venerables prelados, aprovechen e estén firmes en la Fé, se ilustren en las iglesias, e la humilde religion cristhiana se propague e dilate; e de la misma suerte que cresce en lo temporal, se abmente en lo espiritual, despues que la Isla Hispañola, sita en el Mar de las Indias, reducida á la religion cristhiana, oprimada por muchos siglos con el yugo de los infieles, por la solicitud e potente Armada de Nuestro Carísimo hixo en Cristo Don Fernando, Rey de Aragon, de Sicilia, de Castilla e de Leon, de immortal memoria, e de la Reyna Doña Isabel, entonces esposa de dicho Rey; eriximos e ynstituimos las yglesias cathedrales en dicha isla, es á saber: la Hiaguatense Metropolitana, la Bagustense, et Magustense, pidiéndonos dicho Rey e Reyna sobresta materia, e Concediéndoselo con el consexo de Nuestros hermanos e con la plenitud de Nuestra aposthólica potestad, como todo mas plenamente se conthiene en Nuestras letras despachadas. Empero: Constándonos que dicha Isla e

---

* Pacheco y Cárdenas, *Colección de documentos inéditos*, I 34, 29-35. For the translation see pp. 118-21.

lugares para la permanencia de dichas yglesias sean incómodas, ansí por su situacion como por la dificultad de conseguir las cosas necesarias e que fuera desta se hallaba otra Isla llamada San Xuan, en el mismo Mar Océano, suxeta á la misma xuresdeccion; e que ansí mismo las tierras, villas e lugares de la Isla Hispañola de Santo Domingo, de la Concepcion e de San Xuan de dichas Yslas, eran al propósito e acomodadas para iglesias cathedrales e para prelados que les presidieran; Nos, deseando mirar e proveer del conveniente e oportuno remedio, ansí de prelados como de la comodidad de dichos pueblos; e habiendo xuntado consexo para mas madura deliberacion, con Nuestros venerables hermanos; e deseándolo xuntamente en grande manera, el sobre dicho Rey Don Fernando, el cual, como Rey de Castilla e de Leon, e General Gobernador e Administrador de dichos Reinos, por la Serenísima Carisima hixa Nuestra Doña Xuana, á los cuales Reinos dichas Yslas están sugetas e anexas; e suplicándonos tambien lo mismo Nuestros amados hixos Pedro Hiagustense e García Bagustense e Alfonso Magustense, electos en la administracion e gobierno de dichas yglesias Hiagustense, Bagustense e Magustense, llamadas ansí por los dichos respectivos; Nos, usando de la abtoridad e plenitud de potestad, Suprimimos e extinguimos á las dichas yglesias, perpetúamente, e para exaltacion e alabanza de Dios Omnipotente, e de la militante iglesia, Señalamos e Damos Título de Civdades, á las tierras ó lugares de Santo Domingo, de la Concepcion, e de Sant Xuan, e erixidas en cibdades se llamen yglesias cathedrales; una en Santo Domingo, otra en la Concepcion, e otra en Sant Xuan; e sus Obispados se nombren, uno de Santo Domingo, otro de la Concepcion, e otro de Sant Xuan; los cuales, en sus dichas Yglesias, veneren e reverencien á Nuestro Dios e Señor, e á sus santos; prediquen el Santo Evangelio, e enseñen á los ynfieles, e con buenas palabras los conviertan á la veneracion de la Fé católica; e ya convertidos, los instruyan en la religion cristhiana, los den e administren el

Santo Sacramento del Bautismo; e ansí convertidos como á los
demas fieles de Christo, que viven e moran en dichas Yslas;
e á los que á ellas aportasen, los administren e fagan que los
administren los Santos Sacramentos de la Confesion, de la
Eucaristia e los demás; e ansí mismo procuren que dichas
nuevas Islas se fagan e fabriquen con buena forma e con convenientes edificios; e en dichas yglesias, cibdades e obispados,
se erixan parroquiales con sus propios párrocos, dignidades,
administradores e oficiales, e que los tales sean personas
idóneas. E ansí mismo se provean de cura de almas, canongías,
prebendas e demás beneficios eclesiásticos, e puedan erixir e
ynstituir yglesias regulares de cualesquiera órdenes, segun
xuzgaren que conviene para el mayor abmento del culto divino
e de los fieles; e dichos obispos goçen e usen de las ynsignias
episcopales, xuresdeccionales, previlexios e ynmunidades, gra-
cias é indultos, de los cuales los demás obispos gozan por
derecho ó por costumbre; e dichas yglesias Erixemos, Creamos
e Constituimos para siempre es á saber: la de Santo Domingo,
de la Concepcion e la de Sant Xuan, e tambien las eriximos e
Nombramos por cibdades; segunda vez: Santo Domingo, la
Buenaventura, Azua Salvaleon; San Xuan de la Alaguana,
Vera-Paz, Villanueva de Yaquinos; Concepcion de Santiago,
Puerto de Plata, Puerto-Real, la Redena Hava, Salvatierra de
la Cabaña e Santa Cruz; e Concedemos e asignamos á todos los
fieles ynquilinos e habitantes en las tierras, villas e lugares de
Sant Xuan e á sus yglesias toda la dicha Isla de Sant Xuan con
sus destritos e diócesis; de suerte que cualquiera de los obispos
que por tiempo fueren de dichas Islas de Santo Domingo, Concepcion e Sant Xuan pueden exercer e usar en sus cibdades e
obispados toda la xuresdeccion, abtoridad e potestad episcopal,
e puedan pedir e percibir los diezmos, primicias e otros derechos episcopales, de la manera que los demás obispos de la
Provincia de Sevilla, en la ulterior España, por derecho o ley
los piden e perciben, excepto del oro, de la plata e otros metales

e piedras preciosas, los cuales Declaramos están exentos e libres thocante a esto.

Tambien Queremos que las referidas yglesias de Santo Domingo, de la Concepcion e Sant Xuan, sean sufragáneas de dicha Provincia é Iglesia de Sevilla e á su Arzobispado que por tiempo fuere por derecho Metropolitano; e concedemos e reservamos al Dicho Rey de Castilla e de Leon, para siempre, el derecho del Patronato e de presentar personas idóneas para dichas yglesias vacantes de Santo Domingo, Concepcion e Sant Xuan, al Pontífice Romano, para que por él sean puestos en el cargo de dicha presentacion, es á saber: obispos, pastores.

Todo lo conthenido en la página de Nuestra suspension e estincion, ereccion e creacion, ynstitucion, concesion, asignacion, suxecion de descreto e reservacion, nenguno se atrava nin sea osado á falsificarlo nin pervertirlo; mas si alguno pronunciare intentarlo, se declarará por incurso en la yndignacion de Dios Omnipotente, e de sus Apóstoles San Pedro é San Pablo.—Dado en San Pedro, en el Año de mil quinientos e once, á ocho de Agusto, en el Año octavo de Nuestro Pontificado.

Registrado.

THE REDONATION OF TITHES*
(Ferdinand, 1512)

Redonación de los diezmos, y concordia entre Los Reyes Cathólicos Fernando e Juana y los primeros obispos de las Américas. Burgos, 1512

In Dei Nomine Amen. Manifesto sea á todos los que el presente instrumento de capitulacion e ordenacion vieren, como el año del Nacimiento de Nuestro Señor Jesu Cristo de mil e quinientos e doce años, en la indiccion quinta decima, á ocho dias del mes de Mayo, en el año nono del Pontificado de Nuestro

---

* Hernáez, *Colección*, I, 21-25; García Gutiérrez, *Bulario*, pp. 31-34; Frasso, *Tractatus*, I, cap. 19. For the translation see pp. 121-26.

muy Santo Padre Julio por la divina providencia Papa segundo,
en presencia de mi, Francisco de Valencia, canonigo de Palencia, Notario publico por la authridad apostolica é Secretario
del muy Reverendo in Cristo Padre Obispo de Palencia, los muy
altos y muy poderosos Principes, Don Fernando, Rey de Aragon
é de las dos Sicilias é de Jerusalem, Rey Catolico, é Doña Juana
su hija, Reina de Castilla é de León, etc., Nuestros señores de la
una parte, é cada uno de sus Altezas por si y en su nombre, por
la mitad que respective le pertenece de las Islas, Indias y tierra
firme del mar occeano, por vigor de las Bulas Apostolicas á
sus Reales Majestades por el Papa Alejandro VI de felice recordacion concedidas, cuyos tenores de verbo ad verbum, uno
despues de otro se sigue, é son tales: [Aquí se insertan las tres
Bulas de arriba: la *Inter coetera* de 1493, quarto nonas Maji;
2a *Dudum siquidem* de 1493, sexto Kal. Octobris; 3a *Eximiae
devotionis* de 1493, quarto nonas Maji]. Con los Reverendos en
Cristo Padres, Don Fr. Garcia de Padilla, Obispo de Santo
Domingo, é Don Pedro Suarez de Deza Doctor en Decretos,
Obispo de la Concepción que son en la Isla de Española, e Don
Alonso Manso, licenciado en teologia, obispo de la Isla de
San Juan, como Electos Obispos en las Iglesias Cathedrales por
nuestro muy Santo Padre, Julio Segundo, en las dichas Islas
nuevamente criados y erijidas, por sí y en nombre de los Obis-
pos sus Successores, que despues de ellos fueren en las dichas
Iglesias, é de las personas á quien toca lo de suso contenido, de
la otra parte, asentaron é capitularon lo siguiente:

Primeramente que sus Altezas, porque los dichos obispos
tengan a cargo rogar a Dios por sus vidas y Reales Estados, e
por sus animas quando de este mundo partieren, é de los Reyes
que en sus Reinos succedieren, é de los fieles christianos, que
adquiriendo y descubriendo las dichas Insulas murieron, les
hacen merced, gracia y donacion, desde ahora para siempre
jamas, de los diezmos, á sus Altezas pertenecientes, de las
dichas Islas, é hán por bien que los llevan segun é por la forma

que á sus Altezas pertenecen é los hán llevado por concesion y donacion, que de ellos les hizo el Papa Alejando sexto de felice recordacion, como parece por la Bula, que sobre ello su santidad á sus Altezas concedio, cuyo tenor es este que sigue. [Véase la Bula anterior expedida en 16 de noviembre de 1501.]

Los cuales Diezmos es voluntad de sus Altezas que se partan por los dichos Obispos, Iglesias, Clerecia, Fabricas y Hospitales é otras cosas que adelante iran especificadas. E los dichos Obispos, por si y por sus succesores y en nombre de sus Iglesias y Clerecia, promoten desde ahora que guardaran é cumpliran lo susodicho y lo adelante contenido. E con expresa condicion que lo así guardaran é cumpliran, les hacen sus Altezas la dicha gracia y donacion, y no de otra manera.

Item que las Dignidades, Canongias, Raciones y Beneficios, que asi ahora, como de aqui adelante serán criados é instituidos, conforme á la Ereccion hecha de las dichas Iglesias asi en las Cathedrales como en las otras todas, de las dichas Islas, Española é de San Juan, asi esta primera vez, como todas las otras que aconteciere vacar, sean a presentacion de sus Altezas, como cosa del Patronato Real.

Item que todos los otros Beneficios que vacaren é se proveyeren despues de esta primera nominacion é provision, se provean á hijos legitimos de los vecinos é habitadores, que hasta ahora é de aqui adelante han pasado ó pasaren de estos reinos á poblar en aquellas partes, y de sus descendientes, y no á los hijos de los naturales de allá, antes que fuesen á poblar los cristianos. Y esto hasta que otra cosa sus Altezas ó sus succesores determinen ó provean sobre ello, y que estos sean proveidos por suficiencia, precediendo oposicion y examen al modo de los hijos patrimoniales del Obispado de Palencia, con tal condicion que los tales hijos de vecinos, de dentro de año y medio despues que sean proveidos, sean obligados de llevar ratihabicion y aprobacion de sus Altezas y de sus succesores de los tales Beneficios, la cual presentarán ante el Viso Rey y

Gobernador y Jueces de apelacion que son ó fueren en las dichas Islas, é no la llevando el dicho termino pasado ipso facto vaquen, y sus Altezas y sus succesores puedan presentar otras nuevas personas á los tales Beneficios que asi vacaren, pero todavia conforme á lo susodicho.

Item que por virtud de la Bula de Nuestro muy Santo Padre, Julio segundo, concedida para la declaracion del habito que han de traer los coronados, los dichos Obispos hagan luego la dicha declaracion de esta manera: Que traigan corona abierta, tan grande como real castellano al menos, y el cabello de dos dedos bajo de la oreja que sea algo mas largo siguendo muy poco hacia tras, y la ropa de encima sea tabardo, ó capuz cerrado, ó loba cerrada ó abierta, qual quisiere: con tanto que sea la ropa tan larga que al menos como un palmo llegue al empeine del pie; y que asi las ropas de encima como las otras aparentes no sean coloradas ni verdes claras, ni amarillas, ni de otra color deshonesta.

Item que los dichos Obispos ni sus succesores en las Islas, no puedan ordenar de corona á ninguno, si no supiere hablar ni entender latin, ni puedan ordenar, al que tuviere dos ó tres hijos varones, mas del uno, por que no es de creer que ninguno querra todos sus hijos para clerigos, y esta condicion se guarde con los que mas hijos tuvieren.

Item que en el guardar de las fiestas, se guarden las ordenadas por la Iglesia y no otras algunas, aunque por promesas y votos, y que en los sínodos no se acrecienten más fiestas de las que hoy se guarden en la dicha Isla Hispañola y que si quieren acrecentar mas fiestas de las que hoy se guardan en la dicha Isla Hispañola, sea solamente para que la Iglesia las solemnice, y no para que los cristianos las guarden; por que segun las calidades de las haciendas de las dichas Islas, de otra manera no se podrian sustentar en ellas los cristianos.

Item que los dichos Obispos han de llevar los diezmos conforme á la Bula concedida por nuestro muy Santo Padre, y no han de llevar diezmos ni otra cosa alguno del oro, ni plata, ni de otro ningun minero, de perlas ni de piedras preciosas; y que lo que les perteneciere conforma á la Bula lo lleven en frutos como en Castilla y no en dinero, como se ha llevado algun tiempo. Y que por esta causa ni por otra alguna no apartarán los Indios directe ni indirecte de aquello que ahora hacen para el sacar del oro, antes los animarán y aconsejarán que sirvan mejor que hasta aqui en el sacar del oro, diciéndoles que es para hacer guerra á los infieles y las otras cosas que ellos vieren que podrán aprovechar para que trabajen bien.

Item que el Arzobispo de Sevilla Metropolitano de las Iglesias é Obispados de las dichas Islas, ó su Fiscal, puedan estar y residir en cualquiera de los dichos Obispados y ejercer las cosas que como Metropolitano le pertenecen conforme á derecho, y que no pueda poner por oficial el dicho Metropolitano á ninguno de los Prelados de las dichas Islas.

Item que ningunas personas de cualquier calidad, condicion, preeminencia y dignidad que sean, no puedan sacar oro, ni traer personas que lo saquen sino estuvieren sometidas á la jurisdiccion de sus Altezas y á las ordenanzas que allá se guardan, ó guardaren por los legos, en cuanto á sacar y fundir del oro y pagar los derechos que a la sazón pagaren por el dicho oro que sacaren.

Item que los que tuvieren Indios en las minas, ni los Indios que en ellas anduvieren durante las demoras, no puedan ser convenidos, ni traidos, ni arctados, ni llamados por sus causas ni ajenas, durante el dicho tiempo por ningun juez, por que eso se les da por inducias de pan y vin cojer, por cuanto aquel es fruto de la tierra y se ha de dar en lugar del otro segun que se da en Castilla.

Item en las causas civiles, los que se eximieren por la corona, pierdan los Indios y lo que tuvieren en las minas señalado, seyendo la causa profana, que seyendo la causa eclesiastica, bien se puede ventilar ante el juez eclesiastico sin incurrir en pena.

Y los dichos Don Fray Garcia de Padilla, Obispo de Santo Domingo, y Don Pedro Suarez de Deza, Doctor en Decretos, Obispo de la Concepcion, y Don Alonso Manso, Licenciado en Theologia, Obispo de la Isla de San Juan, visto y entendido todo lo en esta capitulacion contenido, é cada cosa é parte de ello, lo otorgaron é ovieron por bien, por si, y en nombre de los Obispos que les sucedieren en las dichas sus Iglesias, é de los que fueren proveidos en las Dignidades Canongias é Raciones y otros Beneficios, que asi suspensos, como no suspensos, en ellas se crian. Y prometieron y se obligaron en cuanto á ellos toca y atañe, de lo guardar, é cumplir enteramente, y hacer que las otras personas, á quien esto, asi de presente como de futuro, toca, ó tocar puede, que lo guarden, é cumplan sin ninguna falta. El cual otorgamiento ficieron en presencia del muy reverendo y muy magnifico señor, Don Juan de Fonseca, Obispo de Palencia, Capellan mayor y del Consejo de sus Altezas, y en sus manos prometieron como legales y fieles Prelados, y scientificos y honestos varones, de guardar y cumplir todo y cada cosa y parte de ello, é aora, ni en ningun tiempo no venir contra algo de todo lo susodicho. En testimonio de lo cual, otorgaron este instrumento en forma autentica. Dado en la ciudad de Burgos á ocho dias del mes de Mayo de mil é quinientos é doce años; é por mas firmeza firmaron aqui sus nombres, a lo cual fueron presentes por testigos los nobles señores, Lope de Conchillos, secretario de la Reina nuestra Señora, é el Licenciado Zapata y el Doctor Carvajal, del Consejo de sus Altezas, llamados y rogados.

E yo Francisco de Valencia, Canonigo de Palencia, Notario publico por la autoridad Apostolica, á todo lo que dicho es, en uno con los dichos testigos, presente fui, é vi firmar sus nombres á los susodichos muy Reverendos señores obispo en mi registro. Por ende este publico instrumento de capitulacion y asiento de mano agena fielmente fice escribir é con este mi signo é nombre acostumbrados lo signe é subscribi. En testimonio de verdad rogado é requirido. Francisco de Valencia, Apostólico Notario.

TO AMBASSADOR VICH AT ROME*
(Ferdinand, 1513)

El Rey:

Mosen Gerónimo de Vich, de mi Consejo y mi embajador en Corte de Roma: porque entre las otras mercedes y beneficios que (sobre el reglón) de Dios, nuestro Señor, habemos recebido, el mas principal es las victorias que en Su ayuda habemos habido contra los infieles enemigos de nuestra santa fe católica, sojuzga[n]do y reduciendo á la obediencia de nuestra Santa Madre la Iglesia muchas tierras y provincias que estaban ausentados della, y convertiendo muchas ánimas de los infieles que en ellas habitan, por el bautismo, a su Redemptor, y continuando en este sancto propósito, como cosa que mas deseo en este mundo; ahora ha placido a la Providencia divina que, allén destas islas y tierras descubiertas en la parte de las Indias del mar Océano, descubrir una grand parte de tierra, que, así por su grandeza, como por no se haber podido descubrir al deredor, que en sola una parte de costa se han descubierto mas de mil y quinientos leguas, como porque han hallado en ella diversos géneros de animales que en las otras islas no se han fallado animales de cuatro pies, se cree que es Tierra firme, la qual está poblada de grande multitud de gente que parecen mas razonables y mas capaces, instruidos y doctrinados en las cosas de nuestra sancta fé que los que fasta aquí se han fallado, de que espero que nuestro Señor será muy servido; y deseando que tanta multitud de ánimas se salve y á nuestra sancta fe católica se aserquen toda, no teniendo respeto á los grandes

---

* Pacheco y Cárdenas, *Colección de documentos inéditos*, I 39, 264-70. For the translation see pp. 127-30.

gastos y trabajos que en ello se acercan, inviamos agora una
generosa armada, así de navíos como de gente, para que, juntamente con otra gente de armas que por nuestro mandato y á
nuestra costa estan en la dicha tierra, sojuzguen a aquellas
bárbaras naciones, las traigan al yugo y obediencia de nuestra
sancta Madre la Iglesia y las aparten de la infidelidad en que
estan y de diversos y grandes errores con que el enemigo las
tiene sujuzgadas. Y para que nuestro deseo se compla en ha-
cerlos cristianos, demas de la gente de guerra, son necesarias
personas espirituales, para que, consu doctrina y ejemplo, los
animen y enseñen, y con palabras y con obras traigan al ver-
dadero conocimiento de la salud de sus ánimas: Y porque las
tales personas, unas han de ser para lo ir a hacer en persona, y
otras para lo favorecer y encaminar desde acá; y el [Patri-
archado al margin] muy Reverendo en Cristo Padre Juan de
Fonseca, arzobispo de Rosano, nuestro capellan mayor y de
nuestro Consejo, de claro linaje y de los principales nobles
destos reinos, como sabéis, desde el principio que las Indias se
descubrieron hasta agora, y al presente por nuestro mandato,
se ha ocupado y ocupa en la provision y governacion dellas,
y por su industria y vigilancia, diligencia y cuidado, con muy
probada facilidad, sin otro interes alguno, salvo por servir
á nuestro Señor y cumplir nuestros mandamientos, ha sido
y es causa muy principal de muchos bienes que en las dichas
Indias han sucedido y suceden, y siempre continúa sus trabajos
para en lo porvenir, con mucho celo que las ánimas de todas
aquellas gentes se conviertan á nuestro Señor; y se espera,
segun la grandeza de la tierra, que, dempues de sojuzgada, con
la ayuda de nuestro Señor, se instituirán de diversos títulos de
iglesias en ella; suplicareis de nuestra parte a nuestro muy
Santo Padre, por virtud de la nuestra carta de creencia que va
con este, que habiendo consideracion a lo subsodicho y al servicio tan señalado de nuestro Señor y acrecentamiento de la
nuestra sancta fe católica que dello se espera seguir mediante

su ayuda, plega á su Santidad que sobre las iglesias que se
irigieren de aquí adelante en la dicha tierra de las Indias—que
generalmente toda la provincia llama Castilla del Oro—in-
stituya al dicho arzobispo don Juan Rodriguez de Fonseca,
universal Patriarca de toda ella, conforme a los otros Patri-
arcados que hay en la Iglesia, de cuya institución, segund sus
méritos y doctrinas, exemplo y fidelidad, y la mucha esperiencia
que tiene en las dichas Indias, y gran deseo y fervor de convertir
á las gentes que en ellas se fallan á nuestra sancta fe católica,
esperamos en nuestro Señor será muy servido, a nuestra sancta
fe católica aumentada y reducidas á ella las almas de la gran
multitud de gente que la dicha tierra habitan; y que la iglesia
prencipal y cabeza del dicho Patriarcado sea en el lugar que
el dicho Don Juan de Fonseca, con licencia y consensu nuestro
señalare en la dicha tierra; porque agora, hasta mas saber della,
no se puede bien señalar, porque, sabida, se señalará mas có-
modamente, [margin: Nuestra Señora de la Antigua] y porque,
en la dicha tierra hay muchas y diversas provincias, como arriba
se dice, y así ha de haber muchas y diversas iglesias cathedrales,
placiendo a nuestro Señor, entretanto que la tierra se sojuzga,
es necesario que en la provincia donde agora está el pueblo de
los cristianos, que es en la provincia que se han de llamar Bética
Aurea, y la iglesia del pueblo se llama Nuestra Señora de
Antigua, le plega criar y regir un obispado de la iglesia cathedral deste nombre, debajo del dicho Patriarcado; y porque el
devoto Padre fray Juan de Quevedo, fraile de la orden de San
Francisco de la Observancia, predicador que agora es de nuestra
Real Capilla, el cual, por su vida y exemplo y mucha prudencia
e iminentes letras y mucha doctrina, ha regido diversos oficios
de provincial y guardian de la provincia del Andelusia muchos
años, y esperamos, por la mucha experiencia que dél se tiene en
las dichas cosas, será nuestro Señor muy servido en que él sea
proveido con este dicho obispado; y nos le enviamos á requirer,
con este cargo y el bien de lo mucho que en el puede servir á

nuestro Señor y ha nos acebtado, de ir luego a la dicha armada á
entender en la conversion de la dicha gente: Por ende suplicareis
a su Sanctidad Nos conceda dos faculdades: la una porque nos
y los subsecores en este Corona Real de Castilla, ó la persona
que para ello señalaremos en nuestro nombre, puede agora y
en de aquí adelante limitar y señalar los límites y diócesis en
la dicha tierra, así para las dichas iglesias y obispado de
Nuestra Señora de Antigua de la provincia de Darien que ahora
se llaman Bética Aurea, y el presente se ha de instituir y criar,
como para las que adelante se instituiran y criaran; la otra ha
de ser para hacer la particion y division de los diezmos de las
dichas iglesias de Nuestra Señora de Antigua y de las que
adelante se criarán e instituirán, y para señaler los réditos del
dicho Patriarchado los cuales diezmos, puesto caso que tenemos
gracia y donacion dellos concedida por la sede apostólica,
porque vayan luego prelados a entender en la conversion de
aquella gente bárbara, los daré, en nombre de la serenísima
Reina, mi muy cara y amada hija, así como se fueren criando
las dichas iglesias, ecepto las tercias, que esto ha de quedar
para la Corona Real destos Reinos, y perpetuamente; y pues
nos habemos de facer la donacion de los dichos diezmos, razon
es que el repartimiento dellos, así de los que se dieren al Patriarchado, como a los Obispados, se faga por la persona que
nombraremos para ello, y que su Sanctidad nos invie la dicha
comision; y la comision para facer la cria de la dicha iglesia
de Sancta María de Darien venga dirigida al dicho muy Reverendo in Christo Padre Arzobispo de Rosano, nuestro capellan
mayor; y que, como veis, esto es caso que comple tanto al servicio de nuestro Señor y a la conversion y salud de las animas
de tan innumerables gentes y acrecentamiento de nuestra sancta
fe católica; por servicio Nuestro que en todo dad la solicitud
y diligencia que convenga, como de vos esperamos, y supliqueis
y procureis con su Sanctidad y con los muy Reverendos Cardi-
nales que os pareciere que podrá en ello aprovechar, y invieme

el despacho de todo lo subsodicho lo mas brevemente que po-
díeredes, que en ello me sirvireis mucho. De Valladolid, a 26
dias del mes de julio de 1513 anos. Yo el Rey. Refrendada del
secretario Conchillos.

THE APPOINTMENT OF BISHOP JULIÁN GARCÉS*

Bulas de Ereccion de la Santa Iglesia de Tlaxcala llamada
Carolense, hoy Puebla de Los Angeles
Que son conducentes para la inteligencia de los sucesos de
la Nueva España, y también para la Santa Iglesia Carolense
de la Peninsula de Yucatan.
Don Pedro de la Vega, de el Consejo de S. M. su Secretario,
y Oficial Mayor de la secretaría de el Consejo, y Cámara de las
Indias de la Negociación de la Nueva España, certifico, que en
la misma Secretaría se halla la Ereccion de el tenor siguente:

I

PROCLAMATION OF BISHOP GARCÉS

Frater Julianus Garces, Dei & Apostolicae Sedis gratia
Episcopus Carolensis in Nova Hispania, universis & singulis
praesentibus & futuris, salutem in Domino sempiternam. Cum
Invictissimus [Rex] Romanorum & Hispaniarum utriusque
Siciliae &c, Carolus & Regina Joanna, atque idem Carolus Rex
in Imperatorem electus, divini amoris igne succensi, zelo Domus
Dei aestuantes, in orthodoxae Fidei propagationem semper in-
tenti post non pauca Regna & Dominia ab infidelibus erepta, ac
luce veritatis perfusa, animo proposuissent Insulas & continens
nostris incognitas penetrare, ut illarum incolas & habitatores ad
verum Dei & Redemptoris nostri cultum Fidemque reducerent:
inque ejus rei exequutionem Ferdinandum Cortes, virum egre-
gium, ab Insula Cubae cum paratissima optimeque instructa
classe transmisset, Deo id agente, in Continentem amplissimam

---

* García Gutiérrez, *Bulario*, pp. 323-33. For the translation see pp. 136-46.

terram quae Sancti Joannis de Ulua finibus clauditur appulsus,
Ferdinandus praefatus cum exercitu superatis montibus pro-
grediens ad Mexici Provinciam maximeque Tenuxtitlan, Urbem
lacui incumbentem, fusis fugatisque non semel hostibus haud
sine magna labore pervenisset, pluresque subinde fuissent ex
incolis ad Fidem conversi & baptizati, structaeque nonnullae
Ecclesiae ac Monasteria pro Civitatibus in urbe Tlaxcaltechae,
nondum Episcopo constituto, Dominus noster Clemens Papa VII,
eidem Provinciae et Civitati Paterno cupiens subvenire affectu,
Ecclesiam Cathedralem ad supplicationem ejusdem Potentis-
simi Regis Caroli ac Reginae & ejusdem Caroli in Imperatorem
electi, creari et erigi constituit, necnon ab Invictissimo Carolo
Carolensem appellari Civitatem voluit: ac de ejusdem & Regi-
arum Majestatum consensu, Nos praenominatum Fratrem Juli-
anum Garces Episcopum & Pastorem dictae Civitati praeficiens,
ejusdem Diocesis terminos praefigi curavit, prout in ejusdem
Pontificis ac Caesarae & Reginae Majestatum Litteris de limita-
tione terminorum super hoc concessis plenius continetur: & ad
erectionem Dignitatum, Canonicatuum & Praebendarum, aliorumque Ecclesiasticorum Beneficiorum cum Cura & sine Cura,
ac alia in praemissis Litteris Nobis commissa, facultatem concessit: quarum tenor de verbo ad verbum sequitur & talis est:

II

PRESENTATION BY CHARLES V

D. Carlos &c. Por cuanto Nos, aceptando las letras y buena
vida, méritos y exemplo de el R.P.D. Fr. Julian Garcés, de la
Orden de Santo Domingo, nuestro Predicador, le presentamos
al Obispado de Yucatan, e Santa María de los Remedios, en
las nuestras Indias de el Mar Océano, que es la primera Tierra
que en aquella Provincia se descubrió, á la qual despues los
Christianos que más adelante pasaron, pusieron por nombre la
Nueva España, é Su Santidad por nuestra suplicación y pre-
sentatión, le hizo gracia y merced de el dicho Obispado, con

título de la dicha Yucatan y Santa María de los Remedios, porque á la sazon era donde residía el mayor número de Christianos, y de ello le mandó dar sus Bulas, y despues, á causa de que aquello quedó sin población de Christianos, y se pasaron adelante y han estado y están poblando las dichas Tierra en la Nueva España y otras Provincias: por lo qual Su Santidad á suplicación nuestra y de el dicho Obispo D. Fray Julian, mandó declarar que el dicho Obispado y límites de él, se entendiesse y estendiesse en los límites de la Nueva España que por Nos le fuessen señalados y limitados, y de ello le mandó dar y dió su Bula y Breve declarándolo assí; su tenor de las quales dichas Bulas y Breves, uno en pos de otro, es como se sigue:

III
Sacri apostolatus ministerio
(Leo X, 1518)

Leo Episcopus, Servus Servorum Dei, ad perpetuam rei memoriam.

Sacri Apostolatus Ministerio meritis licet insufficientibus superna dispositione Praesidentes, ad universi orbis Provincias, & loca, ea praesertim quae Omnipotentis Dei Misericordia Christianae veritatis lucem nostris temporibus incoeperunt agnoscere, frequenti meditatione intendimus, ut in illis orthodoxae Fidei cultus augeatur, & Christiana Religio propagetur, ac eorum incolae & habitatores Venerabilium Praesulum Doctrina & Authoritate suffulti, in eadem Fide semper proficiant, ipsaque loca maxime insignia dignioribus Titulis attollantur, & majoribus honoribus; praesertim cum id Christianorum Regum pia vota exposcunt, & cognoscimus in Domino salubriter expedire. Sane cum clarae memoriae Ferdinandus Aragonum & Siciliae Rex, qui etiam dum viveret Regnorum Castellae & Legionis Gubernator fuit, ad laudem & gloriam illius cujus est terra & plenitudo ejus, ac universi qui habitant in ea, pluribus jam annis elapsis, validissimam classem comparasset, eamque ad novas Insulas in

Occeano Indico inquirendas destinasset, ac inter alias Hispani-
olam Elisabetham nuncupatam, valde notabilem Insulam hujusmodi classe repertam, temporali suae ditioni subjecisset, ac in
ea Sancti Dominici & Conceptionis Beatae Mariae Cathedrales
Ecclesias erigi obtinuisset; paulo antequam ab humanis disce-
deret similem classem circiter duo millia hominum habentem
ad alias Insulas in eodem mari inquirendas misit, eique Dilectum filium Petrum de Arias Capitaneum praefecit; qui cum per
plures dies navigasset ad regionem quandam tandem pervenit,
vulgo Yucatan nuncupatam, tantae magnitudinis ut adhuc in-
certum sit an Insula aut Terra continens sit, eamque sub invocatione ejusdem Beatae Mariae de Remediis vocavit, ac in ea
juxta litus maris oppidum sive pagum cum Parochiali Ecclesia
sub eadem invocatione extruxit; cumque Charissimus in Christo
filius noster Carolus Castellae & Legionis, ac aliorum Regnorum
praedictorum Rex illustris, ejusdem Ferdinandi Regis non modo
Regnorum haeres & Successor, verum & virtutum imitator com-
perisset dictam Terram sive Insulam per multas leucas in longi-
tudine & latitudine a suis perlustratam esse, & a pluribus
hominum millibus habitari, Coeloque salubri ac solo fertili
gaudere, ejusque incolas & habitatores rationis & humanitatis
capaces esse, facileque orthodoxae Fidei nostrae adhaerere,
ejusque mores & praecepta libenter amplecti, nec parvam ipsius
Terrae sive Insulae partem suae ditioni subjecerit, in eaque
plura oppida condi fecerit & in illis Parochiales Ecclesias erigi
obtinuerit, speretque multo majorem ejus partem sub ipsius
ditione venturam, ac discussis errorum tenebris ad lucis verita-
tem perventuram & Christum totius humani generis Redemptorem cognituram fore, ac propterea summopere desideret
dictum oppidum sive pagum juxta litus maris, ut praefertur,
extructum, in Civitatem quae Carolensis appelletur & illius
Ecclesiam praedictam in Cathedralem sub invocatione Beatae
Mariae de Remediis erigi. Habita igitur super iis cum Venerabilibus Fratribus nostris matura deliberatione, de illorum Con-

silio, praefato Carolo Rege super hoc Nobis humiliter supplicante, ad Omnipotentis Dei laudem & gloriam, ac honorem
Beatissimae & Gloriosissimae Virginis Mariae ejus Genetricis,
cum totius Coelestis Curiae jubilo, Authoritate Apostolica tenore
praesentium, oppidum sive pagum Insulae Beatae Mariae de
Remediis hujusmodi, in quo magnus numerus fidelium de prae-
senti habitat, in Civitatem quae Carolensis appelletur; illius
vero Parochialem Ecclesiam praedictam in Cathedralem Ecclesiam sub dicta invocatione Beatae Mariae de Remediis pro uno
Episcopo, Carolensi nuncupato, qui in dicta Ecclesia erecta &
illius Civitate ac Diocesi verbum Dei praedicet ac earum incolas
infideles ad praefatae orthodoxae Fidei cultum convertat & conversos in eadem Fide instruat & doceat atque confirmet, eisque
Baptismi gratiam impendat & tam illis sic conversis quam aliis
omnibus fidelibus in Civitate & Diocesi praedictis pro tempore
degentibus & ad illas declinantibus Sacramenta Ecclesiastica &
alia spiritualia ministret & ministrari faciat, ipsiusque Ecclesiae
erectae aedificia & ad formam Cathedralis Ecclesiae redigi faciat & procuret, ac in Ecclesia & Civitate erectis, necnon Diocesi
praedictis, Dignitates, Canonicatus & Praebendas, aliaque Beneficia Ecclesiastica cum Cura & sine Cura erigat & instituat & alia
spiritualia conferat & seminet, prout Divini Cultus augmento &
ipsorum incolarum Animarum saluti expedire cognoverit, cum
Sede & aliis insigniis & jurisdictionibus Episcopalibus, Privilegiis quoque, immunitatibus & gratiis quibus aliae Cathedrales
Ecclesiae & earum Praesules in Hispania, de jure vel consuetudine utuntur, potiuntur & gaudent, seu uti, potiri & gaudere
poterunt quomodolibet in futurum, perpetuo erigimus & instituimus & eidem Ecclesiae oppidum sive pagum per Nos in Civitatem erectum, pro Civitate, & partem Terrae sive Insulae Beatae
Mariae de Remediis hujusmodi, quam ipse Carolus Rex positis
limitibus statui jusserit pro Diocesi, illorumque incolas & habitatores pro Clero & Populo concedimus & assignamus, ita ut ipse
Episcopus Carolensis qui pro tempore fuerit, in illis Episco-

palem jurisdictionem, authoritatem & potestatem libere exerceat & ex omnibus inibi pro tempore provenientibus, praeterquam ex auro & argento, ac aliis metallis, gemmis & lapidibus praetiosis, quod hoc libera esse decernimus, Decimas & Primitias de jure debitas, caeteraque Episcopalia jura exigat & percipiat, prout aliis in ulteriori Hispania Episcopis in suis Civitatibus & Diocesibus de jure & consuetudine id licet; necnon jus Patronatus & praesentandi infra annum propter loci distantiam Personam idoneam, ad dictam Ecclesiam Carolensem, quoties illius vacatio, excepta hac prima vice, pro tempore occurrerit, pro tempore existenti Romano Pontifici per eum in ejusdem Ecclesiae Episcopum & pastorem ad praesentationem hujusmodi praeficiendam praefato Carolo & pro tempore existenti Regi Castellae & Legionis in perpetuum concedimus & reservamus. Nulli ergo omnino hominum liceat hanc paginam nostrae Erectionis, Institutionis, Concessionis, assignationis, Decreti & Reservationis infringere, vel ausu temerario contraire; si quis autem hoc attentare praesumpserit, indignationem Omnipotentis Dei, ac Beatorum Petri & Pauli Apostolorum ejus se noverit incursurum. Datum Romae, apud Sanctum Petrum, anno Incarnationis Dominicae millesimo quingentesimo decimo octavo, nono Kalendas Februarii, Pontificatus nostri anno sexto. Ic. Galianus Mutus Marti. Contreras Bc. Acolytus.—

IV

Devotionis tuae

(Clement VII, 1525)

Clemens Episcopus, Servus Servorum Dei. Venerabili Fratri Juliano, Episcopo Carolensi, salutem & Apostolicam benedictionem.

Devotionis tuae probata sinceritas, quam ad Nos & Apostolicam Sedem gerere dignosceris, promeretur ut Personam tuam intimis affectibus prosequentes petitionibus tuis, per quas tuae Diocesis & aliarum circumvicinarum omnium, praesertim

in partibus infidelium consistentium Ecclesiarum honor & venus-
tas, ac in eis Divinus Cultus accrescat & ipsi infideles, eorum
caecitate abjecta, ad orthodoxae Fidei lumen conversi Christiano
Dogmate imbuantur, prout & Catholicorum Principum devotio
requirit, quantum cum Deo possumus, favorabiliter annuimus.
Dudum siquidem felicis recordationis Leo Papa X Praedecessor
noster, ad supplicationem Charissimi in Christo Filii nostri
Caroli Romanorum & Hispaniarum Regis illustris, in Imperatorem electi, qui etiam Castellae & Legionis Rex existit, in Yucatan Indiae maris Insula, suis classe & auspiciis ab infidelium
manibus erepta, oppidum insigne primo in eadem Insula in
Civitatem erectam & quamdam Parochialem Ecclesiam tum immediate post eandem erectionem in eodem oppido a Christifidelibus constructam sub invocatione Beatae Mariae de Remediis
in Cathedralem Ecclesiam pro uno Episcopo Carolensi nuncupato, qui in dicta Ecclesia ac illius Civitate & Diocesi verbum
Dei praedicare, ac Pontificalia exercere & Alia per Episcopos
fieri debita facere deberet, cum sede & aliis insigniis ac Jurisdictionibus Episcopalibus, privilegiisque, immunitatibus & gratiis quibus aliae Cathedrales Ecclesiae & illarum Praesules in
Hispaniarum Regnis de jure vel consuetudine utebantur, potie-
bantur & gaudebant, perpetuo erexit & instituit, ac ipsi Ecclesiae
ab ejus primaeva erectione hujusmodi tum vacanti de Persona
tua providit, teque illi praefecit in Episcopum & Pastorem, prout
in diversis ipsius Praedecessoris desuper confectis Litteris plenius continentur. Nobis nuper pro parte tua petitio continebat,
quod cum limites & confines Diocesis Carolensis adhuc des-
tinati non sint, ex eo quod Christiani Hispani praedicti, auxiliante Domino ulterius progredientes, in certa Provincia Nova
Hispania appellata, aliud oppidum Tenuxtitlan nuncupatum
acquisivere, ipse Carolus Rex in Imperatorem electus pro ipsius
Ecclesiae Carolensis maiore venustate, ampliorique Diocesi &
dictrictu, & ut commodius statum tuum juxta Pontificalis exigentiam Dignitatis decentius tenere valeas, limites & confines Dio-

cesis Carolensis hujusmodi in Provincia & oppido Tenuxtitlan hujusmodi seu ipsum oppidum Tenuxtitlan ac ejus districtum pro limitibus & confinibus hujusmodi assignare intendat; quare tam pro parte tua quam ejusdem Caroli Regis in Imperatorem electi, Nobis fuit humiliter supplicatum quatenus assignationem praedictam postquam per dictum Carolum Regem facta foret, approbare & confirmare, aliasque in praemissis opportune providere de benignitate Apostolica dignaremur. Nos igitur te a quibusvis Excommunicationis, Suspensionis & Interdicti, aliisque Ecclesiae sententiis, Censuris & poenis, si quibus quomodolibet innodatus existis, ad effectum praesentium dumtaxat consequendum harum serie absolventes & absolutum fore censentes, hujusmodi supplicationibus inclinati, assignationem praedictam, si illa, ut praefertur, per ipsum Carolum Regem fiat, postquam, ut praemittitur, facta fuerit, Apostolica Authoritate tenore praesentium sine alicujus praejudicio approbamus & confirmamus, eique perpetuae & inviolabilis firmitatis robur adjicimus, ac omnes tam juris quam facti defectus, si qui forsan intervenerint in eadem, supplemus; ita quod tu et Successores praefati praemissa & alia in Litteris ejusdem Praedecessoris contenta, ac reliqua omnia quae in Ecclesia Beatae Mariae & oppido dictae Insulae facere et exercere poteratis in dicto oppido Tenuxtitlan & ejus districtu vel aliis limitibus consignandis, ut praefertur, facere & exercere, teque ac Episcopos Carolenses Successores tuos, non dictae Beatae Mariae sed de Tenuxtitlan aut de aliis limitibus consignandis hujusmodi, vos debeatis in omnibus & per omnia perinde ac si in erectionibus hujusmodi & aliis Litteris praedictis oppidum Tenuxtitlan cum ejus districtu seu alii assignandi limites hujusmodi nominata, ipsumque oppidum & districtus, seu alii limites ut praefertur assignandi, dictae tuae Ecclesiae Carolensi in suam Diocesim assignata & applicata fuissent, de speciali gratia indulgemus ac statuimus & ordinamus. Non obstantibus praemissis ac Apostolicis, necnon in Provincialibus & Synodalibus Conciliis editis

generalibus vel specialibus Constitutionibus vel Ordinationibus,
ac dictae Ecclesiae & Juramento, Confirmatione Apostolica, vel
quavis firmitate alia roboratis, statutis & consuetudinibus, ceteris
contrariis quibuscumque. Nulli ergo omnino hominum liceat
hanc paginam nostrae Absolutionis, Approbationis, Confirmationis, Suppletionis, Indulti, Statuti & Ordinationis infringere
vel ei ausu temerario contraire. Si quis autem hoc attentare
praesumpserit, indignationem Omnipotentis Dei ac Beatorum
Petri & Pauli Apostolorum ejus se noverit incursurum. Datum
Romae apud Sanctum Petrum anno Incarnationis Dominicae
millesimo quingentesimo vigesimo quinto, tertio idus Octobris,
Pontificatus nostri anno secundo.

V

DELIMITATION OF DIOCESE

(Charles V, 1526)

Por ende Nos usando de los dichos Bulas, y Breve, e Declaraciones de Su Santidad, que de suso van incorporadas, y de
cada una de ellas, assí como mejor podemos, y de Derecho
debemos, de suplicación y expreso consentimiento de el dicho
Obispo D. Fr. Julian Garcés, declaramos, y señalamos, y de-
terminamos por límites de dicho Obispado de Yucatán, y Santa
María de Remedios, las Provincias, y Tierras siguentes: Primeramente la Provincia de Tlaxcaltechle inclusive, y San Juan
de Ulúa, que confina con Aguas vertientes, hasta llegar á
Matlata inclusive, y la Villa Rica de la Vera-Cruz, y la Villa
de Medellin, con todo lo de Tabasco, y dende el Rio de Grijalva,
hasta llegar á Chiapa. Los quales términos, y límites, y Provincias de suso declarados, queremos, y mandamos, que sean ahora,
y de aquí adelante, quando nuestra merced y voluntad fuere,
habidos por términos, límites, y distrito de el dicho Obispado
de Yucatan y Santa María de los Remedios, lo qual todo, y cada
cosa, y parte de ello el dicho R.P.D. Fr. Julian, y los otros
Obispos que por tiempo fueren, durante esta nuestra voluntad,

pueda usar, y exercer el Oficio y Jurisdicción de Obispo, conforme á las Bulas de Su Santidad, retiniendo, y reservando, como retenemos, y reservamos en Nos, y en nuestros Sucesores de la Corona Real de Castilla, poder y facultad para mudar, variar, alterar, y revocar, quitando, ó añadiendo los límites, y términos, y distrito, que quisiéremos, ó por bien tuviéremos en el dicho Obispado é Provincias de el, en todo, ó en parte, como viéremos, que mas conviene al servicio de Dios, y nuestro. Y mandamos á nuestro Governador, ó Juez de Residencia, que ahora es, ó por tiempo fuere de la Tierra, que luego con la parte de el dicho Obispo, ó con la Persona que para ello nombrare, haga poner, y ponga en los dichos términos, y límites, y distrito de el dicho Obispado, que de suso va declarado, marcos, y mojones de piedra notorios, y conocidos, que queden por la dicha Tierra por señales de los límites de el dicho Obispado. Dada en Granada á diez y nueve dias de el mes de Septiembre, año de el Nacimiento de nuestro Salvador Jesu Christo de mil, y quinientos, y veinte y seis años. Lo cual todo, y toda cosa, y parte de ello, como de suso se contiene, el dicho Fr. Julian por sí, y por sus Sucesores, dixo, que consentía, y consintió. Yo el Rey. Yo Francisco de los Covos, Secretario de su Cesárea y Católicas Magestades la fice escribir por su mandado. Mercurinus Cancellarius. Fr. G. Episcopus Oxomensis. Dr. Carvajal, indignus Episcopus Canariensis. El Dr. Beltrán G. Episcopus Civitatensis.

VI

INSTITUTION OF DIOCESE OF TLAXCALA

(Garcés, 1526)

Post quarum quidem Litterarum Apostolicarum praesentationem & receptionem, ut praemittitur, factas, fuimus pro parte Domini nostri Caroli debita cum instancia requisiti, ut ad executionem Litterarum Apostolicarum & contentorum in eisdem procedentes, in praefata nostra Cathedrali Ecclesia ad honorem

Beatissimae Virginis in dicta Civitate Tlaxcaltechalae Dignitates, Canonicatus & praebendas ac Portiones aliaque Beneficia
& Officia Ecclesiastica quotquot & prout melius expedire videri-
mus, tam in Civitate, quam per totam Diocesim erigeremus &
institueremus. Nos igitur Julianus Episcopus & Commissarius
Apostolicus praefatus, attendentes petitionem hujusmodi fore
justam & rationi consonam, volentesque ut veri obedientiae filii
imperia Apostolica Nobis directa reverenter exequi, ut tenemur,
commissionem praedictam acceptavimus & eadem Authoritate
Apostolica qua fungimur in hac parte, praefata Caesarea
Catholica Majestate instantibus & petentibus, praedicta Civitate
Tlaxcaltechalae ad honorem Dei & Domini nostri Jesu Christi
Beatissimae Mariae Matris ejus, in cujus & sub cujus titulo per
praefatum Sanctissimum Dominum nostrum in Cathedralem
Ecclesiam est erigenda; tenore praesentium erigimus, creamus
& instituimus in dicta Cathedrali Ecclesia. . . . Quae omnia &
singula de instantia, petitione & consensu dictorum Dominorum
Regis Caroli in Imperatorem electi, ac Joannae Reginae Matris
ejus, eadem Apostolica Authoritate qua fungimur in hac parte
& melioribus modo, via atque forma quibus possumus & de jure
debemus, erigimus & constituimus, creamus, facimus, disponimus & ordinamus cum omnibus & singulis ad id necessariis &
opportunis, non obstantibus contrariis quibuscumque & illis
praecipue quae Sanctissimus Dominus noster praefatus in suis
Litteris Apostolicis voluit non obstare; & ea omnia & singula
omnibus & singulis praesentibus & futuris, cujuscumque status,
gradus, ordinis, praeeminentiae, vel conditionis fuerint, intimamus & insinuamus & ad omnium notitiam deducimus &
deduci volumus per praesentes, mandamus praedicta Authoritate in virtute Sanctae Obedientiae omnibus & singulis supra-
dictis, ut ea omnia & singula, quemadmodum a nobis instituta
sunt, observent & observari facient. Et eadem Authoritate mandamus & ordinamus, quod omnes Dignitates & Canonici, necnon
Portionarii integri, cum teneantur ad celebrandum per Heb-

domadam respective, tempore praesentationis sint in aliquo
Ordine Sacro, & tempore institutionis aut provisionis sint Pres-
byteri, & praesentatio aliter facta sit ipso jure nulla, exinde sine
privatione, aut vacatione & declaratione possit alius praesentari
& institui, qui in dictis ordinibus fuerit constitutus. Item eadem
authoritate ordinamus, quod si causa aliqua supervenerit ex qua
nobis vel Decano, aut ejus locum tenenti, necessarium vel ultra
supradictos dies ad Capitulum vocare teneantur, & sicut in
diebus ordinariis Capitulares adesse. In quorum omnium &
singulorum fidem & testimonium praemissorum praesentes Litteras, sive praesens publicum instrumentum exinde fieri, & per
Notarium publicum infrascriptum subscribi & publicari man-
davimus, nostroque nomine roboravimus. Sigillique nostri pro-
prii jussimus & facimus appensione communiri. Datis & actis
Granatae in Hospitio nostro sub anno a Nativitate Domini
MDXXVI. Omne subscriptione & linea est per me Notarium
infrascriptum approbatum. Julianus, Episcopus Carolensis. Et
quia Ego Christophorus de Peregrino, Clericus Segoviensis,
publicus Authoritate Apostolica Notarius, praemissis interfui,
ideo praesens instrumentum manu aliena Scriptum, Signoque &
nomine meis consuetis, signavi una cum dicti Reverendi Domini
Fr. Juliani Episcopi Carolensis nominis subscriptione & dicti
Sigilli appensione in testimonium veritatis rogatus & requisitus.
Christophorus de Peregrino, Notarius publicus.

Porque en las otras erecciones de los Obispados de Islas, y
Tierra firme se hacían supresiones de Dignidades, y Canongías,
hasta que la renta abastasse, ahora para que dicha erección
fuesse mas clara, y pura, no se hicieron supresiones, antes se
determinó por las Cesáreas y Cathólicas Magestades de el Rey
é la Reyna, nuestros Señores, de anexar las Dignidades de
Arcediano, y una Canongía al Obispo de Yucatan, alias Carolense, en Nova Hispania como antes siempre se hizo á los
primeros Obispos. Por ende Nos el dicho Obispo Carolense por
la Autoridad de nuestro Santíssimo Padre, como por las Bulas

de Su Santidad insertas en la dicha erección parecerá, y por el expreso consentimiento y mandado de Sus Magestades, y los de el su Consejo de las Indias, anexamos, y aplicamos en nuestra Persona, sobre nuestra cabeza ponemos la dicha Dignidad de Arcedianasgo, é una Canongía con sus frutos, é rentas, por nuestra vida dumtaxat, de manera que al nuestro Sucesor no hayan de pasar, ante Sus Magestades despues de nuestra vida las hayan de proveer, como los otros Beneficios de aquella Tierra, e Obispado. Y porque es verdad, firmamos la presente Cédula de nuestro nombre, y tambien la firmó el Secretario de el dicho Consejo de las Indias. Fecha á primero de Diciembre de mil quinientos, y veinte y seis años. Julianus Episcopus Carolensis.

Esto fue aprobado por los Señores Presidente, y de el Consejo de las Indias en nombre de Sus Magestades, ante mi Juan de Sámano, á quien fue mandado por los dichos Señores, que en testimonio lo firmase de mi nombre. En Granada á primero de Diciembre de mil quinientos, y veinte y seis años. Juan de Sámano.—Concuerda con la Erección que se halla en la referida Secretaría de la Nueva España. Madrid, y Abril treinta de mil setecientos quarenta y nueve anos.

Pedro de la Vega.

THE INSTITUTION OF ZUMÁRRAGA*

I

CONSISTORIAL ACT ERECTING THE CATHEDRAL OF MEXICO

Acta Consistorial de la Errección de la Cathedral de Mexico. Consistor. 12 Ag. 1530

Ad relationem Rmi. Cardinalis de Valle, fuit erecta in Cathedralem Ecclesia coepta et facienda in Civitate Mexicana

---

* García Gutiérrez, *Bulario*, pp. 257-77; Icazbalceta, *Zumárraga*, Appendix II, pp. 68-69. For the translation see pp. 154-67.

in India; et quod episcopus vel alii deputandi possit extinguere numerum Canonicatuum et Dignitatuum: et ex nunc tota illa regio fuit assignata pro diocesi, donec erunt erectae aliae ecclesiae. Fuit erecta ecclesia sub invocatione Assumptionis B. Mariae Virginis, cui provisum fuit de persona Fratris Francisci, Ord. Min—A.C.R.R., fol. 207 V. 2, 187.

II

PAPAL PROVISION FOR ZUMÁRRAGA

(Clement VII, 1530)

Hoc est quoddam instrumentum sumptum ex quibusdam litteris Apostolicis, suo vero sigillo plumbeo munitis, cum cordulis canapis, cujus tenor de verbo ad verbum sequitur, et est talis:

Clemens Episcopus, servus servorum Dei. Dilecto filio Francisco de Zumarraga, electo Mexicanen, salutem et apostolicam benedictionem.

Apostolatus officium, meritis licet insufficientibus, nobis ex alto commissum, quo Ecclesiarum omnium regimini divina dispositione praesidimus, exequi, coadjuvante Domino, cupientes, solliciti corde reddimur et solertes, ut cum de Ecclesiarum ipsarum regiminibus agitetur committendis, tales eis in Pastores praeficere studeamus, qui gregem Domini suae curae creditum sciant non solum doctrina verbi sed etiam exemplo boni operis informare, commissas sibi Ecclesias in statu prospero et tranquillo velint et valeant, auctore Domino, salubriter regere et feliciter gubernare. Sane Ecclesia Mexicanen, quam olim Parrochialem in Cathedralem Ecclesiam ereximus et instituimus hodie, necnon sui patronatus et praesentandi personam idoneam ad ipsam sic erectam Ecclesiam, tam ac prima vice quam quoties illa pro tempore vacaret, charissimo in Christo filio nostro Carolo, Romanorum imperatori, semper augusto, qui etiam Rex existit, ac pro tempore existenti Regi vel Reginae Castellae et Legionis, reservavimus et concessimus, de fratrum nostorum consilio pariter et assensu, Apostolica auctoritate, per alias nostras litteras, prout in illis plenius continetur, ab ejus prima erectione hujusmodi vacante, Nos ad ipsius Ecclesiae Mexicanen, provisionem celerem et felicem, ne longae vacationis exponatur incommodis, paternis et sollicitis studiis intendentes, post deliberationem quam de praeficiendo illi personam utilem et etiam fructuosam, cum eisdem fratribus habuimus diligentem, demum ad te, Ordinis Minorum Fratrum Professorem in probatu et aetate legitima constitutum, cui apud Nos de religione, zelo, litterarum scientia, vitae munditia, morum honestate, spiritualium providentia et temporalium circumspectione, aliisque multiplicum virtutum donis, fidedigna testimonia perhibentur, direximus oculos nostrae mentis, quibus omnibus debita meditatione pensatis de persona tua nobis et eisdem fratribus ob tuorum exigentiam meritorum accepta eidem Ecclesiae Mexicanen, de simili consilio, necnon de consensu ejusdem Caroli Imperatoris providimus, teque illi praeficimus in Episcopum et Pastorem, curam, regimen, et administrationem ipsius Ecclesiae Mexicanen, tibi in spiritualibus et temporalibus plenarie committendo in illo qui dat gratias et largitur praemia confidentes, quod dirigente Domino actus tuos praefata Ecclesia Mexicanen, sub tuo felici regimine, gratia tibi assistente divina, regetur utiliter et prospere dirigetur ac grata in eisdem spiritualibus et temporalibus suscipiet incrementa. Jugum igitur Domini tuis impositum humeris prompta devotione suscipiens curam et administrationem praedictas sic exercere studeas sollicite, fideliter et prudenter, quod Ecclesia ipsa Mexicanen gubernatione provida et fructuosa administratione gaudeat se [tibi] commissam, tuaeque praeter aeternae retributionis praemium, nostram et Apostolicae Sedis benedictionem et gratiam ex inde uberius consequi merearis. Dat. Romae, apud Sanctum Petrum, anno Incarnationis Domini millesimo quingentesimo trigesimo, quarto nonas Septembris, Pontificatus nostri anno septimo. D. de Viterbo—

A. de Sancta Cruse—Jo. della Casa—P. Lambertus—Jo. Molluer—N. de Ariza—Fr. Branconius Spallazelus—A. de Villareal.

Et ego Didacus de Arana, Notarius Apostolicus, auctoritate
Apostolica, Cordubensis Dioecesis, hoc praesens transumptum
mea propria manu ex dictis litteris Apostolicis originalibus
fideliter sumpsi in oppido Madrid, Toletanae Dioces., anno a
Nativitate Domini, millesimo quingentesimo trigesimo tertio,
die vero vigesima nona Maii, Pontificatus ejusdem Domini nostri
Papae anno decimo, indictione sexta, et cum dicto originali
correxi, praesentibus ibidem Rdis. Patribus Fratre Petro de
Nieva, et Fratre Gundisalvo de Medina, Ordinis Minorum, et
Martino de Laris, laico, Caligurritanae Dioecis. ad hoc vocatis
pariter atque rogatis, ideo in hanc publicam formam redegi, et
signo meo consueto signavi, nomineque meo roboravi in fidem
omnium et singulorum, rogatus et requisitus. Didacus De Arana,
notarius apostolicus.

III

ERECTION OF THE CHURCH OF MEXICO

(1534)

Erectio Ecclesiae Mexicanae Quae Eadem Est cum Coeteris
Ejusdem Provinciae

Joannes de Zummarraga,[1] Dei et Apostolicae Sedis munere
Episcopus et servus Ecclesiae Mexicanae, cujus sub Christi Dei
Evangelio aeterno militanti, gratia et pax a Deo Patre, et ejus
consubstantiali Unigenito Filio, pacis auctore, qui sui Divini
Corporis effuso Sanguine donavit nobis omnia delicta delens,
quod adversus nos erat Chirographum decreti, quod erat con-
trarium nobis, et ipsum tulit de medio, affigens illud Cruci
pacificans per Sanguinem Crucis ejus, sive quae in terris sive
quae in coelis sunt. . . . atque, ut rem effectui commendarent,

---

[1] The two *m*'s are surely the mistake of a copyist.

me inutilem et omnino ad tantae rei executionem inhabilem, cum apud illos plurimi non deessent qui mea sententia cumulate valerent suis sanctissimis votis satisfacere, ex angulo mei Franciscani Instituti semi-sepultum extraxerunt et in primum Mexicanensem nominaverunt, et elegerunt Episcopum. Quorum piae Petitioni, et Electioni Sanctissimus D. N. Papa Clemens, hujus nominis septimus, paternali affectu (ut par est) condescendens, Apostolicas Litteras per manus Regias, nobis suppeditandas solerti cura destinavit, quas quidem litteras, in membrana more Romano conscriptas, Apostolico plumbo in filis sericis rubei croceique coloris pendente, sanas, integras, non vitiatas, non cancellatas, nec in aliqua sui parte suspectas, sed omni prorsus vitio et suspicione carentes, is qui regium agebat negotium, coram magno coetu in praecipuo Templi sacro loco, Sancti Spiritus invocato favore, nobis praesentavit. Quas quidem ea qua decuit reverentia et submissione suscepimus et legimus. Series vero earum de verbo ad verbum est quae sequitur:

Sacri apostolatus ministerio
(Clement VII, 1530)

Clemens, Episcopus, Servus Servorum Dei, ad perpetuam rei memoriam.

Sacri Apostolatus ministerio, meritis licet insufficientibus, superna dispositione praesidentes ad universi Orbis Provincias et Loca, ea praesertim quae Omnipotentis Dei misericordia Christianae veritatis lucem nostris potissime temporibus inceperunt agnoscere, frequenti meditatione intendimus ut in illis orthodoxae Fidei cultus augeatur, et Christiana Religio propagetur, ac eorum Incolae et habitatores, venerabilium Praesulum Doctrina et auctoritate suffulti, in eadem Fide semper proficiant, ipsaque loca maxime insignia dignioribus titulis attollantur, et majoribus honoribus decorentur; praesertim cum id Catholicorum Regum, et etiam Caesareae Majestatis pia vota exposcunt, et cognoscimus in Domino salubriter expedire. Sane cum oppidum Mexicanense in Indiis maris tirreni Indici nuncupati, olim auspiciis clarae memoriae Ferdinandi Aragoniae Regis, et Elisabethae, Reginae Castellae et Legionis Regnorum, per dilectum Filium, nobilem Virum Petrum Arias militem Segoviensem, eorum gentium, armorum ad easdem Indias destinatorum, Exercitus Generalem Capitaneum noviter repertis, et e manibus infidelium illas tunc occupantium ereptis, ac ad ditionem et dominium eorum et pro tempore existentium Regum eorundem Regnorum redactis, illisque in temporalibus subjectis, quae [sic] eisdem regibus, dum vixerunt, et deinde Charissimo in Christo Filio nostro Carolo, Romanorum Imperatori semper Augusto, dictorum Regnorum nedum haeredi et Successori, verum etiam in desiderio orthodoxam Fidem ubique exaltandi imitatori, ac sub eorum obedientia et dominio, ratione dictorum Regnorum, ex tunc successive eodem Petro Capitaneo Gubernatore permanentibus consistens: admodum insigne existat, longumque et latissimum et distinctum territorium circum circa habeat; adeoque in eo ultra viginti millia vicinorum vel Incolarum, quorum plures Fideles, tam noviter conversi quam etiam alii forenses et de diversis mundi partibus ad illud habitandum confluentes commorentur et resideant, ac in eo inter alias Ecclesias, Monasteria, pia loca, ex devotione Regum Majestatis et Capitanei praedictorum inibi constructa: una Parochialis Ecclesia sub invocatione Beatae Mariae Virginis, cum structuris et aedificiis convenientibus, ad quam omnes ipsi Fideles pro Missis et Divinis Officiis audiendis ac Ecclesiasticis Sacramentis suscipiendis, tamquam ad eorum Parochialem Ecclesiam recurrunt, etiam consistit; ac idem Carolus Imperator summopere cupiat eamdem Parochialem Ecclesiam in Cathedralem, ipsumque oppidum in Civitatem Mexicanensem erigi, et instrui. Nos habita super his cum venerabilibus Fratribus nostris S. R. E. Cardinalibus matura deliberatione, eodem Carolo Imperatore nobis super hoc humiliter supplicante, ad laudem et gloriam Omnipotentis Dei et ejusdem Beatae Mariae

Coelestis, necnon ipsius Fidei exaltationem, Apostolica auctoritate, tenore praesentium, supplicationibus Caroli Imperatoris
hujusmodi inclinati, de eorumdem fratrum consilio pariter et
assensu, oppidum Mexicanense ac Parochialem Ecclesiam Beatae Mariae, hujusmodi in Cathedralem Mexicanensem, sub invocatione ejusdem Beatae Mariae nuncupandam, pro uno
Episcopo Mexicanensi, qui inibi et in illius Civitate ac Diocesi
verbum Dei praedicet, et infideles ad eandem Fidem convertat;
ac tam illos sic conversos quam alios praedictos Fideles in
eadem Fide expertius instruat, doceat et confirmet, ac Sacramenta Ecclesiastica eis ministret, et ministrari, ac praedictam
erectam Ecclesiam illiusque aedificia ad formam Cathedralis
Ecclesiae redigi, faciat; ac in Civitate et Diocesi praedictis
Collegiatas, et Parochiales, ac alias Ecclesias, Monasteria,
Capellas, Hospitalia, Oratoria, et alia loca pia, ac in illis respectiva in numero, et cum dotibus, ac qualitatibus decentibus
per eum assignandis, specificandis, majores, Principales, Abbatiales, Conventuales, et alias Dignitates, personatus, administrationes, et officia etiam curata, et electiva; necnon Canonicatus, et Praebendas, integras et dimidias portiones, Capellanias,
Vicarias, et alia Beneficia Ecclesiastica, cum cura et sine cura,
ac Capitula, necnon Capitulares Abbatiales, Conventuales, et
alias mensas erigat, et instituat respective, ac alia Temporalia,
Spiritualia, Jurisdictionalia, et Pontificalia officia, omniaque et
singula alia quae alii Episcopi regnorum eorumdem facere et
exercere consueverunt, et quae pro divini cultus augmento, et
Fidei hujusmodi exaltatione, ipsorumque Fidelium animarum
salute expedire cognoverint faciat, et exerceat: ac omnibus et
singulis aliis privilegiis, praerogativis, praeeminentiis et gratiis
quibus alii Episcopi praedicti de jure et consuetudine, ac alias,
utuntur, potiuntur, et gaudent, ac uti, potiri et gaudere libere
et licite valeat: necnon in eadem Ecclesia Mexicanensi Capitulum Canonicorum, et Personarum, Episcopali, et Capitulari
mensis, ac sigillo et insigniis, jurisdictionibus, privilegiis, et

praeeminentiis Episcopalibus et Capitularibus, erigimus et instituimus: ac Incolas et habitatores dictae Civitatis eum nomine
decoramus; necnon eidem erectae Ecclesiae pro illius Civitate
Civitatem erectam, et pro Diocesi Terras, Insulas, Loca et Oppida, quae idem Carolus Imperator, vel ejus Consilium Indiarum nuncupatum, positis limitibus et confiniis necessariis,
statui et assignari jusserit: ac pro Clero et Populo illorum Incolas et habitatores hujusmodi respective, et pro dote, et etiam
Pontificalis Dignitatis, et pro tempore existentis Episcopi illius
decentiori sustentatione decimas, primitias, et alia jura Episcopalia, Spiritualia et temporalia de bonis, rebus, et fructibus, de
quibus Carolus Imperator vel consilium hujusmodi specificave-
rint et ordinaverint. Itaque idem Episcopus Mexicanensis in
Civitate, et Diocesi praedictis, Episcopalem jurisdictionem,
auctoritatem, et potestatem exercere, ac decimas, et primitias,
et jura hujusmodi percipere et levare ad instar Episcoporum
praedictorum libere et licite valeat, applicamus et appropriamus: necnon jus Patronatus, ut infra annum propter loci distantiam, per se vel alium seu alios ad id etiam ante vacationes
deputandos Procuratores praesentandi Personas idoneas, tam hac
prima vice quam quoties illa pro tempore vacaverint ad Ecclesiam videlicet Mexicanensem, nobis et pro tempore existenti
Romano Pontifici, per Nos et illum respective in ejusdem Ecclesiae Episcopum et Pastorem praeficiendum. At vero omnes
et singulas alias Dignitates, Personatus, Administrationes, Officia, Canonicatus et Praebendas, Portiones, Capellanias, Vicarias, Monasteria, Prioratus, et alia Beneficia hujusmodi, eidem
tempore existenti Episcopo Mexicanensi ac ejus Vicario, seu
Officiali per eum instituendas, ad easdem praesentationes Carolo
Imperatori praedicto, ratione Regnorum Castellae et Legionis
hujusmodi, ac pro tempore existenti illorum Regi vel Reginae
de similibus consilio et assensu reservamus, concedimus, et
assignamus; non obstantibus Constitutionibus, Ordinationibus
Apostolicis, ceterisque contrariis quibuscumque. Nulli ergo

omnino hominum liceat hanc paginam nostrae erectionis, institutionis, decorationis, applicationis, appropriationis, reservationis, concessionis, et assignationis infringere vel auso temerario contraire. Si quis autem hoc attentare praesumpserit, indignationem Omnipotentis Dei ac Beatorum Petri et Pauli Apostolorum se noverit incursurum. Datum Romae apud Sanctum Petrum, anno Incarnationis Dominicae millesimo quingentesimo trigesimo. Quarto Nonas Septembris, Pontificatus nostri anno septimo.

Post quarum quidem Litterarum Apostolicarum praesentationem, et receptionem nobis et per Nos, ut praemittitur, factas, fuimus pro parte Serenissimae Dominae Joannae, et Caroli semper Augusti, ejusdem filii Hispaniarum Regum debita cum instantia requisiti, ut ad complementum Litterarum Apostolicarum, et contentorum in eisdem procedendum, in praedicta nostra Cathedrali Ecclesia, ad honorem Gloriosissimae Virginis Mariae Assumptionis dedicata, et in dicta Nova Hispania fabricata, Dignitates, Canonicatus, et Prebendas, ac portiones, aliaqua Beneficia, et Officia Ecclesiastica quotquot, et prout melius expedire videremus, tam in Civitate, quam per totam Dioecesim erigeremus, et institueremus. Nos igitur Frater Joannes de Zummárraga, Episcopus, ac Commissarius Apostolicus praefatus attendentes petitionem, et requisitionem hujusmodi justas fore, et rationi consonas, cupientesque, ut verus, et obediens filius Apostolica jussa, nobis directa, reverenter exsequi, ut tenemur, commissionem praeacceptavimus, et eadem Auctoritate Apostolica, qua fungimur in hac parte, praefata Majestate instante, et petente, in praedicta Cathedrali Mexicanensis Civitatis in praedicta Nova Hispania, ad honorem Dei, et Domini nostri Jesu-Christi, ac Beatissimae Mariae Virginis, Matris ejus, cujus, ac sub cujus titulo per praefatum Sanctissimum Dominum nostrum Cathedralis Ecclesia est erecta, tenore praesentium erigimus, creamus, et instituimus. . . .

XXIV. Volumus insuper, et de consensu, et beneplacito Serenissimae Majestis, et eadem Auctoritate Apostolica statuimus, decernimus, et mandamus quod omnium decimarum, tam Cathedralis, quam aliarum Ecclesiarum dictae Civitatis, et Dioecesis fructus, redditus, et proventus, in quattuor aequales dividantur partes quarum unam Nos, et Successores nostri Episcopi perpetuis futurisque temporibus, pro onere Pontificalis habitus sustentando, et ut decentius, et juxta Pontificalis officii exigentiam statum nostrum sustentare valeamus, absque aliqua diminutione pro nostra speciali mensa habeamus; Decanus vero, et Capitulum, et reliqui Ministri Ecclesiae, quos supra assignavimus, aliam quartam partem, modo praemisso, inter eos dividendam habeant; a quibus partibus, licet ex Commissione Apostolica, et longaevo temporis usu, moribus, et consuetudine approbata, eadem Catholica Majestas tertiam partem (tertias in Hispania vulgariter nuncupatas) habere, et recipere integraliter consuevit, volens erga Nos suae liberalitatis dexteram extendere, prout extendit circa alias partes, et circa qualitates infra expressas, Nos, et Episcopos successores, ac Capitulum praedictos, ut magis debitores, tanto munere refectos, efficeret, et ut pro eadem, et Regis ejusdem Majestatis successoribus preces effundere teneremur, in nostra, et dictae Ecclesiae nostrae, et Capituli in sua quarta decimarum parte, liberos, et exemptos esse voluit; reliquae vero duae quartae partes iterum in novem dividendas partes decernimus, duas quarum eidem Majestati Serenissimae, in signum superioritatis, et juris Patronatus, ac ratione acquisitionis praedictae terrae, futuris perpetuis temporibus, percipiendas, et levandas, applicamus. . . .

XXXVIII. Et quia, quae de novo emergunt, novo indigent auxilio; igitur litterarum supra dictarum virtute nobis, et successoribus nostris plenissimam emendandi, ampliandi, et ea, quae oportuerit, statuendi, et ordinandi in posterum potestatem reservamus, ut possimus id facere de consensu, petitione, et instantia Regiae Majestatis; tam circa questionem, et taxationem dotis perpetuam, vel temporalem, et limitum nostri Episcopatus, et omnium beneficiorum, quam circa retentionem decimarum, vel divisionem earumdem secundum tenorem Bullae Alexandri, per quam ipsis Regibus Hispaniae fuit facta donatio decimarum (licet ad praesens, per eandem Regiam Mejestatem ad alimenta nobis sint, cum his tamen qualitatibus donata) quae omnia, et singula, instantibus, et petentibus praedictis Dominis meis Regina, et Regibus, dicta Apostolica Auctoritate, qua fungimur in hac parte, et melioribus modi[s], via, atque forma, quibus melius possumus, et de jure debemus, erigimus, instituimus, creamus, facimus, disponimus, et ordinamus, cum omnibus, ac singulis ad id necessariis, et opportunis; non obstantibus contrariis quibuscumque, et illis praecipue, quae Sanctissimus Dominus noster praefatus, in suis praeinsertis Litteris Apostolicis voluit, non obstare; et ea omnia, et singula, omnibus, et singulis praesentibus, et futuris cujuscumque status, gradus, ordinis, praeeminentiae, vel conditionis fuerint, intimamus, insinuamus, et ad omnium notitiam deducimus, et deduci volumus, per praesentes mandamus praedicta auctoritate, et Sanctae Obedientiae virtute omnibus, et singulis supra dictis, ut ea omnia, et singula, quemadmodum a nobis instituta sunt, observent, et observari faciant. In quorum omnium, et singulorum fidem, et testimonium praemissorum, praesentes litteras, sive praesens publicum instrumentum exinde fieri, et per Notarium publicum infrascriptum scribi, et publicari, nostrique sigilli jussimus, et fecimus appensione communiri. Datum Toleti, sub anno a Nativitate Domini millesimo quingentesimo trigesimo quarto.

IV

ERECTION OF THE ARCHBISHOPRIC OF MEXICO

Erección del Arzobispado de México

Capítulo de Una Consulta del Consejo de Indias a Carlos V: Proponen Para Favorecer las Apelaciones que se Hagan Arzobispados en México y en Santo Domingo. Madrid 26-1-1536

Asi missmo, despues que están pobladas las yslas y provincias de Tierra Firme, que como v. magt. terná memoria, ay en ellas diez y seiss prelados proveydos a presentacion de v. magt., de más de otras provincias que, ahunque tienen governadores, no están nombrados prelados, como son la Nueva Galizia y Veragua y Paria y la Nueva Toledo y el Río de la Plata. [Al margen: que se consulte al Cab. de Sevilla (tachedo: "de Toledo") para que envíe su parecer.]

Hasta agora han venido las appellaciones destas al arçobispo de Sevilla como Metropolitano, porque no le havía, ni ay nombrado en todas las dichas yslas y Tierra Firme: de lo qual se siguen grandes ynconvenientes, porque están algunas destas diócesis a doss mill leguas, y la que menos más de mill; y la governación spiritual de aquellas diócesis, teniendo el metropolitano tan lexos, no puede ser qual deve ni la que conviene.

Y por esto, platicado en el consejo, ha parecido que es cosa justa y necsesaria, y que pues ay tantas diócesis, en aquellas partes y tan rremotas destas, y ahún ellas entre sí tan distantes, se procure que nuestro muy santo padre a supplicación de v. magt. haga por agora en todas las Indias dos metrópolis; la una sea en la cibdad de México de la Nueva España, y la otra en la cibdad de Sancto Domingo de la Ysla Spañola, criando los obispos dellas por arçobispos, y que éstos tengan por suffraganios los obispados que por v. magt. fueren declarados.

Y la Bulla desto ha de venir con derogación de cualquier otra concesión que se aya hecho a los arçobispos de Sevilla, pues cessa la cabsa que pudo aver para ello. Y la necesidad de lo que agora se pide es tan evidente, y desta manera se excusarán todos los daños e ynconvenientes que se han seguido y se esperan cada día seguir de venir las appellaciones al arçobispo de Sevilla. Y pues esto toca tan bien al descargo de su rreal conciencia, supplicamos a v. magt. lo mande proveer con brevedad. [Al margen: "Que scriva al Conde."]

Y porque demás desto se han scripto al embaxador de v. magt. que reside en Rroma, otras muchas cosas tocantes al servicio de Dios y bien de aquellas partes, supplicamos a v. mgt. le mande que con cuydado y brevedad entienda en los despachos dellas, y que escriva a este consejo lo que en ellos hiziere, embiando nos las bullas o breves que sobrello expidiere. Nuestro Señor la vida e ymperial estado de v. magt. acresciente con mas rreynos y señorios. De Madrid, a XXVI de Henero de 1536.

Firman: el cardenal García de Loaisa, obispo de Siguenza, el Doctor Diego Beltrán, el doctor Juan Bernal Díaz de Lugo, y el Licenciado Gutierre Velázquez de Lugo. [Afuera: "para responder."]

CONSULTATION OF THE COUNCIL OF THE INDIES
(1544)

Capítulo de una Consulta del Consejo de Indias a Carlos V: Un Capítulo de la Petitión de los Procuradores de la Ciudad de México Propone que se Haga Arzobispado en México para Favorecer las Apelaciones. Valladolid 8-IX-1544

Entre otras cosas que la cibdad de Mexico ha supplicado a v. magt. por una petitión de capítulos que en el consejo se ha visto, hay uno que porque aquella cibdad cada día se puebla y acrecienta y es y se espera que siempre será cabeça de toda la Nueva España, por ser cibdad tan ynsigne y estar en buena comarca; y que en aquella provincia hay ya muchos obispos, y segund la grandeza de la tierra, de necesidad se han de eregir más iglesias cathedrales; y porque se acrecen muchos gastos a las personas de aquella tierra, que tienen negocios pendientes ante los prelados della, a seguir las apelaciones que interponen dellos y de sus officiales a la cibdad de Sevilla, donde rreside la abdiencia arçobispal, donde es agora su metrópoli; y porque también es cosa grave que si alguna persona es agraviada de algun juez eclesiástico en la dicha Nueva España, en presión o descomunyón o en otro género de agravio, haya de navegar cuatro mill leguas de ida y venyda a buscar el rremedio, padeciendo entre tanto los agraviados. Y han suplicado a v. mt. sea servido de mandar escrevir suplicando a su Sad. que erija la iglesia cathedral de México en iglesia arçobispal y metrópoli de las otras iglesias que agora hay y adelante hoviere en la dicha Nueva España.

Hase platicado en el consejo con el rrmo. cardenal de Sevilla, presidente dél, y que como hemos dicho es agora metropolitano de aquellas partes, y con el obispo de Cuenca, presidente de la chancillería desta villa. Y al rrmo. cardenal y a los del consejo a parecido cosa justa que ansy se haga ansy por las rrazones que la cibdad de México declara en su petición, como porque no es justo que falta en aquella iglesia nueva de aquel nuevo mundo la horden que la iglesia unybersal tiene dada en toda la cristianidad para la buena governacion espiritual della; aunque al obispo de Cuenca le parece que por agora se podría deferir este provisión, v. mt. mande en ello lo que fuere servido. Firman: el Cardenal García de Loaiza, arzobispo de Sevilla, el Doctor Juan Bernal Díaz de Lugo, el Licenciado Gutierre Velázquez de Lugo; y el Licenciado Gregorio López.

CONSISTORIAL REPORT
(Cardinal Juan Álvarez de Toledo, 1546)

Relacion Consistorial del Cardenal Juan Álvarez de Toledo sobre la Erección de las Metropolitanas de México, Lima y Santo Domingo. Roma, S. Pedro, 12-II-1546. [Al margen: a.m.;

De Mexico, Sti. Dominici in Insula Hispaniola, Civitatis Regum ecclesiae cathedrales. xii Februarii, 1546.]

Bme. Pater. Alias B. V. ad laudem et gloriam omnipotentis Dei et reipublicae christianae propagationem et augmentum, gloriosae memoriae Ferdinando et Elisabetha, et deinde post, Carolo V Romanorum imperatore semper Augusto suo nepote, Hispaniarum regibus invictissimis, id supplicantibus, quam plurimas cathedrales ecclesias in suis regnis, insulis, terris et Dominiis in magno mari occidentalis oceani positis erexit, instituit et de novo creavit; illasque una cum suis episcopis et dioecesibus, quoniam tunc temporis ita expedire magis videbatur, Metropolitanae Hispalensi ecclesiae et illius Archiepiscopo pro tempore existenti subjecit atque submisit, ut illi suffraganeae essent, et ecclesiam ipsam tanquam matrem recognoscerent et sequerentur.

Verum quoniam procedente tempore experientia ipsa cognitum est, incolas insularum et locorum praedictorum, propter maximam terrarum et maris interpositam distantiam, et leucarum infinita millia, pro eorum apellationibus prosequendis et aliis suis negotiis peragendis, absque magno eorum discrimine et vitae periculo, ac temporis diuturnitate, ad dictam civitatem Hispalensem se transferre, et ipsum Archiepiscopum adire minime posse, quam si S. V. aliquas cathedrales ecclesias in illis partibus in metropolitanas, et ipsarum episcopos in Archiepiscopos erigat et creet, quas et quos, tamquam Metropoles et Archiepiscopos, caeterae aliae ecclesiae et earum episcopi cum suis dioecesibus recognoscant et sequantur.

Idcirco caesarea et catholica Mtas. de cujus iure patronatus regna, terrae, insulae et dominia praedicta existunt, suorum subditorum in hac parte commoditatibus consulere cupiens, accedente ad hoc expresso consensu devotae creaturae S. V., Garsiae tituli sanctae Susannae prbi. Carlis. de Loaysa nuncupati, ad praesens Archiepiscopi Hispalensis, quem pro se et successoribus suis per procuratorem legitimum praestitit, S. V. humiliter supplicari fecit ut tres numero cathedrales metropolitanas, et earum episcopos in Archiepiscopos, cum Archiepiscopali dignitate, iurisdictione et superioritate, ac omnimoda Pallii et crucis delatione, ac aliis metropolitanis insigniis, absque aliis de eorum personis et ecclesiis praedictis de novo faciendis provisionibus seu praefectionibus, erigere et instituere dignaretur.

Videlicet, cathedralem ecclesiam de Mexico in Nova Hispania, cathedralem sancti Dominici in insula Hispaniola et cathedralem civitatis Regum in Provincia del Peru, Joannem de Zumárraga de Mexico, Alfonsum de Fuentemaior Sancti Dominici, et Geronymum de Loaysa civitatis Regum episcopos.

Et cum declaratione, quatenus futura Metropolitana de Mexico suffraganeas ecclesias habeat, videlicet, de Antequera, et de Mechoacan ac de T[l]axcala, ac de Guatimala, et Civitatis Regalis de los Llanos de Chiapa, et instituendas inde Mexico limitibus et terminis cathedrales ecclesias, si, quomodo, quando, Mti. caesarae, et suis successoribus, expedire magis videbitur.

Quas quidem ecclesias sic ut praemittitur in metropolitanas erigendas, et caeteras alias pro suis suffraganeis dandas, et assignandas, a Provincia metropolitanae ecclesiae Hispalensis, cui metropolitico iure subsunt, perpetuo separare, et dismembrare, ac earundem sic dismembratarum ecclesiarum Praesules, necnon cujuslibet illarum civitatum et dioecesium clerum et Populum, ab ejusdem devotae creaturae S. V. Garsiae carlis., et pro tempore existentis Archiepiscopi Hispalensis, metropoliticis dominio, superioritate, visitatore (sic!) et iurisdictione prorsus eximere et totaliter liberare S. V. dignetur. In quo rem in primis Deo gratam, sua clementia dignam et christianae Reipublicae valde necessariam procul dubio faciet, etc. Cum clausulis opportunis et consuetis et in similibus apponi solitis. (a.m.:) Die Veneris xii Februarii, Romae, apud S. Petrum, 1546. Referente Carle Burgen.

CONCORDAT OF 1753*

Benedictus Papa XIV, ad perpetuam rei memoriam

Cum alias, nempe die undecima Januarii proximi elapsi ad proponenda, tractanda, debitoque fine concludenda nonnulla, praesertim quoad disciplinam Ecclesiasticam, Regium Patronatum, atque alia momenta, quae in Tractatu inter Apostolicam hanc Sedem, et cla. mem. Philippum V dum vixit, Hispaniarum Regem Catholicum mense inito, concordato, atqui utrinque comprobato, & confirmato, relicta fuerant per dilectum Filium nostrum Silvium Sanctae Romanae Ecclesiae Presbyterum Cardinalem Valenti nuncupatum nostrum, & dictae Sedis Plenipotentiarium, & dilectum itidem Filium Magistrum Emmanuelem Venturam Figueroa Capellanum nostrum, & Causarum Palatii Apostolici Auditorem charissimi in Christo Filii nostri Ferdinandi earumdem Hispaniarum Regis Catholici Plenipotentiarium conventus, ac subscriptus fuerit quidam Tractatus octo Articulis comprehensus, cujus tenor est qui sequitur:

Numero 1º. Haviendo la Santidad de Nuestro Beatísimo Padre Benedicto Papa 14º, felizmente reinante tenido siempre un vivo deseo de mantener toda la mas sincera, y cordial correspondencia entre la Sante Sede, y las Naziones, Príncipes, y Reyes Cathólicos; no há dexado de dar continuamente señales segurisimas, y bien particulares de esta su viva voluntad acia la esclarecida, devota, y piadosa Nazion Española, acia los Monarcas de las Españas, Reyes Cathólicos por titulo, y firme Relijion, y siempre adictos a la Silla apostólica, y ál Vicario de Jesuchristo en la tierra.

2º. Haviendo, por esto, observado, que en el ultimo Concordato, estipulado el dia 18 de Octubre de 1737 entre la Santa recordacion de Clemente Papa 12º, y la gloriosa memoria del Rey Phelipe 5º, se avia convenido, que el Papa, y el Rey deputasen personas, que reconociesen amigablemente las razones de

---

* Mercati, *Raccolta de concordati*, pp. 422-37. For the translation see pp. 232-42.

una y otra parte sobre la antigua controversia del pretendido
regio Patronato universal, que quedó indecisa; en los primeros
instantes de su pontificado no se olvidó su Santidad de hacer
sus instancias con los dos, aora difunctos, Cardenales Belluga,
y Acquiviva, á fin de que obtubiesen de la Corte de España la
deputacion de personas con quienes se pudiese tratar el puncto
indeciso; y subcesivamente, para facilitar su examen, no dejó
Su Santidad de unir en uno su escripto, que consignó a los
dichos dos Cardenales, todo aquello, que creyó conducente a las
intenciones, y derechos de la Santa Sede.

3º. Pero aviendo reconocido en acto practico, que no era
este el camino de llegar ál deseado fin, y que se distaua tanto
de cortar las disputas por medio de escriptos y respuestas, que
antes bien se multiplicavan, excitandose controversias, que se
crehian aquietadas; de tal modo, que se abria podido temer
una infeliz rotura, incommoda, y fatal a una y otra parte, y
aviendo tenido pruevas seguras de la piadosa propension del
animo del Rey Fernando 6º, felizmente reynante, de un equita-
tivo, y justo temperamento sobre las diferencias promovidas,
y que se iban siempre multiplicando, á lo que se hallaua tambien propenso con pleno corazon el deseo de Su Beatitud; há
Su Santidad creydo, que no se devia pasar en olvido una tan
faborable coyuntura para establecer una concordia, que se
exprimirá en los siguentes Capitulos, que despues se reduciaran
á forma auctentica, y firmaran de los Procuradores, y Pleni-
potenciarios de ambas partes en la manera, que se acostumbra
practicar en semejantes convenciones.

4º. Haviendo la Magestad del Rey Fernando 6º expuesto á
la Santidad de nuestro Beatísimo Padre la necesidad, que ay en
las Españas de reformar en algunos punctos la Disciplina del
clero secular, y regular; su Santidad promete, que individuali-
zados los Capitulos sobre que se deverá tomar la providencia
necesaria; no se dejará de dar, segun lo establecido en los
sagrados canones, en la[s] Constituciones apostólicas, y en el

Santo Concilio de Trento. Y quando esto subcediese (como sumamente desea Su Beatitud) en el tiempo de Su Pontificado promete y se obliga no obstante la multitud de otros negocios, que le oprimen, y sin embargo tambien de su edad muy abanzada, á interponer para el feliz despacho, toda aquella fatiga personal que *in minoribus* tantos años ha interpusó en tiempo de sus predecessores en las resoluciones de las materias establecidas en la Bula *Apostolici ministerii*, en la fundacion de la Universidad de Zervera, en él establecimiento de la insigne Colegiata de San Ildefonso, y en otros relevantes negocios pertenecientes a los Reynos de las Españas.

5°. No aviendose controvertido á los Reyes Catholicos de las Españas la pertenencia del Patronato regio, ó sea derecho de nominar a los Arzobispados, Obispados, Monasterios, y Beneficios Consistoriales, escriptos, y tasados en los libros de Cámara, que vacan en los Reynos de las Españas; siendo su derecho apoyado a Bulas, y Privilegios apostólicos y a otros titulos alegados; y no aviendose controvertido tampoco á los Reyes Catholicos las nominas á los Arzobispados, Obispados, y Beneficios, que vacan en los Reynos de Granada y de las Indias, como ni á algunos otros Beneficios, se declara, que la Real Corona deve quedar en su pacífica posesion de nombrar en el caso de las vacantes, como há echo hastaquí; y se conviene que los nominados para los Arzobispados, Obispados, Monasterios, y Beneficios Consistoriales devan tambien en lo futuro continúar la espedicion de sus respectivas Bulas en Roma del mismo modo a forma hasta aora practicado, sin innovación alguna.

6°. Haviendo, bien si, controvertidose grauemente sobre la nomina de los Beneficios residenciales y symples de los Reynos de las Españas, (exceptúados, como se há dicho, los de los Reynos de Granada, y de las Indias) y aviendo los Reyes Catholicos pretendido la pertenencia y derecho de nombrar en vigor del Patronato universal; y no aviendo la Santa Sede dejado de exponer las Razones, que crehia militavan por la livertad de los mismos Beneficios, y su colazion en los meses apostólicos, y casos de las reservas, como tambien respectivamente por la libertad de los Ordinarios en sus meses; despues de un largo contraste, se ha finalmente abrazado de comun consentimiento el siguente temperamento.

7⁰. La Santidad de nuestro Beatisimo Padre Benedicto papa 14⁰, reserva a su privativa libre colazion, á sus subcesores, y á la silla apostólica perpetuamente cinquenta y dos Beneficios (cuyos títulos se espresaran aora mismo) para que no menos su Santidad, que sus subcesores tengan el arbitrio de poder proveher, y premiar aquellos Eclesiásticos Españoles, que por providad, e ilibatez de costumbres, por insigne literatura, ó por servicios echos a la Santa Sede, se agan beneméritos. Y la Colación de estos 52 Beneficios deverá ser siempre privativa de la Santa Sede en qualquiera mes, y en qualquiera modo que vaquen, aúnque sea por resulta regio; aúnque se encontrase tocar alguno de ellos al real Patronato de la Corona; y aúnque fuesen situados en Diocesis, donde algun Cardenal tubiese qual se sea amplio indulto de conferir; no debiendose en manera alguna atender este en perjuicio de la Santa Sede. Y las Bulas de estos 52 Beneficios deverán expedirse siempre en Roma, pagando a la Dataria, y Cancillería apostólica los devidos emolumentos, segun los presentes estados; y todo esto sin imposicion alguna de pensiones, y sin exaccion de cedulas Bancarias, como tambien se dirá abajo.

8⁰. Los nombres, pues, de los 52 Beneficios son los siguentes:

En las Cathedrales Avila — Arcedianato de Arevalo

Orense — Arcedianato de Bubal

Barcelona — Priorato antes regular, aora secular de la Colegiata de Santa Ana

Cathedral Burgos — Mestrescolía

Burgos — Arcedianato de Valenzuela

Cathedral Calahorra — Arcedianato de Naxera
Calahorra — Thesorería
Cathedral Cartaxena — Mestrescolía
Cartajena — Symple de Alvacete
Cathedral Zaragoza — Arceprestazgo de Daroca
Zaragoza — Arceprestazgo de Belchite
Cathedral Ziudad Rodrigo — Mestrescolía
Cathedral Santiago — Arcedianato de la Reyna
Santiago — Arcedianato de Sta. Thesia
Santiago — Thesorería
Cathedral Cuenca — Arcedianato de Alarcon
Cuenca — Thesorería
Cathedral Cordova — Arcedianato de Castro
Cordova — Symple de Villalcazar
Cordova — Prestamo de Castro y Espejo
Cathedral Tolosa — Hospitalería
Tolosa — Hospitalería
Cathedral Gerona — Arcedianato de Ampueda
Cathedral Jaen — Arcedianato de Baeza
Jaen — Symple de Arzonilla
Cathedral Lérida — Preceptoría
Cathedral Sevilla — Arcedianato de Jerez
Sevilla — Symple de la Puebla de Guzman
Sevilla — Prestamo en la Yglesia de Sta. Cruz de Ezixa
Cathedral Mallorca — Preceptoría
Mallorca — Prepositura Sti. Antonij de San Antonio Vienn.
Nullius Provintiae Toletanae — Symple de Sta. Maria de Al-
    calá-Real
Orihuela — Symple de Sta. Maria de Elche
Cathedrales — Huesca — Cantoría
              Oviedo — Cantoría
              Osma — Mestrescolía
              Osma — Abadía de San Bartolome
Pamplona — Hospitalería, antes regular, aora Encomienda

Pamplona — Preceptoría general del lugar de Olite
Cathedrales — Plasencia — Arcedianato de Medellin
            Plasencia — Arcedianato de Truxillo
            Salamanca — Arcedianato de Monleon
            Siguenza — Thesorería
            Siguenza — Abadía de Sta. Coloma
            Tarragona — Priorato
            Tarazona — Thesorería
            Toledo — Thesorería
Toledo — Symple de Vallejas
Tuy — Symple de San Martin del Rosal
Cathedrales — Valencia — Sacristía major
            Urgell — Arcedianato de Andora
            Zamora — Arcedianato de Toro

9°. Para bien regular despues las colaciones, presentaciones, nominas, e instituciones de los Beneficios que en lo venidero vacarán en dichos Reynos de las Españas; se conviene en primer lugar que los Arzobispos, Obispos, y Coladores inferiores devan en lo futuro continúar proveyendo aquellos Beneficios, que provehían en lo pasado siempre que vaquen en sus meses ordinarios de Marzo, Junio, Setiembre y Diciembre, aunque se halle vacante la Sylla apostólica; y se conviene tambien, que los Patronos eclesiásticos en los mismos meses y en el propio modo prosigan presentando los Beneficios de su Patronato; exclusas las Alternativas de meses que para conferir se davan antecedentemente lasque en lo futuro no se concederan jamas.

10°. Segundo. Qué las Prevendas de Oficio, que actualmente se provehén por oposicion y concurso abierto, se confieran y expidan en lo futuro del propio modo y con las mismas circumstancias que se hán practicado hastaquí, sin innovar cosa alguna, como ni tampoco en orden al Patronato laical de particulares.

11°. Tercero. Qué no solo las Parroquias, y Beneficios curados se confiéran en lo futuro, como se han conferido en lo pasado, por oposicion, y concurso quando vaquen en los meses ordinarios, sino tambien quando vaquen en los meses, y casos de las reservas, bien que la presentacion pertenezca ál Rey; deviendose en todos estos casos presentar ál Ordinario aquel á quien el Patrono creerá mas digno entre los tres que los Examinadores synodales ayán tenido por idoneos, y aprovado *ad curam animarum.*

12°. Quarto. Qué aviendose yá dicho arriva, que deua quedar a los Patronos eclesiásticos ileso el derecho de presentar los Beneficios de Sus Patronatos en los quatro meses Ordinarios, y haviendose acostumbrado hasta aore que algunos Cavildos, Rectores, Abades, y Compañías erigidas con auctoridad eclesiastica, recurran a la Santa Sede para sus elecciones sean confirmadas con Bula apostólica, no se entienda innovada cosa alguna en este caso. Antes bien quede todo en el pie, enque há estado hastaquí.

13°. Quinto. Salva siempre la reserva de los 52 Beneficios echa á la libre Colacion de la Santa Sede, y salvas siempre las demas declaraciones poco antes indicadas; para concluir amigablemente todo lo restante de la gran controversia sobre el Patronato Universal; Su Santidad acuerda á la Magestad del Rey Catholico, y á los Reyes sus subcesores perpetuamente el derecho Universal de nombrar, y presentar indistintamente en todas las Yglesias Metropolitanas, Cathedrales, Colegiatas, y Diocesis de los Reynos de las Españas, que actualmente posée, á las Dignidades *majores post Pontificalem* y á las demas Dignidades en las Cathedrales, y á las Dignidades principales y demas en las Colegiatas, á los canonicatos, porciones, prevendas, Abadías, Prioratos, Encomiendas, Parroquias, Personatos, Patrimoniales, Oficios, y Beneficios Eclesiásticos seculares, y regulares *con cura, et sine cura* de qualquiera naturaleza, que sean existentes al presente, y que en adelante se fundaren (sin que los fundadores reservasen para si, y sus subcesores el derecho de presentar) en los Dominios, y Reynos de las Españas,

que actualmente posée el Rey Catholico, con toda la generalidad
con que se hallan comprehendidos en los meses apostólicos, y
casos de las reservas generales, y especiales; y del mismo modo
tambien en el caso de vacar los Beneficios en los meses ordinarios, quando se hallan vacantes las syllas Arzobispales, y
Obispales, ó por qual se sea otro título.

14º. Y á mayor abundamiento Su Santidad subrroga al Rey
Catholico, y á los Reyes sus subcesores, el derecho, que por
razon de las reservas tenia la Santa Sede de conferir los Beneficios en los Reynos de las Españas, ó por si, ó por medio de la
Dataria, Cancilleria apostólica, Nuncios de España, é Indulta-
rios; dando á sus Magestades el derecho universal de presentar
a dichos Beneficios en los Reynos de las Españas, que actualmente posée, con facultad de usar de este derecho del mismo
modo, que usa, y exerce lo restante del Patronato perteneciente
á su real Corona; no deviendose en lo futuro conceder á nungun
Nuncio apostólico de España, ni á nungun Cardenal, u Obispo
en España, indulto de conferir Beneficios en los meses apostólicos, sin expresa permision de Su Magestad, ó de sus
subcesores.

15º. Sexto. Para que en lo venidero proceda todo con el
deuido systema, y se mantenga ilesa la auctoridad de los Obispos en quanto sea posible; se conviene, que todos los presentados, y nominados por su Magestad Catholica, y sus subcesores
a los Beneficios arriba dichos, aúnque vaquen por resulta de
provistas regias, devan recivir indistinctamente las Instituciones,
y Colaciones canonicas de sus respectivos Ordinarios, sin ex-
pedizion alguna de Bulas apostólicas, exceptuada la confirma-
cion de las elecciones yá arriva indicadas; y exceptúados los
casos enque los presentados, ó nominados, ó por defecto de
edad, ó por que sea otro impedimento canonico tubieren necesidad de alguna dispensa, ó gracia apostólica, ó de qual se fuere
otra cosa superior á la auctoridad ordinaria de los Obispos;
deviendose en todos estos, y semijantes casos recurrir siempre

en lo futuro á la Santa Sede como se ha echo en lo pasado para obtener la gracia, ó dispensacion, pagando á la Dataria y Cancilleria apostólica los emolumentos acostumbrados, sin que esta imponga pensiones, ó exija cedulas Bancarias, como tambien se dirá luego.

16°. Septimo. Qué para el mismo fin de mantener ilesa la auctoridad ordinaria de los Obispos se conviene, y se declara, que por la cesion, y subrrogazion de los referidos derechos de nomina, presentacion, y patronato no se entienda conferida al Rey Catholico, ni á sus subcesores alguna Jurisdiccion eclesiástica sobre las Yglesias comprehendidas en los expresados derechos, ni tampoco sobre las personas, que presentará, ó nombrará para las dichas Yglesias, y Beneficios, deviendo no menos estas, que las otras (en quienes la Santa Sede conferirá los 52 Beneficios reservados) quedar sujetas á sus respectivos Ordinarios, sin que pueden pretender esempcion de su Jurisdiccion, salve siempre la suprema auctoridad, que el Pontifice romano, como Pastor de la Yglesia Universal tiene sobre todas las Yglesias, y personas eclesiásticas, y salvas siempre las reales prerrogativas que competen a la Corona en consequencia de la regia proteccion, especialmente sobre las Yglesias del Patronato regio.

17°. Octavo. Haviendo su Magestad Catholica considerado que por razon del Patronato y derechos cedidos á si, y á sus subcesores, que dando la Dataria, y Cancilleria apostólica sin las utilidades de las expediciones y annatas; seria graue el incomodo del herario pontificio; se obliga á hacer consignar en Roma a título de recompensa por una sola vez, a disposicion de Su Santidad un capital de trecientos y diez mil Escudos romanos, que á razon de un tres por ciento rendirá anualmente nueve mil y trecientos Escudos de la misma moneda, suma en que se há regulado el producto de todos los derechos arriva dichos.

18°. Haviendo nacido en los tiempos pasados alguna controversia sobre algunas provistas echas por la Santa Sede en las Cathedrales de Palensia y Mondoñedo; la Magestad del Rey Catholico conviene en que los provistos entren en posesion despues de la ratificacion del presente Concordato. Y aviendose tambien, con ocasion de la pretension del regio Patronato universal, subscitado de nuevo la antigua controversia de la imposicion de pensiones, y exaccion de cedulas Bancarias, así como la Santidad de nuestro Beatísimo Padre para cortar de una vez las quejas, que de tiempo en tiempo se subscitavan, se avia manifestado prompto, y resuelto á abolir el uso de otras pensiones, y Cedulas Bancarias con el unico disgusto de que faltando el producto de ellas, necesitaria contra su deseo sujetar el herario pontificio a nuevos devitos, respecto de que el provento de estas cedulas Bancarias se empleava por la mayor parte en los salarios, y en los honorarios de aquellos Ministros, que sirven á la Santa Sede en los negocios pertenecientes al govierno universal de la Yglesia;

19°. Del mismo modo la Magestad del Rey Catholico no menos por su heredada devocion acia la Santa Sede, que por el afecto particular con que mira la Sagrada persona de su Beatitud, se há dispuesto á dar por una sola vez, un socorro, que sino en el todo, á lo menos alibie en parte el herario Pontificio de los gastos, que está necesitado á hacer para la manutencion de los expresados Ministros, y de consequencia se obliga á hacer consignar en Roma seiscientos mil Escudos romanos, que ál tres por ciento producen anúalmente diez y ocho mil Escudos de la misma moneda; con que queda abolido para el futuro el uso de imponer pensiones y exigir Cedulas Bancarias, no solo en el caso de la Colacion de los 52 Beneficios reservados á la Santa Sede, en él de las confirmaciones arriva indicadas, en él de recurso á la misma Santa Sede para obtener alguna dispensazion concerniente a la Colacion de los Beneficios; sino tambien en qual se sea otro caso; de tal manera que en lo venidero queda extinguido para siempre el uso de imponer pensiones y exigir Cedulas Bancarias; pero sin prejuicio de las yá impuestas hasta el tiempo presente.

20°. Otro Capitulo de controversia avia tambien, no ía en orden al derecho de la Camara apostólica, y Nunciatura de España sobre los Espolios y frutos de las Yglesias Obispales vacantes en los Reynos de las Españas; sino sobre el uso, exercicio y dependencias de dicho derecho; de tal modo que se hacia necesario venir sobre esto a alguna concordia, ó composicion. Para evitar tambien estas continuas diferencias, la Santidad de Nuestro Beatísimo Padre derogando, anulando, y dejando sin efecto todas las Constituciones apostólicas que ayan precedido, y todas concordias, y convenciones que se han echo hasta aora entre la Reverenda Camara apostólica, Obispos, Cavildos, y Diocesis, y qual se sea otra cosa que aga en contrario, aplica desde el dia de la ratificacion de este Concordato, todos los Espolios, y frutos de la Yglesias vacantes exactos, e inexactos a aquellos usos pios que prescriven los sagrados canones; prometiendo que en lo venidero no acordara por nungun motivo á qual se sea persona eclesiástica, aunque sea digna de especial, ó especialisima mencion facultad de testar de los frutos y Espolios de sus Yglesias obispales, bienque fuese para pios usos, salvas las yá acordadas, que deveran tener su efecto; concediendo para lo futuro á la Magestad del Rey Catholico, y á sus subcesores la eleccion de economos y Colectores (con tal que sean personas eclesiásticas) con todas las facultades oportunas, y necesarias para que dichos efectos, vaxo de la real proteccion sean por estos fielmente administrados, y fielmente empleados en los usos expresados.

21°. Y Su Magestad en obsequio á la Santa Sede, se obliga á hacer despositar en Roma por una sola vez, á disposicion de Su Santidad un Capital de doscientos, treynta tres mil trecientos treynta y tres Escudos romanos, que impuesto ál tres por ciento rinde anualmente siete mil Escudos de la propia moneda. Y

demas de esto, Su Magestad acuerda que se asignen en Madrid
á disposicion de Su Santidad sobre el producto de la cruzada
cinco mil Escudos anúales para la manutencion y subsistencia
de los Nuncios apostólicos. Y todo esto en consideracion y
recompensa del producto que pierde el herario pontificio en la
referida cesion de Espolios, y frutos de las Yglesias vacantes,
y en la obligacion que hace de no conceder en lo futuro facultades de testar.

22°. Su Santidad en fee de Sumo Pontífice, y Su Magestad
en palabra de Rey Catholico prometen mutuamente por si
mismos, y en nombre de sus subcesores la firmeza inalterable,
y subsistencia perpetua de todos y cada uno de los articulos
precedentes, queriendo y declarando que ni la Santa Sede, ni
los Reyes Catholicos hán de pretender respectivamente mas de
lo que viene expreso, y comprehendido en los dichos capitulos;
y que se aya de tener por irrito, y de ningun valor ni efecto
quanto contra todos, ó alguno de ellos se aga en qual se sea
tiempo.

23°. Para la validazion y observancia de quanto se ha convenido; sera firmado este concordato en la forma acostumbrada,
y tendrá todo su efecto, y entero cumplimiento luego que se
consignarán los capitales de recompensa, que se han expresado,
y echa, que sea la ratificacion.

En fee de lo qual nos los infrascriptos en virtud de las
facultades respectivas de Su Santidad y de S. M. C. hemos
firmado el presente concordato, y sellado con nuestro propio
sello en el Palacio apostólico del Quirinal en el dia 11 de
henero del 1753.

El Cardenal Valenti

Manuel Ventura Figueroa.

Subinde vero dictus Ferdinandus Rex Tractatum hujusmodi
approbaverit, confirmaverit, ratum habuerit, & alias prout in
Scriptura desuper confecta, cujus tenorem praesentibus pro
expresso, & inserto haveri volumus, uberius continetur: Hinc

est quod Nos Tractatum praeinsertum ratum itidem habere, stabilique, ac perpetua firmitate subsistere, & inviolabiliter servari cupientes, motu proprio, ac ex certa scientia, & matura deliberatione nostra, deque Apostolicae potestatis plenitudine Tractatum praeinsertum a praedicto Ferdinando Rege approbatum, confirmatum, & ratum habitum, ut praedicitur, tenore praesentium perpetuo ratificamus, ac ratum habemus, ac promissa per dictum Silvium Cardinalem nostrum, & praedictae Sedis Plenipotentiarium in Tractatu praedicto sincere, & inviolabiliter ex nostra, ejusdemque Sedis parte adimpletum, & servatum iri in verbo Romani Pontificis promittimus. Decernentes praesentes Litteras nullo unquam tempore de subreptionis, obreptionis, & nullitatis vitio, vel intentionis nostrae, aut alio quocumque quantumvis magno, & excogitato defectu notari, & impugnari posse, sed semper, & perpetuo firmas validas, & efficaces existere, & fore, suosque plenarios, & integros effectus sortiri, & obtinere, ac inviolabiliter servari debere. Non obstantibus quibusvis Apostolicis [Litteris], ac in Universalibus, Provincialibus, & Synodalibus Conciliis editis generalibus, vel Specialibus Constitutionibus, & ordinationibus, ac quatenus opus sit nostra, & Cancellariae Apostolicae regula de jure quaesito non tollendo, ceterisque contrariis quibuscumque. Quibus omnibus, & singulis illorum tenores praesentibus pro expressis, & ad verbum insertis habentes illis alias in suo robore permansuris ad praemissorum effectum hac vice duntaxat specialiter, & expresse derogamus, caeterisque contrariis quibuscumque. Datum Romae apud Sanctum Mariam Majorem sub annulo Piscatoris die vigesima Februarii anno millesimo septingentesimo quinquagesimo tertio. Pontificatus nostri anno decimo tertio. D. Cardinalis Passioneus. Loco (   ) Annuli Piscatoris.

PRAGMÁTICA SANCIÓN*

(Charles III, 1767)

PRAGMATICA

SANCION

De Su MAGESTAD

EN FUERZA DE LEY

PARA EL ESTRAÑAMIENTO DE ESTOS

Reynos á los Regulares de la Compañia, ocupacion de sus
Temporalidades, y prohibición de surestablecimiento en tiempo
alguno, con las demás precauciones que expresa

Año 1767

EN MADRID

En la Imprenta Real de la Gazeta

Para despachos de oficio quarto mes

SELLO QUARTO   AÑO DE

MIL SETECIENTOS Y SESENTA I SIETE

DON CARLOS POR LA GRACIA DE DIOS Rey de Castilla,
de Leon, de Aragon, de las dos Sicilias, de Jerusalén, de Na-
varra, de Granada, de Toledo, de Valencia, de Corcega, de
Murcia, de Jaén, de los Algarbes, de Algecira, de Gibraltar,
de las Islas de Canarias, de las Indias Orientales, y Occidentales, Islas, y Tierra-Firme del Mar Oceano: Archiduque de
Austria, Duque de Borgoña, de Brabante, y de Milan, Conde
de Absburg, de Flandes, Tirol, y Barcelona; Señor de Vizcaya,
y de Molina, &c. = Al Serenisimo Principe D. Carlos, mi muy
caro y amado Hijo; a los Infantes, Prelados, Duques, Mar-
queses, Condes, Ricos-Hombres, Priores de las Ordenes, Co-
mendadores, y Sub-Comendadores, Alcaydes de los Castillos,
Casas-fuertes, y llanas; y á los del mi Consejo,
Presidente, y Oídores de las mis Audiencias, Alcaldes, Alguaciles, de la mi Casa, Corte, y Chancillerías; y á todos los

---

* From the archives of the Society of Jesus, *Hist. Soc. Centr. Arch. S.J.*, Vol. 185,
folios 22-33. For the translation see pp. 246-53.

Corregidores, é Intendentes, Asistente, Gobernadores, Alcaldes mayores, y ordinarios, y otros qualesquier Jueces y Justicias de estos mis Reynos; asi de Realengo, como los de Señorio, Abadengo, y ordenes de qualquier estado, condicion, calidad y preeminencia que sean, asi á los que ahora son, como á los que serán de aqui adelante, y á cada uno y qualquiera de vos: SABED, que habiendome conformado con el parecer de los del mi Consejo Real en el Extraordinario, que se celebra con motivo de las resultas de las ocurrencias pasadas, en consulta de veinte y nueve de Enero proximo; y de lo que sobre ella, conviniendo en el mismo dictamen, me han expuesto personas del mas elevado carácter y acreditada experiencia: estimulado de gravisimas causas, relativas á la obligacion en que me hallo constituido, de mantener en subordinacion, tranquilidad, y justicia mis Pueblos, y otras urgentes justas y necesarias, que reserve en mi Real ánimo: usando de la suprema autoridad económica, que el Todo Poderoso ha depositado en mis manos para la proteccion de mis Vasallos, y respeto de mi Corona: He venido en mandar estrañar de todos mis Dominios de España, é Indias, é Islas Filipinas, y demás adjacentes á los Regulares de la Compañia, asi Sacerdotes, como Coadjutores ó Legos que hayan hecho la primera profesion, y á los Novicios que quisieren seguirles; y que se ocupen todas las temporalidades de la Compañia en mis Dominios, y para su execucion uniforme en todos ellos, he dado plena y privativa comision, y autoridad por otro mi Real Decreto de veinte y siete de Febrero al Conde de Aranda, Presidente de mi Consejo, con facultad de proceder desde luego á tomar las providencias correspondientes.

I. Yo he venido asimismo en mandar que el Consejo haga notoria en todos estos Reynos la citada mi Real determinacion; manifestando á las demas Ordenes Religiosos la confianza, satisfaccion, y aprecio que me merecen por su fidelidad y doctrina, observancia de vida monástica, exemplar servicio de la Iglesia, acreditada instruccion de sus estudios, y suficiente número de

Individuos, para ayudar á los Obispos, y Párrocos en el pasto espiritual de las Almas, y por su abstraccion de negocios de gobierno, como agenos y distantes de la vida ascética, y monacal.

II. Igualmente dará á entender á los Reverendos Prelados Diocesanos, Ayuntamientos, Cabildos Eclesiásticos, y demás Estamentos, ó Cuerpos políticos del Reyno, que en mi Real Persona quedan reservados los justos, y graves motivos, que á pesar mio han obligado mi Real ánimo á esta necessaria providencia: valiendome unicamente de la económica potesdad, sin proceder por otros medios, siguiendo en ello el impulso de mi Real benignidad, como Padre y Protector de mis Pueblos.

III. Declaro, que en la ocupacion de temporalidades de la Compañia se comprenden sus bienes y efectos, asi muebles, como raíces, ó rentas Eclesiásticas, que legitimamente posean en el Reyno; sin perjuicio de sus cargas, mente de los Fundadores, y alimentos vitalicios de los Individuos, que serán de cien pesos, durante su vida, á los Sacerdotes; y noventa á los Legos, pagaderos de la masa general, que se forme de los bienas de la Compañia.

IV. En estos alimentos vitalicios no serán comprendidos los Jesuítas estrangeros, que indebidamente existen en mis Dominios dentro de sus Colegios, ó fuera de ellos, ó en casas particulares; vistiendo la sotana, ó en trage de Abates, y en qualquier destino en que se hallaren empleados: debiendo todos salir de mis Reynos sin distincion alguna.

V. Tampoco serán comprendidos en los alimentos los Novicios, que quisieren voluntariamente seguir á los demás, por no estár aún empeñados con la profesion, y hallarse en libertad de separarse.

VI. Declaro, que si algun Jesuíta saliere del Estado Eclesiástico, (a donde se remiten todos) ó diere justo motivo de resentimiento á la Corte con sus operaciones ó escritos; le cesará desde luego la pension quo vá asignada. Y aunque no debo presumir que el

Cuerpo de la Compañia, faltando a las mas estrechas y superiores obligaciones, intente ó permita, que alguno de sus In[di]viduos escriba contra el respeto y sumision debida á mi resolucion, con titulo ó pretexto de Apologias ó Defensorios, dirigidos á perturbar la paz de mis Reynos, ó por medio de Emisarios secretos conspire al mismo fin; en tal caso, no esperado, cesará la pension á todos ellos.

VII. De seis en seis meses se entregará la mitad de la pension anual á los Jesuítas por el Banco del Giro, con intervencion de mi Ministro en Roma, que tendrá particular cuidado de saber los que fallecen, ó decaen por su culpa de la pension, para rebatir su importe.

VIII. Sobre la administracion y aplicaciones equivalentes de los bienes de la Compañia en obras pias; como es dotacion de Parroquias pobres, Seminarios conciliares, Casas de Misericordia, y otros fines piadosos, oídos los Ordinarios Eclesiásticos en lo que sea necesario y conveniente: reservo tomar separadamente providencias, sin que en nada se defraude la verdadera piedad; ni perjudique la causa publica, ó derecho de tercero.

IX. Prohibo por ley y regla general, que jamás pueda volver á admitirse en todos mis Reynos en particular á ningun Individuo de la Compañia, ni en cuerpo de Comunidad, con ningun pretexto ni colorido que sea; ni sobre ello admitirá el mi Consejo, ni otro Tribunal instancia alguna; antes bien tomarán á prevencion las Justicias las mas severas providencias contra los infractores, auxiliadores, y cooperantes de semejante intento; castigandolos como perturbadores del sosiego público.

X. Ninguno de los actuales Jesuítas profesos, aunque salga de la Orden con licencia formal del Papa, y quede de Secular ó Clerigo, ó pase á otra Orden, no podrá volver á estos Reynos sin obtener especial permiso mio.

XI. En caso de lograrlo, que se concederá tomadas las noticias convenientes, deberá hacer juramento de fidelidad en manos del Presidente de mi Consejo; prometiendo de buena fé, que

no tratará en público ni en secreto con los Individuos de la
Compañia, ó con su General; ni hará diligencias, pasos, ni
insinuaciones, directa ni indirectamente á favor de la Compañia;
pena de ser tratado como reo de Estado, y valdrán contra él las
pruebas privilegiadas.

XII. Tampoco podrá enseñar, predicar, ni confesar en estos
Reynos, aunque haya salido, como vá dicho, de la Orden; y
sacudido la obediencia del General; pero podrá gozar rentas
Eclesiásticas, que no requieran estos cargos.

XIII. Ningun Vasallo mio, aunque sea Eclesiástico Secular ó
Regular, podrá pedir Carta de hermandad al General de la
Compañia, ni á otro en su nombre; pena de que se la tratará
como reo de Estado, y valdrán contra él igualmente las pruebas privilegiadas.

XIV. Todos aquellos, que las tubieren al presente, deberán
entregarlas al Presidente de mi Consejo, ó á los Corregidores y
Justicias del Reyno, para que se las remitan y archiven, y no
se use en adelante de ellas; sin que les sirva de óbice el haberlas
tenido en lo pasado, con tal que punctualmente cumplan con
dicha entrega; y las Justicias mantendrán en reserva los nombres de las personas que las entregaren, para que de este modo
no les cause nota.

XV. Todo el que mantubiere correspondencia con los Jesuítas,
por prohibirse general y absolutamente, será castigado á pro-
porcion de su culpa.

XVI. Prohibo expresamente, que nadie pueda escribir, de-
clamar, ó conmover con pretexto de estas providencias en pró ni
en contra de ellas; antes impongo silencio en esta materia a
todos mis Vasallos, y mando, que á los contraventores se les castigue como reos de lesa Magestad.

XVII. Para apartar altercaciones, ó malas inteligencias entre
los particulares, á quienes no incumbe juzgar, ni interpretar las
órdenes del Soberano; mando expresamente, que nadie escriba,
imprima, ni expenda papeles ó obras concernientes á la ex-

pulsion de los Jesuítas de mis dominios; no teniendo especial licencia del Gobierno, é inhibo al Juez de Imprentas, á sus subdelegados, y á todas las Justicias de mis Reynos, de conceder tales permisos ó licencias; por deber correr todo esto baxo de las órdenes del Presidente y Ministros de mi Consejo, con noticia de mi Fiscal.

XVIII. Encargo muy estrechamente á los Reverendos Prelados Diocesanos, y á los Superiores de las Ordenes Regulares, no permitan, que sus Súbditos escriban, impriman, ni declamen sobre este asunto; pues es les haria responsables de la no esperada infraction de parte de qualquiera de ellos: la qual declaro comprendida en la Ley del Señor Don Juan el Primero, y Real Cedula expedida circularmente por mi Consejo en 18 de Septiembre del año pasado, para su mas puntual execucion: à que todos deben conspirar, por lo que interesa el órden público, y la reputation de los mismos individuos, para no atraherse los efectos de mi Real desagrado.

XIX. Ordeno al mi Consejo, que con arreglo á lo que vá ex-presado haga expedir, y publicar la Real Prágmática mas estrecha y conveniente, para que llegue á noticia de todos mis Vasallos, y se observe inviolablemente, publíque, y executen por las Justicias y Tribunales territoriales las penas, que ván declaradas contra los que quebrantaren estas disposiciones para su puntual, pronto, é invariable cumplimiento; y dará á este fin todas órdenes necesarias con preferencia á otro qualquier nego-cio, por lo que interesa mi Real servicio: en inteligencia, de que á los Consejos de Inquisicion, Indias, Ordenes y Hacienda, he mandado remitir copias de mi Real Decreto para su respectiva inteligencia y cumplimiento. Y para su puntual, é invariable observancia en todos mis Dominios, habiendose publicado en Consejo pleno este dia el Real Decreto de 27 de Marzo, que contiene la anterior resolucion, que se mandó guardar y cumplir segun y como en él se expresa, fue acordado expedir le presente en fuerza de Ley, y Pragmática Sancion, como si fuese hecha,

y promulgada en Cortes, pues quiero se esté, y pase por ella, sin contravenirla en manera alguna, para lo qual, siendo necesario, derogo, y anulo todas cosas que sean, ó ser puedan contrarias á esta: Por lo qual encargo á los muy Reverendos Arzobispos, Obispos, Superiores de todas las Ordenes Regulares, Mendicantes, y Monacales, Visitadores, Provisores, Vicarios, y demás Prelados, y Jueces Eclesiásticos de estos mis Reynos, observen la expresada ley y Pragmática como en ella se contiene, sin permitir que con nungun pretexto se contravenga en manera alguna á quanto en ella se ordena: Y mando á los del mi Consejo, Presidente, y Oídores, Alcaldes de mi Casa, y Corte, y de mis Audiencias, y Chancillerías, Asistente, Gobernadores, Alcaldes mayores y ordinarios, y demás Jueces y Justicias de todos mis Dominios, guarden, cumplan y executen la citada ley y Pragmática sancion, y la hagan guardar y observar en todo y por todo, dando para ello las providencias que se requiran, sin que sea necessaria otra declaracion alguna de esta, que ha de tener su puntual execucion desde el dia que se publíque en Madrid, y en las Ciudades, Villas y Lugares de estos mis Reynos, en la forma acostumbrada; por convenir asi á mi Real servicio, tranquilidad, bien, y utilidad de la causa pública de mis Vasallos. Que asi es mi voluntad, y que al translado impreso de esta mi Carta, firmado de Don Ignacio Esteban de Higareda, mi Escribano de Camara mas antiguo, y de Gobierno de mi Consejo, se la dé la misma fé y credito, que á su original. Dada en el Prado á dos de Abril de mil setecientos y sesenta y siete años.
Yo El Rey. Yo Don Joseph Ignacio de Goyeneche, Secretario del Rey nuestro Señor, le hice escribir por su mandado. = El Conde de Aranda. = Don Francisco Cepeda. = Don Jacinto de Tudó. = Don Francisco de Salazar y Aguero. = Don Joseph Manuel Domínguez. = Registrada. = D. Nicolás Berdugo, Theniente de Cancillér mayor. = Don Nicolás Berdugo.

PUBLICACION

En la Villa de Madrid á dos dias del mes de Abril de mil setecientos y sesenta y siete, ante las Puertas del Real Palacio, frente
del Balcon Principal del Rey nuestro Señor, y en la Puerta de
Guadalajara, donde está el público Trato, y Comercio de los
Mercaderes, y Oficiales; estando presentes Don Juan Estevan
de Salaverri, D. Juan Antonio de Peñaredonda, D. Benito Antonio de Barreda, D. Pedro Ximenez de Mesa, Alcaldes de la
Casa, y Corte de S. M. se publicó la Real Pragmática sancion
antecedente con Trompetas, y Timbales, por voz de Pregonero
público, hallandose presentes diferentes Alguaciles de dicha
Real Casa, y Corte, y otras muchas Personas, de que certifico
yo D. Francisco Lopez Navamuel, Escribano de Camara del
Rey nuestro Señor, de los que en su Consejo residen. Don
Francisco Lopez Navamuel.

Es copia de la Real Pragmática sancion original, y su Publica-
cion, de que certifico.

There is no intention here to propose a complete library on the Patronato. That would be a very large task. Moreover, it would go counter to the objective set down at the beginning of the work; namely, to lift the fundamental evidence out of the host of critical writings and to let the fathers of the institution address the reader directly in their own words. The important large documents can, for the most part, be found in print, and those works form the backbone of the list that follows. Those few that were taken from unprinted original sources have their provenance indicated on the spot. All books mentioned in the text are enumerated below for convenient reference. Beyond that are found several select titles touching upon the theory of the system in its legalistic aspects, where there is much controversy. To assist the reader the indications [C] and [R] are appended to designate respectively the canonist or the regalist interpretations of the authors. Many of the chapters reflect the records whose filmed copies reside in the Jesuitica Collection of the St. Louis University Library and the similar collection at Loyola University in Chicago. These extensive archives of an order widely active in the Spanish empire furnished background for the book. As they are well catalogued, their individual sections are not reproduced in this place.

Abbo, John A. and Jerome D. Hannan. *The Sacred Canons*. St. Louis, 1952.

Aquinas, Thomas. *Summa theologica*. Taurini, 1928.

Astráin, Antonio. *Historia de la Compañía de Jesús en la Asistencia de España*. Madrid, 1928.

Ayarragaray, Lucas. *La iglesia en América y la dominación española*. Buenos Aires, 1920.

Bancroft, Hubert Howe. *History of Mexico*. San Francisco, 1883.

Bannon, John Francis and Peter Masten Dunne. *Latin America*. Milwaukee, 1958.

Baronio, Cesare. *Annales ecclesiasticae*. Mansi edition. Lucca, 1738.

Barraclough, Geoffrey. *Papal Provisions*. Oxford, 1935.

Bede, Venerable. *Ecclesiastical History of the English Nation*. New York, 1910.

Bishop Tamaron's Visitation of New Mexico in 1760, translated and edited by Eleanor B. Adams. Albuquerque, 1954.

Borah, Woodrow. "Collection of Tithes in the Bishopric of Oaxaca." *Hispanic American Historical Review*, XXI (August 1941).

———— "Representative Institutions in the Spanish Empire in the Sixteenth Century: III, The New World." *The Americas*, XII (January 1956).

Bravo Ugarte, José. *Historia de México*. México, 1941.

Carbia, Rómulo. *La Revolución de Mayo y la iglesia*. Buenos Aires, 1941.

Castaneda, Carlos E. *Our Catholic Heritage in Texas*. Austin, 1936-1942.

Codex iuris canonici . . . fontium annotatione . . . auctus. Roma, 1917.

Colin, Francisco. *Labor evangélica de los obreros de la Compañía de Jesús en las islas Filipinas. Nueva edición ilustrada con copia de notas y documentos para la crítica de la historia general de la soberania de España en Filipinas, por Padre Pablo Pastells*. Barcelona, 1900-1902.

Corpus iuris canonici. Richter-Friedberg edition. Leipzig, 1879-1881.

Corpus juris civilis. Schoell-Kroll edition. Berlin, 1912.

Corpus juris civilis: Codex Justinianus. Krueger edition. Berlin, 1904.

Cuevas, Mariano. *Historia de la iglesia en México*. El Paso, 1928.

Davenport, F. G. *European Treaties Bearing on the History of the United States and Its Dependencies*. Washington, 1917.

Decorme, Gerardo. *Historia de la Compañía de Jesús en la República Mexicana*. Guadalajara, 1914.

———— *La obra de los Jesuitas en México durante la época colonial*. México, 1941.

De la Costa, H. Review of Luis Weckmann, *Las bulas alejandrinas de 1493 y la teoría política del papado medieval*. *Traditio*, VII (1949-1951).

Denzinger, Henrici. *Enchiridion symbolorum.* Twenty-ninth edition. Freiburg in Breisgau, 1953.

Díaz del Castillo, Bernal. *Verdadera historia de los sucesos de la conquista de la Nueva España.* México, 1904.

Dunne, Peter Masten. *Pioneer Jesuits in Northern Mexico.* Berkeley, 1944.

Egaña, Antonio de. *La teoría del regio Vicariato Español en Indias.* Roma, 1958. [C]

Enciclopedia universal ilustrada europea-americana. Espasa-Calpe edition. Barcelona, 1920.

Encina, Francisco Antonio. *Historia de Chile desde prehistoria hasta 1891.* Santiago, 1940-1954.

Encinas, Diego de. *Cedulario Indiano recopilado. Reproducción facsimil de la edición única de 1596.* Madrid, 1945-1946.

Fernández de Navarrete, Martín. *Colección de los viajes y descubrimientos que hicieron por mar los españoles desde fines del siglo XV, con varios documentos inéditos concernientes a la historia de la marina castellana y de los establecimientos españoles en Indias.* Second edition. Madrid, 1859.

Fisher, Lillian. *Champion of Reform.* New York, 1955.

Fita, F. "Primeros años del episcopado en América." *Buletin de la Academia de Historia* (Madrid), XX (1892). [C]

Frasso, Pedro. *Tractatus de regio patronatu Indiarum. Questiones aliquae desumptae et disputatae in alia quinquaginta capita partitae.* Madrid, 1775. (Original edition, 1677-1679) [R]

Gabut, Johan Anton. "Vita Sti. Pii V." In *Acta sanctorum.* Antwerp, 1680. (This *vita* is found under May 4.)

García Gutiérrez, Jesús. *Apuntes para la historia del origen y desenvolvimiento del regio patronato Indiano.* México, 1941.

———— *Bulario de la iglesia Mexicana.* México, 1951.

García Icazbalceta, Joaquín. *Biografia de D. Fr. Juan de Zumárraga, primer obispo y arzobispo de México.* México, 1881.

———— *Nueva colección de documentos para la historia de México.* México, 1886.

Giménez Fernández, Manuel. *El Concilio IV Provincial Mejicano.* Seville, 1939. [C]

Gómez Hoyos, Rafael. *Las leyes de Indias y el derecho eclesiástico en la América española e islas Filipinas.* Medellin, 1945. [C]

Gómez Zamora, Matias. *Regio patronato español e indiano.* Madrid, 1897. [C]

Guerin, P. *Les conciles.* Parisiis, 1868.

Gustavson, Carl. *Preface to History.* New York, 1956.

Hanke, Lewis. *First Social Experiments in America.* Cambridge, 1935.

Hannon, Philip M. "Going In through Their Door." *America,* C (January 10, 1959).

Hedde, R. "Pragmatique sanction." In *Dictionnaire de theologie catholique,* Vol. XII. Paris, 1930-1950.

Hernáez, Francisco Javier. *Colección de bulas, breves, y otros documentos relativos a la iglesia de América y Filipinas.* Brussels, 1879.

Herr, Richard. *The Eighteenth Century Revolution in Spain.* Princeton, 1958.

Herrera y Tordesillas, Antonio de. *Historia general de los hechos de los Castellanos en las islas i tierra firme del mar oceano.* Madrid, 1601.

Holleran, Mary Patricia. *Church and State in Guatemala.* New York, 1949.

Hughes, Philip. *A History of the Church.* New York, 1934-1947.

————— *A Popular History of the Catholic Church.* New York, 1951.

Jordan de Asso y del Rio, D. Ignacio y D. Miguel de Manuel y Rodríguez. *El ordenamiento de leyes que D. Alfonso XI hizo en las Cortes de Alcalá de Henares, El año de mil trescientos y cuarenta y ocho.* Madrid, 1847.

Kearney, Edward W. *Philip II and the Castilian Cortes: A Study in Sixteenth Century Absolutism.* Unpublished thesis. Loyola University (Chicago), 1955.

Kenny, Michael. *Romance of the Floridas.* Milwaukee, 1934.

Kirsch, J. P. "John XXII." In *Catholic Encyclopedia,* Vol. VIII. New York, 1907-1914.

Lanning, John Tate. *Academic Culture in the Spanish Colonies.* Chapel Hill, 1940.

Las siete partidas. English translation by Samuel Parsons Scott. Chicago, 1931.

Las siete partidas del rey don Alfonso el Sabio, cotejadas con varios códices antiguos. Madrid, 1807.

Legón, Faustino J. *Doctrina y exercicio del patronato nacional.* Buenos Aires, 1920. [C]

Leturia, Pedro. "La bula del patronato de las Indias españoles que falta en el archivo Vaticano." *Studi e testi,* No. 125 (1946).

—— "Die Heilige Stuhl und das Spanische Patronato in America." *Historisches Jahrbuch,* Band 46, Heft 1 (1926).

Levellier, R. *Organización de la iglesia y ordenes religiosas en la virreinato del Peru en el siglo XVI.* Madrid, 1919. [R]

Lietz, Paul Stanton. "Don Vasco de Quiroga: Oidor Made Bishop." *Mid-America,* XXXII (January 1950).

Mansi, Giovanni Dominico. *Sacrorum conciliorum nova et amplissima collectio.* Martin-Petit edition. Parisiis, 1901-1924.

Mansilla, D. Review of José Goni Giztambide, *Historia de la bula de la cruzada en España* (Vitoria, 1958). *Hispania sacra,* XX (1957).

Mariana, Juan. *Historia general de España.* Toledo, 1601.

Mecham, J. Lloyd. *Church and State in Latin America.* Chapel Hill, 1934.

Medina Ascensio, Luis. *La santa sede y la emancipación Mexicana.* Guadalajara, 1946.

Mercati, G. *Raccolta de concordati in materia ecclesiastiche tra la Santa Sede e la autoritá civili.* Roma, 1919.

Moeller, Charles. "Christ, Order of the Knights of." In *Catholic Encyclopedia,* Vol. III. New York, 1907-1914.

Mónica, Sor. *La gran controversia del XVI siglo.* Madrid, 1952.

Monumenta historica Societatis Jesu: Epistolae et instructiones Sancti Ignatii. Madrid, 1903-1911.

Morelli, D. Cyriaci [Domingo Muriel]. *Fasti Novi Orbis et ordinationum apostolicarum ad Indias pertinentium breviarium cum adnotationibus.* Venetiis, 1776.

Novísima recopilación de las leyes de España. Madrid, 1805.

Nowell, Charles E. "The Treaty of Tordesillas and the Diplomatic Background of American History." In *Greater America.* Berkeley, 1945.

Ots Capdequí, J. M. *El estado español y las Indias.* México, 1941.

Ots Capdequí, J. M. *Manual de historia de derecho Español en las Indias.* Buenos Aires, 1943.

Pacheco, Joaquín F.; Francisco de Cárdenas; y Luis Torres de Mendoza. *Colección de documentos inéditos, relativos al descubrimiento, conquista y organización de las antiguas posesiones españoles de América y Oceania, sacados de los Archivos del Reino, y muy especialmente del de Indias.* Madrid, 1864-1884, 1885-1932.

Padden, Robert Charles. "The Ordenanza del Patronazgo, 1574." *The Americas,* XII (April 1956).

Parkman, Francis. *The Jesuits of North America in the Seventeenth Century.* Boston, 1867.

Pastor, Ludwig von. *History of the Popes from the Close of the Middle Ages.* English translation. London, 1891-1934.

Pattee, Ricardo. *Gabriel García Moreno y el Ecuador de su tiempo.* Quito, 1941.

Phillimore, Walter George Frank. *Ecclesiastical Law.* London, 1921.

Powell, Philip Wayne. *Soldiers, Indians, and Silver: The Northward Advance of New Spain, 1550-1600.* Berkeley, 1952.

Prescott, William Hickling. *The History of the Reign of Ferdinand and Isabella the Catholic.* McKay edition. Philadelphia, 1893.

Prestage, Edgar. *Chivalry: A Series of Studies To Illustrate Its Historical Significance and Civilizing Influence.* London, 1928.

———— *The Portuguese Pioneers.* London, 1933.

Puga, Vasco de. *Provisiones, cédulas, instrucciones de su magestad: ordenanzas de oiditores y audiencia, para la buena expedición de los negocios, y administración de justicia: y governación desta Nueva España: para el bueno tratamiento y observación de los Indios, dende el año 1525 hasta este presente de '63.* México, 1563.

Recopilación de leyes de los reinos de las Indias. Madrid, 1681.

Ribadeneyra, Antonio Joaquín de. *Manual compendio de el regio patronato Indiano.* Madrid, 1755. [R]

Rippy, J. Fred and Jean Thomas Nelson. *Crusaders of the Jungle.* Chapel Hill, 1936.

Rodríguez Valencia, Vicente. *El Patronato regio de Indias y la santa sede en Santo Toribio de Mogrovejo (1581-1606).* Roma, 1957. [C]

Sacrosancti et oecumenici concilii Tridentini canones et decreta. Parisiis, 1910.

Schäfer, Ernesto. *El consejo real y supremo de las Indias, su historia, organización y labor administrativa hasta la terminación de la casa de Austria.* Seville, 1935.

———— *Índice de la colección de documentos inéditos de Indias.* Madrid, 1947.

Shiels, W. Eugene. "Church and State in the First Decade of Mexican Independence." *Catholic Historical Review,* XXVIII (July 1942).

———— "Francisco Pablo Vásquez and the Independence of Mexico." *Mid-America,* XXX (July 1948).

———— *Gonzalo de Tapia.* New York, 1934.

Simpson, Lesley B. *The Encomienda in New Spain.* Revised edition. Berkeley, 1950.

Sipos, Stephanus. *Enchiridion juris canonici.* Roma, 1954.

Solórzano Pereira, Joannes de. *Disputationem de Indiarum jure, Tomus Primus sive De justa Indiarum Occidentalium inquisitione, acquisitione et retentione.* Madrid, 1653. [R]

———— *Politica Indiana.* Madrid, 1646. [R]

Suárez, Francisco. *De fide.* Vives edition. Parisiis, 1858.

Trevor-Davies, R. *Spain in the Age of Decline.* New York, 1957.

Ullmann, Walter. *The Medieval Idea of Law.* London, 1946.

Uriarte, Manuel José. *Diario de un misionero de Mainas,* edited by Constantino Bayle. Madrid, 1952.

Vander Linden, H. "Alexander VI and the Bulls of Demarcation." *American Historical Review,* XXII (October 1916).

Vargas Ugarte, Ruben. *Historia de la iglesia en el Peru, 1511-1568.* Lima, 1953.

Vasconselos, José. *Historia de México.* México, 1956.

Walton, Clifford Stevens. *The Civil Law in Spain and Spanish America.* Washington, 1900.

Weckmann, Luis. *Las bulas alejandrinas de 1493 y la teoría política del papado medieval.* México, 1949.

Weismann, Elizabeth Wilder. *Mexico in Sculpture.* Cambridge, 1950.

Wernz, Franz Xavier. *Jus canonicum,* edited by Pietro Vidal. Roma, 1927.

Zavala, Silvio. *Philosophy of the Conquest of America.* México, 1953.

INDEX

About this book

King and Church was designed by William Nicoll of EDIT, INC. It was set in the composing room of LOYOLA UNIVERSITY PRESS. The text is 12 on 14 Bodoni Book; the reduced matter, 10 on 12; and the notes, 8 on 10. The display type is Bodoni Book (Mono 875).

It was printed by PHOTOPRESS, INC. on WARREN'S 55-pound English Finish paper and bound by A. C. ENGDAHL AND COMPANY, INC. in BANCROFT cloth.

IMPRIMI POTEST: John R. Connery, S.J.
Provincial of the Chicago Province
January 27, 1961
IMPRIMATUR: ✠ Albert Cardinal Meyer
Archbishop of Chicago
February 1, 1961